After the Bitter Comes the Sweet

苦尽甘来

After the Bitter Comes the Sweet

How One Woman Weathered the Storms of China's Recent History

YULIN WANG RITTENBERG

with Dori Jones Yang

ISBN: 1506167098
ISBN-13: 978-1506167091

Cover design by Kathryn Campbell
Printed in the United States of America

Published by East West Insights
www.eastwestinsights.com

DEDICATED TO MY HUSBAND,
whose unwavering spirit and the strong ideals
enabled me to finish this book,
and to my four darling children,
who endured with me the decade of harsh challenges

CONTENTS

PROLOGUE

MY HUSBAND, SIDNEY, and I had just gone to bed when the knock came. Sudden and sharp, it jolted my body. They had come for him.

Sidney sat upright and put his hand on my shoulder, as if to protect me. "Stay here. I'll answer it." He slipped on his bathrobe over my old tattered long johns and padded to the front door of our apartment. My new set of flannel underwear was in the wash, and he had insisted I wear his good pair of long johns to bed, so I would be warm on this night, February 21, 1968, reported to be the coldest of the winter.

I strained my ears to hear the words he exchanged with an unfamiliar male voice at the door. When Sidney came back to the bedroom, he said, "The deputy director wants to talk to me about a new work assignment."

Dread deepened the shadows around me. No one gets a special assignment at 11 o'clock at night. Paralyzed in silence, I watched Sidney put on his clothes.

Both of us had known this moment was coming, sooner or later. For nearly two years, China had been roiling in the latest political movement, the Great Proletarian Cultural Revolution. An American, Sidney had eagerly—perhaps too eagerly—jumped into the fray. One of the few foreigners who had joined the Chinese Communist Party, always outspoken and frank, Sidney began making speeches to huge crowds around the country. To him, the Cultural Revolution was a much-needed democratic correction, a chance to speak out against all that was unfair in China, a return to the idealistic values of Mao Zedong that had so attracted him.

Twenty years earlier, Sidney had arrived in China with the United States Army after World War II and traveled throughout the country. Appalled, Sidney had witnessed frozen corpses lying in the streets, starving women selling sex for bowls of rice, and corrupt officials hoarding grain for profit during a famine. Sidney had traveled by donkey to the hillside caves of Yan'an, where he lived with the founders of the Chinese Communist Party when they were still underground. He had cut off all ties to his homeland in order to stay behind and help the Communists because he deeply believed they offered a better future for my country.

In our twelve years of cross-cultural marriage, we had sparred frequently in fiery arguments. I was stubborn as a rock, Sidney often said. Sometimes I berated him for having his head in the clouds, too willing to sacrifice our family happiness for what he considered the greater good. Still, I had never met a more selfless, idealistic man. Plus, he was razor-sharp smart and relentlessly upbeat, and he made me laugh.

Six months before that knock on the door, a black cloud had descended on us. Sidney lost his beloved job as an English-language editor and trusted leader at Radio Peking. Large-character posters, many written by our friends and colleagues, appeared on the walls at our workplace, accusing him of being a "bourgeois politician." A group photo that included China's top leaders was published in an official magazine, with Sidney's face blacked out. Ominous signs. On Christmas Day, he was placed under house arrest and told to prepare for interrogation.

Then my work permit was taken away, so I couldn't even go into my office. After seventeen years of hard work, this felt like a personal betrayal. The Party had given me an education and entrusted me with a good job, and I was as loyal as Sidney was. My husband was no bourgeois politician; he had abandoned the luxuries of American life to serve the people of China. Why was he being treated like an enemy?

The schools closed down amidst the political turmoil, so our exile from work was lightened by the chance to spend all day, every day, with our four children, ranging in age from two to ten. They played games and sang revolutionary songs. But after we put them to bed, Sidney and I sketched out scenarios of disaster. He had already spent six years in prison, unjustly accused of being an American spy. Yet after his release in 1955, he had reaffirmed his faith in Chairman Mao Zedong, who personally admitted that Sidney's imprisonment was a mistake. Once again, Sidney had chosen to stay in China and return to work. That's when I met and married him, defying my parents, who refused to attend my wedding to a foreigner.

Now young people calling themselves Red Guards were rampaging, and civil war had broken out in some cities. The military had recently reasserted control, but ordinary life was disrupted. We could only guess what kind of power struggle was going on among China's leaders. This time, I worried that Sidney might even be expelled from China and sent away from us. Or worse.

Fully dressed in a dark brown corduroy suit, Sidney came over to the bed and kissed me.

What could I say at a moment like this? "Stick to the facts," I warned him. I knew that they would try to force him to make a false confession, which could make his troubles worse. "No wild talk."

Distressing as things were, I never dreamed that those would be the last words I would say to my husband for ten long years.

He nodded and walked softly into the other two rooms of our apartment, to kiss each of our children good-bye.

Then the front door opened and shut, and he was gone. Trembling, I jumped up and looked out the window, unable to believe this was really happening. The front entrance of our three-story apartment building, the Foreign Experts Building at Radio Peking, was on the other side, so I could not see the car that took him away. Freezing air crept in through the glass. Clouds covered the moon.

I got back into bed but couldn't sleep. I tossed and turned, then sat up and stared at my hands. Now what? Would Sidney come back tonight? Were they taking him to the office for questioning? Or to prison? The future blurred.

I had always been levelheaded: a sturdy, reliable girl and a pragmatic, clear-thinking woman. Daughter of a worker, raised in wartime poverty and chaos, I had learned to be self-reliant. I assumed I could handle anything. But I feared for our children, who had always lived in the relative comfort afforded to us as a "foreign" family in Beijing. Born and raised in China, they were sweet and innocent. How might they suffer because of their father's troubles? My youngest child, a chubby-cheeked boy who looked more American than his sisters, couldn't even talk yet. Maybe Sidney would come home before dawn and this nightmare would end.

Half an hour later, another knock on the door startled me, this one louder and more insistent. Willing my fingers not to shake, I put on my bathrobe and opened the door.

Several soldiers barged into our living room, together with a man from the Army Management Team that had been running our office at Radio Peking.

"Wang Yulin." One of them addressed me by my full name. "We don't think it would be suitable for you to continue living here. We're going to move you."

Something exploded inside my head. Clearly, they had taken Sidney off to prison. And now they had come for me, too. "What about my children?" I pleaded.

"They'll go with you."

PART I

Chapter One

Escape in the Night

MY MOTHER WOKE me up in the middle of the night, jerking my arm. Only four years old, I whimpered.

Her voice was urgent. "Get up. Now."

"I'm sleepy," I protested. Why did Mama sound so harsh?

"The Japanese devils are coming. We have to leave. Now. "

"I don't want to!" But my sister-in-law got me up, slipped on my outer clothes, and prepared me to leave our cramped rooms that opened onto a ramshackle courtyard, the only home I had ever known.

Around me, everyone was working in haste, in the dark. Papa gathered up his woodworking tools, essential to his livelihood as a carver and furniture maker. My brother and two oldest sisters collected what family possessions they could carry: pots and pans, dried food, padded clothes we might need next winter. They wrapped our things in quilts, tied them, and attached the ropes to long poles to carry on their shoulders. My third sister, age seven, strapped small packages of her belongings to her back.

Confused, I sat on a wooden stool and watched the strange, subdued bustling. In the flickering light of the lantern, their motions seemed jerky. They spoke in urgent whispers, although there was no one to disturb. Despite the late hour, the air hung heavy and humid. It felt like the hottest night of the year.

Mama directed the packing with short, firm words. "No, we can't take that jar. Too heavy. Wrap a few in this towel."

Her feet had been bound as a child, so she could only hobble in unsteady steps. My sister-in-law was luckier; her feet had been bound but then released after her marriage, at my mother's insistence. Since she could walk with steady strides, my sister-in-law carried me out of the house.

The street was teeming with people fleeing Beijing. Chaos had broken out following news of military skirmishes on the outskirts of the city, where Chinese troops were trying to stop Japanese aggression. Rumors were flying that the Japanese army would march through the city gates and into the streets of Beijing any day now. Just a few days earlier, Japanese and Chinese troops had clashed at the Marco Polo Bridge on July 7, 1937.

That date became known as one of China's national days of shame—the beginning of Japan's full-force invasion of our country. Six years earlier, the Japanese army had occupied Northeast China, then called Manchuria, and later advanced all the way to the Great Wall, about forty miles north of Beijing. From there, Japanese troops had taken over the eastern part of our province, Hebei. But at that moment, in July 1937, war erupted just outside Beijing, the former imperial capital. Frightening rumors were swirling about Japanese brutality. No one wanted to get trapped by the fighting or victimized by ruthless foreign soldiers.

That fateful night, everyone was rushing in the same direction, almost in silence. We flowed through the gates of the massive city walls, over potholed, broken roads out into the countryside, fleeing toward the south and west, away from the Japanese army advance. Shuffling along in an ever-growing flow of people, my family headed for the hills, the Taihang Mountains west of Beijing.

Day after day, we hiked. My feet had never been bound, but they hurt from the endless walking. My little legs grew tired. Blisters broke out on my feet. I begged to stop and rest, but we couldn't. Sometimes Sister-in-Law carried me. Other times, Mama took my hand. After sundown, we hid behind rocks or in a cave and tried to sleep. Mama cradled me in her arms, to protect me from the sharp stones. We quickly finished the dried food we had brought and purchased cheap corn-bread buns from local villagers. We drank water from streams.

Many women balanced a long pole on their shoulders, carrying small babies in baskets on one end and belongings on the other. The fields were green with ripening crops, but the road was so dusty that I could taste the grit between my teeth. By midmorning, the sun beat down intolerably. Sweat poured down our bodies. Some said it was the most humid summer in living memory. By noon, we were exhausted and not only hungry but unbearably thirsty, too. Sometimes we trudged all day long and could not find water anywhere. Occasionally I cried as I walked, and my tears mixed with drops of sweat as they rolled off my face.

Eventually, no matter how valuable or needed our belongings were, we had to discard or sell them. All along the road, we saw possessions that people had dropped. One by one, my father even had to sell or abandon his woodworking tools. Some once belonged to his father, also a carpenter. My grandfather, who came to Beijing when he was fourteen years old after floods wiped out his village, had learned woodworking as an apprentice. He crafted such finely carved furniture that he had been hired to work in the emperor's palace. He even earned an imperial rank as a grade five official, with the right to wear a round cap with a red button—his prized possession, saved even during later years of rising debt. Later, Grandpa went on to carve the figures of young children surrounding the Goddess of Mercy at the Buddhist shrine at the eastern gate to the city of Beijing.

Following in his footsteps, my father had started work at age thirteen as a "carver," the name given to cabinetmakers and carpenters. Papa joined with other young men to form a band of sworn brothers who worked together to build homes and furniture.

But now, as a war refugee, my tall and handsome father had to leave behind most of these precious tools, his means of making a living. We simply couldn't carry them any longer. All we could save was our lives.

Pressing us on was dread of the Japanese. Our fellow refugees told horror stories of how the "Japanese devils" raped women and killed babies.

One day, on a winding dirt road in the mountains, our fears materialized: Japanese soldiers came in sight. Scrambling up the mountainside to evade them, we hid behind rocks and bushes. At age four, I couldn't take it anymore. I started bawling.

"Throw that baby down!" someone shouted. "If the Japanese hear the crying, they'll come after us all!"

Sister-in-Law clamped one hand over my mouth. She pointed down the mountainside at the Japanese troops. Then she drew her other hand across her neck in a slicing motion. Rigid with terror, I stopped crying.

The Japanese did not pursue us, so the immediate crisis passed. But I never forgot that moment of sheer fear.

Chapter Two

Japanese Devils

WHEN I WAS small, I didn't have a name. The only name my parents ever called me was "Xiao Lao," literally "Little Old," but actually meaning, "The little child of our old age." It was the common way of referring to the youngest child in any family, and I was my mother's youngest. She gave birth to twelve children, and only five of us were alive when we left Beijing. We were so poor that two of her children actually starved to death before I was born. So I suppose it was natural not to bother to name me until they knew I would survive. Besides, in those days it was common for a Chinese girl to live out her whole life without a name of her own.

But I came about my name in a traumatic way, shortly after my family emerged from hiding in the mountains and settled in Shanxi Province. We waited there that horrific summer of 1937, as the Japanese army swept south through Hebei Province and marched relentlessly along the railway routes, winning battle after battle, leaving behind soldiers to control the cities they had seized. Within months they had conquered all of coastal China, as far south as Shanghai.

We found a temporary place to live in a small town. By then, Papa had only a handful of tools left, but he used them to do odd jobs around our neighborhood. My brother helped him at first. My sister-in-law went to neighboring houses, offering to cook or sew, but no one could afford help.

In Shanxi, my father quickly discovered that he could not earn enough money to feed us all. My stomach was always gnawing with hunger. My father knew he would eventually have to move to a big city, but he waited until the fighting calmed down.

As a small child, I heard no news about the larger world. I am sure my father listened carefully to rumors in the streets, as the Japanese army swept southward. He must have heard about the Nanking Massacre, Japan's six-week orgy of barbarism after it took over our nation's capital that December. Japanese soldiers looted homes and raped and murdered as many as 300,000 Chinese citizens. Perhaps my father even knew that the Chinese army was poorly trained and equipped, wearing cloth shoes and fighting with outdated weapons against the superior force of Japan's well-disciplined troops. China didn't have antiaircraft weapons, so Japan's fighter jets could attack with impunity, almost anywhere in China. No one had any idea how long the war would last.

All my parents knew was that the Japanese army was invading our country, and no Chinese could stop them from doing whatever they wanted.

Small detachments of marauding Japanese soldiers even crossed the mountains. My father, out working, kept his ears open for any hint that they might be coming to the small town where we lived.

My mother feared most for Second Sister, then seventeen years old. Tall and slender, with large eyes and arched brows, she was the family beauty. Her name was Yulin, which means "jade forest." She was a cheerful, vivacious girl with a warm heart. She often played with me. Mama and Papa loved her and had bright hopes for her future. A pretty girl could attract a wealthy husband. That might help us all.

But beauty meant danger in a country occupied by foreign troops. So every day, my mother would muss up Second Sister's hair and smear black ashes on her face to make her look ugly.

I giggled at her, smudged up like that. She laughed back and dabbed ash on my little nose.

One morning, when I was out of the house with my father, Japanese troops suddenly arrived on our street. They barged into our courtyard, shouting in pidgin Chinese: "Girls! Girls!"

Mama quickly hid Second Sister in a corner of the courtyard, behind a stack of cornstalks. But the Japanese soldiers found her. When they poked their bayonets into the cornstalks, she shrieked, and they dragged her out. My mother screamed and tried to protect her, but one soldier kicked her away. Another grabbed Mama by the arms and held her. A Japanese officer raped Second Sister, right in front of my mother's eyes.

When I came home, Mama was weeping profusely, cradling Second Sister, whose eyes had an empty, shocked stare.

"Japanese devils. They hurt her," Mama told me. I was too little to understand.

After that, Second Sister fell into a deep depression, shrinking from contact with other people. She would help with the chores, but seldom spoke. Even I couldn't make her smile.

Mama and Papa agonized over what would become of her, whispering in the courtyard while she slept.

Some months later, friends introduced a well-known Chinese traditional medicine practitioner, who fell in love with my second sister and asked her to marry him. He was quite a bit older than she was and exceedingly fond of her.

The wedding feast was a modest affair, but my mother, relieved to have found a good match despite Second Sister's trauma, smiled through it. The bridegroom grinned happily as he looked at his beautiful wife. But Second Sister's face showed no emotion at all.

After the wedding, she went to live with him, and he treated her like a precious gem. But soon my sister came down with a mysterious sickness. She returned to our home and was confined to bed. Sometimes she would become delirious in the middle of the night and yell for our mother: "Ma, give me a knife!"

"For what?" Mama asked.

"To kill the Japanese!"

Her screaming frightened me. "She is having a nightmare," my mother told me as she tried to calm her down.

Whatever Second Sister's sickness was, it never healed. One day, she died.

Afterwards, my mother was seized by a stroke that paralyzed half her body. Mama would stand in the doorway, half-dazed. We would say, "Mama, come eat," but she would answer, "No, I have to wait for Second Daughter. She'll be here soon."

Mama seemed to have no feeling, no awareness of anything around her. If I brought her something to eat, she would keep staring into space and just open her mouth, or she'd shake her head to show that she didn't want to eat.

So few of Mama's children had survived beyond childhood. And then, suddenly, for the second daughter to be raped—and to die! It was a terrible wound.

Later, when I registered for school, I needed to have a real name. Mama gave me my dead sister's name: Yulin.

I later changed the way the name was written, selecting a different character for "lin," with the same sound. I was never as beautiful as she was, but fate had a better life in store for me.

Chapter Three

Hunger and Despair

AFTER SECOND SISTER'S rape and death, our family deflated. Without Mama's constant motion, her pestering and caring, all energy drained out of us. Without Mama's strength and protection, we all felt lost. I saw what happens when a mother gives up.

Even as a very young child, I breathed in the foul scent of hopelessness.

By then we were living in a bigger city, back in Papa's home province, where we had moved so that he could earn enough to support us. It seemed inevitable that the Japanese would take over all of China, so we could not escape them, no matter where we went.

Beijing seemed too dangerous, so Papa led us back across the Taihang Mountains to the city of Shijiazhuang, about 170 miles southwest of Beijing. Shijiazhuang means "Stone Family Village," but it was not a village. Rather it was a medium-sized city, sitting in the plains at the junction of two railroads.

Although the Japanese army controlled Shijiazhuang, day-to-day rule was exercised by a puppet government of Chinese collaborationists under the Japanese. We were told this was the Kuomintang, or Chinese Nationalist Party, but it was not the official Kuomintang (KMT) of Chiang Kai-shek, which was still fighting the Japanese in the South and West.

At first, my father tried again to use his carpentry skills doing odd jobs, but few people had enough money to pay him. So my father became a street vendor. He nailed together a wooden stand on which he sold cigarettes, peanuts, melon seeds, and candy. When I was five or six years old, I would sometimes help him at the stand. But when he took a break and left me in charge, I didn't know how to figure up prices or use the scales. Sometimes Chinese soldiers would come by, grab a pack of cigarettes, and make off with it.

One day I ran after them. "You owe us ten cents!" I cried. "My daddy will be back soon, and he—"

A soldier turned abruptly and cuffed me on the head. "I'm your daddy!" he said, using a Chinese insult implying my mother was a whore. "I'm risking my life fighting at the front lines, and you want to take my money!"

When my father heard about this, he stopped letting me help him sell things.

Not everyone was cruel. A local Chinese man allowed us to rent a room in his large compound, where we thought we would be safe. Our family of eight squeezed into one Japanese-style room. Sliding paper panels in a wooden frame closed off a sleeping area against one wall. All of us slept on one bed, a wooden platform covered with a tatami mat. We thought we were lucky because we each had a quilt.

Young as I was, I could feel the constant tension in our crowded home. My mother seldom spoke, but when she did, she quarreled with my father. Although I admired both of them, my parents never got along with each other. I never really understood why. Theirs was an arranged marriage, and not a good match. Papa, who married at the age of sixteen, was tall and handsome, and never seemed satisfied with Mama, who was short and plain.

My brother, then over twenty, had learned the watch-repair business at an early age as an apprentice to a friend of Papa's. In Shijiazhuang, he got a job at a small shop. My brother had a good engineering mind and became an expert at watch repair. But in wartime, no one had much money to spend on such luxuries, so he didn't earn much.

Sister-in-Law managed to find some work she could do at home. A man living on our block was organizing the women to sew army uniforms for the collaborationist soldiers who worked for the Japanese. She would bring home material to sew uniforms, ten at a time.

My special daily task, starting from the age of five, was to go down to the railroad tracks and pick up used bits of coal that had not been entirely consumed in the flames. In those days, all Chinese trains had classic coal-fired steam engines with chimneys and thick black smoke. At every station, the workers shoveled out the burned-up coal to make room for fresh coal. Sometimes, they did this between stations, too, tossing the used embers out alongside the tracks.

My father made me a little three-clawed stick with which I could pick up the coals without burning my fingers. I would bring them home in a little tin bucket. That was our fuel for both cooking and winter warmth.

Almost every morning, I would go down to the tracks to collect these bits of coal. Other poor kids would be there, too, scrounging for half-burned coal. A group of raggedy children would run along the railroad tracks, racing to get the biggest embers. At a young age, I learned that life was a struggle. But I also felt a heavy responsibility; if I didn't bring back enough coal embers, Mama would not be able to cook food for the whole family. I could not do big things for my family, but I could pick up embers. As young as I was, this task made me feel important.

In the afternoons, I'd go out with my mother to hunt for edible weeds. That's what we lived on. Sometimes, I was mildly poisoned when I picked and ate the wrong weeds. I had to learn the hard way: if you break the stem and white liquid seeps out, don't eat it.

Mama often told me, "Manna doesn't fall from heaven. You have to work hard for everything you eat. Other people can save you, but only temporarily. The only way to get by is to work hard your whole life." Even though she didn't have a job, at first, I could see that she, as a woman, spent every minute feeding and caring for us. Hard work was not a virtue but a harsh fact of life. And self-reliance was essential for survival.

My father built a square stove of clay bricks in the open-air courtyard. A big steel wok sat on top, and underneath we burned branches, wood, or the coals that I collected. Even when it was raining, snowing, or windy, we cooked outside. While Mama was ailing, Sister-in-Law took over the cooking. Third Sister showed me ways to help, grinding the cornmeal or chopping the vegetables.

We almost never had meat. On good days, when Papa brought home some money, we made steamed buns from cornmeal batter, adding chopped weeds or salty pickled vegetables. Otherwise, we lived on thin gruel made from millet or corn, with the bitter weeds we had gathered. If we were lucky, the gruel had a few pieces of turnip floating in it. We would add a bit of garlic for protection against disease.

On bad days, we had nothing to eat but *doubing*, a kind of hardtack made from leftover soybean husks that people normally fed to the pigs for roughage. Thick and heavy as a brick, doubing was tough and tasteless, edible only after you soaked a piece in hot water. Sometimes I had to pick out pig hairs and grit that cracked my teeth. Pig hair is tough, not like human hair; you can't chew it or swallow it. Still, there were some terrible days when Sister-in-Law would say, "If we can't get our fill of food, we can fill up on water."

Even though I could barely remember our happier days in Beijing, I often longed for the food we had eaten there, especially at Lunar New Year celebrations.

Sister-in-Law told me how she and Mama would prepare food for two weeks before the holiday, because starting on New Year's Eve, a woman was not supposed to touch a knife for two weeks. Even in those easier years we couldn't afford pork meat, but Mama would splurge and buy pork skin, which was cheap. I salivated as Sister-in-Law told me how Mama would chop it into small pieces, boil it, and save all the juice. Then she chopped carrots, soybeans, and turnips and made a slow-cooked stew with gravy. This she packed in a big jar that was kept cold outside. The vegetables and meat jelled together and became firm. Mama would bring it in, cut out small squares, and serve this with steamed buns. Men enjoyed these small squares as appetizers along with warm rice wine.

"This was in one jar," Sister-in-Law said. "We always had two more." A second jar, she told me, stored a mixture of a little bit of meat with potatoes and vegetables. The third contained steamed buns, *mantou*.

I remembered well eating those steamed buns. Even when cold, they tasted wonderful! I recalled going outside to steal one, hiding it in my shirt to eat when I got hungry. I also recalled how Mama would make us new clothes each Lunar New Year.

During the hungry years, these memories seemed like forbidden luxuries. We could not even afford to eat real rice or white flour. We never had new clothes.

I couldn't understand why we were still so poor when everyone in our family worked so hard. Often Papa left home for two or three weeks at a time, building houses. There was no way to mail money back home. Mama's cash would run out long before he returned. Sister-in-Law's work sewing clothes for the army brought in a limited income, but there was never quite enough money.

During those hard years in Shijiazhuang, my eldest sister came back to live with us. Big Sister had married at seventeen, before I was born. Her husband was an opium addict and eventually became impossible to live with, so she returned home to her birth family. Her mother-in-law permitted Big Sister to take away only the younger of her two sons, three-year-old Peilian. Though he lived under the same roof with us, Peilian was not considered a member of our Wang family.

Several years later, Big Sister learned that her husband had died from his addiction somewhere on the streets of Beijing. Her mother-in-law did not go to claim the body, because that would have made her responsible for the burial, and she couldn't afford the expense. Big Sister also heard that her mother-in-law, desperately poor, had sold the older son, Peiquan, at the age of six, to be an apprentice to a Beijing opera troupe. Whenever his name came up, Big Sister's eyes looked tormented.

My parents didn't hesitate to take her back. But as a widowed daughter, Big Sister had low status in our family. Each year, at Lunar New Year, she had to spend the entire night sitting out on the street. According to local custom, a widow wasn't allowed to look at the lantern in her mother's home on New Year's Eve, or the whole family would suffer bad luck.

The return of Big Sister and her son made our living situation even more unbearable. The entire family was already sleeping on one platform bed. My mother and father kept close to one wall with Elder Brother and his wife against the other wall. Third Sister and I cuddled up in the middle, although my mother worried about her girls growing up in bed between these married couples.

After Big Sister and her son joined us in that crowded bed, Papa complained every morning. Peilian would grind his teeth at night and wake Papa up. One neighbor told my father, "Use the boy's shoe. Put the toe of it in his mouth and let him chew that." My father tried this, and Mama argued, "You cannot do this! It is cruel!" Papa said, "I work hard the whole day. At night I need my rest! I cannot rest because of the noise he makes!" Renting an additional room was out of the question.

Finally, Papa asked the landlord for permission to build a small room on one side where Elder Brother and his family could stay. The landlord agreed, and Papa built it. Then we had an entrance, with one small square table. On the right side lived my mother and her daughters, and on the left, my brother's family. What a big difference!

Another solution came as a gift. My father had learned some simple treatments in Chinese traditional medicine and volunteered to help whenever one of the neighbors had a health problem. He knew many medicinal herbs and had learned massage and acupuncture. Papa sometimes made medicine for people, but he never allowed the women to touch it, nor would he reveal any of his recipes to us. Most Chinese medicine was practiced only by men and taught to their sons.

Papa learned the Chinese traditional method of easing headaches and curing minor illnesses. A kind and generous man, Papa was very successful at helping people who had one particular affliction, an egg-sized lump in the back of the neck. My father used two fingers to massage the area. He would lift these two fingers to face the sun and blow his breath on them, then start his massage. Within about a week, the lump would be gone.

He earned such a fine reputation as a healer that he was addressed as *Da Ye*, "Master," by our neighbors. Most of his patients were too poor to pay him in cash. Our landlord was moved by my father's good deeds. He emptied out a small storage room, put in a small bed, and offered it to us, free of charge. My father moved in and was relieved. He said, "At last! I can get some sleep!"

Being so poor, we had very few possessions. But one day, a beggar stole a small pocket watch my father carried around. My father's friends found out who the thief was and brought the watch back. They offered to beat the guy up, but my father refused. "I think he's learned his lesson," Papa said.

Later, he told us, "If you treat people well, people will treat you well. If you hold bitterness in your heart, your whole life will be destroyed." I didn't fully understand what he meant until many years later.

I also didn't understand how hard things were on my mother. When Mama was three years old, she had been forced to undergo the common ritual of foot binding. Her feet were broken; the toes were folded back on top of her feet and tightly bound with a cloth three or four yards long. Mama told me how she cried and begged not to have her feet ruined, but my grandmother insisted, even though they were a simple working family of chimney makers. In those days, the smaller the feet, the greater the beauty. The imperial palace selected ladies-in-waiting based on the smallness of their feet.

By the time I saw them, Mama's feet were deformed stumps, about four or five inches long. She walked everywhere with short, stunted steps that made it seem she was walking very fast.

The practice of foot binding had begun with the wealthy, who prided themselves on ladies who did not need to work. Rich women wore tiny embroidered shoes and lounged about in courtyard gardens. But the practice had spread to all classes, so that every Chinese family did it to their young girls, in order to ensure a decent marriage. It was painful and cruel, a form of torture for girls and a severe restriction on the freedom of women. In theory, married women were not supposed to take jobs outside the home. But in reality, all poor women, in the cities and the farms, had to work constantly. Foot binding made no sense at all for poor families like ours.

After the emperor was overthrown in 1911, foot binding went out of fashion, and it gradually stopped. My mother refused to allow it for any of her daughters, even for Big Sister, who had been born in 1910. Sister-in-Law, who moved into our house when she was seventeen, had feet that were tightly bound during her childhood. But Mama told her, "Because of bound feet, I have suffered so much! I came from the old days. But now people's attitudes are changing, and I don't want you to suffer this way. Go ahead and unbind your feet."

It took time, loosening the bandages little by little, and Sister-in-Law's feet spread out. They weren't tiny like my mother's or normal like my eldest sister's either, but in between, like a size six. Once Sister-in-Law told me, "I'm so glad that your mama insisted on unbinding my feet. That was one of the first things she said when I moved in: those bandages—off with them!"

In a quiet way, Mama defied other customs, too. In Beijing, in those days, a daughter-in-law was not allowed to come to the table until after the whole family had finished eating. Then she ate by herself. Although most families followed this custom, my mother always treated Sister-in-Law like a member of the family. So we all ate together at the table.

But Mama was strict about other rules at mealtime. Elbows were not allowed on the table. We were instructed to use only one hand to eat. When we finished, we had to ask Papa's permission to leave the table. Back in Beijing, my dad had insisted on one other rule: leave a little bit of food left in the bowl. Such a gesture means that you have plenty of food and good luck. If you wipe the bowl completely clean, it means that you will starve. But after the war began, we had to drop that nicety. We were too close to starving already.

Chapter Four

A Different Fate

AFTER THREE OR four months of silence, Mama slowly began to recover from her stroke and the trauma of Second Sister's death. We knew she was getting better when she began to bicker with my father. Most of my parents' fights had to do with being poor. When father returned home, my mother would quarrel with him about how difficult it was to feed us. She threatened to go out and get a job, but he forbade it.

As it happened, I was the reason Mama's spirits came back.

Unlike my father, Mama believed girls should be educated. Back in Beijing, she had sent my third sister, Guilin, to school against his wishes. But when we left suddenly, her education had stopped after just a year or two. During the war, without his carpentry tools, my father didn't have money to continue her education. He said, "If the family she marries into wants to support her education, that's fine with me." But Guilin, just three years older than I, was too young to find a husband yet.

The year I turned seven, Mama argued with my father about me.

"Xiao Lao needs to go to school," Mama insisted one night as we were eating. I looked up from my bowl astonished. Third Sister had told me school was a wonderful place to meet little friends and get away from the grind of everyday home life.

My father glanced at me. "Whatever for?"

"I don't want her to be illiterate like me," Mama said, with a fire in her eyes I hadn't seen in years. "Although I can see, I'm like a blind person. You have to idea how terrible it feels, not being able to read a single word."

"It would be a total waste," Papa said. "Why should we spend the money to put this daughter through school when she is going to get married and belong to another family?" This was the traditional argument against educating girls. I

20

had heard it many times.

Mama's eyes took on a steely look. "This daughter won't be like the others. I want her to have choices."

Papa just shook his head. Thinking of Second Sister, I felt somber.

"This is our last chance, our youngest child," Mama persisted. She had a stubborn streak, which I inherited.

"If I had money, I'd send Peilian to school," Papa said. I knew this was true. Papa spent hours teaching his little grandson to read at home. Although my father had only six years of schooling himself, he often read history books. "As it is, we have to save up to send Xukuan to school," Papa said. That was Elder Brother's son, who was several years younger than I. As the only grandson with the family name, little Wang Xukuan would have priority over my sister's son. To my father, both grandsons had priority over me.

"Of course," Mama agreed. "Once Xiao Lao learns to read and write, she can help Xukuan. An education is something no one can ever take away from her."

Papa lifted his bowl of thin soup and emptied it. "We can't even buy decent vegetables. How can we find money for school?"

"I'll go out and find work," Mama said. "I'll sweep floors if I have to."

"No, you won't," Papa said.

Ours was a very traditional Chinese family, and normally my father made all the decisions. We were taught to obey him always. But to make sure I got an education, my mother defied him. In ways that mattered, large and small, Mama always loved me and took care of me. Papa had a good heart but he never questioned Confucian attitudes of obedience and male supremacy—not until years later. Plus, he was seldom at home and paid little attention to the children.

I was thrilled. Mama's strength and determination was back. She would protect us. And she would make sure I had a different fate than Second Sister.

≈

True to her word, my mother found a job, laboring as a charwoman in a Japanese military hospital. It was about twenty miles away, in a part of town called "East of the Bridge." In those days, the city of Shijiazhuang was divided into two sections—East of the Bridge and West of the Bridge, although in those wartime years there was no actual bridge. We lived West of the Bridge.

Mama's job was too far away for her to walk every day, so after working twelve-hour shifts, she spent the night there, sleeping on a long platform bed shared with many other Chinese workers. Most of the Japanese soldiers at the hospital were seriously wounded, and many died. Part of her job was to remove corpses. This short, skinny woman, with deformed feet, had to half-carry, half-drag each heavy dead body to another room.

My mother also cleaned hospital wards. Some wounded soldiers took their suffering out on her and the other Chinese workers. Mama told us that many of them had terrible tempers and treated her like an animal—beating her, shouting at her, and kicking her from behind as she went from room to room. Mama remembered hearing *baka*, "fool," frequently barked at her.

Mama endured this abuse so she could enroll me in a girls' primary school. She spent every penny of her earnings on my schooling, and she even saved part of her meager food rations to feed me. At first, I was too little to understand the sacrifice she was making.

But she would say, "Study hard, girl. Don't be like your mother, going through life like a blind person. All I know how to do is stand in front of the cook stove and take care of my husband. I know nothing about what goes on outside of our door. When people bully me, I don't even know what to say! And don't think that because you're a girl you're not as good as the boys. Learn well, and stand up for yourself!"

≈

School changed my life. I was so happy for the chance to learn that I could hardly control myself. In my heart, I set a high goal—to be the best student.

Each morning, I would scramble out of bed to pick up half-burnt cinders down by the railroad tracks. After that, I would come home, grab a piece of cornbread that had been slapped on the inside of the wok, and eat it as I walked to school.

Every school used the same books, and we studied each lesson for two days. Small children tend to retain experiences in a deep place and recall them clearly, even many years later. So I can still recite several of the first-grade lessons, like this one:

> *Darkness is over.*
> *A new day begins.*
> *Sister and brother get up early.*
> *The sun is almost rising.*
> *Arise! Greet the sun.*

≈

We had to memorize everything. Teachers did not allow us to ask questions. They just told us what we had to learn, and we did our best to remember. It was like forcing food into the mouth of a goose to fatten it up.

We didn't have pens or pencils but learned to write with a Chinese ink brush. We learned our sums on the abacus. I studied hard and became the best student in my class. After that, I set an even higher goal: I decided to be a doctor. Or maybe an engineer! At school, anything seemed possible.

But at home, things were still grim. While I was in school, Third Sister got a job. At age twelve, she went to work for a Japanese family—taking care of their two children, cleaning their house, and buying the food. Often she was beaten. Sometimes she came home with bruises on her face and arms. Tears streamed down her swollen cheeks.

"Please, please! Don't make me go back there," she pleaded. "If you just don't make me go back, I'll do anything else. I'll go out and beg for food."

Mama shook her head sadly. "You have to do this work, because we don't have enough food to feed everybody. Stick it out somehow. You'll be okay when we find you a mother-in-law."

Poor Third Sister! She cried and cried, but it was no use.

At this early age, buffeted by forces beyond my family's control, I learned that expressing emotions doesn't do any good. I tried to suppress my own feelings and soldier on. For poor people like us, it was the only option.

≈

Each day, after I got home from school, I would help Sister-in-Law sew buttons onto the military uniforms that she made. Sometimes after supper I would go to a classmate's house to do homework together. Returning home, I had to run and hide from drunken Japanese soldiers, who tried to grab Chinese girls—of any age. Once I had to pound on the door of a closed shop to hide inside.

The older I got, the more I chafed at how wrong this was. I couldn't understand why Japanese soldiers were allowed to beat, rape, and pillage at will. China was our country, not theirs. When they began to face defiance in parts of China, the Japanese began a scorched-earth tactic called the Three All Policy—kill all, loot all, destroy all. Villages that harbored resisters were burned to the ground. Nobody could stop them.

As I spent more time in school, I became aware of politics. To me, it seemed that politics did nothing but divide people. The Kuomintang, the puppet regime under the thumb of the Japanese, ran my school. Our principal, installed by this collaborationist government, was a self-important man from the South—with a big belly that showed he had plenty to eat.

Every morning, the school day opened with exercise drills, followed by our recitation of the Will of Dr. Sun Yat-sen, the Chinese leader who had inspired the revolution that overthrew the emperor in 1911. Then the principal would lecture the students, going on and on about political topics, including Dr. Sun's Three Principles of the People. We learned to respect Dr. Sun, who had traveled the world to gather support for China's freedom and who had died shortly before the Chinese achieved it. His political philosophy was appealing: he advocated nationalism, democracy, and improving people's livelihood. But under the Japanese occupation, democracy was a cruel joke. And even I could see that no one in power cared about my family's livelihood.

Dr. Sun was dead, and we didn't have enough to eat. All this political talk cut into our classroom time, and we students found it annoying and tedious. The teachers asked the principal to shorten his lectures, but their efforts were in vain.

Yet politics was everywhere, sometimes just under the surface. One teacher was a Mr. Liang, a little man with a moustache. I found out later that he was an agent for Chiang Kai-shek's military intelligence. Another teacher, Mr. An, told us about the "liberated areas." We knew these were regions of China not occupied by the Japanese, but we didn't realize that he was telling us about places run by the Communists. In those regions, he taught us that students went to another kind of school and learned harvest dances. He told us that in liberated areas everyone had enough to eat, and nobody went hungry. When school authorities entered the classroom to inspect, Mr. An would go back to the regular lesson, math or history.

When I was in fourth grade, some students started a campaign against the principal. We came to school for knowledge, not for his speeches of political nonsense every morning! He made our teachers angry, and most students hated him. The older students composed a jingle to curse the principal, and one tall boy from sixth grade came to our class, closed the door, and taught it to us. He recited one line at a time, and we repeated it until we remembered and could say it all together:

A big old crow flew in from the South.
He could talk, and he could laugh,
He could write and he could recite.
One two three! Two two three!
What a dirty bastard was he.

The conflict between students and teachers, on one side, and the puppet principal, on the other, became more and more bitter. Finally, the animosity rose to the point where the physical education teacher would shout, "Attention! Dismissed!" before the principal got a chance to give his morning lecture.

The principal struck back. "Good children of the party," he addressed us, meaning the puppet Kuomintang Party. "It is time to hunt down the secret Communist elements. They are making the trouble."

I went with some schoolmates to speak with the principal. We asked him, "What is the Communist Party? What do you mean by Communist elements?"

"Communist elements kill people and burn down their homes," the principal told us. "They don't even spare little children!"

We all looked at one another with wide eyes. Where were these monsters? Could they be worse than the Japanese soldiers?

The principal said, "There are definitely Communist elements behind the trouble here. Otherwise, how could everyone leave before my lecture? You mustn't be taken in by them!"

We asked Mr. An about the liberated areas where they did harvest dances. He responded by singing a song. "The sky is blue in the liberated areas," he sang, a line I recognized as praising the Communist Party.

"Oh," I said, "I get it. So the liberated areas are where the Communist Party is?"

"Shhhh!" he cautioned. "The Communist Party is the people's party, helping the people liberate themselves, so that everyone has food and housing. Just as we have capitalists in the city, they have landlords in the country. But the Communist Party gives the land to the farmers, and they are no longer beaten and bullied by the landlords."

That sounded good to me. But who was telling the truth? And what good did the Communists do if Japanese soldiers still terrified us all?

Teacher An often talked so much about these political matters that we couldn't finish our class work. This bothered me. Mama always reminded me of the importance of learning, of taking advantage of every possible minute to learn as much as I could. She taught me a ditty:

An inch of sunlight, an ounce of gold,
An ounce of gold can't buy an inch of sunlight.
If you don't try hard while you're young,
When you're older, you'll regret it in vain.

How hard it was for Mama to put me through school! I knew I had to learn everything I could to repay her kindness. While I loved to hear Teacher An tell stories about the liberated areas, I worried about the lost class time. Several friends and I decided to express our concerns and ask Teacher An to let us finish the class work before telling us stories.

They asked me to speak for the group. I wondered why he would listen to a poor girl like me, but I decided to try. I swallowed hard before opening my mouth. "Teacher An, sir. We're getting behind in our class work," I said. "Because you take too much time telling stories."

He frowned and shook his head, and I quaked. Maybe it was a big mistake to speak up. But he agreed. "Okay. I'll give you makeup classes."

This was the start of a lifetime conflict in my mind: People in authority told me politics would make life better, but I often felt impatient with political and ideological activity when it cut into time needed to learn skills and get things done.

As the war dragged on, my father's construction business dried up. He found very few jobs that employed a whole team; he could only find small jobs for one or two people.

After getting to know my classmates, I began to wonder, *Why are we so poor? Other kids have enough to eat. Why can't I even touch barley, or chicken, or apples? Why do we never ever have a decent meal?*

What do I mean by poor? I was seventeen years old before I had my first piece of fruit, after I got my first job. Mama told me that when she was married, they borrowed an apple to put in the middle of the table for the wedding feast. No one dared eat the apple, and it was returned afterwards to the neighbor from whom it was borrowed. Even though my family members were all honest, hardworking people, we were never able to do much more than simply survive. The more I learned about the larger world outside our family compound, the more I worried about that. It seemed unfair, but there was nothing I could do about it.

In 1945, just before the war ended, I graduated from primary school. I was number one in my graduating class of forty-odd students. But I knew that would be the end of my education. Mama was proud of me—and also relieved that she could quit her grimy hospital job and sleep at home. Now I could read. For her, that was enough.

One day, my music teacher visited us at home. She had strongly encouraged my singing and believed I had promise to become a professional singer. "Yulin is not on the list of middle school entrants," she said. "I'm sure she could pass the exams. What's the problem?"

"We have no money," Mama said. Middle school charged tuition, and even families with money didn't waste it on educating daughters beyond sixth grade.

"But it doesn't take much money," the teacher protested.

"Teacher, we have nothing," Mama replied. "Yulin not only can't afford school, she has to go to work to bring some money in for the family to survive."

So after graduating first in my class, I went back to picking up half-burned coals, pulling up edible weeds, sewing on buttons and stuffing cotton in jackets, and helping my father sell cigarettes. Still, I couldn't help dreaming of going on to middle school. After a few days, I got up my courage to broach the subject with my father.

He laughed. "Useless!" he said. "What good would it do?"

"Girls can work and earn money, too!" I said. "With more education, I could get a better job."

A sad look crossed his face. "You little wench. What do you know?" He shook his head. "You want to work? I'll get you a job."

Third Sister, home for a brief stay, shivered. "You don't want to work," she said.

I gave up. Mama had sacrificed for me. Now it was time I helped out the family.

A few days later, Papa came home with news. A textile mill was looking for old people and young people to work the night shift, running the cotton gins. They were willing to hire children as young as twelve. Papa had accepted a job for himself—and he agreed to take me with him.

Together we headed off for my first job: night shift at the cotton mill.

Chapter Five

Liberation

I FELT VERY GROWN-UP, having my first paying job, but I also worried; Papa said the work at the textile mill involved machines and could be dangerous for a twelve-year-old child. Mother warned me to listen to my father, avoid going anywhere alone, and always stick close to him while walking to and from the factory in the dark.

The cotton gins were small electric units, installed at waist height over a conveyor belt. Standing in a long row at stations along the belt, workers fed cotton bolls into the machine in front of them. The machine divided cotton fiber from the seeds, working lightning fast. The supervisor always pushed us, "Quick! Quick! You cannot stop. Too slow!" So without thinking, I had to continuously pick up cotton and feed it into the hungry machine.

If you got sleepy, you might go to scoop cotton bolls, not realizing that your hand was still over the machine. If your hand touched the machine, it made a big *BRRRR* sound, and it would stop. The first time I did this, my heart jumped into my mouth, and I quickly snatched my hand back to safety. The supervisor yelled at me. "Stupid girl! Don't touch!" The second time I did it, he got even angrier. But it was hard to stay alert on the night shift.

One night, after I had worked there for about five months, there was an accident. The little boy next to me got sleepy, and while putting cotton into the machine, his hand went in—and he couldn't pull it out! The boy screamed. His blood spurted all over the white cotton bolls. I jumped back and grabbed my own hands. His machine screeched to a stop, and the supervisor turned off the electricity for the whole factory. I couldn't stop watching as a grown-up worker extracted the boy's arm from the machine. His hand was mangled beyond repair. Horror washed over me as I witnessed the bloody pulp that was left.

Any injury was strictly the worker's problem. The factory would not pay any hospital expense or medical care. The boy was fired.

This tragedy could just as well have happened to me. Back home, when I told Mama, she refused to let me continue working there. She said, "No more! I don't want you to lose an arm!"

Relieved but also disappointed, I went back to the dull life of helping with the sewing.

≈

One day, I heard a great shouting on the street: "The Japanese Devils are all washed up! They surrendered!"

The streets underwent a remarkable change. The haughty conquerors of yesterday were now shuffling down the street, heads low, bowing constantly to every Chinese they met. We children came out and shouted at them gleefully. Many Chinese pedestrians shoved and beat the disarmed, defeated Japanese soldiers who had tormented us for so long.

But the devils' departure made no difference for our family's poverty, and we couldn't get Second Sister back.

The first time I heard the word America was when people shouted, "American relief supplies are here!" Our family was issued one drab olive U.S. Army blanket. We had no idea what Americans were like, but we were impressed by the fact that these strangers across the sea were sending us supplies.

As soon as the Kuomintang government of Chiang Kai-shek took control of our city, I heard in whispers that Communists were being rounded up and executed. No one dared to discuss this out loud, let alone object. Even if only one member of the family had joined the Communist Party, the whole family would be arrested. In fact, the Number Six Jail was a notorious jail where suspected Communists were subjected to all kinds of cruel torture. We heard of people dragged off to the jail and never heard of anyone being released.

"See? Politics is dangerous business. Don't even talk about it," my father warned. "If anyone asks, just say we are loyal Chinese citizens."

I thought, *Teacher An must be a Communist. I have to keep his secret so he doesn't get in trouble.* I tried not to imagine what it would be like for him in the Number Six Jail.

Once, I had gone to Teacher An's living quarters. It was the barest, poorest-looking place I had ever seen. I was shocked. "You're even poorer than my family," I said, "not like the other teachers."

He told me that Communists served the people and couldn't think of their own comfort. He said Communists sided with the poor workers and peasants against the rich and powerful who made our lives miserable. After that, I no longer believed that the Communist "bandits" killed people and burned their homes. Instead, I admired them for their selflessness and service to others.

Things were getting very tense in our city. Rifle fire crackled all around our little house. Rumors flew along the street. Everyone in our compound rushed down into the earthen cellar in which the landlord stored his cabbages.

"The Communists share property and wives!" My father cautioned all our neighbors to keep their women out of sight. My parents started discussing possibilities for getting Third Sister and me married off, to protect us. On that very day, they found a husband for Guilin, a worker in the Da Qing Textile Mill. Soon after, they were married.

It wasn't possible to have the traditional sedan chair to fetch the bride in or to have the usual celebrations with loud drums and cymbals and a big feast. The wedding was a modest dinner held at the man's family home, East of the Bridge, and we attended.

The groom wore a western-style hat with two tall feathery sticks in the hatband. Third Sister was dressed in the red bridal garments my sister-in-law had worn, with a red headband. My brother-in-law sawed on his *erhu*, the Chinese two-stringed fiddle, and we got a friend to pipe on the *suona*, a small, shrill folk trumpet, said to have been brought by the Huns and named after a town in Turkey. That was all the wedding music we had.

My mother gave Third Sister a piece of white cloth to take with her to her new home; it was to be shown to her father-in-law and mother-in-law the next morning, to prove by spots of blood that she had been a virgin. Otherwise, her new family would bully her all her life for being a "bad girl" and treat her with contempt. My mother really worried about this test for us; she wanted us to be treated with respect and kindness in our future families.

Symbolizing the journey from her father's home to the husband's home, Guilin was carried in a chair from one room to another. Together the bride and groom kowtowed: to ancestors, to parents, then to each other. Her new husband entered the wedding chamber with a bow and fired off four arrows—one into each corner—to drive out evil spirits, then carried Guilin into the room.

To tease the new couple, we put the traditional walnuts, dates, and other lumpy things under the thin mattress on the bridal bed. At some weddings, little kids hid under the bed while older people hid outside, near the window, which had been cracked open so they could hear. The couple would have difficulty sleeping because it was so uncomfortable! In exasperation, they would say, "Raw walnuts!" These words in Chinese sound the same as "giving birth." Listeners outside would snicker, while the kids giggled under the bed—so the new couple got no rest the whole night. The teasing was all part of the wedding fun. It was one time in our drab lives when everyone could laugh.

The next morning, after the white cloth had changed hands, the bride was served dumplings that were purposely undercooked. The in-laws would ask, "Raw?" She would say, "Yes, raw!" This means "have a baby." Everyone would applaud, hoping that new members would be born into this house, happily and safely.

The second day the bride was given a piece of cloth to make into a pair of pants. A girl with little sewing experience might fail, bringing suffering upon herself. But a job well done made the husband's family happy. The third test was to cook for the whole family. If a bride didn't do well, her mother-in-law would teach her, but with a criticizing attitude.

These were traditional "regulations" for becoming a wife. Legally, the groom's mother had the right to beat her daughter-in-law at any time, for any reason. So the bride wanted to do well and please her mother-in-law right from the start.

Mama told me this was my destiny, as well. She betrothed me to a man who fried dough twists for a living—again, out of fear that I would be "Communized." Since I was young, the wedding was postponed, but at least Mama thought I had a protector.

After Third Sister's wedding, the combat outside Shijiazhuang intensified. Citizens were ordered by the Kuomintang government to dig trenches to protect the city from the Communists. Following the ancient imperial custom, families were organized into groups of ten, and one man from every family had to do hard labor for the government. Since my brother had a job at a watch shop, Papa agreed to go. He not only had to get up very early to dig ditches but also had to round up men from other families to do this work with him. The trenches were more than ten feet deep, and Papa told us his crew had to dig about a thousand cubic feet of earth.

The Communists must have been close to the city, because there was constant strafing from KMT planes. When we heard airplanes overhead, we ran into the cellar. After the planes left, we came out and picked up a lot of bullets in our courtyard.

One day, the strafing went on far longer than usual, and it seemed closer. Then, all of a sudden, the firing stopped. But we still didn't dare come out of the cellar. Then we heard some men in the courtyard, shouting, "Anybody here? Old Grandfather! Old Grandmother! Don't be afraid! We're the army of the poor. You have nothing to fear!"

I could hear their voices from inside the cellar, where I huddled with Mama, Big Sister, and Sister-in-Law, hoping the soldiers hadn't come for us. "Old Grandfather" and "Old Grandmother" were terms of respect, not like anything we had heard from the Japanese or the Kuomintang soldiers.

My father left the cellar to go to the latrine. We heard a soldier speak to him. "Don't be afraid, Grandfather. What's your name? What do you do?"

"My name is Wang. I'm a carpenter."

"Great! A worker!"

"And who are you?" There was fear and suspicion in my father's voice.

"We're from the Eighth Route Army. We liberate the poor. Do you understand?"

I had never heard this term, "liberation," applied to people. It sounded like the word meaning "untie" or "release"—like untying a goat to let it eat freely in a field.

A young soldier ran up. "Company Commander, where are we going to rest?"

"Right here. This is a worker's home. Grandfather, is it all right if we rest here and boil some drinking water?"

"Yes, that's okay," said my father, still wary.

I was amazed to hear their polite tone. What armed soldiers ask permission?

"Isn't there anyone else in your family?"

"We have a whole big family here."

"Oh. Well, where are they?"

"Hiding in the cellar."

"Can you get them to come out? Tell them that we won't hurt anyone."

My father called out, "Everyone come out! It's all right."

We emerged from the cellar, full of curiosity. No one had ever heard of soldiers who were polite and helpful, rather than pillaging and bullying people.

A tall soldier asked me, "Little Girl, whose family do you belong to?"

Frozen at the sight of soldiers in our courtyard, I could not respond. I was fourteen, but still so short that people often called me Little Girl or Little Sister.

"What's wrong, Little Girl?" he said. "We're the army of the poor. We've been fighting for you. There's nothing to be afraid of."

"You look just like us," I said. Each young man had a cap with a red star on it, but otherwise they were dressed in old, often-mended clothes. Only one of them had a rifle slung over his shoulder.

"Of course, we're the same."

"Our principal told us you had red noses and green eyes," I said, teasing them like brothers.

Everyone burst out laughing, and they asked me my name.

"Wang Yulin," I answered.

"So you are in school?"

"I finished sixth grade," I said proudly. "But we don't have any money, so of course I can't go to school anymore."

The commander said, "Don't worry, Little Girl. In the liberated areas, schools are all free. You don't need money to go to school."

"Really!" I exclaimed, wide-eyed. No longer afraid, I took his hand and led him in to see our modest rooms. One young soldier pointed at our clothes stand and said, "Is that for taking pictures?" Then I realized that these must be country boys who knew nothing about cities and city people. In rural areas, no one had more than one or two sets of clothing.

One soldier asked, "What do you have to eat?"

"I can go collect some edible weeds for you," I said.

"Aren't there any rich people's storehouses that have food?"

"Yes, there are," I said. "I have seen them when I went out collecting coals. I can show you."

After I led them to the building, the soldiers flung open the storehouse doors. Floor to ceiling, it was crammed with more sacks of flour and rice than I had ever imagined existed in the entire city. The soldiers handed me a sack and then started handing them out to people on the streets.

"Can we really take this food?" a woman asked.

"You can," said a Red Army commander. "This is called *Kai Cang Ji Pin*,'throwing open the granaries to feed the poor.'"

I had never heard of that, but it sounded wonderful. Poor people lined up to receive sacks of flour, which they hastened home on their shoulders.

I took my sack home and gave it to Mama. It contained wheat flour of a fine quality we hadn't eaten since leaving Beijing.

My mother and sister-in-law used the flour to make huge stacks of *laobing*, delicious Chinese griddle cakes. We hadn't eaten like that in as long as I could remember!

After dinner, the commander came back to our courtyard. He asked my father, "Grandfather, do you know a shortcut to the area called East of the Bridge?"

"Yes," said my father. "My third daughter's in-laws live over there."

"Could you take us there by the shortcut? We want to liberate the people on the other side of the bridge. We have to go in the darkness of night."

"Can do," said my father. "We can leave at twilight."

My father took a kerosene lantern and led the way. When he returned, he told us, "They don't allow any noise when they're on the march; they move in total silence. All the way, we had to pick our way among corpses. I have never seen such polite soldiers, neither beating nor cursing. When we got there, the commander said, 'Grandfather, you go back now. We're going to have to fight.' In all my life, I have never seen an army like this."

My mother said, "They all call me 'Grandmother,' and they were so thankful when I gave them some laobing to eat."

Then I told everybody, "And they are going to let me go to school, without paying any money!"

Our city of Shijiazhuang was officially liberated on November 12, 1947. It was the happiest day of my life. If this was Communism, I wanted more of it.

Chapter Six

My Own Liberation

THE SOLDIER'S PROMISE was not empty. Two months later, in early 1948, I entered Shijiazhuang Girls' Middle School. It was a boarding school, with tuition, textbooks, meals, and lodging—all free. What a wonderful new world! All of a sudden, I had no worries about food, shelter, and education.

I was beside myself with joy. We girls stayed in the school dormitories and were fed three meals a day. Some students complained about the monotonous diet, but for me, it was heaven.

At school, they usually served us steamed corn bread with yellow bean sprouts, sometimes varied with millet. Corn bread was considered cheap food, but the kind served at school was made solely of cornmeal—no wild weeds or vegetables in it! The first time I had anything stir-fried, it was bean sprouts with a thin watery sauce, served with corn bread. I dipped my corn bread in the sauce from the beans and savored the flavor as if it were food from the emperor's table. This was the same "discovery" that Sidney told me he made in prison: if you soak the powdery corn bread in cabbage soup, it is so tasty!

Other students who watched me were surprised: "You eat everything!"

"This is delicious!" I told them.

"But those are just bean sprouts."

And I said, "I have never eaten this before. If you'd lived on the pigs' bean-cake and wild weeds, you'd know how good this food really tastes."

At the end of every meal, my bowl would be clean. I was so grateful, I would skip back and forth to class. Far and away, this was the happiest I had ever felt.

Having grown up during a time we now called the "Old Society," I had to adjust to what seemed to me a whole new world. Before, when I hunted for coal cinders, I was just one kid among the beggars. But now I lived with my classmates, and I had to learn how to talk to educated people. I loved making new friends. Every morning I hummed to myself as I washed my face, and every night I listened to the breathing of the other girls. Fifteen of us slept on a long wooden bed, with only a coal burner to heat the room. But I fell asleep with a smile on my face.

Although I was nearly fifteen, I was in seventh grade, what we called grade one of middle school. Still, I was not the oldest in my class. War and poverty had disrupted education for most of us.

Our school didn't have many students, and their educational levels varied widely. Some of them came from the old guerrilla bases and were much older and less educated. They were serious about learning, and they wore a kind of uniform that looked like the Eighth Route Army, except there were no insignia. The teachers were all very conscientious. Most of them came from a college called North China Associated University, in the old liberated area. Some other teachers were held over from the KMT school system.

Since Shijiazhuang was the first big city to be liberated, the Communist Party began many pilot projects there. The Party, then headquartered a few hours outside our city, declared that Shijiazhuang would be "our Moscow"—where Communist policies were first implemented in an urban setting.

Ours was the first middle school for girls, and received special attention from the top leadership. The teachers were always inquiring after our health, our living conditions, and our studies. To me, this attention was novel and amazing. None of the teachers questioned whether it was worthwhile to educate girls.

Many of our teachers had lived in the Shanxi-Chahar-Hebei region, which had been a Communist guerrilla base against the Japanese. Under our teachers' guidance, we girls organized a song and dance team and created modernized versions of the traditional, familiar harvest songs and dances, called *Yangge,* to educate city folks about the meaning of Liberation.

It was propaganda; that's true. But I believed in it with all my heart. For the first time in my life, people outside my family reached out and offered me a chance at a better life. I had never expected this. I was so full of joy that I wanted to shout it in the streets. And I did.

Throughout 1948 and 1949, the Red Army liberated many Chinese cities, one after another. Every time a town was liberated, students from our school would go out in the street and create a celebration. So in addition to doing our class work, we were very busy!

As the People's Liberation Army (PLA) paraded through the city, we girl students would follow, telling everyone through our songs and dances that a new day was dawning. People would flock into the street. We used simple instruments that anybody could play—the *suona* trumpet, round Chinese drums, and cymbals. We would shout slogans and sing the songs for which the Chinese Communist Party had become famous, including "The East Is Red" and "The Sky in the Liberated Areas Is Bright and Clear." The dances were easy to learn, and we twirled with bright scarves. Sometimes the local people would join in and dance with us. We carried a picture of Mao Zedong in a stiff frame and a slogan that was written in big characters on a long piece of cotton cloth: "Celebrate the Liberation of"—followed by the name of the latest city.

Our group would stop in each little neighborhood to put on a short musical play, about ten minutes long. Through these plays, we showed people the need to eliminate the bad ways of the Old Society, which we learned to call "feudal." We called on the poor to begin a new life full of hope in the new society and to send their children to school. Sometimes I would see girls look at me with that same wide-eyed amazement I had felt just months earlier. *School? Really?*

In one skit, I was cast as a male worker, because everyone said I looked strong. It was a story about a wife whose husband and mother-in-law wouldn't allow her to attend literacy classes or take part in social activities. They thought that her only role in life was to stay at home and take care of her husband and children. But then the husband went to a training course and learned about the role of women in the new society. He changed his thinking, then supported his wife in learning to read and write and helping to overthrow the old feudal values.

Every time I acted in a skit or danced in the streets, my heart flooded with joy. I eagerly learned the new words and ideas. I felt released from the tight bonds of poverty and the old ideas that had always oppressed women. I knew I was lucky to be living at this moment in history. To me, this *was* Liberation.

After the long years of war and occupation, most people in Shijiazhuang and the surrounding areas lived in grinding poverty, and they could immediately see the impact of the Communist policies. Even if the poor understood nothing about Marxism, they felt tremendous gratitude for Mao Zedong and the Communist Party. At last, they had full bellies and opportunities to work for a better future.

One weekend when I was home, a district committee was taking the first census after Liberation. They registered every family in a big book, writing down names of the parents and the number of members in the family. They came to our house and asked me my mother's name. Because of the traditional way in which we addressed each other, I did not know.

Girls keep the last name of their father. Growing up, they are called "Number 1," "Number 2," "Number 3," etc. The last one born is called "Xiao Lao," meaning "the child of our old age," as I was called. When my mother was young, daughters weren't given any other name. When they grew up, they were called so-and-so's wife or so-and-so's mother.

That day I learned that my mother's original family name was Li, which means "plum." When she married my father, whose family name is Wang, meaning "king," this gave her the name "Wang Li." Most women had no given name, so they just added the character *Shi*, which means "clan." My mother's name, Wang Li Shi meant she was Mrs. Wang, from the Li clan. Later, I found out that she did have a personal name, a nickname from her childhood, but it was considered bad luck to mention it after marriage.

However, my brother and sisters did have formal given names because we knew our genealogy and family history. Papa kept a thick book handed down from his great-great-great-grandfather, which designated the names to be used for male and female descendants for five or six generations. Under that system, when a child is born, the name is already set. But only the sons use these names for their children.

My father followed this tradition in naming us. Our names all had to have the second character *lin*, meaning "forest": Xiulin, Guilin, Weilin, Yulin. Today, younger generations in China no longer follow this naming tradition. My siblings and I are the last ones in our family to carry all the family's names.

Traditional language was changing for me at school, and it got me in trouble at home. In Chinese, *nin*, the formal version of "you," is used for addressing elders while *ni*, informal "you," is used to address peers and younger people. My parents had brought me up to use nin when addressing them, but our teachers insisted on being addressed informally, as comrades. I got used to speaking with everyone that way.

One Sunday at home, my father told me to get him some tea water. And I asked, "Papa, do you want the whole glass?" I used the informal address without even thinking. I turned to go up the few steps into the next room and received a hard kick from behind. I hit the steps, which banged my nose and scraped my face badly. I sat there, stunned.

"You go to school, huh!" Papa shouted, standing over me, his face distorted in a scowl. "What kind of person did you become? Not respecting your parents? How dare you address me as "ni"! Now stop crying. I will teach you how to respect people."

I hadn't realized how important this was, but very clearly that day, I got it. My father was not violent in general, but he was very strict. I was angry at being kicked, but my mother explained to me later why it was wrong of me to show disrespect.

I lost that battle, but I did succeed in getting Mama to cancel my betrothal.

At school, we learned about many topics that had once been taboo. Our hygiene teacher, a man in his sixties, told us that he had never been allowed to teach this subject before. He taught our class full of girls about menstruation, pregnancy, and other things that made us hide our faces in embarrassment.

He said, "I used to not dare to teach these things, and now you don't dare to look me in the face. But these are all things that you need to know."

Before these lessons, we used to use strips of old clothing for sanitary napkins. When we washed them out, we would throw them in some dark corner, never even thinking of drying them in the sun to reuse them. We didn't dare let anyone see them. Now, we learned to use sanitary paper, and if we did use cloth, to wash the cloths and then hang them up in the sun to dry.

My mother upbraided me for this "indecent exposure." I argued that we had learned this in school. Even so, she said, I could carry out these new sanitary measures only at school, not at home.

I continued to pour every ounce of strength into my studies. I became the number one student in the sciences, and I dared to tell others my big dream: to become a doctor or an engineer. I loved singing, and, similar to my primary school teacher, my current teacher felt I should study singing and make it my career.

Besides leading the Yangge team, I ran track. I became very good at running—perhaps because as a child, I had to chase the trains and pick up coal embers. The physical education teacher trained me in long-distance running, more than four hundred meters. I made the school team and was selected as the entrant for the citywide long-distance running events. I came in first, winning the championship in girls' long-distance running for our city. As the school's star track athlete, I was getting to be well known in Shijiazhuang.

One day, when I was studying in the classroom, an older student named Luo Huarui came over to talk with me.

"I've been paying attention to you," she said. "You do well in your studies and you're always willing to help other people. You get along with everyone—and you're from a worker's family. We have an organization that can help improve your understanding and also help you in your studies. Would you be willing to join?"

Everything was still new to me. I asked her, "If I joined, what would I be doing?"

"You would raise your consciousness and become a better person and a more effective one," she said.

I didn't know what "raise my consciousness" meant. "Would I have to pay?"

"No," she answered, a little amused. "It would not cost you anything."

"Then maybe I can join," I said. "My family has no money. I'll think about it."

The organization was the Communist Youth League. To join it was not the same as joining the Communist Party, but it was a step in that direction and a firm commitment. Still, in those days it was a potentially dangerous one because the Chiang Kai-shek government was still fighting to suppress Communism.

I had to think twice about getting involved in anything political. In China, politics was not about casting ballots. It was a life-and-death struggle. Before Liberation, we had seen those accused as Communists disappear into the Number Six Jail, never coming back out again. And now, after Liberation, I knew that the Communist Party investigated people suspected of being Kuomintang spies.

In fact, the new regime did check out every single family I knew. Who had joined or ever helped the Kuomintang? Who had been a member of the Kuomintang's Three Principles Youth League? Those individuals had to report for questioning, make a self-criticism, and write down exactly what they had done for the Kuomintang. Those records would prove damaging in years to come, more than anyone imagined.

Even though the Communists had taken control of Shijiazhuang's government, the city was still very much in a state of civil war. Many people opposed and feared the Communist Party, especially older people. Sometimes they even killed those they believed to be Communists. At school, our teachers called them "counterrevolutionaries." Government control had changed hands so many times in the past forty years that many ordinary people doubted this Communist-run government would stay in power. After all, the Communist Party had no experience running anything larger than a rural region.

"Don't ever join any political party," Papa warned me. "They're all trouble. If you do, it could bring disaster to the whole family."

From birth, I was trained to obey my father in all matters. But I was beginning to think for myself. "The Communist Party has been good to us," I retorted. "They're helping poor people."

He glowered. "No. I forbid it. The family's safety is more important than anything else. Remember that!"

But I was stubborn like my mama. I understood why my father opposed it, and how dangerous it might be for the whole family. But I defied my father and secretly joined the Communist Youth League on December 26, 1948, Chairman Mao's birthday. I joined with several other students in the induction ceremony. Comrade Luo led us in a simple oath, with clenched fists raised, after which we were officially members. It turned out that Luo was the leader of our league branch.

The main reason I joined was gratitude to the Party, which had changed my life in such positive ways. I had gained so much from being able to attend school that I wanted to spread the benefits to others. Although Americans today look at me with skepticism when I say so, many Chinese of my generation understand and remember this feeling of joy and gratitude. Our lives had truly changed overnight.

I took my youth league membership very seriously. I felt it was my duty to help other students with their lessons, so I began to do math coaching during off-hours or between classes. I also did other social work, took part in youth league training courses that the city Party committee held, and organized political activities for our branch of the league.

Every week I attended youth league meetings, which included students from other schools, both boys and girls. At the meetings, all the leaders talked about was how we could help other people. Some students would ask, "What is the Communist Party? What do they do?" And our leaders taught us, saying, "The Communists are on the side of the poor. We serve the people." My teachers showed us what this meant through their actions. To me, what mattered most was how people treated others. I loved the Party because I could see how they had helped me, and how they taught me to help other students at my school.

Because of the constant fear of Kuomintang informers, our meetings were held in secret. During the day we attended classes, so we usually met at night, at some place away from school, outside the city in the suburbs. My teacher warned me to be very cautious at night, because there were gangs of disgruntled former power-holders and dispossessed landlords who harassed people on the streets.

Sometimes on a weekend night, when I was at home, a schoolmate would come get me for a league meeting. I would tell my mother it was just a school meeting.

She insisted I always walk with another person for company, and I agreed. I hated walking alone, especially passing graveyards. All graves were dug outside the city, along farmers' fields. Wooden coffins were buried with little mounds built up on top of them. A board stood at the head, showing the name of that person with birth and death dates, plus the name of the deceased. I was afraid of ghosts. An older classmate told me that was ridiculous; no modern person believed in ghosts. But I couldn't help feeling afraid. That's when I learned to whistle and sing to keep up my courage.

In March of 1949, three months after I joined the youth league, I was one of a few students sent from my school for a week's cadre training program. We learned that the youth league was a young reserve force for the Communist Party of China, which represented the interests of the poor and oppressed, working for the liberation of the entire human race. I ardently wanted to be part of that. I learned a lot of big words, like "proletariat" (in Chinese this means "propertyless class"), "capitalist," and "feudal." I learned that even during the Japanese occupation, the Party organized the distribution of land to the landless and land-poor peasants, behind the battle lines. This was a big deal. When farmers had control over their own land and didn't have to give grain to the landlord, they produced more food for everyone to eat. I could see this on my plate each meal.

What I observed, in fact, was that the Communists really did help poor people. Some families had too many kids, and the mother had never worked, and they gave more grain to those large poor families. Sometimes they found jobs for people. They let poor kids like me go to school without paying. They kept repeating the slogan: "This party belongs to the workers and the peasants, not to the rich people." And I believed that. I trusted the Communist Party with all my heart.

The focal point of our training was, "Always remember the good that the Party has brought you!" We were taught, above all, to be thankful and loyal to the Party. That early training invaded my thinking so deeply that I could never shake it, even when Party policies changed.

≈

After Liberation, Big Sister, Xiulin, decided to look for work. She was hired as a nanny by the new mayor of Shijiazhuang, Ke Qingshi, nicknamed "Big Nose Ke." My big sister demonstrated that she was honest and could do the work of several people: she cleaned house quickly, cooked well, and took very good care of their children. Xiulin worked for this family most of her life.

When asked about her family history, Xiulin explained to the mayor's wife about her two sons—the older one sold by her mother-in-law, the younger one with her parents. With the help of Mayor Ke's family, Big Sister began putting notices in newspapers all over the country, trying to find Peiquan. Finally, in response, someone from Shaanxi Province contacted the mayor's office.

My sister was so excited! What would her son look like after all these years? He had been sold at age six; now he would be in his late teens. The mayor insisted that Xiulin take the train to meet the Peking Opera Group, and she recognized her son immediately.

My sister spoke with the man in charge of the group. "Can I bring my son with me and let the mayor see him? So we can thank him?"

He said of course, because the mayor was a powerful leader. The mayor was pleased to see this handsome young man who was also very good at Peking opera. But the story of his childhood was a sad one. Like the apprentice in the movie *Farewell My Concubine*, Peiquan had been beaten mercilessly by his masters and had led a very hard life.

The mayor asked him, "What do you want to do? Continue to sing the Peking opera?"

"No! I hate it," Peiquan said. "What I want to do is to work in a factory and go to night school."

The mayor's office asked the opera group to do this favor—to let Peiquan go. Of course they agreed. Peiquan vowed never to sing another line of opera again. He worked, studied, and became a chief engineer.

Meanwhile, Guilin pursued a career in the People's Liberation Army. She never finished primary school before she started working at age twelve; she married at nineteen.

After Liberation, the PLA was checking every government agency to uncover any corruption and correct it: they reviewed the quality of workers' performance, the accuracy of the books, and the behavior of people in charge of company finances. Guilin's husband managed a textile factory's financial books. Soon after they were married, he was arrested and imprisoned for three years for having acquired some factory money in a shady transaction.

Guilin believed he was a dishonest person. Her in-laws did not allow divorce, so she joined the PLA by herself—without telling any of us. While I was in middle school, Guilin continued her education in the army. She studied very hard and became a doctor's assistant, learning how to assess patients and dispense medicine. Eventually she became a pharmacist.

My father's fortunes took an upswing as well. He had made a contribution by helping the PLA soldiers liberate the other half of Shijiazhuang, and now the new local government asked him to do road work and to build army barracks, houses, and furniture for retired Red Army soldiers. He earned good money, and Mama finally had enough to feed us. We were taught to thank the Communist Party for all this—and for the overwhelming fact that I was actually studying at school.

In 1949, when I was in ninth grade, I came down with a severe case of colitis that nearly killed me. I stayed at home sick for more than two months and shrank to a shadow of my former self. My parents had no money for a doctor. Instead, they prayed at a Buddhist temple for my recovery. Confident of his own healing power, my father fed me some herbal medicine that tasted like ashes—a powder that he mixed with water. But I got worse and worse. After Liberation, I had the right to hospital care for free. But my parents didn't know that.

In our compound lived an elderly couple named Li, who sold fried dough twists for a living. They were fond of me and often gave me little treats to eat. I called them "Godfather" and "Godmother." Thinking that I was doomed, they brought a wooden board for me to be laid out on when I died.

One day, two of my teachers showed up, to see why I had been absent from school for so long. One teacher told my mother that the principal, worried about a star student, had sent her to inquire about me. By then, I was already in a coma. Without even asking my parents' permission, they quickly wrapped me up, and using the wooden board as a stretcher, carried me to the hospital.

The hospital doctor shook his head and said it was too late to save me. I was placed in an area for the terminally ill, but the doctor continued to care for me. My mother refused to leave my side. She wet my lips with water and slept at the door to my room every single night.

After what seemed an endless time, the hospital found the right medicine for me. After a series of injections, I "came back from the dead." My parents gave thanks at the temple for my deliverance. They told me that I should work hard to repay the blessing. For weeks, I recuperated in the hospital until I was able to eat normally. After a short time at home, I returned to school.

Here's how this incident was written up in our school publication:

> One day, student Wang Yulin took sick and was unable to move. Teacher
> Yang Ting immediately got the women teachers together to carry the student to
> the hospital on a litter. Local people saw these teachers in grey uniforms, carry-
> ing the student to the hospital, and it became a local legend at once. People said,
> 'Look how concerned the Communist Party is for the welfare of the people!
> Who ever heard of such a thing!'

(Reprinted from the Memorial Publication of the City
of Shijiazhuang on the 50th Anniversary of the Former Girls
Middle School, now called Middle School #17).

By October 1, 1949, when Communist Party Chairman Mao Zedong declared that "The Chinese people have stood up" and announced the formation
of the People's Republic of China, I was already deeply committed to his cause.
Our youth league members danced in the streets to celebrate the Liberation of
all of China.

I never dreamed that one day I would meet Chairman Mao.

Chapter Seven

Party Secrets

BY THE END of 1949, the Red Army occupied every major city in mainland China, and Chiang Kai-shek had fled to Taiwan with his corrupt government. He still claimed the right to rule all of China, but nobody expected him to come back soon.

Still, it was considered risky to be a Communist. A lot of people didn't dare to join the Party, and all Communist Party meetings were still held in secrecy at that time.

Early in 1950, I became a part-time staffer at the city office of the Communist Youth League. I also was appointed vice chairman of the city's China/Soviet Friendship Association and was congratulated by Mayor Ke for this organization's achievements. We all admired the Soviet Union as China's big brother, guiding us and collaborating with us on projects to modernize and strengthen our country. Organizations that exchanged culture and nurtured friendship with the Russians were important. For the first time, I met foreigners and marveled at their yellow hair, bulbous noses, and thick beards.

Such work filled me with pride, since not too long ago it had been unthinkable for girls to take leadership roles. But I didn't forget traditional girlish matters. At school, I crafted some lovely pieces of embroidery. My teacher told me that all my pieces would be included in a special permanent display. I was excited and honored, but sad to find out that my artwork belonged to the school. I never got to keep even one.

By the time I was approached to apply for full Communist Party membership, I was eager to join. Everything I had witnessed about the Party was positive, from its policies toward women to the personal example of selfless service set by its members. After years of feeling adrift and ignored, I finally had something to believe in, and I believed with every fiber of my being. To me, Communism was about hope.

One spring day in 1950, I joined the Communist Party of China. The Party flag, red with a yellow star, adorned the wall of a classroom. Four of us girls joined on that day. We stood facing the flag and took an oath of loyalty to the Party, after which the branch secretary, Wang Wanying, shook hands and congratulated each of us in turn. We vowed to fight all our lives for Communism and to set an example for other students. My chest swelled with pride. At seventeen, I was an insider, working shoulder to shoulder with people I admired to build a better China.

We had frequent meetings, always secret. One Sunday, during my weekend visit home, a classmate came by and said, "Wang Yulin, let's go. It's time for the Party meeting."

When my dad heard "Party meeting," he realized that must mean the Communist Party. He picked up the big cleaver that Mama used for chopping vegetables. With bulging eyes, he came after me, yelling, "What! Who told you to join the Communist Party? I'll kill you! You bring the whole family trouble!" Wielding that knife, he chased me, and I ran out of the house—I literally ran for my life! I was terrified. I knew he meant it. Still, I didn't think of quitting. My defiance was small compared to the sacrifices others had made.

A few weeks later, my life changed drastically. It began with a simple message: "The principal wants to talk with you. It's urgent."

When I entered his office, alone, the principal closed the door and addressed me in a quiet, serious tone. The central Communist leadership in Beijing—called "Central"—needed a small group of absolutely dependable people for a confidential task. They had to be Party members and crackerjack students. The school had decided to send me.

I would go away to live in a secret location, on a secret assignment, for months or possibly years. No one would know where I was or what I was doing. "The Party's orders," he called it.

"When?" I asked. "Right after graduation?"

The principal shook his head. "No. It's urgent. You must leave right away. Before the end of the school year."

My heart sank. It was an honor to be chosen—both thrilling and scary. Of course, I accepted. Orders were orders. But I didn't want to go. I hated to leave my friends, especially before completing middle school. I had worked so hard to finish my schooling through ninth grade. The principal promised to write an official letter stating that I was a middle-school graduate. But I didn't get to take my final examinations, which were only a few weeks away, and I never received a graduation certificate.

In a letter to my parents, I explained as best I could. "Don't worry," I wrote, but I knew they would.

Shortly afterward, I left by train directly from the school. I traveled with two other students to Jingxing, a coal-mining center in western Hebei Province. From that train station, we were taken by car to a secret hideout in the mountains called Kulongfeng, where we were to live and work.

Kulongfeng literally means "a crack in the hole"—and that's just what it was. A strange geological formation left a deep bowl in the ground, and at the bottom of the bowl was a huge rock with a cleft in it, forming a long, deep cave. The cave was only visible after you went down in the bowl. This was the site of the Party's secret relay station for its radio communications. The saying was: "Not even the atom bomb could destroy this radio station!"

We were to be trained as technical staff for this relay station. It was not a broadcasting station, but only a transmitter station, receiving signals and passing them on. Beijing had just been liberated, and if the capital city were to be lost to the Kuomintang again, we were told, announcers would join us and our cave would become a full broadcasting station. We were to stand by until the situation in Beijing was judged to be stable.

Our equipment, housed in a long cave, looked a little like a power station. The machines were six feet tall and covered with steel plates. We were warned not to touch the metal, especially during the rainy season. They were worried about electrical conduction during thunderstorms. We just watched the gauges and turned the plastic tuning dials very carefully. I worked in that cave eight hours a day.

Our living quarters were in other caves nearby. My cave didn't have a door, but in winter, a thick cotton curtain hung over the entrance. We had very narrow beds and a stove inside, so we could heat our water and keep warm. It was a comfortable cave, very nice. But from the air, or from the outside, nobody would guess that people lived there. At first I lived alone, since I was the only girl there. All of us shared a primitive outhouse with two deep holes and a shed made of cornstalks, in the style of the local farmers. I would clear my throat as I approached it to make sure no man was inside.

The deputy chief of our central radio station had been transferred to this mountain hideout when the Communists took over Beijing. Although he had formerly worked for the Kuomintang, he was a highly skilled radio engineer, and he taught us, step-by-step, everything we needed to know. I was the youngest worker there, and everyone was especially nice to me. The stationmaster was a kind and good man. His wife—we called her Mama Du—treated us young workers like her own children.

In those days, everyone was on the "supply system." Our clothing, shoes, food, soap—all our daily necessities were issued, along with cash equivalent to the cost of five pounds of millet. The nonsmokers, like me, had nothing to spend our money on. Every meal we ate together, and the food was simple peasant food, such as millet porridge, coarse corn bread, salted vegetables, fried cabbage, and turnip soup.

I would go with the others to wash my clothes in the river. To save on soap, we picked a type of wild seedpod to use when scrubbing our clothes. While we washed, we would chat, sharing about our families. We trusted each other completely and spoke openly about whatever was on our minds. Sometimes we clambered about in the surrounding hills, picking wild fruit and wildflowers, and we'd sing. We also had water fights.

For the sake of secrecy, we were not permitted to associate with the local people. But sometimes the others would get me to scale the wall from our compound to the peasant home next door, and from there I would go to the marketplace to buy some peanuts and persimmons. The persimmons were the first fruit I had ever tasted, and I was already seventeen years old! The local peasants, who wore towels on their heads, smiled when they saw me. I never understood how they could keep those towels gleaming white, without modern soap.

In the evenings, the stationmaster and his deputy taught us technical skills and guided each of us in building a little radio set. I was ecstatic the night I could hear a broadcast coming from the set I had built! But the deputy stationmaster grabbed my little radio and dashed it to the ground.

"Not up to the standard," he said.

Hurt and insulted, I broke into tears. I didn't know at the time that he actually had designs on me. "I'll teach you to build a first-class radio," he said. He wanted to spend more time with me.

In every other way, life was good. The twenty or thirty of us there all felt close to each other, and there was lots of fun and merriment. There were very few, if any, cares or worries.

One day as I was washing my clothes, a man came down to the river. When

I looked up, I recognized one of my middle school teachers, Mr. Wang. He had been transferred to this area to do youth league work. The next Sunday, I went to visit him and stayed several hours, laughing and talking and eating dinner. It was dark by the time I started for home.

There is a Chinese saying: "The newborn calf doesn't know to be afraid of the tiger." I had forgotten that there were wolves in the mountains. After I had hiked quite a ways along the trail, I thought I saw eyes glaring at me in the dark. I was terrified, certain that I would be eaten by wolves.

Then I heard the voices of my comrades calling out from far away, looking for me with torches and calling my name. Finally I knew I would be safe. When I joined them and returned to my cave, the stationmaster scolded me for going off at night by myself. He explained that revolutionary cadres were expected to follow discipline, and that for me to risk being attacked by wolves was a serious mistake.

But I felt the close kinship of the group around me and didn't mind being scolded. I had been told that the Communists treated everyone like brothers and sisters. And now, from my own experience, I knew this was true.

Many years later, after working in Beijing at a much higher standard of living, I fondly recalled Kulongfeng and wondered where the jolly, carefree life of those days had gone—days when we all felt like members of one big revolutionary family. We gave up the comforts of home to work for a higher cause, but it didn't feel like a sacrifice. Chinese people of my age often recall those early days of idealistic Communism in the 1950s with nostalgia.

Once they allowed Mama to journey to Jingxing to see me. It was the first time in her life that she had ever ventured away from home by herself. She worried about how I was doing on my first job, with both the work and the social aspect, especially since this was my first time dealing with men. Mama left Kulongfeng excited and proud. She said, "My baby girl is working very well! It's a wonderful job, and they treat my daughter like family."

━━

At the Lunar New Year, which we Communists called "Spring Festival", the old stationmaster decided that we could celebrate with the local farmers. We invited people to a party at our station, but we were still not allowed to tell our neighbors what work we were doing. We put on a musical drama called *Wang Xiulan*, a long play about a pair of young lovers, with melodies we had composed ourselves. The farmers enjoyed it and clapped heartily at the end.

The only cloud in my life was a problem that developed with the deputy stationmaster. He was about thirty-five, an expert technician, and a very good teacher. A girl of seventeen, I was naive and inexperienced with men. For our musical drama, I sang the lead, portraying the lovely Wang Xiulan. Even though no one agreed that he was right for the part, the deputy stationmaster insisted on playing the role of my lover.

During the celebration after the performance, he deliberately got me tipsy, but my comrades chased him away before he could go any further. He then sent me a note, by messenger, asking me to bring him my homework. I took him my homework, but quickly excused myself and didn't let him coax me into staying at his place.

Mama Du noticed that the deputy stationmaster was always sending me notes and trying to get me to see him. She told her husband and then came to talk with me.

"Have your parents spoken with you about finding a husband?" she asked.

"A husband!" I said. "I'm only seventeen."

"That's right," she said, nodding. "I've noticed, too, that you're young for your age. But you have to be careful who you associate with. You need to know who someone is before you get close to them."

"Don't worry," I said. "If I ever get interested in anyone, I will discuss it with you, for sure."

One day, after the technical study and before the evening meal, the deputy stationmaster invited me to take a walk with him. "I used to get paid in gold, because of my technical skills. I had money, but I never married," he told me. "You can look me up whenever you have questions, and in three days' time I can help you build a really good radio set."

What he didn't know was that I looked down on him. First, because he had previously been with the Kuomintang, for whom I had little respect. Second, I sensed that he was manipulative in trying to get close to me. He talked tough to others, but was always simpering and grinning around me. And third, at seventeen I had no interest in getting married or becoming romantically involved with anyone. Instead, I was bent on training myself to be an excellent technician and launching a successful career.

One day, not long after Chinese New Year, the director took me aside for a private meeting. "The higher-ups want you to move to Beijing," he told me. "They need a lot of cadres there."

My face flushed with joy. The location of Radio Peking headquarters, Beijing was the capital of the country now that the Communist Party had consolidated power, and it was once again a safe place to live.

"What kind of work?" I asked, trying not to show how eager I was to leave.

"Not sure. Important work."

In those days, cadres had to change jobs often, and usually no one told us the reason. Of our team at Kulongfeng, I was the only one chosen to go to Beijing. I guess someone looked at my dossier, which contained my family history. As the daughter of a worker, I had a "good" class background and was considered reliable. Plus, I was educated. Even though I had only a junior high school education, I could read and write. The leaders said I took my work sincerely and had a good attitude.

After my experience with the deputy director, I was both relieved and enthusiastic to move on to the central radio station, Radio Peking, in early 1951. At last, I could move back to the city where I was born—with a great job and wide-open possibilities. Radio Peking was to play a major role in unifying the country and rebuilding the nation. After nearly a year living in a cave, this was a big promotion.

In Beijing, I was assigned to analyze statistics in the personnel department, which we called the "Cadres Department." This meant keeping track of such statistics as the number of employees at each level who came from each class background (capitalist, intellectual, worker, peasant, or army) and the level of education they had achieved. I had access to the secret personnel dossiers of almost everyone at the Broadcast Administration. Every three months, we had to report to the central government.

This was a totally new challenge for me. It was not technical, so it didn't help me get closer to my dream of becoming an engineer. But it was important, and it was an opportunity to learn yet another set of skills. Besides, it showed how highly they trusted me, even though I was barely eighteen.

Not long after the move, to my great surprise, my new boss, the head of the Cadres Department, summoned me for a talk.

"Comrade Wang Yulin," he said, "your boyfriend from the country is pining for you."

I gasped. That guy was still after me? What nerve!

"If you are willing," he continued, "we will transfer you back so that you can be with him. His technical knowledge is valuable, and we need to take care of him."

"What do you mean, 'take care of him?'" I said. "There was nothing whatsoever between us."

The personnel chief's eyebrows rose. "All right then," he said. "If there's nothing there, we'll forget it."

I was relieved to hear that. But this episode jolted me, so I made three rules for finding a husband in the future:

We needed to share basic views in common.

He shouldn't be too much older than I was, nor should he be younger.

He had to be honest, and our relationship had to be one of mutual respect; he mustn't see me as someone to keep house for him.

Despite my firm decision, I kept getting love letters and phone calls from the deputy stationmaster. Irritated with his persistence, I ignored the letters and hung up on the calls.

Several months after our first talk, the chief called me in again.

"That deputy stationmaster is still in a bad mood," he said. "We told him that you denied any feeling for him, but he doesn't accept it. He's in low spirits, losing sleep, not eating well. He's a valuable asset, and the organization is thinking of transferring you back there."

My face grew hot and my hands shook in fury. My work assignments were up to the Party, but my marriage should be my own choice. This was not the Old Society anymore. I don't know where I got the courage, but I flatly refused him. "You're trying to force this on me," I said. "I never had any emotional ties to him, and I will never accept a transfer back there!"

"Don't be so stubborn!" he said. "Think what's good for the Party."

But I wouldn't budge. Since I flew into such a temper, they finally gave up on this effort. Also, the old stationmaster had confirmed that there had been nothing between us.

The whole incident shook me up. The possibility that time spent with a respected older man could get misconstrued as interest in starting an amorous relationship hadn't occurred to me before. Could I really affect someone else like that, to the extent that he fell into a sulky mood and it affected his work?

After this, I was more careful in my contact with all men. Everyone at the Broadcast Administration ate together in a big canteen building. I became cautious about what where and with whom I would sit. When someone invited me to see a movie, take a walk, or have a meal together, I now had to worry about what it might lead to. If I received a letter that seemed to be angling for a relationship, I would refuse to open all subsequent letters from that person.

But that led to trouble, too. People would say, "She aims too high. We ordinary people aren't in her sights. She'll end up an old maid." Adding to the pressure, my mother would send me letters that my brother had scribed for her, asking anxiously whether I had a "target" yet.

Despite the tension my feelings on marriage caused, I was too busy to worry much about it. Outside of my regular work, I attended night school and also volunteered as a tutor for comrades who needed after-hours schooling. I made up my mind to just watch and wait, until I found someone who could be a true companion, someone I could talk to about whatever came up, a mutual love that would endure all my life.

Chapter Eight

Building the New China

IN THE EARLY 1950s, Beijing felt like the center of the universe. On October 1, 1949, Chairman Mao had stood on the Tiananmen Gate Tower of the former emperor's palace and declared that the Chinese people had at last taken control of our destiny. On that date, the capital of the country officially moved back to Beijing after decades in Nanjing. The Communist Party took the reins of the government, and the People's Liberation Army quickly consolidated and moved troops into all of China—except Taiwan, Hong Kong, and Macau. The Communists finally had *carte blanche* to pursue their egalitarian dreams in China. It was an exhilarating time.

As a Communist Party member who had joined before 1949—and with impeccable proletarian roots as the daughter of a worker—I held my head high in the new China. After four decades of warlords, chaos, famine, and war, we in the Party were building socialism in China, the most populous nation on earth. We planned to industrialize and modernize our country, which had once been regarded as the "sick man of Asia." If socialism could win and work in China, it could spread throughout the world. Everything seemed possible.

Among the first things the Party did after Liberation were to undertake highly successful campaigns that rid China of two scourges: opium and prostitution. For more than one hundred years, China's governments had failed to stop the spread of opium addiction, introduced by British traders in the nineteenth century, yet the Communist Party eliminated it completely in just a few years. The Party also reeducated prostitutes and placed them in new jobs and, when possible, marriage. After centuries of foot binding and oppression, Chinese women like me had access to education and good jobs. These social reforms convinced me even more that the Party was capable of achieving its aims of rescuing the poor and downtrodden—including women.

At Radio Peking, our goal was to make sure everyone in China—and in the world—knew of the great progress being made. In those days before television, radio was the most modern means of communication, and we worked at the cutting edge. We were part of the Central Broadcast Administration, but everyone referred to our work unit simply as "Radio." The cozy companionship of our months in the cave station had ended, but it felt heady to step onto the national stage in a responsible job at such a young age.

When I arrived in Beijing, the ancient gray city walls still stood, although they were torn down later to allow for a freer flow of traffic in a modern city. Young people crowded into Beijing to take jobs in the government, and promotions followed rapidly. We went to work with enthusiasm and confidence.

Many government offices took over Western-style buildings in the former Foreign Legation quarters. The emperor's palace in the old Forbidden City became a museum, open to all. The Communist Party of China and the central government set up headquarters next door in Zhongnanhai, in elegant buildings around the Central and South Lakes in what was once an imperial garden and servants' quarters. The leaders worked in a secure area behind thick, high walls, but put up a sign at the gate saying, "Serve the People." October 1 became our new National Day, and each year I went out into the streets to witness ever-grander parades. Once I caught a glimpse of our highest leaders, Chairman Mao Zedong and Premier Zhou Enlai, on the viewing stand atop the old imperial gate, Tiananmen. These were the great men of the country and the world, and my heart flooded with wonder when I saw them.

At first I shared a room with three other girls from the office in an area called Mahua, which means "fried dough twists." We took the tram bus to work, about forty minutes each way. In those early days, we did not receive paid salaries. The state provided everything: housing, food, toilet paper, and other personal supplies, plus a little bit of cash each month. I would use my cash to buy peanuts, which were five cents a packet.

After several months, the state decided to change to salaries commensurate with each level of the bureaucracy. When I first started getting paid this way, my salary was 87.50 yuan per month. At today's exchange rate, that is less than 15 U.S. dollars. But in those days, it was more than enough for me to pay for food, clothing, and all other expenses—except housing, which was provided free. I put most of it into savings. But I did make one big purchase: a navy-blue, western-style suit with a skirt. I never wore it, but it made me feel very sophisticated.

Once I settled into my new job, I began to attend night classes. It had always bothered me that the Party had pulled me out of school just as I was finishing junior high school. I knew it would take more than three years, but I was determined to eventually earn my high school degree. I would attend class after dinner and not get home until 11 o'clock. Still, some days I had to work till nine or ten o'clock at night, so I had to miss class and I had little time to study. My education had to bubble along on the back burner. Work always came first.

Although the early 1950s were exciting, my life was very simple: from dorm to work to school. I didn't have time for exploring the city. I ate my meals at the Radio cafeteria, and there were always several choices: two different meat dishes, a vegetable dish, and rice or noodles or buns. To me, this was heavenly. Only occasionally would I go to a restaurant.

In 1954, I was transferred to a new assignment as a confidential secretary to Mei Yi, the director of the State Broadcast Administration. My job was to manage the classified documents that came down from the central leadership, as well as handle logistics for the director. At age twenty-one, I was awed that they trusted me with this responsibility.

Mei Yi was a very high-ranking cadre, a vice minister, who had worked for decades in the Party's propaganda organizations. He was also famous for translating Nikolai Ostrovsky's *How the Steel Was Tempered* into Chinese. Mei Yi was a tall man with a brilliant mind, a thick Cantonese accent, and messy handwriting. He treated me with fond indulgence, like a father.

I kept his appointment book and set up meetings for him. Around the office, I developed a reputation of being *lihai*, which means "tough." Sometimes the director would ask me to pass on his orders, and then I had to follow up to see that the work was completed. I was straightforward, sometimes blunt. Still, everybody liked me. A lot of men wrote me love letters. I hated that.

I also did some work for the deputy director, Wen Jize, an old cadre from the revolutionary days, when the Party was based in the caves of Yan'an. He walked in small steps, leaning forward slightly, because there was a steel brace fitted around his lower ribs. An underground Communist for many years, Wen Jize's ribs had been broken by the Kuomintang when they arrested, beat, and jailed him. All of us admired Deputy Director Wen as a revolutionary hero. Sometimes he would ask me to copy passages from an article or a book that analyzed the nation's political situation. He would quote from these passages when he gave speeches, which he did often.

After I took on this job, the leaders entrusted me with the keys to a cabinet that contained secret documents. Because of this, I was allowed to live in my own room—a rare privilege for a single person. At that time, the Broadcast Administration did not have its own dormitory, so it took over the Jincheng Hotel, the "Golden City Hotel," for staff housing. I lived there on the second floor, in a small square room with one bed and one table. I shared a bathroom down the hall. I was not afraid to live alone, since I knew everyone at the hotel; they were my colleagues. This hotel was more convenient to the office, and my privacy was ensured.

In the early 1950s, Director Mei Yi told me that I had been selected to go to the Soviet Union for training as a radio sound engineer, although the date was not set. I began to imagine an exciting future for myself. I had long dreamed of becoming an engineer, and the idea of living abroad, possibly in Moscow, captivated me. Some colleagues and I began to take Russian language lessons from a Russian couple working at Radio, for two hours a day. After three years, I could carry on a simple conversation and read some short items in *Pravda*, the Soviet Communist newspaper. Now, I've forgotten almost every word of Russian.

My work as a confidential secretary was hard, and I was cut off from most people, except for the leaders at Radio Peking. Every time a mass political movement came along, which was about every two years, I would be sent out to collect data on whoever or whatever was being investigated.

The first political campaign I experienced directly was the *San-fan*, "three evils," campaign of 1952. The purpose was to root out corruption, waste, and bureaucracy within the Party and government. If someone reported the theft of something valuable from the office, I was in charge of investigating and trying to estimate the value of the stolen goods. Actually, very few people stole in those days, but it did happen sometimes. It was my job to collect these numbers and total them for the whole Broadcast Administration. This was tricky because sometimes a cadre would want to show off and get approval from his higher-ups, so he would falsely accuse a colleague. Sometimes, the value of the so-called stolen goods was exaggerated.

I understood why this campaign was necessary, but I was troubled by the case of Driver Guan. I was in charge of the team of drivers at Radio, dispatching them to deliver and pick up Radio officials who were attending meetings in other parts of Beijing. Part of their job was to repair the cars whenever there was a mechanical problem. After work, the drivers would drive the cars home and keep them there. Sometimes, they would take a few tools home, too, so they could fix the cars at home. One driver I knew as a good and honest man, Driver Guan, was accused of stealing because he had left a few tools at his home. These were really small tools, nothing expensive. Driver Guan was subjected to serious criticism and humiliation, in meeting after meeting, where he was called a thief. Before Liberation, he had worked for the Kuomintang, so even though he was a simple driver, he was viewed with suspicion. People didn't believe him when he said he had just taken the tools home to use them to repair the car. Driver Guan didn't lose his job, but he was in low spirits for a long time.

To me, it seemed unfair to punish a man so severely for a small infraction. But I could do nothing to help him. I was glad when the campaign ended; that focus on political and ideological infighting filled me with impatience. Besides, after that campaign, everybody became very tense and self-protective, careful not to talk too freely with others. You never knew what others might report about you. I could really feel this difference. In the countryside, when I worked in the cave, we had friendly, open relationships with our comrades. But after San-fan, in Beijing, people were cautious and guarded. To me, this was unfortunate but necessary.

That winter, I was sent to a rural area outside of the city of Hangzhou to investigate a man the Party suspected of having joined a counterrevolutionary group. I had to travel about thirty miles through the countryside, sitting on the back of a flatbed tricycle. At the village, I went to the local police station to locate my contacts.

The police chief seemed shocked: "You've got some nerve, girl. Things are pretty tense down here, with assaults, rapes, robberies . . . and you come down here by yourself? Never heard of such a thing!"

He gave me a few contacts, and I put up for the night in a local inn. It was bitterly cold, and my fingers were freezing as I sat there compiling my data. One of the inn staff members felt sorry for me and gave me a warming pan for my hands, which helped.

After three days of work in the countryside, I caught the train back to Beijing. I traveled in a "hard sleeper" compartment, with bunks for four people. I got to talking with my fellow passengers and discovered that all four of us were cadres sent out on trips to investigate other people. One of the cadres was a young man who took an interest in me and tried to find things we shared in common. Even though I snubbed him, he suggested that we exchange addresses and write each other.

This started me thinking again. Contact with the opposite sex was becoming complicated. When I revealed that I was single, men acted like I ought to welcome their advances. I thought of a colleague of mine in the secretary group: she was close to forty, had never been married, and had all the problems I associated with the traditional "old maid" persona—bad temper and nagging.

At the office, I had cultivated a reputation as a young woman indifferent to suitors. The minute a young man expressed romantic interest, I would cut him off. I didn't want to end up an old maid. But with my busy work schedule and Russian lessons, I had no time for dalliances, let alone marriage and children. Besides, I would be going to Moscow someday.

But for now, I was still in China and when I returned to Beijing, I heard there would be a general raise in pay. Director Mei Yi called me in and asked me whether I would yield my chance for a raise to some of my older colleagues, since I was young and would have many opportunities.

Out of respect for my elders, I did yield my raise—never imagining that I would go for the next thirty years without one! During this time, when people asked me what my pay grade was, I would say, "*bu zhang ji*" which means "minister level." In Chinese, this phrase has the same sound as "never go up in pay grade." Everyone who heard this understood and laughed.

Chapter Nine

Meeting Sidney

ON MAY 2, 1955, my colleagues in the secretary group were gossiping about a foreign man who had been released from prison and was now coming to work at Radio Peking. He had a foreign name but everyone knew him only by his Chinese name, Li Dunbai. One day, he came to our office and went straight to a meeting with Director Mei Yi.

This man's story amazed us. He had lived in the caves of Yan'an during the revolutionary days, and he personally knew many of the Party's top leaders, including Chairman Mao and Premier Zhou Enlai. They trusted him so much that they let him not only work for Radio Yan'an but join the Communist Party of China, even though he was American. He had been imprisoned for six years on charges of spying, yet he had remained loyal to the Communist cause. When he was released, the Party declared that he had been wrongfully imprisoned and apologized to him. He had asked to come back to work at Radio, even though his ex-wife, Wei Lin, worked there.

"That's stupid," I said. "Why would he want to work with his ex-wife? That could be awkward."

"It's not necessarily awkward," said one colleague. "Some people just don't care about such matters. Wei Lin waited for him for three years, and then she divorced him and married someone else."

"Well, that's not right," I said. "If you really love someone, and you know he's not an evildoer, then you should wait for him. No matter how long it takes!"

My colleagues laughed at me. "You're a victim of feudal education!" one said. "Nobody believes that old stuff about how a wife has to stay loyal to her husband, no matter what."

"Maybe," I said. "My mother and father never got along from the day they were married—yet they never divorced, and they raised a bunch of children who turned out pretty good . . ."

Somebody said, "But this couple wasn't close, emotionally."

"Then why did they even get married?" I asked.

"Little Wang, you're too young. You don't understand these things. What would you have done?"

"What would I have done? If I were his wife, I would have waited until his case was cleared up! I wouldn't pay any attention to what people were saying."

Little did I know that the foreign man himself overheard me. His English name was Sidney Rittenberg, and he was in the next room, discussing his new work assignment as a foreign expert and advisor with Director Mei Yi. After serving them tea, I had neglected to shut the door all the way when I went back to my office, adjacent to the director's. (At the time, I could not know that Sidney would go on to tease my lifelong habit of not shutting doors throughout the nearly sixty years of our marriage.)

Director Mei Yi called me in after Sidney left. "Little Wang, Li Dunbai is just out of prison, a bachelor, all by himself, and probably doesn't know anything about how to manage his life. I'm giving you the job of helping him buy what he needs and get his life in order. Watch your short temper and blunt habits of speech. Don't be sharp with him! Get him settled into his apartment."

So I got a Broadcast Administration car and took Sidney to his new quarters in Mahua, where I used to live when I first arrived in Beijing and where Director Mei currently called home. Sidney had been assigned a large two-room apartment—much roomier than most people's—though he had to share a bathroom.

I took Sidney to the Xidan shopping district to buy clothes. We had *jiaozi*, a type of dumpling, together at a corner restaurant. We ordered a kind called "lovebird jiaozi," a mixture of pork and beef. But the name meant nothing to me, at the time, since I felt no romantic attraction.

When the server took our order, I asked Sidney how many dumplings he wanted.

"Sixty," he answered.

"Impossible!" I said. "I can eat fifteen, at most."

"Sixty," he repeated. "Try me."

I ordered eighty altogether, and there were none left at the end.

How can this man eat that much? I thought, but I kept it to myself. For a girl brought up in poverty, never able to taste jiaozi at all as a child, his appetite seemed excessive. But I had no idea what kind of appetite a man can build up in prison.

After dinner, I helped him hang up his clothes, stow his belongings, and get his place in order. Although he had met China's most powerful leaders, to me he was just Li Dunbai, a man who needed some help. At the time, I was really busy with work and night school, so the only time I was available to help Sidney at home was on weekends.

On the very first weekend, Saturday afternoon to be exact, I poked my head inside the shuttle bus that he and other other high-ranking cadres took to and from work as it was pulling away from the office. "Li Dunbai," I said in my most official voice. "Don't go out tomorrow. I'm coming to see you."

In my innocence, I had no idea how that sounded to people on the bus. They teased Sidney all the way home. "You're under orders to wait for a visit from a young lady tomorrow," they hooted.

The next day, Sunday, I returned to Mahua, organized Sidney's clothes, and put the wash in the basket for the orderly to take out. Then we went for a long walk, during which I felt that we were talking and arguing as though we had known each other for years. He spoke Mandarin Chinese so fluently that I didn't think of him as a foreigner at all.

I called him Lao Li, meaning "Elder Li," according to the common custom in China. That is what everyone at the office called him. He was thirty-four at the time, but to me, at age twenty-two, he was yet another older man at work.

That night, we went to a Peking Opera performance of *Sou Gu Jiu Gu*, which means "Finding and Rescuing the Baby Emperor." The story is about a peasant who gives up his own baby in order to save a former emperor's infant son from destruction.

After the opera, we walked the streets again, stopping to enjoy snacks from the street stalls, which I discovered we both loved. But what an argument we had! Sidney, his head stuffed with doctrine after his long years in prison, insisted that it was a bad play. "Who cares about those old feudal emperors and nobles!" he said. "They're all reactionaries, and they all belong in in the garbage bin of history."

"That's a very narrow viewpoint," I said. "The baby emperor was a human being, a baby! Everyone cares about this story."

We had arguments like this all the time. But I found that, rather than creating distance between us, they brought us closer. We both enjoyed our debates, which were never disrespectful, even though our opinions differed widely. I judged every situation based on human relations while Sidney saw everything in terms of ideology. To me, his views were too rigid; humane treatment mattered more than the Party line. But we both could see the other's perspective. If I knew I was right, I wouldn't give in, and he told me he admired that.

But that came later. In those days, I thought to myself, here's an interesting new friend with whom I can talk and argue. Despite the difference in our ages, he treated me as an equal.

Chapter Ten

Marrying a Foreigner

ONE SUNDAY SOON after I met Sidney, Ma Yingquan and his wife invited me to go rowing with them in Beihai Park. Ma, in charge of Radio's administrative office, was an old cadre from the mountains who had worked his way up from lowly orderly to his present position. From Shanxi Province, he had a thick accent and an earthy, rural sense of humor.

To my surprise, when I arrived at the dock with Ma and his wife, I saw Sidney there, too.

"Why?" I asked Ma.

"It's just right," he said. "We two in one boat and you two in another."

I felt awkward. *Helping this man is a duty given me by the leadership*, I thought. *Going rowing in the park with him is another story.*

But more surprises were in store. After rowing a while, Ma suddenly took his boat back to the shore, and he and his wife ran off, saying, "You two go ahead, we have something we have to do."

We both knew that Ma had deliberately set us up, planning an outing to this romantic setting and then skipping off and leaving us alone. We both swore at him, but we kept on rowing around, talking, and then going ashore and snacking till it was time to go back. This was the first indication to me that somebody thought I should form a closer relationship than I was ready for.

Sidney told me a little about his life before coming to China. He described the social-activist work he had done in America as an organizer of workers and young people. To me, it sounded like the same sort of thing that the Communist Party was doing in China, the kind of good works that had attracted me to the youth league as a teenager.

One thing Sidney didn't talk about was his time in prison. He had spent the entire six years in solitary confinement, and I found out only years later that the cruel mistreatment had pushed him into a mental breakdown. Sidney insisted on taking the blame for his imprisonment; he said he was working hard to correct his bourgeois thinking. But I knew that Chairman Mao himself had admitted Sidney's imprisonment was wrong. Even our glorious Communist Party could make terrible mistakes.

At the Broadcast Administration, Sidney was treated as a hero. He had joined the Party during its pre-Liberation days in Yan'an. He had shared simple meals with Chairman Mao and other top Party leaders, such as Zhou Enlai, Zhu De, Liu Shaoqi, and Peng Zhen. He had watched movies with them and danced with their wives, even with Mao's wife, Jiang Qing. By the time I met Sidney, he had a high level of clearance to read confidential Party documents.

Some people were in awe of him. But to me, Sidney was just an interesting man. With more life experience than most men I knew, he had a lot to talk about, and I found it fun and relaxing to spend time with him. He had a witty way of commenting on life and made me laugh. Even though he had studied at one of America's best colleges while I had yet to finish high school, he admired my proletarian background.

It was true that there were many differences between us, but I never thought of Sidney as looking different. He had thick black eyebrows, deep-set brown eyes, and a strong nose. But the only thing I noticed about his looks was that he had exceptionally large round eyes; later I discovered that this was the effect of the thick lenses of his black-framed glasses. I told him he had tricked me! His eyes were not as big as they looked. From the time I was a little girl, I always thought the most attractive people were those who were tall and had large eyes. At 5'7", Sidney was not very tall, but he was two inches taller than I was.

Often both of us worked late, till nine or ten at night, and we would go out for a late-night snack afterwards. Sometimes we would take long walks under the streetlights of Beijing's main thoroughfare, Chang'an Avenue. In one alley near Xidan, many small vendors sold snacks: wonton soup, sesame flat bread, noodles, fried rice. We would each buy something we liked, then find a space to sit on long benches and talk as we ate. The food was tasty and cheap. I introduced him to some Beijing specialties, such as almond jelly, red bean puree, and Peking duck rolls.

Just across the street from our office was a movie theater, and we often went to the movies together. Sometimes we had completely different reactions to films. I openly told him my opinion, and he told me his. Our different viewpoints made us laugh.

Sometimes, during the day, he came to my office. He was on the list of people who could read secret documents, and it was my job to call each of the people on the list when there were documents to read, in order to understand the Party line. Sidney was then the only Party member in the English section with access to these secret documents. Later, if he finished his work before I did, he would wait in his office till I was ready to leave. Because he lived in Mahua and I lived at the Jincheng, he would walk with me as far as Xidan before we went our separate ways.

As I learned more about him, I came to admire Sidney's character. Even after his horrific experience in solitary confinement, he never abandoned his loyalty to the Party; he had chosen to stay in China rather than return to America. It amazed me that he could love my country that much. At work, he trained many Chinese people in English translation and developed a reputation as a good-hearted man always ready to answer a question, no matter how basic. I often heard people calling, "Lao Li!" to ask him for help with grammar or usage. He was a crack translator, able to read a document for the first time and simultaneously translate it into English. He was an expert, but he didn't put on superior airs, as some Chinese intellectuals did. He treated ordinary workers as equals and asked about their families. If a cleaning woman was mopping the floor, Sidney would wait or else walk to the side, so as not to interfere with her work. I knew he came from a "bad class background" as the son of a wealthy American family, but I could see from his actions that he was a better Communist than most.

My character is different from Sidney's, and I could see that right away. If you accuse me of wrongdoing, and I think it's unfair, I will jump through the roof. I get openly angry and argue back. I cannot accept things I don't agree with. I thought, *If somebody put me in prison and forced me to live alone in a dark room for six years, then released me with a brief apology, how would I feel?* Yet I never heard Sidney complain. That quality in a human being is rare.

Still, I never thought of marrying him.

About a month after our rowboat date, in June of 1955, I received a surprising note from Sidney. He gave a brief introduction about himself, as though I didn't know him, and suggested that our relationship ought to develop into love and possibly marriage.

It made me angry. I had been warding off romantic approaches for years, and here was yet another—and from an American, not even a Chinese! I wrote him back, rejecting any idea of romance and announcing that I was cutting off all relations with him. Nobody was going to push me around.

But I was in an awkward spot. I had already promised to go to the Sun Yat-sen Park with him that same evening. Of course, I had to carry out my promise. In the warm, clear air of early summer, we walked under the trees, talking about nothing and everything. I felt natural with him. Then we sat on a park bench and something amazing happened: Sidney put his arm around me and hugged me. Not only that—he kissed me! I actually found myself kissing a man, for the first time in my life. In my mind, you didn't kiss someone unless you had decided that he was the one you were going to marry. To my surprise, the kiss felt good. Wonderful, actually.

"I'm serious, Yulin," Sidney said. "I want to marry you. We could have a great internationalist family." This was jargon for working together to bring Liberation to every country in the world. Between committed Communists, this passed for romantic.

Marriage! A family! I didn't know what to say. This was not a future I had imagined.

Sidney continued, "You should know that I'm not only an American—I'm a Jew."

"A Jew? What's that?"

By the time he finished a brief explanation, the park patrol was shining flashlights on our bench to see what we were up to. We stood up.

"At least tell me you'll consider it," he said.

"Li Dunbai, thank you very much," I said, in my most formal tone. "I will consider it." He claims I accepted his proposal that night, but that's not how I remember it. Anyway, I didn't turn him down.

As I turned away from him to walk home, my mind was clanging with contradictory thoughts. This man was twelve years older than I was, and he had been married twice before—once in America and once in China. He came from a country so alien and distant that I could not even imagine it. Still, I liked his humor and his intelligence. He reassured me he had no intention of leaving China, ever. He was more committed to Communist ideals than even the reddest of the Party members I knew. He was intriguing and full of fascinating insights, facts, and quotes from famous people. He opened me up to worlds far beyond my knowledge. When we talked, time flew by. It never occurred to me to think that there might be any political danger in marrying an American, although it was the height of the Cold War and our two countries were enemies. He loved China and the Communist Party almost as much as I did.

I didn't like this talk of marriage and family. But I wanted to see him again. Soon.

One night, Sidney invited me to have Peking duck at the famous Quanjude Duck Restaurant. The duck dinner was amazing and the conversation engrossing. When I got back to Radio Peking after dinner, I found that I had lost the keys to the cabinet where we kept the top-level secret Party documents. Appalled, I rushed back to the restaurant to ask if they had found my keys, but it was closed. A worker there said I would have to wait till the place opened the next day.

I begged a friend, Yang Zhaolin, (who later served as the director of the Radio Administration and was a good friend of ours), to take the night shift for me in the central editorial office—promising that I'd repay him for the favor by inviting him out to dinner. He was so responsible and so worried about the secret documents that he slept in my office that night. Early the next morning, I rushed back to the restaurant. They had found my keys! What a relief.

Director Mei Yi let me off without punishment, since I was usually very careful and hardworking. But he criticized me severely: "Having fun is fine—but not at the risk of the keys to the secret documents that are placed in your care!"

I was so remorseful that I cried like a baby. For the first time in the five years since I had moved to Beijing, my reputation of being responsible and trustworthy was tarnished. My comrades kept teasing me about this for years: "Wang Yulin got involved in lovemaking and lost the office keys!"

The very next time we got together, Sidney began pressing me to set a date for a wedding.

"Okay, I will marry you," I told him. "Definitely. Don't worry. But there's no reason to be in such a hurry!" I needed to finish up my schooling and get my high school degree. Besides, I hadn't told anyone in my family about him. I wasn't ready. I figured we could wait a few years.

He said he was willing to wait.

≈

In August 1955, the Central Committee began a new movement called Su Fan, shorthand for "the campaign to eradicate hidden counterrevolutionaries." Instead of targeting the usual class enemies—the Kuomintang, landlords, and capitalists—this campaign aimed to purge "hidden" counterrevolutionaries inside the government and Communist Party. According to the *People's Daily*, "1 to 3 percent" of Party members were secret traitors.

To me, this was scary. Who were these inside traitors undermining our good work?

Again, I was sent out to investigate various suspects. Now that I knew Sidney, who had been falsely accused, I saw these suspects in a different light. Surely, most of them were guilty as charged. Most class enemies harbored angry feelings toward the Communist Party because they had lost power and prestige when we took over the country. But perhaps—just perhaps—some people were innocent. I still loved the Party, but now I knew it could make mistakes. That made me extra careful in my investigations.

Today, few people remember the Su Fan campaign. Yet for me, it was a troubling time. At Radio, two of the accused men committed suicide by jumping off of buildings. One of them slaughtered his wife and children first. This was deeply disturbing and filled my mind with conflict: Why was this man so cruel? Was it because he was wrongfully persecuted? Even if he was really a spy for Kuomintang military intelligence, as charged, what kind of pressure made him destroy his family and himself? What mental torment he must have gone through! Despite the neighbors' criticism of me for "sympathizing with counter-revolutionaries," I wept for that family.

Though I never actually took part in the struggle meetings or the physical coercion of others, I went out and investigated the backgrounds of the accused. This led to more contradictions in my heart. Sometimes, accused men would break down and confess to wrongdoing, but later they would try to recant. It was hard to tell what was true. I suspected they had falsely confessed just to stop the persecution. But once they admitted wrongdoing, they could never take back their words.

These political struggles are too cruel, I told myself. They seemed to contradict the kindness and fairness of the Communist Party. I tried to stay out of it, as much as possible.

The following February, I was in Shanghai on assignment when I suddenly received an urgent telegram from Li Wu, another deputy director at the Broadcast Administration. He told me to return to Beijing immediately, without giving any reason. My work in Shanghai wasn't finished. It didn't make sense, so I telephoned Li Wu, asking why.

"Don't ask any questions," said Li Wu. "Come back at once!"

It sounded serious. Orders are orders; I packed up and took the train back to Beijing.

The day after my return, I asked Director Mei Yi why I was called back. Mei Yi laughed, and said, "Don't you know? You're going to get married on Saturday!"

I was furious. This was my life, and I didn't want other people running it.

Immediately, I ran over to Sidney's office and stamped my foot at him. "What kind of tricks are you up to?"

"It's not me," he said, with a twinkle in his eye. "Li Wu asked me if we were going to get married during the Lunar New Year, and I said we couldn't because you were away. Then he called you back. That was his idea, not mine."

I went to Ma Yingquan's office. "How can I get married on Saturday, with no preparation? I don't even have the right clothes!"

"What clothes?" he said. "We revolutionaries, what do we care about clothes? Just wear whatever you have on."

It was useless to argue. I hadn't wanted the wedding to be that sudden. By then, I wanted to marry Sidney, but I wanted to decide when, where, and how. But everybody else at Radio seemed to want it, and big posters were already up advertising it! So I gave in.

In truth, I was a little frightened about getting married. I didn't know what marriage meant. My mother and sisters were far away, in Shijiazhuang, and I had no one to help me prepare.

Gathering my courage, I wrote to my mother and siblings and told my father in person that I was planning to marry an American. In a letter she dictated to my brother, my mother responded, "You've been so picky all these years, and now you end up picking a foreigner!"

My father said, "Six hundred million Chinese, and you couldn't find one? You're going to marry a foreigner, and then go off to a foreign country with him?"

I argued, "He isn't an ordinary foreigner. He speaks Chinese and he understands China."

But no one in the family showed any sympathy, and not one of them showed up for the wedding. None of them even sent me a wedding gift. Their lack of support intensified my apprehension. Maybe I was making a big mistake.

Although he didn't interfere, Director Mei Yi also opposed our marriage. He told Sidney that he thought our cultural backgrounds were too different. "You'll want to talk about Shakespeare, and she'll want to talk about Peking Opera," he said.

It's true that there were huge gaps between us, in terms of family background, education, culture, and social experience. I had grown up poor. I'd been through hardships, forced to work for a living from early childhood. Sidney was from a well-to-do family and had studied at University of North Carolina and Stanford.

But marriage was a matter of two people joining together, like a cooperative. The two people had to draw on each other's strengths to make up for their own shortcomings, so Sidney and I reached an agreement. We resolved to always be frank with each other. Both of us outspoken, we agreed to deal with each other openly and sincerely, keeping nothing back. Whatever issues we had, we'd put them on the table and discuss them, not letting them fester and cause trouble. We would always respect one another. When there were minor differences, we would accommodate the other Party and not nag.

So, for instance, after our marriage in Beijing, Sidney still insisted on wearing western-style clothes and shoes, while I liked to wear Chinese-style clothes. But this was never a problem for us. We understood and respected each other's choices.

Our wedding was very simple, as were all Chinese weddings in those days.

That Friday, we took a letter of introduction from our Party committee to the local government office at Erlong Lu "Street of the Two Dragons" subdistrict. The woman district leader called me over for a few last words.

"Are you voluntarily getting married?"

I must have looked harried. "Yes," I said.

"He's much older than you. Are you sure you want to do this?"

I steadied my voice. "I'm sure."

"Does he really love you?"

"Yes." I had no doubts about that answer.

Finally, she stamped my marriage license and gave it to us along with a copy of the new *Marriage Law of the People's Republic*. We were formally married.

In those days though, people paid more attention to the wedding photo than to the license. When we met people, they wouldn't ask, "Have you got the license?" but rather, "Have you had your picture taken?"

So we went to the main shopping street, Wangfujing, and had a wedding photo taken together at the famous Beijing Photo Studio.

Now all that remained was the wedding celebration.

The party was held in one of the big conference rooms at Radio Peking. Our mischievous friend Ma Yingquan presided. He had us each describe the course of our love affair, while the guests ate wedding candy scattered around the tables. Then all the guests signed a large piece of red cloth, wishing us a life of great happiness. No feast, no cymbals, no raw walnuts in the bed. The party ended quickly.

Most of the girls I worked with at that time knew nothing at all about sexuality and sexual relations. One of my colleagues, a newlywed, told me how she hated to go home after work because she knew she would have to endure having sex, as if it was some painful and frightening experience a wife owed to her husband. These women didn't even know that sex could be enjoyable.

So on our wedding night, I was apprehensive. Sidney and I talked about having children, and both of us decided that we would wait for a year or so. But how were we to avoid my getting pregnant? In my innocence, I said, "Very simple. We just won't have sex."

Well, that didn't work for Sidney. And we didn't even try it.

Looking back on our simple wedding, Sidney has often said he regrets that I never wore the white bridal dress and that we never had a formal ceremony.

"Let's have another wedding now, even after all these years of married life!" he has suggested.

But marriage is not about a ceremony. It's about a lifetime of love and caring. Otherwise, you can have an elegant ceremony and a huge celebration, yet one year later end up getting divorced. That's not for us.

Chapter Eleven

Living the Dream, Ignoring the Shadows

As a result of my marriage to Sidney, I was transferred out of my job of managing secret documents. Sidney was a Party member and treated like a hero, but he was, after all, a foreigner, and regulations forbade that sort of relationship for people handling secrets.

My new job was in the technical department, where I was to learn sound engineering. I liked the work and the chance to learn a new skill, but I also felt this forced shift revealed the higher-ups' lack of confidence in me. I distinctly did not like that. Neither my loyalty nor my trustworthiness had changed; why had they changed their opinion of me? But it was the Party's decision, so I accepted that it must be for the best.

I learned quickly how to handle studio recordings and how to produce montages. In fact, I was so good at it that I was put in charge of producing programs to be sent to Moscow as part of our exchange agreement with Radio Moscow. I worked against tight deadlines, and often the tape would be rushed to the airport as soon as I finished the program.

Mostly from the Soviet Union, our equipment was outdated even then. We used big open-reel tape machines. Often, three of us would have to tune in material from four to six different tape machines at the same time. We rotated through three eight-hour shifts a day, so my work hours kept changing.

During the big parades across Tiananmen Square on May Day and National Day, I often got to be the chief sound technician, recording the ceremony from a pit beneath the flagstaff in the square. From this vantage, I could clearly see all the national leaders, including Chairman Mao and Premier Zhou Enlai, standing on the balcony of the Tiananmen gate. We would record their speeches and the singing of the national anthem and mix the sound for broadcast throughout the country and the world.

Before long, I became pregnant. This news filled me with joy. Sidney suggested that I quit night school, but I refused. After all the effort I had put into my studies, I insisted on finishing my education—and I made it! Later in life, I was extremely hard on my grandchildren, insisting they finish their education—mainly because it was simultaneously such a struggle and privilege for me. I never took it for granted.

As my belly grew bigger the following winter, Sidney often held my arm as we walked across the icy courtyard. One day, I was watching my step when he suddenly dropped my arm. I looked up and saw his former wife, Wei Lin, coming toward us.

She walked by quickly, without smiling or acknowledging us, but I was furious. "What's wrong with holding my arm?" I asked Sidney. "I'm your wife."

"I don't want to hurt her feelings. You know she's not happy in her marriage, and she can't have babies. I don't want to rub it in by showing how happy I am."

"Her feelings? What about my feelings?" I asked. "Tell me the truth. Do you still love her?"

This was our first fight. I felt terribly hurt. Sidney claimed he thoroughly disliked Wei Lin, who had asked to divorce her second husband and remarry Sidney after she realized he was being treated like a hero. When he refused, because he was engaged to marry me, Wei Lin had turned hostile toward him. He told me he dropped my arm that day simply because he felt sorry for her. But he was married to me now, and I felt he shouldn't retain any attachment to former flames.

≈

Although I didn't realize it at the time, it was a good thing I was no longer handling personnel matters. The next political campaign struck harder and closer. In February 1957,

Chairman Mao published a speech encouraging people to openly express their opinions about the Communist Party leadership, as long as it was constructive criticism. He called it "the policy of letting a hundred flowers bloom and a hundred schools of thought contend." We soon nicknamed it the "Hundred Flowers Movement." Hundreds of intellectuals believed Chairman Mao's promises that they could freely air their grievances and be heard. This unleashed a flood of letters and articles and big-character posters criticizing the Party. Two prominent men even openly suggested power-sharing in a multiparty system.

But very shortly, the campaign was crushed. In July 1957, Mao cracked down on all those who had spoken out, starting the "Anti-Rightist Movement." The Communist Party investigated and persecuted all those who had trusted Mao and had spoken openly. They were labeled as "rightists," meaning they weren't sufficiently left leaning or pro-Communist. As such, they were openly criticized and punished, usually sent to the countryside to do manual labor, sometimes for months, sometimes for years. Some of the critics were even charged with being counterrevolutionaries—for us, equivalent to the word "traitors."

When I heard about people being persecuted that I did not know personally, I assumed they were guilty: class enemies who were undermining the good work of the Party. But soon many people I did know were being accused as well, including colleagues at Radio Peking who were good people.

To me, the most distressing case was that of Wen Jize, the deputy director of the Broadcast Administration. I was shocked one day to hear that he had been labeled a rightist. How could anyone question the loyalty of Wen Jize? He was the revolutionary hero whose ribs had been broken in a Kuomintang jail.

I no longer worked with him, but I knew him well. Wen Jize was sincere and honest and kept meticulous records. He was a gentle man with a good heart, a loyal Party member who made many speeches and had access to high-level leaders. But after Liberation, some people were jealous of him. Many Party members, in fact, grew envious when some of their old comrades were promoted to high positions. After being labeled a rightist, Wen was demoted and given a job as an ordinary clerk in the records office at Radio. He worked at that low-level job for twenty years.

During the Anti-Rightist Movement, I didn't see Sidney much. He worked during the day, and I worked at night. But when I did ask him about the campaign and the attack on Wen Jize, he said that lower-level Party people had probably made a mistake.

Sidney faced an awkward situation in the English section. The Party insisted he had to identify a rightist, but there was no one who was really a rightist. So he had to pick one man he knew was not really a rightist, and that man was attacked. Yet after being accused, that man really believed he was a rightist. He sincerely did a self-criticism and tried to examine what rightist thoughts he had been harboring without realizing it.

I was deeply confused. Like Wen Jize, this man had poured his whole heart into his job. Why would the Party accuse him of being a rightist? You can tell a person's attitude by his behavior over time. If someone's heart is in the wrong place, eventually he will say something to reveal himself. Maybe he can hide it for a few months, but it is impossible to hide for years. I could not believe that either accused man was a bad guy pretending to be good.

"Sidney," I said, "why don't you visit Deputy Director Wen? He's been a good friend to us." Sidney looked embarrassed, but he refused. After spending six years in prison, he couldn't risk being seen as someone who sympathized with a man labeled as "rightist."

The Anti-Rightist Movement shook me. If you ask people to speak up and give their opinions, you shouldn't punish them for it. It looked like the Party had deliberately tricked them. Just because someone offers suggestions does not mean he or she is out to overthrow the government.

I still believed in the Communist Party, but now I felt something was wrong with its policy. Somebody, at some level, was making wrong decisions. From childhood, I was taught that the purpose of Party policy was to serve the people. But after these political movements ruined people's lives, I had doubts. Where was that spirit of fairness?

Years later, Deng Xiaoping, one of the leaders in charge of the Anti-Rightist Movement, admitted that 99 percent of those charged as rightists were innocent. Later, I also found out that every movement had quotas. Each organization had to identify a small percentage of their workers as rightists, counterrevolutionaries, or corrupt—whatever label the movement was targeting. Like Sidney's experience, even if no one in your work unit was a counterrevolutionary, you had to provide a person to attack and that person would have to prove he wasn't guilty. The purpose was to find a "live target." In the criticism of this target, the intellectuals were supposed to learn to think like proletarians. In reality, this was a new twist on the traditional mantra of China's imperial rulers: "Kill the chicken to teach the monkeys a lesson." The actual result was that Chinese intellectuals learned to self-censor their thinking and utterances; rather than thinking like proletarians, they became very careful not to say what they thought.

≈

During those years, I was absorbed by pregnancy, childbirth, and child rearing. Sidney and I were building a family, and my values were shifting. To me, nothing was more important than nurturing and protecting my loved ones.

During the late 1950s, it seemed that everyone was having babies. China was at peace, and the economy was growing. Chairman Mao encouraged us to have big families. "Of all things in the world, people are the most precious," Chairman Mao is reported to have said in 1949. No one worried about overpopulation. For the first time in at least fifty years, it seemed, China could feed its people. We were proving that Communism could work in China—far better than any previous system. With more young people, we believed that China could modernize even faster.

In March 1957, I gave birth to our first child, Xiaoqin. She came sooner than I expected—just a year after our marriage. Sidney gave her the English name of Jenny. When I went into labor, Sidney rushed me to Xiehe, the former Rockefeller hospital (also called Union Hospital) and left me lying on a stretcher in the corridor while he rushed back to work.

I was alone, in pain, and calling for the nurse.

"What are you shouting about?" said the nurse. "You think you can have a baby without hurting? We won't bring you into the delivery room till the baby's head begins to come out."

The nurse brought me food, but I was hurting too much to eat. "If you don't eat, where are you going to get the strength to give birth?" The nurse scolded me.

I spent sixteen hours like that, in the hospital corridor, until finally I gave birth to a baby, over ten pounds. In China, such a big newborn was almost unheard of, and I was scarcely big enough to handle it.

Sidney got the news on the phone and rushed back to the hospital. We were both overjoyed at our new daughter. Sidney told me that when he went to look at our child in the room where the babies were kept until the mothers had milk, Jenny saw him and gave a big sneeze.

I made lots of clothes for our new baby, with the help of a Japanese neighbor. Her husband, Yaki, was a Japanese-language expert working at Radio. At that time, we had experts who spoke more than thirty languages. Although I had hated all Japanese during the war, I became fond of Mrs. Yaki, who stayed at home with her children. I told her, "I don't know how to prepare baby clothes." She said, "I will help you!" She showed me how to make long, Japanese-style baby gowns, which all my children wore.

In those days, all Chinese babies wore pants with a slit in the back, so that they could squat and pee wherever they happened to be. Even today, this remains common practice. This tradition works well in the countryside, but it is not well suited to city life. My Japanese friend disapproved. She pointed out to me that babies, when they learn to walk, often fall down and sit in the dirt. So she helped me make baby clothes that did not have the customary slit.

My Chinese neighbors thought this very strange. They would see Jenny's baby clothes and laugh. "How can she pee without split pants?" they would say.

"It's too unsanitary," I would answer. Instead, I made diapers out of cloth, washing them in hot water and drying them in the sunshine. Of course, China did not have disposable diapers in the 1950s.

I had worked right up to the day of delivery, but I took the standard fifty-six-day maternity leave. After that, I went back to work, putting the baby in the nursing room, which was not far from my office, and going back every three and a half hours to nurse her. I would pick her up when it was time to go home.

Sidney and I were so happy with our little baby! I would talk to her constantly, and it seemed as though she understood what I was saying. When I took her to the staff dining room, the chefs were all fond of her. They called her "Big Girl."

In June of 1958, our second daughter Xiaodong (Toni) came along, followed in December 1959 by our third daughter, Xiaoxiang (Sunny).

Our children all shared one character in their given names, as was the Chinese custom. In our case, they were all named Xiao, meaning "to understand"—literally, "to dawn on." Qin means "diligence." Dong means "the East." Xiang means "to soar." Later, our son was named Xiaoming, Ming meaning "enlightenment." When they were small, we always spoke to them in Chinese and called them by their Chinese names. We did not use their English names until many years later.

When Jenny was a year old, with me working and another child on the way, I put her in one of Beijing's finest nursery schools, Fragrant Hills Child Care Institute. This was a private boarding school, run by an independent child-care specialist who enjoyed the appellation "democratic personage," meaning a good non-Communist individual. The school went from preschool to sixth grade. All the teachers were graduates of a teaching-training institute, with teaching degrees.

When Toni was a little over one, we sent her to a nursery school run by Radio Peking near the Mahua residential compound where Sidney had lived before we were married. When Sunny was a little over a year old, we put her in the same nursery school as Jenny, near where we lived.

In Beijing in the late 1950s, most educated young women entrusted their babies to day care while they returned to work. It was the modern way. Long before the women's liberation movement in the West, Chinese women held substantial jobs and expected to contribute to society. Very few young mothers stayed at home with their children.

My children lived at school for two weeks, after which they would come home for one night, Saturday. They needed to be back at school on Sunday evening.

Though the school fees took up all of my salary, we were thankful for the nursery schools, because we felt that the children got expert care and schooling there—better than we could possibly give them, busy as we both were.

In 1957, shortly after Jenny was born, we were very lucky to have my mother come to live with us. We had moved to the Radio's newly built Foreign Experts Building, into a two-bedroom apartment. We had no kitchen, just a hot plate for boiling water but no stove or refrigerator. We ate most of our meals in the foreign experts' dining room, which served both Chinese and Western food.

Mama couldn't get used to the elegant dining room, with its high-priced food: she insisted on cooking for herself on the hot plate and eating at home. Outside, along the edge of the building, she cultivated her own little vegetable garden, with eggplant, peas, squash, and corn.

Mama would cook for us, too, and she was a wonderful cook. According to Sidney, "Mama was a cook like Schubert was a composer." Back in Shijiazhuang, she used to cook with a big wok for my father and his crew of apprentices. And she knew the art of noodle making, throwing the dough back and forth between her two hands—sometimes throwing it six feet away—until it was worked into super-thin noodles. Then she would fling the long chain of noodles into a pot and cook them—one long noodle for each pot!

Sidney loved Mama's cooking, especially dishes like braised ribs or sweet-and-sour ribs. Or the delicious little "eggplant pockets" Mama would make, with tasty ground pork sandwiched between two slices of eggplant.

At first, Mama didn't know Sidney. "So little hair," she would grumble. But after she came to live with us and got to know him, he became her favorite. She was always making tasty little morsels to tempt him into eating more. Especially when Sidney was trying to lose all his surplus weight—his "capitalist stomach"—she would ambush him unexpectedly with his favorite food.

"Dunbai," she would say, "A man is iron, but food is steel. If you go hungry, how will you feel? How can you work if you don't eat enough?"

Or she would play tricks like, "Here, taste this for me and tell me if it's okay."

Having come from the Old Society, Mama couldn't get into the habit of spending money. She would say, "You're living in heaven today—you have money to spend. But you have to think about the times when there was no money."

She would take the little scraps of soap that were too small to use, put them all together, melt them down, and work them into new cakes of soap.

I had been sending Sidney's business shirts to the laundry, but Mama would hold up the washed and pressed shirts disdainfully, and say, "Look, you call this washing?" Then she'd throw the shirts on the floor, pick them up, and wash them herself. Like magic, they would be pearly white when she got through with them. We couldn't figure out how she could get them so clean—much cleaner than the laundry.

She taught the children to love cleanliness too. When she would sweep the floor, one of the little tots would follow her with a little whisk broom. When Mama cultivated her vegetable garden, the children would follow her with tiny spades and hoes. Mama taught our children to wash their own little socks, handkerchiefs, and underwear.

Once, when Mama wasn't feeling well, Sidney went down to the most famous old Beijing tea shop to get her some of the very best tea, since it was one of her real pleasures. He brought back a quarter pound of tea leaves from a special tea that grew on only one tree, cultivated exclusively for the emperor in the old days.

Mama thanked him, and was happy to get this special tea, but she actually never touched it. Instead, she would collect the tea leaves left in the cups when we had guests, take those soggy tea leaves outside in the sun, and when they dried out she would put them in a little tea can of her own. And that's what she would drink. High-class tea was for other people, not for our Mama.

When Mama wasn't feeling well, and Sidney would ask her what was wrong, she would say, "Oh, you young people can't understand. This is a sickness from the Old Society." She thought everything bad came from the Old Society, where her life had been mired in poverty.

Encouraged by Mama, we taught the children to be generous. I would cut an apple or a pear into two unequal pieces, and ask the elder daughter, "Which piece will you give your little sister?" At first, she would offer the smaller piece to her sister. Then I would explain that it was better to give Little Sister the bigger piece and keep the smaller one for herself. They learned in this way to treat sharing as natural and as a matter of honor. We also taught the children to take care of guests and to let guests at the table have first choice of their favorite dishes.

We had a problem with the little tots picking and tearing at Sidney's books on the bookcases. We solved it by putting the littlest tot in charge of "protecting Daddy's books." When we assigned responsibility, that child took it seriously and solemnly warned others away.

I tried to set an example for my children so they would listen to me. Sidney and I never quarreled in front of them, and we didn't hit them or yell at them. If one girl made a mistake or behaved badly, I would put her in the bathroom. "Think it over," I would say. "When you realize what you did is not right, knock on the door, and I will open it for you." Then I would close the door. The child would stay there a while, then knock on the door and come out, saying, "I was wrong." I would say, "Why?" And she would say, "I shouldn't have done that. That's being bad. Next time I won't do that." And I would say, "Okay. Go play with your sisters."

Our children all care for each other and help each other to this day. And the sight of an elderly Chinese woman who reminds them of their grandmother may bring tears to their eyes.

My father lived nearby in a little enclave of old-style Beijing mud-brick homes, with just one room opening onto a courtyard. I helped get him a job as master of woodworking at Radio Peking, where he made even the complex acoustic paneling for the broadcasting studios.

Like Mama, my father grew to feel differently about my marriage. Once he told me: "Actually, I had met him [Sidney], because I used to run into him at the drinking-water station when we lived at Mahua. He was genial and always respectful and polite. I didn't realize that this was the foreigner you were going to marry. Otherwise I would have agreed to it."

My father was a man of strong integrity. Any work that he did was certain to be done well. Our chief engineer at Radio Peking, Huang Yun, was very picky, but he said, "I can never find anything wrong with the work that Old Man Wang does. He is very conscientious."

Papa would take our children back and forth to nursery school on his bicycle. His bike was actually an old model that he had bought long ago, but it always looked new. His room was the same way—always spic-and-span.

On the way to and from school, he would regale the children with tales from the ancient chronicles, such as the *Three Kingdoms* and *Heroes of the Marshes*. They grew up knowing all about heroes like Guan Gong, Zhang Fei, and Zhao Zilong. Influenced by my father, our eldest daughter grew up with a keen interest in Chinese history and literature. By telling these ancient stories to the children, my father infused them with subtle lessons, teaching them to be honest and upright people like the heroic figures.

After we moved to the new Foreign Experts Building, our lifestyle changed dramatically. We now had room to entertain and a common dining room that served palatable food, so we could invite guests to dinner.

We would make coffee for guests on weekends. Actually, we were known in the foreign community for our great coffee. We would buy the beans and roast them ourselves, pouring out a fresh, jet-black brew. Of course, I didn't allow the children to have it. Once, they stole a few swallows from what was left over in the guests' cups. They all made ugly faces and spit out the coffee. "How can they like this bitter stuff!" exclaimed little Jenny. But the girls all loved one American dish I learned how to make: brownies.

Our three little girls would sing their nursery school songs for our guests. They were adorable, talented little girls, who made me feel very proud. I thought about how wonderful their lives were compared to mine growing up! I didn't really have a childhood, but they had a great one.

I had very little interest in the guests who would visit. They were mostly Sidney's friends and spoke English, which I didn't understand. When we didn't have guests, Sidney often went out to do his Party work: educating foreigners in Chinese Communist Party policy and Chinese affairs. At first, he asked me to go with him. I only went once. His friends were polite to me, but they spoke in English. So the next time, I refused to go. "I don't want to sit there like a dummy," I said.

Of all the high-level leaders Sidney had befriended in the caves of Yan'an, the one who kept in closest touch with us was Zhou Enlai, the premier of China. Zhou often met with the foreigners living in Beijing, as if that were part of his job. In large groups, Zhou was serious and intellectual, but we sometimes had dinner with him with just a few close friends, and then he would relax, laugh, and joke. Once Sidney and I took two of our daughters to a musical performance at a theater. Our seats were in the second row, and as it happened Premier Zhou sat directly in front of us. One of the girls complained that she couldn't see, so Zhou placed both girls on his lap to watch the show.

During those years, Sidney worked hard long hours, including weekends. Sometimes I complained, since weekends were the only time when we could all be together. But he always put his work above family, as the Communist Party taught us to do. Whenever anyone asked him to do something extra, to take on another task or work overtime, he would do it. "For the revolution," he said. I didn't like it, because I wanted him to spend more time with the family. But I understood.

Chapter Twelve

College Student

IN LATE SUMMER of 1960, I was suddenly sent off to college. I had completed my high school education at night school just before giving birth to my first child, but I had never dreamed of being able to go to college.

One day when I was rushing home from work, eager to get back to my three tiny girls, Radio Deputy Director Li Wu called me from behind. "Wang Yulin! Wang Yulin!"

"What is it, Comrade Li Wu?" I turned and smiled at Li Wu, a thin older man, the one who had called me back to Beijing for my wedding.

"Good news! The leadership at Radio has decided to send you to college. You're supposed to report to school tomorrow."

"What? College! Me?" I couldn't believe my ears.

"That's right. You'll study English for a few years, as a student/trainee, and we'll continue to pay your salary. If you have any problems, just let me know."

My assignment was to study English at the Beijing Foreign Languages Institute, China's number one foreign language school. The news filled me with excitement. No one in our Wang family, generation after generation, had even finished high school, let alone gone to university. But it would mean living away from home six days a week. My older daughters were toddlers, just two and three years old, and the youngest, Sunny, was only eight months old. I worried about leaving her. Mama was busy taking care of the household and the older girls, and a baby needs extra attention.

Mama assured me that she would take good care of Sunny. As the one who had encouraged my education since I was little, Mama was thrilled at the idea of my attending college. The next morning, I picked up Sunny and said, "Your mommy's going off to school, little one." She grabbed a strand of my hair and pulled, as though she understood what was in my heart.

The baby began drinking formula. But since I stopped nursing her suddenly, I had too much milk and it was painful. For several months, I would have to excuse myself from class and go to a bathroom to squeeze out the milk. That meant missing class, and it was hard to catch up.

≈

When I entered the great gates of the university in September of 1960, I felt like Grandma Liu in the Chinese classic *Dream of the Red Chamber*—the countrywoman who entered the rich squire's courtyard and gawked at everything with wondering eyes.

Everything was new, and many things were completely unexpected. Before starting college, I had cut off my pigtails to wear my hair short, a more modern look. But I found that lots of the college girls still wore their hair in braids. They were seventeen, eighteen, or nineteen years old, and here I was, twenty-eight and a mother of three! I was the eldest student by far—older even than some of the teachers, one of whom was only twenty-three.

The upshot was that the teachers and the hundred or so students in my class all called me "Big Sister," a title that carries respect in China.

However, I wasn't really good material for training in English. Physically, I was in the classroom, but in my mind I was always worrying about whether my baby was crying and being properly fed, and how the two older girls were getting along. I phoned Mama, and she said that Sunny wasn't accustomed to formula and kept getting diarrhea. This added to my anxiety. So we hired a nanny, just to care for Sunny. The children called her "Ayi" or "Auntie."

Memorization was not one of my strong points, and I hated it. Learning English meant a lot of memorizing, because many of the rules for spelling and pronunciation made no sense whatsoever. Why is "read" sometimes pronounced like "reed" and other times like "red"? And why are "though" and "thought" and "through" pronounced so differently? In vain, I kept asking the teacher, "Why?" It wasn't like Russian, which was pronounced just the way it was spelled.

In addition to my challenging studies, I had more and more Party work to do as the year progressed, which took up my study time. My responsibilities involved work with the Communist Youth League and as a longtime Party member, I was made branch secretary for my year.

As branch secretary, I was responsible for helping fellow students manage personal matters. For example, once I spoke with a young student from the countryside who wanted a divorce. When I asked him why, he said, "My wife and I have no common language."

"Did you have a common language before?"

"Before, I used to cook and take the food out to the fields for her. My wife used the money from selling farm produce to put me through high school."

"So why is it that your relationship has soured, now that you're in college with all expenses paid by the state?"

"Because now she can't understand anything I talk to her about. She is illiterate."

"This isn't right, to ask for a divorce. She worked so hard in the fields to put you through high school, and now that you're in college, you forget all the support she gave you? Your wife is willingly taking care of your two children by herself. If you want to know what I think, you should not divorce your wife."

In the end, he didn't divorce her, and years later, when he was a retired man in his sixties, he visited me in Beijing. He told me that he and his wife got along very well. "Big Sister, it's good you didn't agree for me to divorce my wife," he said.

Another case was a female student from the Manchu ethnic group who fell in love with an African student and became pregnant with his baby. Dating and having children while in college was against the rules, and she also faced strong prejudice against Chinese girls becoming close with African students. Under great pressure, she was forced to withdraw from her studies.

I expressed sympathy for her, but since it was against the rules there was nothing I could do to keep her in school. But I did befriend her and invited her to our home before she left.

Another student was having major trouble in his studies. He could never answer questions in class, and his pronunciation was very poor—worse than mine. He became depressed and was sent to the mental hospital, but I didn't believe he was really sick.

"Big Sister, help me! They use electric shock treatment, and I can't stand it."

Again, I sympathized, but I wasn't able to do anything for him.

One day, another student chased after me in the courtyard.

"Big Sister! Big Sister!"

"What's wrong?" I turned around to ask her.

"You have to tell Li Lianzhu to take care of his mother. She mistook iodine for eye drops, and now she can't see. Li Lianzhu doesn't even go home on weekends, and the neighbors are very critical of him. You have to persuade him to take care of his mother."

Li Lianzhu was an exceptionally good student, who often stayed at school studying over the weekend. I talked with him, and he promised to go home whenever he could to take care of his mother.

Another time, a female student came to me with a question from Liu Shaoqi's book, *How to Be a Good Communist*. Liu Shaoqi, an old revolutionary, had recently been appointed chairman of the People's Republic of China, head of state.

"Big Sister, how do you explain this statement: 'A Communist should be able to undergo testing by the Party. Even if you are wrongfully accused, you should be able to take it, to consider it the Party's testing of you'"?

The question made me uncomfortable—I thought of Sidney. But now I represented the Party. I answered, "That's what Liu Shaoqi wrote. My own view is the Party may test someone for a short time, but it shouldn't drag out for a long time."

Another question came from a youth league cadre: "Big Sister, the organization is always giving me political work to do, but I have to keep up with my studies. What can I do?"

"That's the same problem that I'm having," I answered frankly. "I don't want to do so much political work, but our class political coach says, 'Who's going to do the political work if we Communists don't do it? Who are you going to shove it off onto?'" The class political coach was one of the professors who, instead of teaching, was in charge of coaching the students in political thinking.

Another student complained, "Teacher Hu is prejudiced. She doesn't help students who find the studies difficult and doesn't call on us to practice in class. Instead, she gives special coaching to the best students. How are we supposed to catch up?"

I had my own feeling about this. I was behind in my studies, but the teacher always called on the ace students in class. Students from peasant or worker families usually had the hardest time, and they couldn't get the help they needed.

I discussed this with the political coach, but he only gave me some empty talk. "Your job is to get those students to put aside their complaints and put their energy into hard study! We Communists should 'delight in helping.' We should be 'the first to endure and the last to enjoy.' You should set an example by your own actions." His words were quotations from the old Confucian classics—highly admirable, but irrelevant to solving the students' problems.

Another responsibility of mine was to decide which students needed supplementary aid: textbooks, food allowances, for example. Once a week, I had to convene a Party branch meeting, and I also attended and gave guidance at the youth league meetings.

College was not the dream life I had expected. I had to stay up late at night to study, and often my Party work kept me from attending review classes I really needed. I missed my kids, too. I felt such heavy pressure from the need to keep up with both my studies and my political work that I had trouble sleeping at night. To help me sleep, I frequently went to the school dispensary to take shots of vitamin B12.

To try to keep up my health, I would get up a little after five in the morning and run eight hundred meters around the campus sports field. But there wasn't always time for that. In fact, time was so tight that sometimes I would cook my lunch by putting noodles in a thermos jug, pouring water from the boiler room into the jug, and letting the hot water cook the noodles.

In 1960, the Chinese and the Soviet Communist Parties openly split apart, and the Soviets withdrew their technical experts from China, leaving many projects unfinished. The newspapers were full of angry articles, calling the Soviet Communists "revisionists" because they had revised their original pure aims of bringing socialism to the whole world. Several dozen students from other schools who had been training in Russian in preparation to go to the Soviet Union were suddenly transferred to our department for English studies. I managed to get one of these new students to replace me as Party branch secretary. This relieved some of the pressure on me.

By the time I returned home at Christmas, I was totally stressed. I asked Sidney, "Was this is your idea, sending me to college? Because you wanted me to learn English?"

Sidney denied it, but he admitted he knew about the plan before I did. At Radio, some of the leaders expected Sidney to return to the United States someday and hoped he would present a good image of China there. Although he had no intention of going back, it made sense for me to learn his language, to help him in his work with foreigners in Beijing. Comrade Li Wu, who was also Party secretary-general at Radio, had discussed the idea with Sidney first, and he had agreed.

So once again, others had made a key decision about the direction of my life. I felt tricked.

Chapter Thirteen

Surviving the Great Famine

SOON AFTER I began college, we experienced severe food shortages. The whole country was in the grip of famine, but it was a famine that I never heard anybody talking openly about. Years later I would discover that tens of millions of people died of hunger between 1958 and 1961, mostly in the villages and rural areas.

But we city people knew nothing about that. All we knew was that a great many people, including many of our students—myself among them—were walking around with swollen faces, arms, and legs. We were suffering from malnutrition edema, though nobody called it that.

There were three causes for the famine. One, the weather was very bad indeed for farmers, with prolonged drought in the North and flooding in the South. This was the official cause that the newspapers blamed.

The second cause was one the Party stressed internally: the unreasonable demands from the Soviet leader, Nikita Khrushchev. After the break with the Soviet Union, Khrushchev demanded that China repay its debt for the Soviet arms and equipment supplied to Chinese expeditionary forces during the Korean War. Originally, this was not supposed to be a debt: the understanding with Stalin was that China would supply the fighting men, while the Soviets supplied the equipment. But with the ugly polemics that broke out between the two countries, the Soviets demanded that both China and North Korea repay them for their equipment. Mao Zedong said that North Korea's Kim Il-Sung had responded to the bill from Moscow by presenting them with a bill in the same amount for services rendered by North Korea to the Soviet Union, so he didn't pay a cent. But China, Mao told us, is a great power; we had to pay.

We responded with grim resolve: we would tighten our belts and repay the hated "revisionists" and "socialist-imperialists" every cent! We were a proud people, especially China's students. We held our heads high, refusing to complain, as we tightened our belts. This meant that trainload after trainload of China's best meats, grains, fruits, and vegetables were shipped to the Soviet Union in payment of the Korean War debt. Only Party members knew about it, and this was a bitter pill when so many Chinese citizens were starving.

But there was a third cause for the famine, a cause that no one talked about: the disastrous failure of the "Great Leap Forward."

Unveiled by Chairman Mao in January 1958, the Great Leap Forward aimed to rapidly modernize China into an industrialized communist economy. Our Party's audacious goal was to surpass the United States and Britain in steel output within fifteen years. Mao wanted this to be a grassroots effort, so tens of millions of farmers abandoned the fields to the very young and very old, while they went off to scour the hills for iron ore, nonferrous metals, rare earths, and other minerals, to be used for the growth of village industry and trade. Farmers had to give up their private plots and join communes, and although the Party exhorted them to increase production for the country, they lost their personal incentive to work hard. Obeying misguided directives from Beijing, some farmers had to switch to crops that were poorly suited to their land. Rural areas claimed huge record harvests, and Radio Peking reported this news, but the reports turned out to be false. By the harvest season of 1960, just as I was beginning college, China faced one of its most devastating famines in history.

In reality, the dislocation of the economy that came with the Great Leap Forward was a major cause of the famine. Tens of millions died because of these disastrously flawed policies. But we students would typically say to one another that our swollen bodies were the result of a virus or something in the water.

To eat, I went out with my fellow students to strip the trees of their leaves. We would dry the green leaves in the sun, grind them up, and mix them with a tiny bit of flour to make "green noodles." If we went harvesting late, someone else would get there first and the leaves would be gone. Every unit (schools, factories, government bodies, etc.) had a quota for the amount of leaves they were to collect. Each unit reported on how well they had met their quota.

I was a city girl and didn't know how to climb trees. I could only take a pole and jump up and down, beating the leaves off the trees. The low branches that stuck out tore my clothes. The highly prized elm leaves and flowers, as well as the leaves of the locust trees, would all be gone by the time we got to them. All that was left for us were the poplar trees. The old folks watching us strip the poplars told us that, even in the famines of ancient times, people didn't eat poplar leaves because they are bitter and make your mouth pucker up. But eating them was better than going hungry, so we ate them.

Of course, being married to a foreign expert, I could have gone home and had access to whatever food I wanted. My friends said, "Big Sister, why don't you go home and eat properly?"

I thought to myself, *A big sister should act like a big sister. How can I run off and fill my stomach by myself?*

Within months, my face, arms, and legs were badly swollen. I was moved into the special dorm for students with edema and was not allowed to take part in the physical exercises. Sidney was deeply worried about me. He brought me a big bag full of meat, fruit, and bread, but I wouldn't accept it. At the time, I was still secretary of the Party branch. "How can I eat this stuff when all the other students are going hungry?" I said.

This was the kind of self-sacrificing idealism the Party taught us. We were always to put the common good ahead of our personal needs and model exemplary behavior for others. Sidney, as worried as he was about my health, agreed with my reasoning and respected me for it.

Suddenly, one day on the playing field, I heard students shouting.

"Chairman Mao has sent a special supply of soybeans for students with the swelling!"

Others shouted, "Chairman Mao has sent us fish!"

After that, each student with the swelling could get a mouthful of fish and a tablespoon of soybeans each day.

We were tearfully thankful for how Chairman Mao cared for us. We decided to leave all the available fish for the most serious sufferers, who were bedridden. I didn't actually get any of the fish, but I was very excited about this help from on high. Instead of blaming Mao's policies for the disaster, we thanked him for the brief relief from it.

Actually, the Party leadership had issued instructions that no Party members were allowed to contend with non-Party people for vegetables or meat. In other words, the well-being of ordinary citizens came first. I remembered the harsh times in Shijiazhuang, when my family couldn't get enough to eat. But in those days, the Kuomintang soldiers would go from house to house, seizing everything valuable. Some folks were beaten and even killed because they resisted the marauding soldiers.

Two different parties, two different worlds, I thought to myself.

Mama was always admonishing me. "Don't forget the harsh days of the past, and don't forget that our good life today is owing to Chairman Mao and the Communist Party!" The poorer a person had been in prerevolutionary days, the more loyal she was to the Party. We were so convinced that the Party had our best interests at heart that we could not imagine that it was in any way responsible for this suffering.

In my mind, the sole culprit behind the famine was Soviet revisionism. Soviet insistence that we pay for the Korean War equipment was what caused the food shortage. We had no idea that it was a nationwide famine, and that millions were starving to death. Nor did we realize the real situation behind the false propaganda about wheat fields that yielded ten times the usual crops, utilizing super-deep plowing and super-dense planting that Chairman Mao advocated. In fact, the fabulous yields were obtained by transplanting pregrown crops from other fields and concentrating them onto a patch of "model land." Without a free press, we also didn't know that the exemplary achievements in industrialization, faithfully reported by Radio Peking and the newspapers, were wild exaggerations.

I even heard that once you got the swelling, your body could never return to normal health. Still, I wasn't afraid; I just accepted it as an inescapable fact. The edema made our bodies tired and our minds sluggish. Quarrels were few; nobody had the strength for them. When we weren't in class, we'd go back to the dorm and lie down. There was very little activity.

When I would go home on weekends, I had to change buses several times and then walk a good distance to get home. When I arrived, tired as I was, I'd pretend to be in great spirits so as not to upset the children.

It wasn't just me suffering; all the comrades around me were in the same boat. There was a strong feeling of "we'll all stick together, and we'll get through it!" In the end, we did get through it—most of the people I knew, that is.

≈

One day in 1961, I got the scare of my life: someone from Radio called me at school to tell me that our second child, Toni, had taken violently ill at her nursery school. Sidney sent a car to fetch me.

The nursery-school teacher on duty told me that the children had eaten some pears with the noon meal, and that afterwards she'd noticed that little Toni, just over one year old, was unusually quiet and listless. The teacher put Toni to bed and took her temperature; it was way below normal.

Without another word, the teacher, pregnant at the time, wrapped my baby up and rushed her to a newly established neighborhood clinic nearby. Once Toni got to the clinic, she began having convulsions.

Terrified, I rushed to the clinic and then sat there helplessly, with Sidney holding my hand, as they worked on Toni with an old-fashioned pulmotor, a mechanical device that pumped oxygen into her lungs. All I could do was weep on Sidney's shoulder and plead with the medical staff to do everything they could.

Twice, the doctor came over to tell us that our child had stopped breathing, but that they would continue their best effort to revive her—and twice she came back to life. Finally, her breathing was stable enough to transfer her to the Friendship Hospital, where the chief of pediatrics, Dr. Arthur Zhang, was a good friend of ours.

At the hospital, Toni suddenly became paralyzed on one side, from eyelids to toes. Dr. Zhang worked on her tirelessly, using both Western medicine and Chinese acupuncture. Just as the staff shook their heads over our baby, a dramatic event turned the tide.

First, Toni was seized with violent diarrhea. When the first bout ended, Dr. Zhang was leaning over her, listening with his stethoscope, when suddenly Toni's paralyzed left arm rose up and struck him in the face!

We were overjoyed: Our child was back. She was going to be okay!

We never did find out what caused the problem. But we didn't care about the cause—our child was alive! Dr. Zhang judged that it might have been some sort of toxic dysentery. I stayed home to care for Toni, and after a couple of weeks, she was back in nursery school. Fortunately, none of our other children took sick.

Mama's comment on Toni's recovery was simple and direct, as usual. "I knew she'd be fine. How can a baby die under socialism?"

This statement, coming from a woman who had lost eight of her twelve children in the Old Society, was not as strange as it may seem. To her, capitalism meant the Old Society, where babies often died and corpses littered the streets. Socialism had transformed her life so drastically that it seemed to her almost like magic.

Sidney and I both felt intensely thankful for the neighborhood clinic that saved Toni. Like the "barefoot doctors" in country villages, the neighborhood clinics were a product of Mao Zedong's Great Leap Forward. If that little clinic hadn't been there—and if Toni's teacher hadn't taken immediate action when she spotted something wrong—our daughter wouldn't be here today. Although

I worried about long-term aftereffects for many years, Toni not only survived but grew up to become a talented doctor herself and now runs four clinics in North Carolina.

Despite evidence to the contrary, we all wanted to believe that nothing bad could happen under socialism.

Chapter Fourteen

Old Auntie and the Amaryllis

IN 1961, THE Great Leap Forward ended, and the Party switched to more pragmatic policies, allowing farmers to use private plots and sell some of their produce in free markets. While we heard some Party members criticize these policies as "capitalist," they did help increase the food supply. The Great Famine ended, we students had more to eat, and my swelling went away, with no long-term effects.

My life returned to normal: studying six days a week at college and visiting Sidney and the girls on weekends. Still, it took me longer than usual, six years, to finish my education.

During the boiling hot summer of 1964, I went to a village with my classmates to take part in the Party's "Four Clears Movement." This was part of a campaign by Chairman Mao to teach people in the countryside about socialism. We students were sent to help achieve the four objectives of the campaign, which were to evaluate local government expenditures, give a clear account of warehouse inventory, clear up inequities in the distribution of collective farm income, and straighten out local finances.

The main targets of this movement were the rural cadres, who were routinely subjected to investigations, whether or not there was probable cause. Most of the student groups were assigned to audit village books, investigate local cadres' behavior, and visit neighboring collectives to gather information.

Fortunately, my part was simpler: to write a history of a village that was now functioning as a "people's commune," where villagers shared the land and the work and took care of each other. We didn't have to find wrongdoing, only stories that would illustrate the lingering effects of class struggle in the villages. We spent a month in one village about thirty-five miles from my campus in Beijing.

Two other girls and I stayed with poor peasant families. It was against the rules to stay with a cadre or a well-to-do family, and we were required to eat the same food as the poor family we lived with. We gave our host families our grain ration tickets and thirty fen (worth about twelve cents) for our food every day. Although our food was simple, it was fresh and tasted good. Every third day, we switched to a different home.

I found it relaxing to talk to the peasants, who had no pretensions. I never had to worry about their backgrounds and whether or not they might be the object of some political struggle. These were honest, reliable people, and I assumed I could learn much from their attitudes toward life.

The first task our three-girl group was given was to write about the life of an elderly village widow. She was a hospitable woman, a little over fifty, which was considered old in those days in the Chinese countryside, but she lived in a tiny mud-brick hut with unbelievably foul air. As luck would have it, we had been assigned to interview the least sanitary person in the village—in fact, the villagers mockingly called her "The Health Department." We addressed her by the more respectful title of "Old Auntie."

Her home consisted of two small rooms separated by a dirty piece of cloth in place of a door. In the outer room there were pig slops and chicken feed, a large urn for water, and a pile of coal dust for making into coal briquettes. The inside room was Old Auntie's bedroom.

The first time I went into the bedroom, I had to cover my nose against the foul air. A close look at the *kang*, "brick oven-bed," on which she slept revealed that there were chicken droppings all over it. Greenbottle flies flew about the room.

"Have a seat, have a seat," Old Auntie said.

I looked around but saw nothing to sit on.

"Don't worry about us—we're not tired," we said, as with one voice. We decided to interview her outdoors, sitting on stools in the dirt of her courtyard. Nobody wanted to touch Old Auntie, for fear she had fleas.

Although I had grown up fighting starvation, I realized quickly that rural poverty was even more severe than what I had experienced in the city. At least we had had access to water and were able to keep our home environment neat and clean. Plus, we had a basic knowledge of how to prevent some sickness. I had never seen such primitive living conditions, even during the time I lived in a cave.

One day, the old lady gave each of us a bowl of *congee*— stewed rice porridge with vegetables. My classmate poked me in the ribs to whisper, "Big Sister, there are two big flies in your bowl."

Startled, I felt my stomach churn at the sight.

"What's the matter?" asked Old Auntie. "Doesn't the congee taste good?"

"It's fine, it's fine," we chorused.

"We don't have anything good to eat in the villages," she said. "All we can offer you is grain that's fresher than what you get in the city."

"It is indeed fresher," we agreed.

Then I asked, "Auntie, you hatch your chicks on the kang?"

She said, "They hatch quickly on the warm kang, and it's easier to take care of them in there."

When she saw that we had all laid down our chopsticks and weren't eating, she asked anxiously, "Is something wrong? Why aren't you eating?"

Little Zhu, one of the other students, quickly changed the subject. "How many pigs do you have?"

"I have about a dozen, and two of the sows are just about to birth new litters. You can see how loveable the little piglets are!"

"You care for those pigs as though they were children," I said. "Look how sleek they all are!"

She said, laughing, "If you don't take care of them, they don't fatten up."

She went on to tell us how she hovered around the sows constantly when they were about to give birth, and after they gave birth she watched carefully to see that the mother pig didn't accidently crush the little shoats. I was afraid the conversation was taking too long, so I started asking questions about her life.

"Auntie, you used to be a servant in a landlord's home, right?"

She said, "That was long ago."

Little Zhu said, "We heard that you gave birth to a daughter in the grain storehouse."

"That's right," she said. "Fate has dealt me a hard life. I was married twice, and both husbands died. So did all my children."

We paused in silence. In traditional China, to be a childless widow was the worst possible outcome in life.

"It's not so bad, Auntie," I said. "Look what a good life you have now."

Despite the primitive conditions of her home, she totally agreed. "That's all thanks to Chairman Mao," she said. "Look how fat I've become. Folks all say I'm the picture of prosperity! They don't know that before the Liberation I was nothing but skin and bone."

"What did your husbands do?" I asked.

"They both had a hard life. Both worked as hired hands for the landlord; both got sick and couldn't afford a doctor, so I had to sit by helplessly and watch them die. I had one child with my first husband and another with my second, but neither one lived."

Pangs shot through my heart. I remembered my own childhood illness, when my parents thought they could not afford medical care. But at least I had survived. "What kind of work did you do?" I asked her.

"In the landlord's home, I had to mill the flour right up till I was almost ready to give birth. Then the landlord ran me out of his house. I begged him to let me have the baby there, but he said, 'You're a widow. It will bring me bad fortune if you have your baby here!' I left, but I had no place to go. Some of the neighbors built me a grass hut, where I stayed in the bitter cold winter and where I gave birth. I had no milk, so I carried the baby out into the fields to dig for weeds to feed her. But alas! When I got back home, the baby was dead."

With three small ones of my own, I could feel her loss. Compared to that grass hut, this filthy hovel must have felt like paradise to her.

"What did you do after the baby died, Auntie?"

"I went begging in the streets. Until Liberation."

In spite of the dirty clothes and bad air, I found myself loving this old woman. I wondered if the leaders had purposely placed me in this old woman's house, to see how I would withstand the test. Fifteen years after Liberation, this was a good reminder of the life I myself had lived, before the Communists. How easy it was to forget, living with my American husband and relatively privileged family. Even this filthy hovel represented a better life for Old Auntie. And her upbeat spirit inspired me. How could I possibly complain about my life?

When Auntie was out, I cleaned and swept the whole house, although there was no way that I could keep it clean. As soon as I cleaned up the chicken droppings in one area, chickens in another would mess things up again. I also washed her clothes, in spite of my fear about fleas. They were the filthiest I had every touched. I washed them with soap and hung them out to dry. When she returned, she was astonished. She peered about the room, looking right and left. "I don't recognize the place. You even washed my clothes!"

"We didn't know whether you would like this," I said.

"Like it? I love it!"

I hoped she would see how much better life was with clean clothes and a well-swept house, but I never knew.

During the month I spent in the village, I grew close to Old Auntie. When we went back to the city, she gave us several beautiful amaryllis plants. These elegant long-stemmed plants had gorgeous blossoms: huge red trumpets that filled me with cheer.

"Don't forget me," she said. "When you look at these flowers, think of your Old Auntie."

After we got back to school, I kept thinking about her and seeing her kindly face. Our English Department was producing some entertainment at that time, so I wrote and directed a little skit about Old Auntie. The professors and students applauded it. That weekend at home, I told Sidney about it, and he smiled. Not only was I learning English but I was deepening my social consciousness. After the destructive campaigns and disastrous famine, meeting Old Auntie was a welcome reminder of the good that Communism had done for China's poorest people.

As for the amaryllis, I planted it in a flowerpot and placed it in our sitting room. One day, Mama mistakenly poured a full pan of what she thought was water into the flowerpot, but it turned out to be grease! However, the amaryllis kept its head erect and survived. This plant had a place of honor in our home. We called it our "family flower." It would become a symbol of survival against all odds in times to come.

Chapter Fifteen

Meeting Chairman Mao

IN NOVEMBER OF 1965, half a year before the curtain rose on the Great Proletarian Cultural Revolution, I got a call from our English Department telling me to return to Radio immediately. I was afraid that one of our children was sick again, so I rushed home from college without even picking up my things at the dormitory. At that time, I was already more than six months pregnant with our fourth child.

I checked in with Deputy Director Li Wu, and he said, "You and Li Dunbai will go to Shanghai tomorrow. You and some others will be received there by Chairman Mao."

I couldn't believe my ears.

"Go home and get ready!" he said.

I hurried home and asked Sidney what the occasion was.

"It's Anna Louise Strong's eightieth birthday," he told me. "Chairman Mao has invited us to help celebrate. They have arranged a special plane, and we will travel with Liao Chengzhi." Liao was a high-level Communist leader, a man Sidney had worked under at the New China News Agency during the revolutionary time in the caves of Yan'an. Fluent in several languages, Liao did a lot of "united front" work, liaison with foreigners in China.

Anna Louise Strong was a world-famous American writer and radical activist who had been one of the earliest enthusiastic supporters of the Communist movement in Russia, back in the 1920s. Feisty and hot tempered, she had been arrested and deported on Stalin's orders at the same time Sidney was imprisoned, in 1949. Yet at eighty, she was highly admired by our Communist leaders in China, where she now lived full time. Anna Louise had been a close friend of Sidney's since their days in Yan'an, where he helped her translate secret documents and write articles about the Chinese Communist movement. Since my marriage, I had come to know Anna Louise, too, although she spoke no Chinese.

By the time of Anna Louise's birthday, Mao Zedong had achieved nearly god-like status. We viewed Mao as not only the leader of China but the liberator of the world. For me, an invitation to meet him was tantamount to a flight to the moon to meet the Buddha.

Mama told me to be sure to wish Chairman Mao well on her behalf.

Suddenly, I was conscious of my appearance, especially my huge belly.

"I need some decent clothes to wear when I meet Chairman Mao," I told Sidney. As my belly had grown, I had just been wearing bulky jackets and tying my pants with a cotton sash. I went to American economist Frank Coe's place and borrowed a copper-colored maternity jacket from his wife, Ruth.

The government had chartered a special plane for our small group of about fifteen. My first experience flying was not a good one. When we took off, a storm lashed us with wind and rain. The plane pitched and rolled and yawed the whole way to Shanghai. The takeoff and landing were particularly uncomfortable, and I felt nauseated the whole time. I threw up so much that I used up all the little paper airsickness bags on the plane. We traveled on the same plane with George Hatem, an American doctor who, like Sidney, had stayed in China under Communism, and he went around the plane collecting the bags for me until they ran out.

We made it safely to Shanghai, where we stayed at the Jinjiang Hotel, one of the most famous. We were informed that the meeting was not ready yet and that we were first to visit a Shanghai factory. But as soon as we arrived at the factory, Liao Chengzhi received an urgent phone call, asking us to return at once to be received by Chairman Mao at the former French Club, renamed the Jinjiang Club, across the street from our hotel.

As we walked across the street, I could see the large frame of Chairman Mao standing in the outer doorway of the club, shaking hands with each of the guests. I began to shiver with excitement.

When I approached Chairman Mao, he must have noticed how tense I was, because he began to speak casually with me to calm me down.

I was introduced as "Wang Yulin, wife of Li Dunbai."

In a very gentle voice, he asked, "Where are you from?"

"I'm from Beijing." I couldn't believe I was shaking hands with the Great Helmsman.

"What does your father do?"

"He's a carpenter," I said, trying to steady my voice.

"Ah, a proletarian, a worker—great!"

Then he held on to my hand and looked me straight in the eyes. "Comrade Wang Yulin, we gave Li Dunbai a hard time; our Party locked him up for six years. Our Communist Party made a mistake. We are really sorry."

My eyes widened. I was too moved to say anything.

"How many children do you have?" the chairman continued.

"Three."

"And the fourth is about to be born?"

"Yes, in three more months."

"Well, take care of your health."

"I thank Chairman Mao for caring."

We were led to a conference room where we sat in upholstered chairs along three walls around the perimeter of the room. There were a dozen foreigners, all trusted Communist intellectuals, and about half a dozen high-ranking Chinese in attendance. Chairman Mao sat at the front, next to Anna Louise Strong, and began chain-smoking his favorite brand of cigarillo—Gongzi, which means "worker."

Of all the things that Mao said that day, two things made the deepest impression on me. At the beginning, he asked for permission to smoke, and he asked for a show of hands as to how many present were smokers. When fewer than half of us raised our hands, he commented, "On this, too, I find myself in a minority."

I couldn't imagine what the "too" meant. How could the Chairman of the Communist Party be in a "minority"? In those days, every word Chairman Mao uttered was parsed for deeper meanings. But what startled me most was what he said next.

"Who knows, a situation might arise where I'll have to go back to the mountains and start doing guerrilla warfare all over again!" He tossed his head back and laughed heartily, but no one else laughed. Fifteen years after Liberation, why would we need guerrilla warfare? The faces of the propaganda chiefs in the room turned white.

At that time, Mao's meaning was obscure. But looking back, I now realize that he was already struggling with other leaders of the Party who had taken away his power over the economy after the disastrous failure of the Great Leap Forward. To reconstruct the broken economy, President Liu Shaoqi and Deputy Premier Deng Xiaoping were reversing many of Mao's policies and downgrading his beloved agricultural communes, leaving Mao in a minority within the top leadership. Underneath his calm surface, Mao was probably roiling with anger at them and trying to figure out how to use his godlike stature with the Chinese masses to regain full power. That is one reason he had left Beijing for Shanghai, where he was consolidating support for his comeback.

As I listened to Mao speaking that day, I wondered whether we would also meet his wife, Jiang Qing. She appeared toward the end of the reception and invited us to a formal luncheon in a dining room next door. She played the part of a gracious hostess.

At the luncheon, I was seated just opposite her. Sidney had told me about meeting her in the caves of Yan'an, when she was a beautiful young movie actress. She looked younger than I expected, but I thought her color seemed pasty, as though she were ailing.

"Comrade Jiang Qing, how's your health?" I dared to ask her.

"Not bad," she said. "Only my stomach's not too good."

As she spoke, she called over one of the servers and told her to take two of the tangerines on the table and warm them up. "With my stomach problem," she explained to me, "I can't eat cold food, so I eat warmed-up tangerines."

Jiang Qing didn't seem to relate to anyone around her. She did not take part in the political discussion and did not even talk to anyone. She certainly did not look like part of a political power about to take over the country. In fact, nobody was paying much attention to her.

⁓

That night, Premier Zhou Enlai invited us to dinner in the ballroom, along with a large group of visiting Japanese youth. The choral group of the East Sea Fleet entertained us with music. Their main number was the new chorale, "Long March Suite," composed by Zhou's old friend, General Xiao Hua. In the middle of the performance, Zhou Enlai surprised everyone by jumping to his feet and calling out, "Wait a minute! Why did you skip over the verse about crossing the Great Snowy Mountains? That was composed by Comrade Xiao Hua personally!"

Looking embarrassed, the young conductor paused. "We haven't rehearsed that verse," he said. "We don't know it."

"Never mind, I'll lead you," said the premier. He walked out in front of the choir, took the baton, and sang out in a clear tenor voice, leading them in singing that verse. Later on, we thought that this little incident might have reflected the pre-Cultural Revolution political struggles, but Xiao Hua was not yet in trouble at that point, so it's hard to say.

After we returned home, Mama wanted to hear every detail about our meeting with Chairman Mao. But my mind quickly shifted to personal matters. Not long afterward, on February 15, 1966, our son, Xiaoming, was born. We had not planned on having another child, but all of us were agog over this new addition to our family.

To me, it seemed an auspicious time to bring a baby into the world. Sidney was not only honored and trusted at work but had been received by Chairman Mao himself. In just a few months, I was about to earn my college degree and move back home, where I could care for my children and take up a new job at the Broadcast Administration. After the Great Famine and the damaging Sino-Soviet split, China was growing again and seemed stable and at peace.

As it happened, our son could not have been born at a worse time.

Chapter Sixteen

Fury over Furniture

IN AN ODD twist of fate, Sidney and I had the worst argument of all our married life, just before the storm of the Cultural Revolution blew our lives off course. While attending college at the Foreign Languages Institute, I was still considered to be a cadre employed by the Broadcast Administration, so the state continued to pay my salary. Sidney's salary was high in those days—higher even than the pay of Chairman Mao and Premier Zhou Enlai. As a foreign expert, he was paid on a different scale than Chinese citizens. His income was more than enough to cover the family's expenses, so I put all of my income in the bank and saved it. We never thought much about money. Still, it annoyed me when I found out that Sidney had emptied my bank account, without informing me, and spent all my savings on antique furniture. This was not just any furniture, but extremely valuable yellow rosewood chairs and tables made by the finest craftsmen in the Ming Dynasty, more than four hundred years ago.

In 1960, Sidney had been chosen to join an elite team tasked with translating the fourth volume of Mao Zedong's writings into English. This work was so secret that even I didn't know about it until years later. One of his colleagues on that team was a scholar named Ji Chaoding. Elder Ji was a collector and connoisseur of classical Chinese furniture, and he began to take Sidney to antique shops in Beijing. Elder Ji feared that embassy personnel were buying up these rare, beautiful pieces and shipping them out of the country—a great loss for China. Most Chinese citizens, with their low salaries, couldn't afford to buy such luxuries. He encouraged Sidney to purchase some of these gorgeous antiques and keep them in China, with the promise that he would one day donate them to the Palace Museum in the Forbidden City. Sidney began to buy antique furniture, and he reassured Elder Ji that he would eventually donate all of it to the museum. In the meantime, it would decorate our home in Beijing, showing off the finest Chinese artistry to our foreign visitors.

At first, this seemed to me an extravagant expense and a bourgeois luxury—certainly not the way I would have spent my salary, if I had known. But I quickly fell in love with these handcrafted chairs and tables and chests, with their elegant curved arms and delicate legs. Perhaps, as the daughter of a cabinetmaker, I had more appreciation for wooden furniture than for other types of art. But mainly, these items were just stunning. One tall screen was covered with porcelain painted in vivid colors, with blossoms and leaves. One heavy rosewood table was carved so that it looked exactly like bamboo. To me, they represented the beauty of China, my country, my heritage. I felt inspired by the time and effort that went into their creation. It was an immense privilege to have them in our home. Each time I returned from the hubbub of college life to my husband and children, the furniture calmed my spirit.

One Saturday in the spring of 1966, not long after I had given birth to our son, I came home from college, and all this lovely furniture was gone. My heart nearly stopped beating. Our living room was barren, with only a few ugly standard-issue chairs and tables left behind.

"Lao Li! Where is our furniture?"

"We donated it to the Palace Museum. Don't you remember?" Sidney said. "I told you last weekend."

"No, I don't remember any such thing. Why did you do it?"

"Elder Ji has passed away now, so I thought it was time to give these treasures back to China."

"But it was ours."

"It was not right to keep it here for our personal enjoyment. It belongs to the people of China."

It was then I noticed one piece remained: a low tea table with one leg that was not original. Sidney told me the Palace Museum had refused to accept it. The rest of our nineteen pieces of lovely furniture had disappeared forever. The porcelain screen, the elegant curved armchairs, the delicately carved tables. I had not had a chance to run my fingers along the smooth wood and say good-bye.

Perhaps he had said something about donating the furniture, but I had no idea that he meant to give away every piece of it that week. I thought he meant to donate it "someday." Certainly, he had not obtained my consent or asked my input on which pieces to donate and which to keep. He just gave it all away. Our most precious possessions. For all the Party's talk of equality between men and women, he made this major decision without my input. To me, that was disrespectful in the extreme.

I have never been so angry in my life, before or since. I screamed at him.

"What does it matter?" he responded. "Why do you always have to be so stubborn! You're like a block of granite."

It was our worst moment.

To this day, Sidney claims that I had agreed to the donation, but I have no recollection of it. I was so angry at him that I stayed at school and didn't return for the next few weekends, even though I had a newborn baby at home. He came to school to talk to me, but it took a long time for me to cool down.

Many years later, around 2000, our eldest daughter took an American friend and client, Craig McCaw, to the Palace Museum in Beijing and was astonished to find two pieces of our Ming Dynasty furniture on display. They stood in a special exhibit hall that was accessible only by payment of several thousand U.S. dollars. The docent told them that any of these pieces would sell for several million U.S. dollars. The furniture was labeled, "Donated by Li Dunbai of Britain." They credited him but didn't even get his country right.

When Craig returned to the hotel, he said to Sidney, "You really are an idealist!"

In retrospect, Sidney chose the right moment to give away that furniture. In the Palace Museum, it was protected from the ravages of Red Guards, who had been instructed to destroy "the Four Olds"—everything that was historical or traditional. If the furniture had remained in our house, we could not have protected it.

It turned out that it was not the antiques but our lives that were hacked to pieces by the Red Guards. The turbulence in our home reflected a deeper tumult that was churning beneath the surface of China.

Chapter Seventeen

The Storm Begins

IN MAY 1966, just weeks before I expected to take my final exams and complete my university education, a flurry of *dazibaos* appeared on our campus. A dazibao is a poster with a revolutionary message, handwritten in ink in large Chinese characters on newspapers and pasted on walls. It is a peculiarly Chinese form of protest.

The first of them seemed innocuous enough. Some students were protesting a method of education called "sudden attacks against the students." These were, in effect, pop quizzes. We were accustomed to preparing for big exams, and these unannounced quizzes seemed unfair. If students weren't prepared that day, they might fail, and that could harm their final grade for the course. The poster writers, all anonymous, said they backed this movement, which actually started at other schools, and claimed that Chairman Mao himself encouraged students to protest against "sudden attacks."

I agreed with the protest but was too busy to think much about it. A few days later, though, I was startled by another set of dazibaos. These criticized our school's Party committee for enforcing the "Six Prohibitions" that came from the Beijing Municipal Party Committee. As a Party member, I knew that these six things were not permitted: putting up dazibaos in public places, holding meetings off campus, meeting with students from other schools, photographing dazibaos, demonstrating in the streets, and surrounding the homes of suspected enemies.

Obviously, someone—whoever produced these dazibaos—felt the Six Prohibitions were unfair. But how could ordinary students openly defy Party policy? Immediately, I assumed this was another attack by rightists, similar to what happened in 1957. Some rebels were trying to undermine the authority of the Communist Party. It never occurred to me that someone in the highest leadership could possibly be sanctioning this attack.

When I went to study in the library (there was no room to study in the dorm, where we lived eight to a room), there was yet another dazibao, this one written in blazing big characters. It was titled "Black Gang Boss—Chen Yi."

This shocked me even more. Chen Yi was a national hero. A famous military commander during the revolution and the war against Japan, he now served as China's foreign minister, vice premier, and a member of the Party Political Bureau. He was one of the twenty most powerful rulers of the country. As foreign minister, he was ultimately in charge of our school, the Foreign Languages Institute. To Sidney and me, he was also a personal friend.

The dazibao accused Chen Yi's foreign ministry of carrying out a policy of "Sell out the nation in return for praise from foreigners." That smelled like a charge of treason. It also described the policy of the Foreign Languages Institute as "a bourgeois reactionary line," opposed to Chairman Mao's proletarian revolutionary line. The poster was signed, "5.16 Red Guards."

I knew that 5.16 probably stood for May 16, but I didn't understand why they picked that date. What had happened on May 16? Who were these "May 16 Red Guards"? What were they guarding? And why were they attacking a good comrade like Chen Yi?

We knew Chen Yi to be a cheerful, hearty, humorous veteran of the revolution, very strong on principle. I recalled a time when Sidney and I had dinner with Anna Louise Strong, Premier Zhou Enlai, and Marshal Chen Yi. We were struck by the easy camaraderie between the old revolutionaries.

At the table, Zhou had commented on a current slogan: "Everyone can be a poet!" He said, "That's an exaggeration. At least, I know I'm no poet. I wrote a poem in classical style and sent it to Chen Yi for comment. He sent it back with a note, saying, 'I can't comment on this poem, because it's not a poem.'" We all knew that Chen Yi, sometimes called "The Poet Marshal," was an expert at poetry.

Later, when it was time to offer a toast to the health of Anna Louise Strong, Chen Yi insisted that the premier take the lead, because he was higher in rank. But Zhou Enlai said, "No, you have to do it. You're a marshal. I'm not a marshal." As a Commander of the People's Liberation Army, Chen Yi had led the troops that drove the Kuomintang out of Shanghai and brought about victory in 1949. He was one of ten top military commanders to receive the title of "marshal" in 1955 from Chairman Mao.

By the farthest stretch of imagination, I couldn't accept that Chen Yi was a bad person, let alone a "black gang boss."

I rushed back to the dorm to find some of my classmates. Several of us gathered under a big tree in front of the classroom building and talked things over. We all felt that this was another rightist attack on the Party. Maybe this was a test of our loyalty. We had to do something about it, but we didn't know what.

One of my classmates and close friends was Wang Fengzhen, a lively, talkative girl from a peasant family near Shijiazhuang. She had been assigned to study Russian in the Soviet Union, but after the Sino-Soviet split she was instructed to learn English instead. Solid and honest, she and I saw eye to eye on most things and became very close.

Although we opposed the dazibaos attacking Chen Yi, we did agree with the ones protesting pop quizzes. Still, we felt that the critics had a bad attitude, and the criticism in the dazibaos was not raised in good faith.

Later, five of us female students met in a corner of the campus and decided to take up the fight to defend the Communist Party and the socialist system. First, we decided to report what was going on to the Party central leadership. At that time, we weren't aware that similar things were going on at other schools.

We set off on foot for the Central Committee headquarters at Zhongnanhai, around fifteen miles away. I knew the way, because I had often been to Party headquarters when I worked at Radio. It took about five hours to walk there from the university district. As we walked, we continued our animated discussion of the situation at our college.

"I'm sure this is a rightist attack on the Party," said Wang Fengzhen. After the Anti-Rightist Campaign, we learned to call anyone who opposed Party policy a "rightist." At best, they were bourgeois people who didn't understand why only Communism could build China. At worst, they were class enemies out to destroy the Party.

"I agree," said Chen Xiuzhen, a fellow student. "We have to do our part to defend the working class." In the jargon of the time, this meant to defend the Communist Party and its leaders.

"But why do they point the spear of their attack at Chen Yi?" I asked. This baffled me. Chen Yi's policies were far from controversial, and I had always considered him above any doubts—close to Mao and the revolutionary heart of the country.

"There's got to be some big conspiracy behind this," said Xiuzhen. "I think they're counterrevolutionaries. They use the dazibaos to influence public opinion for an overthrow of the government."

"But how did they get to be so powerful?" asked Fengzhen. "We have to look into the backgrounds of these May 16 people. Why are they so active, right at the beginning of a new movement? They must have been plotting behind the scenes for a long time."

It was getting very late, and there were few people on the streets. It was just the five of us, talking excitedly about our first impressions of the thunderous Cultural Revolution that was about to startle the world. It was puzzling, and even though we were students, none of us could imagine the source of the discontent.

Only much later did I learn what had happened on May 16: the Politburo had discussed a secret document stating that representatives of the capitalists had sneaked into the Party and the government, forming a gang of "counter-revolutionary revisionists." It charged that these Party cadres were plotting to seize power and turn the dictatorship of the proletariat into a capitalist dictatorship. Like the Soviets, they had "revised" their Communist views and were now undermining the Party.

In effect, Chairman Mao was accusing some Party leaders of being "capitalist roaders"—trying to return China to capitalism by allowing private farm plots and markets. That's what Liu Shaoqi and his allies had done to try to revive the economy after the disastrous famine that followed massive collectivization in the Great Leap Forward. To do so, they had pushed Mao to the side, reversing his economic policies, and Mao was trying to make a comeback. Now there were charges that some Party leaders, still unnamed, "waved the red flag to oppose the red flag." That's what had emboldened the 5.16 Red Guards. They were guarding Chairman Mao himself, in his effort to grab total power. Most of us trusted Mao so much that we would never have believed this.

Finally, we arrived at the reception station for the central office of the Party. It was after dark, and the street lamps were on. A middle-aged man confronted us, saying, "You should go to the reception center for the External Affairs Office of the Central Government, not here."

Setting aside our fatigue after that long hike and disregarding our empty stomachs, we walked another half mile or so to the External Affairs Office.

There we met with a young secretary to Chen Yi, a man named Kang. We were pleased to find that his viewpoint was the same as ours. We were more certain than ever that we were right: this was an attempt by bad elements to seize power! We believed we were the loyal ones.

Secretary Kang supported our view and promised to relay our information to the leadership—presumably to Chen Yi, who was in charge of the External Affairs Office. We wrote our ideas down in a letter, signed it, and left it with him. When other students learned of our "long march" to Party headquarters, we were called "the girls of steel."

On the long walk back to school, stomachs still empty, the five of us decided to set up an action center in our class, exchanging information, analyzing the situation, making plans, and watching for every opportunity to counterattack against the bad elements. Whatever this plot was, however big it was, we had to work to stop it.

But quickly we realized that we were not in a position of power at our school. The tide was against us. The dominant force was the blizzard of dazibaos posted everywhere—and the crowds of excited students that gathered to read and comment on them. Among students, protecting the status quo was not popular.

Still convinced this was a test of our loyalty, we decided that our activities had to be carried out secretly: a secret organization, secret meetings, secret exchanges of information, secret plans, secretly organized action. We felt as if we were like the underground revolutionary heroes who worked under the "White Terror" in the old days of Kuomintang China. We would join with the underground Party loyalists everywhere and stop this foul scheme to overturn our beloved Communist Party.

An article in *People's Daily* announced the beginning of a new revolution in China, later called the Great Proletarian Cultural Revolution, although it had nothing to do with culture. In inspiring language, the paper announced that China was rotten from within and the Party needed to be cleared of "revisionists." Students needed to organize to remove these internal enemies through class struggle. A high tide is rising! A new day is dawning! It is right to rebel.

On university campuses, these words were electric. My friends and I put on armbands and became Red Guards, too. But unlike the rebels who wrote the dazibaos, we felt we were the true Red Guards, defending the genuine proletarian revolutionaries in the Party.

Oddly enough, my husband had the opposite reaction when the Cultural Revolution started. At Radio, he believed he was witnessing young people trying to reawaken revolutionary fervor and speak out against the rigid bureaucracy that had stymied progress in recent years. To him, this rebellion was a breath of fresh air and a chance to right wrongs. But Sidney and I spent so little time together, we didn't have a chance to compare notes.

Chapter Eighteen

Making Revolution

WITHIN A MONTH, our school's leading Party committee and all the school leaders had become completely immobilized and were no longer able to lead. We found out that the mayor of Beijing had been dismissed, although we weren't sure why, and ordinary Party members like me weren't sure what direction to follow. The Beijing Party committee was no longer giving us guidance. The whole city was gripped by chaos and confusion.

Inspired by Mao's words, "It is right to rebel," students were "making revolution" full time: putting up and reading dazibaos, holding rallies, criticizing professors, and staging political debates. Young people, who had missed out on the real revolution, now gathered along major Beijing avenues, held up giant pictures of Chairman Mao, and shouted slogans.

The student rebels continued to criticize the authorities, and no one seemed able to stop them. I couldn't figure out who was in control of the Party and why attacks on trusted professors were allowed. Some students blossomed with excitement and empowerment, but I felt confused and unsettled.

Classes came to a halt—not just at our college but at primary and high schools, too. Final examinations were canceled. No one even mentioned graduation. It seemed trivial compared to this earth-shattering movement.

After six years of study, living away from my small children for six days a week, completing almost all my course work, I would not have a chance to earn my college degree. Yet I barely had time to contemplate that loss.

On June 9, 1966, the central leadership of the Foreign Affairs Ministry sent a work team to take over our school. Its director was Vice Foreign Minister Liu Xinquan.

At first, the work team's attitude was cold toward us five girl activists. They paid no attention to us. Nor would they meet with us or speak with us. Instead, they were very warm toward the rebellious students who put up the radical dazi-baos, always chatting with them in their offices, talking and laughing.

We took a dim view of the work team and called them "the rightist work team." The five of us mailed off a confidential report to the central Rarty leader-ship, expressing our views on the work team. But there was no response.

Before long, a huge new barrage of dazibaos, in great black characters, ap-peared all over the campus: "Down with Chen Yi!" "Down with the sinister Party committee!" "The Foreign Ministry is Revisionist!" "We dare to pull the emperor down from his horse, though we die from a thousand cuts!" This last is a famous quotation from the classical Chinese novel *Dream of the Red Chamber*.

These posters covered the walls in the dormitory hallways, in the library, in the dining hall, and in the classroom buildings. I saw them as sinister signs of the perfidy of the rebels.

But I was pleased when I noticed some new posters calling for "Work Team—Get Out!" "Oppose the Work Team Entering the School!"

I didn't know who put up those posters, but I hoped they might turn the tide. However, soon one member of the work team sought us out, summoning the five of us to their office in the school administration building.

"The situation's pretty clear now," he said. "Those people are out to get rid of the work team, to drive us out. In this way, they hope to sabotage the leading role of the Party and the Foreign Ministry. We want you to keep us posted on what's going on with these slippery fish. We need to call them out."

We agreed, and from then on we defended the work team because it repre-sented the Party's leadership. But we explained that our viewpoint wasn't exactly the same as that of the work team. We opposed pop quizzes, and we felt that some professors deserved criticism.

To me, the biggest issue was how students were selected for admission in our school. I had long suspected there was a bias against accepting students from truly proletarian families of workers, peasants, and soldiers. Most students came from urban families that were educated or privileged. There was a great disparity between rural and urban students in terms of their levels of education and their ability to absorb schooling. The rural and blue-collar students tended to run into big problems in their studies, and many of them gave up and dropped out.

Our professors usually ignored these struggling students in class instead of engaging them. The teachers didn't coach them outside of class and didn't bother to answer their questions, even though it should have been extra important to train members of the proletariat. During evening study hall, the teacher on duty usually paid no attention to the students who needed help with their studies. To me, after growing up in a poor family, this issue mattered a lot more than all the empty talk in most of the dazibaos.

For example, there was one rather petite girl student, Ma Xuelian, who was from a rural village. She studied very hard, but she was a slow learner. In her third year, the school ordered her to withdraw. This came as a harsh blow to other students from poor families. We went to the political-ideological coach to plead for her, but it was no use. She was forced to drop out. Just imagine what a crushing defeat it was for this poor country girl, who brought with her the highest hopes from her family and fellow villagers, only to return in disgrace.

At that time, all students at our school considered themselves Red Guards, loyal to Chairman Mao, but we were divided into two camps—the majority and the minority. Students in the majority faction called for overthrowing all professors, labeling them "reactionary academic authorities." Since we were learning foreign languages, many of our professors had studied abroad, and the majority rebels quickly labeled them as spies or bourgeois reactionaries. Anyone with a foreign connection was suspected of spying. These charges were posted all over campus, and the professors had no way to respond.

We five girls were in the minority. We felt that it was wrong that some teachers refused to help students from rural or blue-collar backgrounds, but we didn't agree to oppose all of the professors. Many of the charges against them were unfounded. And we didn't agree with the demand to let students make the school's business decisions. The rebels said, "The schools belong to the students."

In retrospect, it's ironic to look back on the late 1960s, where students all over the world rebelled and demanded the right to make decisions at their universities. We had more in common with students in Paris and New York than we knew.

One hot summer day, the majority students forced all of our professors to parade single file around the campus. They wore cardboard signs around their necks that stated their names and labeled them as "reactionary academic authorities." I knew that some of these professors looked down on us blue-collar students, but still it wasn't right to humiliate them like that. Some teachers were advanced in years and in poor health. To treat them like this was shameful.

Some of the majority Red Guards barged into professors' homes and destroyed cultural objects that they didn't approve of—for instance, they smashed the flowerpots on their windowsills. One old professor's wife had a pet cat. The raiders said this was "bourgeois thinking." I didn't agree with any of this. How could flowerpots and cats represent capitalist class thinking?

So the five of us activists set up our own Red Guard organization, naming it "Kang Da Battalion." Kang Da, or "Resistance University," was the famous Yan'an training school for cadres during the war of resistance against the Japanese invasion. We had armbands printed up that said "Red Guard" and "Kang Da." Soon others wanted to join us.

We held our own meeting in the English Department dorm, keeping our discussion secret so as not to be labeled "reactionary elements." We particularly raked Mao's wife over the coals. That summer, we had read about a new leading group called the Central Cultural Revolution Group, and Jiang Qing was appointed its first vice-chairman. From what I had seen of her, I was surprised to see her taking such a high-profile political role.

"She was a movie actress under the Kuomintang, and her personal life was a mess! How does she get to be the main spokesperson for Chairman Mao in the Great Proletarian Cultural Revolution?" one classmate said.

"Jiang Qing is calling on students to 'Attack with words and defend with arms,'" said another. "Actually, that means calling on the students to fight. There's no way of reconciling that with Chairman Mao's call to 'Fight with words, not with arms.'"

"How come Chairman Mao doesn't know the wild talk she's putting out?"

"Jiang Qing is a petty bourgeois revolutionary, not a proletarian!"

But we noticed that whenever Jiang Qing went to a school and supported one faction, that faction immediately took over the school, putting other factions on the defensive. "How does she get all that power?"

"Whatever happens, nobody else must know what we're talking about, or we could get in serious trouble."

In all our discussions, the one person we never suspected was Chairman Mao.

Chapter Nineteen

Pandemonium

THE WHOLE CAMPUS was plunged into chaos. One minute, the "reactionary academic" professors were the targets of a struggle meeting, being paraded around in dunce caps. The next minute, the struggle was directed against members of the school's ruling Party committee. These members would be encircled by a mob of angry students, who would throw questions at them that they never got a chance to answer—although most of the questions were not even answerable.

By mid-June of 1966, it turned into a struggle between students from blue-collar families and those from white-collar families. Big posters went up that said, "Heroic fathers, stalwart sons; reactionary fathers, bastard sons."

This infuriated me. As the daughter of a worker, I had benefited from the Party's preference for the poor, and I strongly believed our professors should spend extra time helping students from less privileged backgrounds. My heart was with the blue-collar students. But as Sidney's wife, I knew firsthand that the son of a wealthy American lawyer could be "redder than red"—more loyal to the Chinese Communist Party than many Chinese were. Even more important, I worried about my four children, all descended from that same urban intellectual American family. None of my proletarian fervor in raising them could change that. We had raised them to be stalwart Communists, and I didn't want anyone calling them "bastards."

These dazibaos led to a new debate all over the campus. Several hundred members of rival factions would hold spontaneous debates in the courtyards. Sometimes students from other schools would come to listen.

This argument split the student body right down the middle. My Kang Da Red Guard group had grown to more than one hundred members. The other side, called the "Red Banner Battalion," was popular, too. They claimed to be the true rebels, and they argued for supremacy of class origin. But on this issue, I was confident we could win many more students to our side. We were still called the minority, but on this issue, it seemed we were in the majority. After all, many of our professors were good examples of loyal Chinese who had returned from overseas because they wanted to rebuild a strong China, even though their parents had been capitalists—and most students realized that. I took heart. Maybe the tide was turning and reason would prevail.

The debate raged for several days, not solving any issues but only exacerbating the feelings of hostility. Each side tried to defeat and dominate the other side, in order to seize power at the school. The animosity intensified.

Finally, we held a great debate on the school's athletic field. A speakers' platform was set up at one end of the field, with two microphones. For our side, our minority group had selected me, from the English Department, and Yang Hanyan, from the Spanish Department. This was an honor, a recognition that I was a Red Guard leader with an opinion worth hearing. But I also yearned to settle this matter, once and for all.

The day was hot and humid, and my shirt was dark with sweat even before the debate began. Yang and I stood at one microphone and two opposing students stood at the other. The debate was not run according to normal rules. Our side would say one line, and the other would rebut one line; then we would reply with another line, and so on. Students in the audience would speak up whenever they chose.

Yang and I argued that you couldn't evaluate a person by the political position or class background of his father. The other side argued that a reactionary father couldn't possibly teach true revolution to his son, so the son was bound to take the reactionary path.

I had prepared several good lines in advance. "The theory of blood lineage is wrong. We should judge people by the way they act, not by their family background."

The opposition said, "Then why are Party members selected based, first of all, on their family origin and on a study of the past three generations of their family?"

Typically, both sides used quotations from Chairman Mao against the other side.

I quoted Mao's statement, "The important thing is a person's behavior."

They countered, "Chairman Mao said that a person's family origin influences them and stamps them with the brand of a class."

The arena for our debate had no seats. Everybody was standing, bunched in little groups with others who shared a definite viewpoint in common. While we were speaking from the podium, these individuals and groups in the audience were arguing with each other. Sometimes they would shout or cheer. The sun beat down harder as the debate progressed. But the cheers energized me, and I felt confident our side was gaining the upper hand.

At the height of the debate, a student rushed up to the podium and said, "Here's a directive from the central leadership."

The noisy excitement immediately dropped to a tense quiet as everyone listened for the new instructions from above. This was the news I had been waiting for.

"At Zhongnanhai Party headquarters, Chen Boda has approved our slogans. He agrees that class determines all. He has written a marginal note on our list of slogans that says, 'Their points are well taken.'"

This sent the majority into a paroxysm of shouting and celebration. Chen Boda was chairman of the Central Cultural Revolution Leading Group, and his word was law.

My heart jumped into my mouth, and I couldn't say another word. The debate was over. It had never been about logic or reason. Right and wrong were determined from above. A few words from one powerful man could settle it.

This also deflated the students who were struggling to overcome "bad class backgrounds," the sons and grandsons of landlords and capitalists and intellectuals, who wanted to prove their loyalty despite their family origins. Now those from blue-collar families were on top of the world. As a worker's daughter, I might once have rejoiced; as Sidney's wife, I could not.

Still, political debates continued. Students who had once been friends and colleagues now were attacking each other like hated enemies. It felt like civil war. At the height of the acrimony, Marshal Chen Yi, the foreign minister, came to our school to meet with the leaders of the two sides, to attempt conciliation.

Once again, my hopes were raised, although I knew Chen Yi's position was precarious. I attended that meeting with my Kang Da friends, who had staunchly supported Chen Yi. We approved of the way he conducted foreign policy and guided our college. Since the big debate, the Red Banner Battalion had grown; they were in favor of either waging a criticism struggle against Chen Yi or overthrowing him altogether. Many of them attended, too. Still, I hoped this would be the day that our loyalty would be rewarded and the rebels silenced.

When Chen Yi entered the crowded meeting room, he spied me on one side, came over, and shook hands. This was natural, since he was a friend of our family.

"So this is where you're in school, Wang Yulin," he said, in his usual gruff, hearty way.

"Yes," I said.

"How are you doing, and how are the children?" he asked.

"They're fine," I replied. "How's your health?"

He said, "Me? Oh, I'm never going to collapse, no matter what."

Then he turned and went around the room, shaking hands with everyone there, both Kang Da and Red Banner students. *Such an upright, dignified man!* I thought. *How could anyone doubt his revolutionary credentials?*

Marshal Chen addressed us students, contending that we were all young people and there were no fundamental differences between us. He confirmed that we all wanted a well-run school. Therefore, we should not dissipate our strength fighting against each other, but should close ranks in a common cause. I cheered.

But he did not succeed in calming things down. The Red Banner students were still powerful, and they kept disrupting and criticizing. They refused to accept him as their leader.

After Chen Yi left, the meeting hastily disbanded.

Then Red Banner people encircled me and pointed their fingers in my face. "Wang Yulin, you defend Chen Yi because you're personal friends. Your group are total royalists!"

Furious, I argued back. "What do you mean, 'royalists'!" *As if supporting the Party leaders were the same as supporting a king!* "A good man is a good man, and that's all there is to it. Look at the foreign policy he has carried out."

As luck would have it, soon afterwards Jiang Qing's speech denouncing the work teams was broadcast on campus, and the official Party theoretical magazine, *Red Flag*, ran an editorial that stated the work teams had been carrying out a "bourgeois reactionary political line."

That immediately branded us as "royalists," since we had been defending the work team. Our prestige went down the tubes, and the Red Banner Red Guards took over all power at the school. They ordered us to make self-criticisms.

Writing a self-criticism meant examining my own life and admitting to mistakes in my political thinking. Even though I did not think I had made mistakes, the Red Banner students insisted I write a new one almost every day, in big black letters on newsprint, and paste it up on the wall. They said that, in supporting Chen Yi, my friends and I had carried out the "bourgeois reactionary line." They said I had "forgotten my roots" in marrying a foreigner, that I had lived a "bourgeois luxury life" and turned against my own working class. I disagreed, but they forced me to admit to these bad thoughts.

As a loyal Communist who had joined the Party in 1948 and served it faithfully for so many years, this was galling. What was wrong with my thinking? Yes, there were times that a private car had picked up Sidney and me and taken us to the opera or the theater. But I didn't wear fashionable clothes, and I normally took the bus everywhere.

But I had to confess to "serious mistakes." I admitted to not really knowing the situation, being confused, not knowing the bad things that some cadres had done, just protecting the status quo. I said that I hadn't understood the true nature of the work team; I just helped and supported it. I said some professors deserved criticism because they had not reached out to help proletarian students. I admitted I did not understand the saying, "Heroic fathers, stalwart sons; reactionary fathers, bastard sons." But mostly I wrote generalizations, saying what a bad Communist I was.

Still the rebels were not satisfied. They kept calling me in and haranguing me, saying that my self-criticism was not sincere and too shallow, that I still hadn't dug up the ideological roots of my error and that I needed to perform more profound self-examination.

Frustrated and angry, I kept writing self-examinations, each one more or less like the others. I didn't really see where I was wrong, so I couldn't write anything in depth. They said my class standpoint was wrong, but where? I was a worker's daughter; my work at Radio should have proved my loyalty. But somehow it didn't. When I admitted that I had carried out the bourgeois reactionary political line, they said, "You're hiding behind big empty labels, to escape real, specific criticism." That was true!

The whole country was turned upside down. Leaders were brought down. Low-level nobodies suddenly strutted around, lording it over other people. Friends turned against friends. No one could be trusted.

Our tormenters tried to get us "girls of steel" to turn on each other, to report "bad thoughts" our friends had expressed in private. One of my friends cracked under pressure, and her snitching caused trouble for the rest of us. After that, I didn't dare share my true thoughts with anyone. Wang Fangzhen could never forgive that girl, to this day, but I understood that the pressure was intense.

Even now, whenever I see college classmates, I instantly recall the ugly things done and said in the heat of the Cultural Revolution—insults permanently branded in my memory. Our Red Guard factions regarded each other as hated enemies, and it's hard to forget those battles. At least our infighting was only verbal; on other campuses there was physical violence, with students and professors killed or maimed.

This self-confession process went on for several weeks during the hottest summer months. I had to stay on campus and could go see Sidney and the children only once a week, on Sundays. Mama took care of them, and they continued their normal life at boarding school during the summer. Sidney stayed out late attending revolutionary meetings at Radio, but on the few occasions we talked, he told me he agreed with my Kang Da stance in support of Chen Yi. I was miserable and wished I could just move back home. That was a bourgeois thought, putting personal life ahead of the revolution, and I tried to suppress it.

By midsummer, a new campaign and slogan took over Beijing campuses: "Great Liaison." This meant sending students to other cities and college campuses to connect with other students and discuss their revolutionary experiences. Premier Zhou Enlai had announced that students were all welcome to travel about the country, and that the trains would carry them without tickets. Later, I learned that the Great Liaison was designed to diffuse the student rebellion, but at the time none of us knew what was going on at Party headquarters.

Suddenly, most of our tormenters disappeared from campus, so there was no one to monitor or discuss my self-criticisms. My buddies and I talked things over and decided that we, the "girls of steel," would go off on a Great Liaison tour of the country, too. It seemed like a good time to get away.

Chapter Twenty

Looking for Answers

I WENT HOME AND told Sidney and Mama that I was going to travel. They didn't object. So I packed my things and went to the train station. This was my first opportunity to see my country. My Kang Da comrades and I figured that traveling around the country and visiting other schools could help us find the solution to the big issue at our school: how to unify the warring factions of students.

In September of 1966, I boarded the train with my friends Wang Fengzhen and Zheng Xuezhen. We didn't need tickets, and the hard seats and aisles were jammed with students. The train was miserably hot, but it was exciting to watch the countryside as it changed from flat fields to steep mountains and then semi-tropical greenery.

We traveled all the way to Chengdu, capital of Sichuan Province in the far southwest. There we found the Red Guard Reception Center, where they assigned us lodgings in a middle school classroom with a dozen other traveling students. We had brought our blankets with us.

Each day, we walked along the streets, reading the dazibaos and listening to little knots of debating students. From what we read in the dazibaos in Chengdu, we could see that there were sharp conflicts and contradictions among different Red Guard groups here, too. These people certainly hadn't discovered the secret of Red Guard solidarity.

After about a week in Chengdu, we took the train to Chongqing, on one of the main new rail lines built after Liberation. Formerly called Chungking, this large city on the Yangtze River had been the wartime capital of the Kuomintang.

We visited the notorious SACO prison and torture chambers, where Communists and liberals were imprisoned during the 1940s. This had been the headquarters of the Sino-American Cooperative Organization, in collaboration with the Kuomintang government. It had been an intelligence gathering operation, run jointly by the head of Chiang Kai-shek's secret police and Rear Admiral Milton Miles, head of U.S. Navy intelligence operations in China. The exhibitions showed evidence of torture and massacre, sanctioned by the United States. I was shocked at what I learned there of American cruelty in China and vowed to ask Sidney about it.

When we listened in on Red Guard debates in Sichuan, we kept our mouths tightly closed—no comment. We were too afraid to speak after what happened on our own campus. But we were not finding the answers we had set out to look for.

⁓

At the end of October, we returned to Beijing and found the campus almost deserted. I had nothing to do at school, so I obtained permission and went back to work at Radio. I was assigned to the Letters from Listeners Office in the English language section. At last, I could use my English language education at work.

Under the control of the military, Radio continued to broadcast every day. But behind the scenes, it was chaos. Labeled a "counterrevolutionary black gang member," Director Mei Yi had had been ousted from his post in May 1966 and had been forced to write self-criticisms. Rebels were struggling to take power there, and Sidney openly sympathized with them.

On National Day, October 1, Sidney had shaken hands with Chairman Mao, who signed Sidney's "Little Red Book" of Mao quotations. A signed copy of Mao's book was a prized possession, and we treasured it. When the rebels had stormed the offices of the Broadcast Administration, Sidney had gone with them. He believed deeply in what he thought was their cause: freedom of speech and real democracy.

Suddenly, Sidney's words, recorded right before the rebels took over, were heard all over China, and Li Dunbai became famous. People would stop him in the street and ask him to sign their Little Red Books. He was seated on the rostrum when 15,000 people attended a mass struggle session against Mei Yi and other leaders of news organizations. The goal of a struggle session was to humiliate, shame, and taunt one person in front of a crowd. Sidney shouted and raised his fist with the others, even when the leaders screamed in pain. Fortunately, I never had to attend such struggle sessions, but I did believe that Radio had fallen into sluggish bureaucracy and needed shaking up.

In December, Sidney and others from Radio were invited to the Great Hall of the People to meet with Jiang Qing, who openly supported the rebels, even when they used violence. On December 31, 1966, Sidney's rebel group seized power at the Broadcast Administration.

After the rebels took control, though, the situation at Radio descended into anarchy. Free speech meant anyone could denounce anyone else. A new set of rebels rose up and tried to overthrow the old rebels, who then acted to quash them, using vicious tactics of bullying and harassment. There was a bitter—but nonviolent—struggle for supremacy between two rebel factions at Radio, just as there had been at my college. It was the "royalists" versus the "rebels," although both groups claimed to be the true rebels following Chairman Mao's revolutionary line. Just as at my college, colleagues who had once worked together in harmony now became bitter enemies.

I didn't want to get involved in the factional struggle, but I couldn't help it. I spoke out in support of Sidney, proud of his bold and progressive revolutionary actions. Some of the other foreign experts got involved, too, but others refused. In fact, a few of them sternly warned Sidney to remember he was a foreigner and to stay out of Chinese politics. But he believed deeply in Chairman Mao's approach as the best future for the Communist revolution.

In March of 1967, the Chinese Communist Party effectively ceased operations. All Party organizations, including the highest-level Politburo, were forbidden from holding meetings; their dossiers were sealed, and their offices were locked up. The Politburo was taken over by the Cultural Revolution Leading Group, led by Chen Boda and Jiang Qing. The only exception, a highly significant one, was that Party organizations in the armed forces were to continue business as usual. This banning of Party activity was so widespread that it even applied to the schools, as well as to all police and security bodies—and the Broadcast Administration. The original Chineses Communist Party—the one that had won my loyalty—was viewed as the creature of Liu Shaoqi, as undermining Maoism, as a barrier to the Cultural Revolution. Only Mao and his leading group were sacrosanct and could not be criticized. As a Communist, my beliefs were not shaken. But the Party I had loved so deeply seemed to be disappearing.

Sidney tried to jump in and unify the two rebel factions at the Broadcast Administration. One day he came home after a particularly contentious mass meeting. In his effort to reconnect the two rebel factions, he had told them he was ashamed of the harsh tactics the old rebels once used against their opponents.

"It's all over for me now," Sidney told me. "In ten minutes, I've gone from the most popular member of the majority to a minority of one."

"Have you eaten?" I asked him. "How about some fried rice?"

He was quiet as we ate. I put my hand over his. "Stick to the truth," I said. "I'll stick with you, whatever comes."

The next morning, at eight, there was a knock on the door. But this time, the news was good: Sidney had been selected to be the new head of the Broadcast Administration! Quickly, our living room filled up with people wanting to be Sidney's friends. I poured them tea and coffee and served them snacks.

This was the way of politics in China; there are always clear winners and losers, no sharing of power. But despite his new title, Sidney had no real power at Radio. He was now the nominal chairman of the "Group of Three," who were in charge of the whole State Broadcasting Administration. At the first meeting, he declined to exercise the power of that position and named himself "advisor" instead. He tried to conciliate the two rebel groups, but now the new rebels wanted to take revenge on the old rebels.

To get away from the infighting, Sidney went out from Radio and became a public speaker, denouncing blind obedience to the Party. Most of Sidney's time was spent making speeches at universities, in factories, at scientific research institutes, and in government offices all over Beijing. He addressed huge crowds at Beijing University, Qinghua University, People's University, the Geological Institute, the Aeronautical Institute, the Telecommunications Institute, the Foreign Languages Institute, and the Academy for Advanced Military Studies. Once he spoke to a meeting of more than one hundred thousand people in Tianjin. In addition to this, he wrote articles that appeared in leading newspapers, including *People's Daily*, *Beijing Daily*, *Guangming Daily*, and others. He encouraged Party members to embrace the ideals of the new revolutionaries. Sidney became a full-time "Cultural Revolutionary."

At our offices at Radio, I saw huge dazibaos on the walls around the building, calling on everyone to learn from "Li Dunbai, International Fighter for Communism." This was a title that Mao Zedong had used for him when introducing him to African freedom fighters in 1963. Sidney's speeches were being cited in newspaper editorials and quoted by Cultural Revolution leaders all over the country.

In the twinkling of an eye, Sidney had become an idol. People regarded him as a man "in the Bethune mold." Like Norman Bethune, a Canadian doctor revered by the Chinese because he had come to China in 1939 to care for the poor and for Communist soldiers, heedless of his own health and safety, Sidney had left his own homeland to support the struggles of the Chinese people. He had worked tirelessly, day and night, for their cause. Even after being wrongfully imprisoned for six years, Sidney remained a staunch friend of the Chinese proletariat.

This praise gladdened my heart, but the tide of popular adulation also seriously worried me. I cautioned him not to run around giving public speeches so much. For one thing, I was concerned about the fact that Sidney had never become a Chinese citizen. In the back of my mind was the possibility that one day people might turn against him, charging him with being a foreigner interfering in Chinese politics.

Sidney had always been an outspoken, frank person who never concealed his own viewpoint, and he would speak up against anything he thought was unfair. I was afraid that his speeches could lead to disaster—perhaps even expulsion from China.

At the end of August, my fears came true. Sidney was suddenly transferred out of Radio. He was instructed to go home and await a "special assignment." On National Day, he was not invited to join Party members on the reviewing stands. One day, a photo appeared in the *Beijing Review*. Taken the previous summer, the photo had originally showed Sidney with Mao, Zhou Enlai, and Jiang Qing; this time Sidney's image had been blacked out of the picture. Gradually, his foreign friends stopped visiting him. Next, a large dazibao appeared at Radio, titled "Bourgeois Politician, Li Dunbai." It was the first of many, the beginning of a campaign in which everything bad that happened at Radio was blamed on Sidney. After another upheaval at Radio, the military took over.

Soon afterwards, my work pass was confiscated; I could not even enter the Broadcast Administration compound to read the dazibaos, although we lived right next door. Armed garrison troops guarded every gate.

In my seventeen years of working at Radio, this was the first time I had ever been deprived of my rights. I was angry and indignant. What had I done to deserve this treatment? No one could explain to me why I wasn't allowed to do my work.

That fall, all schools closed down. Even nursery school teachers came under attack. For the first time, Sidney and I spent all day together, every day, with our four children. The girls were ten, nine, and six years old, and the baby was not yet two. We played games with them and sang Cultural Revolution songs. Sidney taught them to recite poems by Chairman Mao. The children were happy and carefree, playing on the swings, slide, and merry-go-round in the courtyard with their neighbor friends. To avoid trouble, I stayed inside our apartment at the Foreign Experts Building. To pass the time, I knitted sweaters. Generally, we ate at the cafeteria, but sometimes Mama cooked up the best meals we could afford. I watched her and tried to learn how to cook, a skill I had never cultivated.

But I had trouble sleeping. I had seen so many loyal Communist Party members tormented and humiliated. Sidney and I knew the other shoe would drop soon; we just weren't sure how bad it would get.

One winter's day, at the height of the Red Guard terror, a half-dozen young Red Guards came to our home and demanded Sidney's personal diaries and notes. At first, Sidney refused to hand them over. Finally they said that if he showed them the material to prove that it hadn't been destroyed, they would be satisfied and leave.

He was considering meeting their demands, when I broke in, speaking to him in English, but without lowering my voice. "Don't do it!" I warned. "You can't trust them. If you show them the material, they'll grab it!"

They didn't like that at all, since it was probably exactly what they planned to do. They yelled at me. "Have you forgotten that you're Chinese? Why are you helping an enemy agent? Traitor!"

But in the end, they had to leave empty-handed. For one thing, the guards at our gate were all friends of our family and had cautioned them against trying any rough stuff.

After they left, I told Sidney, "You must never believe in people like that! They would take your words out of context and attack you with them."

Sidney was very moved. He said, "As proud as you are of being Chinese, you stood up for the truth—even though it got you called a traitor. I really admire your courage."

To me, I had acted in a way that was just straightforward—not heroic, just very ordinary and natural. In my gut I knew that the Red Guards' action against us was not a good sign. They called me a traitor, which meant that I was being tarred with the same brush as Sidney. How long was this going to last? I thought of the six long years that Sidney had spent in prison the first time and realized that nobody knew how long this would go on.

I thought about our four children: What sort of treatment could they expect? The very thought made me shudder. I feared especially for my youngest child, our two-year-old son, who still couldn't talk. What would happen to him?

On Christmas Day, December 25, 1967, Sidney was placed under house arrest. He was not allowed to go anywhere without permission and was told to prepare for interrogation. The interrogators came to our house, quizzing Sidney daily. One question surprised us: Why did Sidney give away the antique furniture when he did? Did that mean he knew the Cultural Revolution was about to begin?

No one told us clearly why Sidney had been removed from Radio, or why he was now being placed under house arrest and interrogated. But that's how it was with everyone in those days. Staunch Communists were attacked and could not defend themselves. Even President Liu Shaoqi and Vice Premier Deng Xiaoping had disappeared from public view, and they were lambasted daily in the press.

Sidney heard through a secret friend that Jiang Qing herself was accusing him of being an American spy. A strong, ugly word. That sent chills through us both. We stayed up late every night, talking, trying to figure things out. Such crude treatment as we were receiving meant that there were hard times in store for our whole family. We tried to anticipate the worst that might happen.

I gave him the best advice I could. "Just tell the truth and stick with it," I said. "Don't let them scare you into a false confession. Remember—no wild talk."

He did not need to remind me of the first words he had ever heard me say, "If you really love someone, and you know he's not an evil-doer, then you should wait for him. No matter how long it takes."

Finally, on the night of February 21, 1968, just after Sidney and I had climbed into bed, we heard it: that sudden, sharp knock on the door. They had come for him.

PART II

Chapter Twenty-One

The World of One Room

AFTER SIDNEY WAS taken away, my mind felt as murky as an inkpot.

Half an hour later, the second knock shook me out of my stupor. Soldiers barged into my home and insisted on taking my children and me away. Why? On what charges? What had we done wrong? No one explained.

My whole world collapsed around me.

Our baby son and three girls were fast asleep. Little Ming's nanny came running out of the back bedroom and asked, "What's going on?" The sight of the soldiers frightened her. "I'm just the nanny, the *baomu*," she said to them. "I'm not related. I'll just go home."

"We know you're not involved in this," said the man from Radio. "But you have to go with them and keep on taking care of their children, just like before. Go wake them up and get them ready to go."

"Oh, no. I've done nothing wrong!" she insisted. "Please. My husband is a soldier, like you."

"It's an order," one said. The nanny kept begging them, but they paid no attention to her.

My heart was trembling. *Sidney went to jail, and I am going to jail*, I thought. *Why ask the children to go with me? Probably because they are so young and cannot leave their mother.*

"Get moving!" one of the soldiers barked.

I rushed into the bedroom to wake up the girls. "Qin, Dong, hurry up and get dressed."

Toni and Jenny, ages nine and ten, sat up and gazed at me with big round eyes, totally mystified.

Sunny, age seven, rubbed her eyes and turned over. "No. I want to sleep."

I said, "Little Xiang, be a good girl. Listen to your mama and get dressed."

She grumbled as she pulled on the hand-me-down T-shirt she had been wearing that day. The older girls quickly pulled on their clothes. The nanny went to get the baby.

Suddenly, I remembered a Communist hero whose well-known story was often told on the radio. Before Liberation, the Kuomintang jailed him, and they took his six-year-old son to jail, too. The boy grew up there. Later, both the man and his son were executed. My children will grew up like that boy, wandering between prison cells, I thought.

In China, I knew, whether under the emperor, the Kuomintang, or the Communists, the authorities can jail you and question you without any proof that you've committed a crime. Sometimes you languish in prison for years, and you cannot clear your name. I knew from Sidney that prison conditions were grim: low heat, minimal food, little medical care. At times interrogation. My children and I might be going to prison for the rest of our lives. I was sturdy and could handle anything. But my children were young and vulnerable.

My hands shook as I started pulling out extra clothes to take with us, including pants and underwear for Sidney, thinking that we might be in the same prison. He had gone off with my ratty old long johns; they wouldn't keep him warm on freezing winter nights.

"How long will we be gone?" I asked the soldiers.

"Don't pack any clothes," one man said. "We don't have time. You can come back and pick up some clothes later. Hurry!"

In ten minutes we were ready.

The soldiers looked grim, but the girls were talking and laughing, as if we were heading out on a midnight adventure. I didn't mention the word prison or tell them that their daddy had been arrested. They had no idea what tribulations awaited them.

Just outside our courtyard gate, two cars were waiting: an army jeep and a small passenger car. Holding my baby son, I was ushered into the jeep, and the soldiers ordered the nanny to get in the other car with the three girls. As soon as I slid into the backseat, one soldier sat on either side of me, blocking me in. They were already treating me like a prisoner. As if I might try to escape!

My mind went dark with fear. I clasped my little son to my chest and kept looking back at the car behind us, terrified that it might make a turn and carry my daughters off in another direction.

"Where are you taking us?" I asked, but no one would answer. Gazing out on the dimly lit streets, I focused on the direction the driver took. *If he goes straight at the intersection*, I thought, *then I'm going somewhere in the city. If we turn west and head for the countryside, then it's to prison.*

The car went straight.

It's a good thing, I thought, *that Mama's away in Shijiazhuang.* My sister had just come for a visit and taken Mama back with her. Otherwise, how could Mama, in her seventies, have withstood this sudden calamity?

After what seemed like an eternity—but was probably around forty minutes—we pulled up in front of a large, multistory building I didn't recognize. The soldier next to me jumped down and ordered me "Out!" As I entered the building, men in plain clothes lined the two sides of the path. Inside, the soldiers pushed the children, the nanny, and me into an elevator, and it began to rise. At that time I was too tense and too busy soothing the girls to note which floor it stopped on. My son was sleeping on my shoulder, but one of the girls was asking questions I couldn't answer. Another one was crying.

We were escorted to the end of a long corridor, passed behind a big screen, and turned right into a large bedroom.

Sidney was not there.

Three men wearing white service uniforms emerged from the room across the corridor, One soldier pointed to these men and told me, "These men work here. Whatever issues you have, take it up with them. They'll tell you the rules."

With that, the soldiers left.

I looked around our room. There were five single beds, lined up parallel to each other, with about one foot of space between them. One was a full-sized bed, slightly larger, with room for me to sleep with the baby. Each bed had mattresses and quilts. There were also two small easy chairs, with a little table between them, equipped with two lidded teacups. A door led to a modern bathroom. Clearly, this was not a prison. I breathed with relief.

Although I didn't realize this until we were released, this building was the Qianmen "Front Gate" Hotel, right in the heart of Beijing. There were two windows, but the one facing the street was boarded up. A screen covered the small window facing the courtyard. There was no telephone.

As I looked around, an army man who looked to be in his forties entered the room. "Wang Yulin," he said, "you should study while you're here and take care of the children."

Study? A strange thought. I knew he meant studying Mao's writings. "How long will we stay?"

"Not clear," he answered.

"Can we go out?"

"No, of course not."

"What about food?"

"There will be people responsible for bringing you meals," he replied. "It will cost 27 yuan per person per month. You'll be responsible for two-thirds of the nanny's food bill."

Per month? This would be a long stay.

"Twenty-seven yuan? I don't have enough money to pay for that!"

He said, "You will receive your regular salary, and we can give you 100 yuan per month from Li Dunbai's salary."

Muddled as I was, I quickly did the math. I would need 200 yuan a month to pay the nanny and buy food. My pay of 87.50 yuan, plus 100 yuan from Sidney's pay wouldn't cover this. "I still won't have enough to pay those bills," I protested.

"We'll think about that when the time comes," he said.

With that he left, and the three men in white came in. One said, "My name is Li, and I'm in charge of your daily needs."

"Comrade Li," I said, nodding in greeting.

"You cannot call me comrade. Call me Mr. Li," he said. "You are not allowed to shut your door—not even when you're bathing. The windows are not to be opened, and you're not allowed to go outside of the room, even into the hallway. If you need anything, send the nanny. She can fetch your boiled drinking water."

Then he added, in a very severe tone, "Do you understand?"

"Understood!" My fear and confusion had morphed into anger. Clearly, the three men in white were there to guard us, not to serve us. We would be under twenty-four-hour surveillance.

By then, it was around one in the morning. The children were sleepy, so I put them to bed. Then I lay down, hugging my son, but I couldn't sleep. This whole situation made no sense.

Where is Sidney now? What's going through his mind? I thought. *At least we're not in some horrific prison.* But we had definitely been put away, forced to leave our home and stuffed into one room, too small for six people. From the outside, no one could guess that anyone was living here. A big screen blocked off our end of the corridor.

And there was the added injustice of making me pay for our food! I started adding up the numbers in my head. At 27 yuan per person per month, I would need to pay 162 yuan a month to feed the six of us, plus 45 yuan for the nanny's pay. That would mean more than 200 yuan a month. Clearly, I couldn't afford that.

I decided I would tell them I didn't want the nanny. She was there to watch us, I was sure. It wouldn't be comfortable living there with her, and she didn't want to be there anyway. We didn't have room for her. And economically, it was too much of a burden. As long as we were shut up there, I didn't need a nanny.

The next morning, I went across the corridor and raised this with the man named Li. "I can't afford a nanny anymore. One, I'm not working, so I can take care of the children. Two, my economic situation doesn't permit it."

Sternly, he answered, "You may not dismiss the nanny! She can help you take care of the children, so that you can use this time to study and give a clear account of your problem. Now, get back to your room!"

His rebuff jolted me. It seemed like a bad omen for the days ahead. I couldn't dismiss the nanny. Did I have any control over my life at all? I went into the bathroom and shut the door as much as I was allowed to and wept silently. I didn't want anyone to see my emotions.

We weren't in a prison, it was true, but we were imprisoned nonetheless. How could the children bear these cramped conditions, six people living in one room with no fresh air or chance to go out? And for how long?

Sitting there, doubled over with grief and rage, I made up my mind. I would survive—whatever came. Whatever anger I felt, I would choke it back, even if it churned in my stomach. I would struggle through each day until I could see my husband again—whenever that would be. I wasn't sure how, but I would do whatever I could to protect my four children and their future. Hope is a choice, and so is despair. Teeth clenched, I chose hope—as a form of defiance. I would not let them break my spirit.

The next morning, the kids explored their new environment, opening drawers and turning on the faucets. I tried to calm myself and think about how I might lead my life in this tiny territory that we now inhabited. I could not control how long we stayed there, but I could control my own reaction to it. That's one thing Sidney once told me he had learned during his six years in prison. "They control the stimulus, I control the response. They can't break me as long as I use my head," he had explained. And maybe I could find a way to make things bearable, at least for the kids.

But I kept thinking, *Can Sidney's case really be that serious? Jiang Qing had said he was spying for the United States. Could that be true? If so, then why couldn't I see it?* Recalling Chairman Mao's words, "the fox's tail is bound to show," I decided it wasn't possible. If Sidney was an agent there was no way I hadn't seen a single sign of it, in all the years we had been married. He was conscientious and responsible in his work. Even when he wasn't well, he never complained. And he was so warm toward the Chinese comrades around him. Everything Sidney did had always been out in the open; he never hid his opinions or feelings. In fact, he was a lousy liar. I could always see through him.

More than anything, I recalled details of that trip to Shanghai with Sidney in 1965. Chairman Mao had held my hand, looked me in the eyes, and personally apologized to me for keeping Sidney in prison for six years. He told me very plainly, "This was a mistake of the Chinese Communist Party." So why was his wife calling Sidney a "secret agent"? Could the Party make the same mistake twice?

I began to seriously worry about Sidney's health. No one had yet told me he was in prison, but I felt sure of it. He had previously suffered through tuberculosis and hepatitis, and now he was older, forty-seven. How would they treat him? Would they torture him? The previous time they had not physically tortured him but they had given him some damnable drugs that had driven him out of his mind. Would they do that again?

My heaven! Who can give me the answers? I thought, as I watched my children playing in our cramped room. *Why should this disaster fall on our family? We have always strongly believed in the cause and obeyed the Party. I'm so loyal they called me a "royalist," for crying out loud.*

Night after night, I lay wide-awake, clutching my baby and searching for answers, but there weren't any. After the children fell asleep, I'd roll over to face the wall, cover my head with the quilt, and sob. I couldn't let the children see me like that. I didn't want to scar their spirits.

But even during the day, there were times when the sadness inside would overflow, and I would stand at one of the windows weeping uncontrollably.

"Mama! Mama! What's wrong?" The children would put their arms around me and look up, questioningly. But when I looked down into the innocent eyes of my little daughters and my son, who still couldn't even talk, the tears would come faster. The thought that wrenched me most was this: "They're going to be fatherless children."

"Don't cry, Mama," the girls would say.

"You're good kids," I would say. "Mama won't cry." And I would wrap them in my arms. How could I tell them what I was thinking? They were too little. I could only swallow my words.

Chapter Twenty-Two

A Mother's Demands

FINALLY, AFTER ONE weepy episode, I told myself, *Stop it. Now. You can't go on like this every day. You have to fight.* For the sake of their future, I realized that I had to train the children so they would be the finest students when they had a chance to return to school. Whenever that would be.

My mind made up, I charged over to the room across the hall. "Mr. Li," I said. "Since you won't let the children go to school, get me the proper textbooks for their grades, and I'll teach them myself."

"Textbooks?" he said. "Where am I going to get textbooks?"

"From the bookstore," I said. "Buy them. Or borrow them from the education bureau. I can't let my children lose all this time. Otherwise, let them go to school."

"Teaching the children is your problem," he said. "What's it got to do with us? Besides, your job is to oppose Li Dunbai, and to write down the things he did against China."

I kept insisting. Finally, he said, "All right, all right! Go back to your room. We'll make inquiries."

Two weeks went by, and I heard nothing, so I went back across the hall.

"Why aren't the textbooks here yet?" I asked indignantly. "How long do we have to wait?"

Every day I kept after them, demanding that they get me textbooks. One day, the books finally came. From then on, I gave the girls lessons every day, in their three grade levels. This gave me a goal and provided us all with something to do during the endless, dreary days.

There were math textbooks but no language ones, so I taught them, from memory, famous essays by Chairman Mao, especially the "Three Old Essays": "Serve the People," "In Memory of Norman Bethune," and "The Foolish Old Man Who Moved Mountains."

I can still remember Mao's lines about Norman Bethune, meant to inspire future generations of Communists. "We must all learn the spirit of absolute self-lessness from him. . . . A man's ability may be great or small, but if he has this spirit, he is already noble minded and pure, a man of moral integrity and above vulgar interests, a man who is of value to the people." Those were the qualities Sidney and I had aimed for; I wanted our children to learn them, regardless of our circumstances.

Every morning at eight o'clock, our family would begin the day by singing, "The East Is Red"—the song that celebrated Chairman Mao. Then I would teach them the Three Old Essays until the girls could all recite them by heart. Then we'd have three separate math lessons, and the girls would quietly work on their math problems.

I loved watching the girls as they did their schoolwork. They were all good children, like little dolls. Toni and Sunny both had brown hair, like their father, while Jenny had thicker, black hair, like mine. Toni wore her hair in short po-nytails. Of the three, Toni had the worst temper. She was very stubborn and wouldn't do anything she didn't want to do. Sunny had delicate feelings and was sensitive to the smallest slight. Jenny was very smart, intrigued by Chinese literature and history. Toni was fascinated by the idea of being a healer, and she noticed when her little brother was not thriving. Sunny was a whiz at math, with an independent spirit and her own take on things.

The stark reality of our lives forced the children to mature earlier than they otherwise would have. They learned subterfuge—and quiet defiance. As for me, for all the suffering and humiliation, I was determined to find out why they were treating me like an enemy.

For generations, my family had been poor, honest people. I had worked at Radio for seventeen years, and the record was plain: I had always been scrupulous and conscientious in whatever work I had been given to do—sometimes working day and night, sleeping on the office floor, leaving no stone unturned to do my job well. Even if they thought Sidney was a spy—a charge I could not prove or disprove—where was the logic in automatically assuming that I was bad, too? Where was the evidence?

There wasn't a single member of our family who didn't honestly love Chair-man Mao. As far as I could see, everything good that had happened in my life directly grew out of Mao's direction and what he had done for China. As Mama used to say, over and over, "If it weren't for Chairman Mao, our family wouldn't exist!" The only thing she ever objected to that Chairman Mao did was to free the Japanese war criminals; she thought that was wrong.

I set myself two overall aims.

First, I would find out where Sidney was and why they were attacking him with such vile accusations. I would do everything in my power to clear his name—in part because this would have a direct bearing on the children's future. I had to eliminate the stigma of coming from a "bad" family, or their future would be ruined. Second, I would exhaust every possible means to teach my kids to be good, well-educated people, investing all my energy for their sakes.

In order to carry out these commitments, I had to be strong. I would have to go on living and fighting, whatever happened. I could not let myself fall!

But as time dragged on, our confinement to this little room began to affect the children's health. Their appetites declined—especially my son's. He once drank about a quart of milk a day, but after some time in confinement, he could only drink half a pint, and he began pushing away his bowl of rice porridge. Day by day, Little Ming grew thinner and paler. Since infancy, he had always had a weak stomach. I demanded an electric hot plate, so that I could warm milk and eggs for him. But the guards refused. All I could do was warm the milk by pouring the boiled drinking water into a bowl and setting his milk bottle in the hot water—then dropping the raw eggs into the warm milk and stirring, to cook them a little.

At first, Ming would take some of this milk, but then he refused it. I tasted it to see what was wrong. The lukewarm milk was mostly raw eggs and had a kind of gamey flavor—yuck. Then I understood why he wouldn't drink it.

I asked to be allowed to give him some rice porridge or noodles at noon or in the evening, but they refused. They said the cook had no time. I said, "The nanny has nothing to do, she can fix the food." But that wasn't allowed either.

I couldn't stand seeing Little Ming get thinner and thinner. I asked the nanny—the only person allowed to come and go freely—to buy us some lotus root flour, which I mixed with hot water to make a sweetish drink. But after a few days, Ming spurned that, too.

Growing increasingly worried about the children's health and hoping to jump-start their appetites, I instructed them to run back and forth in the tiny space around and between the beds. At night, I would have them do push-ups and sit-ups. Even when they didn't want to run, I would make sure that they did, and I explained the importance of keeping fit.

One day, desperate for fresh air, the children stealthily tore off the paper that pasted the courtyard window shut, so that they could open one of them. The three girls sat there, side by side on the windowsill, holding their little brother so he could get some sunshine.

Very soon, the white-suited men in the opposite room saw what was going on. They scolded me severely and pasted the paper back on. Still, they left enough unpasted space so that we could open the little panes below the main window. Again, the girls held their brother up to the windowsill so that he might catch a little sunshine and fresh air.

After six years of college classes, I started teaching them English sentences. I taught them to understand me when I said, "They're coming!" or "Shut the window!"

Whenever the kids opened the window, I would sit by our open door, my eyes fastened on the room across the hall, and as soon as I saw anyone headed our way, I'd warn the children in English. Then with lightning speed, they would put things back the way they had been. With the passage of time, Mr. Li began "not noticing" what was going on at our window, and we were not interfered with again. We celebrated this tiny victory.

Then one very sultry afternoon, the girls were holding their little brother up to the windowsill so that he could catch a bit of sun, when some of the service personnel in the courtyard below spotted them.

One of them shouted, "Hey, look! What a cute little foreign baby!"

My son was handsome from the start: large eyes, a firm nose, and a wide forehead. Of my four children, he looked the most "foreign."

They called up from below. "Hi, Baby! Come on down and play with us!"

I waved thanks at those good-hearted people, but made a sign to show them that it was impossible.

One of them, a tall, thin young man, caught a little bird in the courtyard tree and held it up toward the baby. "Little foreigner! Would you like to have this birdie?"

Ming still couldn't talk, but he stretched out his two little hands, as if to catch the bird, while his sisters shouted, "Yes, Yes!"

The young man thought for a minute. "Let down a rope, and I'll send the bird up to you."

The three girls looked everywhere for string and thread, tying together whatever they could find to make a long string. The baby went after them, helping. He understood.

I cast the line down, but it was still too short. The young man stood on tiptoe on top of a chair and tied the line around the bird's foot. The children pulled it up into the room, and at last they had something to play with! The children all waved to the young man in the courtyard to thank him.

My oldest daughter, Jenny, said, "Let's untie the bird." Soon it was flying all around the room, with the children chasing after it, shrieking with laughter. They jumped on the beds and waved their hands and twirled. After weeks of tedium, that common sparrow brought mirth and joy into our cramped, airless room.

When they were tired, Jenny said, "Let's let it go. The little bird is tired, too. It won't live long like this." She had learned this wisdom the hard way.

Watching the children having fun made me happy, of course, but it also made me sad. *These lovable kids, why can't they go out in the sun and play? What crimes have they committed, that they should be locked up? Even my two year old, who still can't say "Mama"— is he a lawbreaker? What a towering injustice this is! Who will speak out on our behalf? Have these children lost their freedom just because their father is an American? And because he was too eager and wholehearted in working for the good of China?*

My third daughter's Chinese name is Xiang, meaning "to soar freely." Now, she didn't even have the right to leave the room.

The little birdie was freer than we were.

Chapter Twenty-Three

The Real Accusation

THE CHILDREN'S HEALTH got worse and worse. Sunny got a rash, and her face began to itch. At first it seemed minor. But I couldn't stop her from scratching, and soon the tiny blisters began running yellow fluid, turning her little face and chest into a sticky mess.

I asked to take her to the clinic, but the guards paid no attention.

At night, when we went to sleep, I tied her hands to the bed so that she wouldn't scratch. How could I let this pretty girl grow up with ugly scars all over her face! But the itching was unbearable, and she would break the cords and scratch anyway. The rash quickly spread; my little daughter was in agony.

I marched over to the opposite room again and declared, "My child is sick. She must go to the doctor!"

Mr. Li said, "It's just a rash, isn't it? What can a doctor do about that?"

"It's more than that now," I said. "It's become boils, all over her body. Can't you see it?"

"We'll ask the leaders," he said. "We can't make that decision."

"You've been asking for over a week," I said. "Are you going to wait for the child to die?"

"Who said we would let her die? You're not being reasonable."

"Who is not being reasonable here? Tell me! What crimes have these kids committed? Why can't they see the doctor when they're sick?"

"All right, all right!" they told me. "Go back, and we'll take your demands to our superiors."

To my relief, the next day a doctor came to look at Sunny. He left her some medicine. But after two or three days she still showed no improvement. To control the scratching, I made her mittens out of old cloth and tied her wrists to the sides of the bed again—this time she could move her arms but couldn't reach her face to scratch it up. But it was all in vain because she would break free and scratch her face anyway.

Sunny's threadbare clothes were sticky from her sores, but she had no other clothes to change into. Her two older sisters used the hotel sewing kit to patch her shirt, and soon there were so many patches that you could hardly make out what it had originally looked like.

Her sisters said, "Little Xiang, your clothes can go on exhibit in the museum."

This worried Sunny. "Wait till Papa comes back and sees what kind of rags I'm wearing!"

I shushed the children. "Be careful what you say." I knew they could get in trouble for talking about their father coming back. My sweet kids! Not one of them ever believed that their father could be a spy. They all expected him to be cleared of charges and released soon.

One day, three strangers—two men and one woman—called me over to the room across the hall. They made me stand, and they sat in a row, facing me, inquisition style. Mr. Li was also present, sitting over on one side.

"Your name is Wang Yulin?" one man asked.

"Yes."

"Your husband's name is Li Dunbai?"

"Yes."

"Do you know that your husband is an American secret agent?"

"No, I don't know that." To betray China would have gone against Sidney's deepest values. If he was innocent, as I assumed, how could he prove it? Real spies are taught to lie. So who would believe him when he said he was not a spy?

"How can you not know it?" he said. "The whole country knows it, except for you?"

"Why am I being detained?" I countered.

Glaring at me, the middle-aged woman added, "We ask the questions. You're a disgrace to our nation!" She used the words *minzu bailei,*, meaning "a traitor to my nation and my people."

Anger gripped my throat. So this was the real accusation against me. It was a horrible insult, but was it a crime? How could anyone think I was disloyal to China?

The second man jumped in. "Which of Li Dunbai's contacts do you know?"

"I don't know of any foreign contacts, except for other foreign experts in Beijing."

"What people and organizations does he have contact with in foreign countries?"

"I don't know. The American *Daily Worker* once asked him to write some articles for them, but I don't know whether he wrote them or not."

"How can you not know anything?" The interrogator raised his voice. "Don't play dumb with us!"

"I was away from home, in college, from 1960 to 1967. I came home only on weekends." This was, in fact, a problem. I really didn't know what Sidney had been doing all those years. But it was also the perfect defense.

"He's your husband. He doesn't talk things over with you?"

"I don't know what kinds of things you're talking about."

"Your main problem," said the first man, "is that your class position still hasn't come around. You have to draw a clear line of distinction between you and him. That's your only way out."

I said nothing, but inside I was fuming. How dare they question my "class position"! I grew up as the daughter of a poor worker and had joined the Party before Liberation. "Drawing a clear line of distinction" was a euphemism for denouncing my husband. No way would I do that.

"Okay, let me ask you something else. Tell us how Li Dunbai attacks the working class and the Communist Party when he's at home."

"I never heard him do that." Quite the contrary!

He pressed forward. "What evil things have you done together with him?"

By now I was really angry. "Evil things? He's never done anything evil!"

"What does he teach the children at home? What kind of propaganda has he been disseminating among them?"

"The children come home on weekends; he plays with them and often teaches them quotations from Chairman Mao."

Another glare from the woman, who shouted, "Who's asking you about that? We're asking you what reactionary propaganda he spreads among the children!"

The three of them took turns pummeling me with insulting questions. But to my surprise, when I glanced over at Mr. Li, I noticed that he was looking at me sympathetically.

Then, in a vicious tone, the woman said, "You go back and study hard! Especially pay attention to these three articles by Chairman Mao: 'Message Urging Tu Yu-Ming and Others to Surrender,' 'Whither the Nanking Government,' and 'Farewell, Leighton Stuart.'"

These were all articles I had read many times.

"Examine your own thinking in the light of those writings. You have to change your class position. Your only way out is to draw a clear line of distinction with Li Dunbai! Go back and think it over very carefully!"

After that, they would call me to the room across the hall every three or four days, repeating these demands and insisting that I tell them about Sidney's foreign connections and correspondence. But I had nothing to add. I thought it was strange that they didn't ask me about things Sidney did in China, such as the fiery speeches he had made. Should I be afraid of these interrogators? I believed in the old Chinese proverb: He who doesn't do shameful things has no fear of demons knocking at his door.

They glared and shouted at me, as if certain their behavior would frighten me, but I was not afraid. I knew that I hadn't done anything wrong, and I had never done anything to undermine the government. My heart was at peace. I couldn't understand why they were trying to pin something on me. It made no sense and was a complete waste of time.

One day they said, "We know lots of facts that you are not aware of. Li Dunbai didn't tell you." They held up a stack of papers and waved them at me, saying, "Look! This is all Li Dunbai's testimony! Why don't you testify?"

"If that's his testimony, then you have the information you need. I don't know anything about what he said. You have to ask him."

But when I went back to our room, I did a lot of soul-searching. *Could Sidney really have secret agent connections with America? No! Remember who he is, and how he behaved. Any letters he received would have been lying around all over the place. He never did anything furtive. Sidney's mind is very clever, but his movements are very clumsy. He doesn't conceal anything that he does. In fact, he would make a terrible secret agent. Don't let these questions get to you.*

One day I called the three girls over and said, "Think back and tell me: What has Papa talked to you about?"

"Papa's always teaching us Chairman Mao's poems and getting us to sing Chairman Mao's songs," said Jenny.

"Has he ever said anything bad about socialism?

"Never," the three girls answered in unison.

Little Xiang asked, "Mama, is Papa really a bad egg?"

"What do you think?"

"Papa is not a bad egg!" they all chorused back at me.

I smiled at them and stroked their hair. "You're right. Remember, your father is a good man. There are bad people attacking him."

They nodded solemnly.

But I cautioned them, "Once they let us out of here, don't talk like that, okay? You have to remember to say you're 'drawing a line of distinction' from Papa."

"Why?" my youngest daughter asked.

Her big sister said, "How silly you are! If we don't do that, people will curse at us."

"Right!" I said. "They say your Papa is an American secret agent—a traitor, an enemy to China. You understand that he's not. But don't tell anyone else that your Mama said Papa is not a secret agent. Understand?"

All three little heads nodded in agreement.

I marveled at how they handled such complicated issues at their tender age, yet shook my head at the fact they had to learn these two-faced tactics. I hoped that we could get out of this room someday, that the children could go back to school. If they did, they had to learn not to talk publicly about their father and not to argue back when people said he was a spy. They didn't have to betray him, but drawing a line of distinction might protect them until Sidney could clear his name.

$$\approx$$

As the interrogations continued, Little Sunny's rash got worse. I kept demanding that she go to the hospital for examination and treatment. Since I was not allowed to leave our room, they finally let the nanny take Sunny to the clinic that was attached to the Traditional Medicine Research Institute.

The doctor gave her a kind of Chinese medicine, a yellow fluid, for her face and body. Her two older sisters took good care of her, applying the medicine and covering it with gauze twice every day. The nasty rash gradually got better, and at long last the sores dried up.

But just at that point, a different sickness took hold of my second daughter, Toni.

In the middle of the night, Toni suddenly called out "Mama! Mama!"

"Little Dong, I'm here," I said, and went over to hug her.

She was trembling all over and delirious. "Mama, I'm afraid of the tiger!"

I was at my wit's end. I had Jenny turn on the light and bring the thermometer. Toni had a fever. It wasn't too high, but it scared me. I remembered how she had gone into convulsions and nearly died from a fever as a baby. I demanded that our keepers immediately get her to the hospital.

But the people in charge of us said, "What kind of fever do you call that!"

I was really beside myself. "If my child dies, who's going to be responsible?" I demanded. "She must go to the hospital immediately."

Finally, they called a doctor to our room. He examined her and gave her a shot to break the fever, but by the next day the fever still hadn't come down. After a week, when Toni's fever rose to 103 degrees, they agreed to let the nanny and a guard take Toni to the clinic at the nearby Friendship Hospital. But they wouldn't let me go.

When the nanny got Toni to the clinic, the doctor scolded her for not coming earlier. The doctor also said Toni wasn't eating properly. "What's this poor quality food you're giving her? Don't you get enough to eat?"

Hospital doctors examined Toni, prescribed medicines, and gave her an injection. Thank heavens, within three or four days she recovered and was back to normal.

Meanwhile, the three girls all worried about their little brother, who still couldn't talk, not even to call "Mama." I assured them that it was no problem; he was a very bright child, and once he started talking, they would see that he was fine. Actually, as I pointed out to them, he understood everything we said to him; he just hadn't decided to talk yet.

I reminded them of what had happened with his little stuffed teddy bear, just a few months before we were detained. He used to go to bed hugging his teddy bear, and before dropping off to sleep he would kiss his bear's nose. After a time, the bear's nose began to look icky, and the nanny threw it in the trash. Little Ming cried and cried. Jenny and Toni went downtown and bought him a new teddy bear. But it wasn't his bear, and he totally rejected it, pushing it away and bawling. His sisters tried to fish the old one out of the trash, but they couldn't find it. I reminded them of this incident to show how clever their little brother was, letting us know what he wanted, even though he still couldn't talk.

"He's no dummy," I said. "He'll talk someday, when he's ready." But I feared the long-term effects that our detention might have on him—and on all of them.

Chapter Twenty-Four

Crowded Yet Alone

SOME DAYS SEEMED endless, but others flew by in our little room. I would teach the children daily and rejoice in how fast they learned—so fast that I increased the pace of their lessons. Their curiosity and the eagerness with which they grasped things were like rays of sun in my darkness. When one of my daughters looked at me with bright eyes, keen to see how well she had completed her schoolwork, it would fill me with delight to say, "All correct! Not one mistake!"

I was very exacting. If they got a math problem wrong, I insisted that they do it over several times. Fortunately, I had always loved math, physics, and chemistry, so I was able to teach them with enthusiasm. All that tutoring I used to do for my classmates prepared me well.

Aside from giving lessons, I insisted on the daily regimen, leading the children in jogging back and forth, doing exercises, and taking cold baths. In the tight space, they would run into each other and burst into giggles. All this was to maintain good health—for myself, as well as the children.

Internally, though, I struggled with anxiety and despair. Engaging in all this activity kept me from just sitting around, moping. But I couldn't help agonizing, especially about Sidney. Where was he? How was he getting along each day? Was he buckling under pressure? He was always so ready to admit the Party was right and he was wrong. I just hoped he wasn't confessing to something he hadn't done.

Achingly, I thought about my own father and mother, too. I knew they would be sick with worry, trying to find us. Despite my financial woes, I continued sending thirty yuan a month to Papa to take care of his living expenses—something I had started a few years earlier when he stopped working. As for Mama, I had been supporting her for years, so I arranged to send her twenty-three yuan a month. Although she was now living with my third sister in Shijiazhuang, her grain ration tickets were still listed with my account. At my request, the people in charge of me had been sending the money and ration tickets to her every month. But the keepers had not allowed me to send my parents even a brief note, reassuring them that the children and I were together and all right. Also, I didn't get any news about my parents. My father suffered from stomach trouble and asthma, and my mother had high blood pressure. She had already suffered a stroke once, after the shock of losing Second Sister. What if they needed me and I could not help?

Money worries continued to preoccupy me, too. We had 187.50 yuan in monthly income and total expenses of 187.20. In addition to supporting my parents, I had to pay the nanny's wages and food supplement, our basic food costs, milk for my son, our newspaper subscription, soap, and toothpaste. Each month, we had only 30 fen left over. There was no money to buy milk, eggs, or calcium tablets for the children. I couldn't even afford my sanitary pads. It cost 30 fen each time one of the children visited the hospital clinic. The children were growing, their feet were getting larger, and their clothes were worn and torn. I really didn't know what to do!

I reported all this to the keepers repeatedly, but nothing was resolved. I asked if we could order three portions of food for the six of us. They refused. I asked if I could owe some of the food bill, temporarily, promising to pay it back once I was free, but this wouldn't do either.

My deepest concern was the children's health. They badly lacked sunshine and fresh air. They couldn't eat a lot of meat, especially the fatty meat that we were given. One of them even got diarrhea from all the fat. Repeatedly, I asked Mr. Li if he could bring us dishes other than the fatty meat, but he said no.

Little Ming especially was not thriving as a toddler should. He kept getting thinner, and his stomach couldn't handle the kind of food we were given. I couldn't afford to buy sugar to sweeten his milk. When I asked for some, Mr. Li demanded, "Why do you have to put sugar in the milk? Don't be so particular!"

Once I asked the nanny to buy my son a bunch of grapes, at a cost of a little over ten fen, but I was criticized for this, too. The interrogators said, "You think your son has the right to eat fruit? You should realize what kind of people you are! Don't think it's like it used to be!"

The nanny's attitude became increasingly hostile. Every morning she went out to fetch our hot drinking water, since we were not allowed to step outside our door. But I was the one to get the children to eat, drink their milk, and go to sleep; she did nothing. When I asked her to help, she said, "You're not working, so what else are you going to do if you don't take care of the children?" I was sure she was reporting on us, so I had to watch what I said in front of her. Several times, I demanded to let her go. Even if we were released later on, the children would be going to school or to nursery school, and we wouldn't need a nanny. But the people in charge of us said, "No. You can't decide for yourself whether or not you use the nanny."

Straining under these burdens, I would stand at the window that faced the street, peering through the tiny cracks between the boards that blocked it. Often I would cry very quietly, trying to make sure the children wouldn't notice.

Once I got a glimpse of an elderly lady with tiny bound feet, walking along the street; I called the girls over to see if it was their beloved grandmother.

"It can't be," said Toni. "How could Grandma come over here?"

But I said, "It looks like her. It must be her!"

"It can't be."

But I insisted. "For all we know, your grandma might be living next door to us."

Every day, I'd stand there for a while, like a madwoman, squinting through the cracks to see if I could catch sight of my mama. Weeping silently, I would say in my heart, "Mama, Mama! Where are you?"

Often I would give the fatty meat and some mantou (Chinese steamed bread rolls) to the nanny to take home, hoping that she would be helpful to us. She went home every weekend, and I found out that she lived just a block away from my father. So one day I beseeched the nanny to take a message to my father, to tell him that we were all okay.

"I can't tell him where you are," she said.

"You don't have to say where we are. Just tell him that we're getting along fine, so that he doesn't worry."

"No. I can't do anything for you," she replied.

"I'm just asking you to give him that one sentence. He's very old, and I don't want him to worry."

But no matter how I begged, she wouldn't do it. She even reported me to the keepers. We had always treated her very well, like one of the family. She had been with us for over a year. She had been glad to take the meat from our rations that we hadn't eaten. But now, when she had this opportunity to give me a little peace of mind, she hardened her heart and turned a cold face to me. Even the children noticed her unkindness and began to dislike her.

One day she announced, "Wang Yulin, my wages should be raised by two yuan a month, and I should have another day off every week."

I told her, "You can take another day off each week, because all you do is go get drinking water for us and watch the baby while I'm giving the other children lessons. But I can't afford to pay you more."

But she threatened, "If you don't want to give me a raise, I'll go to the keepers."

Her belligerence troubled me. This was not a matter of her needs as an individual; it was typical of the dog-eat-dog atmosphere being generated by the so-called Cultural Revolution. And after all the selfless dedication I had known in fellow cadres, this woman's attitude stung me.

Our keepers had told me at the start that I could send back for clothes from our old apartment. So one day I said to the nanny, "The children's clothes are torn. Tell the keepers that you need to go fetch some clothes for them. My bank deposit book is in my overcoat pocket. Go to the bank and get me some money."

Very soon after that, Mr. Li came over to speak with me.

"What's going on? You're trying to get the nanny to sneak out and get you some money? Well, I can tell you your bank account has been frozen for a long time. As for the clothes, we have to examine them first, and then we'll give them to you." But they never did.

I hated myself for being silly enough to trust in the nanny, who had become their spy to watch me inside our little room. But I still allowed myself to have illusions about her, as I desperately needed to find an ally.

Crowded in that tiny room, I had to face my troubles all alone.

Chapter Twenty-Five

A Plea to the Premier

AS THE MONTHS passed in confinement, a curious change occurred. I found that the three men across the corridor were no longer treating us like enemies. Sometimes Mr. Li would come over to see us. He would play pick-up sticks with the children, and he began to let the children visit his room. Once when the girls went over to get the Chinese medicine for Sunny's rash, they climbed up on the keepers' laps and discovered that under their white service outfits the men wore military uniforms. Instead of being worried, the children were delighted, since they had been taught to respect the soldiers of the People's Liberation Army.

Jenny exclaimed gleefully, "Oh, you're Liberation Army men!"

Toni chimed in, "No wonder Mama said you can't be service workers—you must be soldiers!"

I had warned them to be careful about how they talked around those men, because they were certain to be public security personnel, reporting our behavior to the authorities.

One day, the waiter who brought our food, Mr. Cui, saw me crying and tried to comfort me. "Wang Yulin, you just stick it out here. You have no idea what a mess things are outside. You would really suffer now if you were outside."

"What's going on outside, Mr. Cui? Tell me." The newspaper was full of revolutionary slogans, but I had no way of knowing what was happening to ordinary people.

He looked over his shoulder to make sure Mr. Li couldn't hear. "It's crazy out there. Groups are fighting each other with sticks. Struggle sessions are spinning out of control. Homes are being looted. People are being tormented and beaten up. If the masses heard that your husband was an American spy, they would beat you for sure. So don't cry. You're a lot better off in here than out there."

This was the most that he had ever said to me in all those months. Before that, he would just bring the food, put it down, then turn on his heels and leave, without saying a word. I was glad he was talking, but the news was disturbing. Had the whole country gone mad?

From time to time, Mr. Li would also tell me about things that were happening outside. For instance, he shared the news about an explosion that had taken place in the Xidan marketplace. But he would never say anything about Sidney.

One day Mr. Li asked me a question that shook my equilibrium. "Wang Yulin, shouldn't we stop sending the money to your father and the grain ration coupons to your mother?"

Shocked, I asked, "Why should I do that?"

"That's what your father said we should do," said Mr. Li.

"What? My father said that? Tell me what really happened! Did he die?"

"Your father's in good health—no problem," he assured me. "I took him the money myself and handed it to him."

But I still didn't believe Mr. Li. "No, tell me the truth. Please! Why don't you want me to send them the money and grain tickets? What's happened? Did my mother die?" I burst out crying.

"Nothing has happened to them! I'm telling you the truth."

After a minute, I began to believe him and calm down. Finally, I said, "Then just keep sending them the money and grain tickets. I want to see the receipt in my father's own hand, and I want to know how my mother is getting along."

He nodded. "Okay. We can continue to send them as usual, if that's what you want."

I spent much of the next few days in tears, fearful that my mother had actually passed away. Mama had been through so much suffering! I needed to see that she was treated well and to have her live with me so that I could take care of her. I knew Sidney felt the same way.

But now that I knew Mr. Li saw my father in person, I began to press him for information. I still could not write letters to my family, but I found out that my mother was still in reasonably good health and still living with Third Sister. But Mama missed us terribly and wept every day. She took the baby's photo with her everywhere and showed it to people.

One day, though, I heard that Mama had an attack of high blood pressure, and I was afraid that she might pass away before I could see her again. I couldn't eat or sleep for three days and three nights. My mother had been battered in the Old Society. After Liberation, her health had improved. Now, Li Dunbai's situation was shattering her again. I put in a request to have her come and stay with us, but again it was ignored. Distress about my parents and my children finally spurred me to take action.

Not knowing where else to turn, I thought of Premier Zhou Enlai, whom I trusted. If he was still in power—and the keepers reassured me he was—he might be able to help us. I had met him a few times at dinners, but I didn't really know him personally. Still, he certainly knew who Sidney and I were, and I knew that he loved children. So I wrote a long, rambling letter and poured out my heart to Premier Zhou.

I sealed this letter in an envelope and then wrote a separate letter to the Central Cultural Revolution Leading Group, asking them to relay my envelope to Premier Zhou Enlai. It was dated August 21, 1968, six months after Sidney's arrest.

In the style of the Cultural Revolution, every statement started with a quotation from Chairman Mao, and so that's how I began my letter to Premier Zhou:

> Chairman Mao's supreme instructions say, "We should have faith in the masses. We should have faith in the Party. These are two fundamental principles. If we doubt these principles, we shall be able to accomplish nothing." Our beloved Chairman also writes, "The enemy will not destroy himself. Whether it's the Chinese reactionaries or U.S. imperialism's forces of aggression in China, they will not leave the stage of history of their own accord."
>
> Dear Premier Zhou: I have some problems on my mind that I can't resolve, because no one has talked with me for more than half a year. I'm writing this letter, interrupting your work, in the hope that you can give me some direction and enlightenment. As you know, I am Li Dunbai's wife. Because of his problem, I have been shut up in a single room together with my four children, deprived of freedom. The children are small: the oldest is only eleven, and the youngest is just two. We have been living in this one room for more than half a year, without ever going out of the door.
>
> There are lots of problems in our life that cannot be resolved. These things are very upsetting to me. For example, when the children get sick we can't get timely medical care. My son's health is poor, and he isn't allowed to go out for fresh air. The food we get has too much fat in it; it's making the children sick. The money we receive from the leadership is not enough for our monthly living expenses.
>
> The children ask me almost every day why they can't go to school and

when they will be able to go out and play with other kids. I teach them from Chairman Mao's works and have taught them to recite his quotations. Every morning, afternoon, and evening, I spend one full hour teaching them to memorize Chairman Mao's Three Old Essays.

All I can do is to weep at night, in secret. That's right; what kind of people are we supposed to be? We're people without freedom. For so many years, I've been loyal to the Party. I have loved the Party and Chairman Mao. When I was fourteen I made up my mind to join the revolution, following the Party and Chairman Mao. After Liberation, my living conditions improved, but I have never spent money recklessly. The leadership can investigate among the masses and find this out.

I experienced the hateful Old Society, and I can never forget how I suffered in the past. My elder sister was only twelve years old when she went to take care of a baby for a rich family. My mother gave birth to twelve children, but only four lived to see Liberation. My mother worked as a servant. When I was thirteen years old, I became a child worker in a factory. My elder brother and my father were both poor workers, unemployed for a long time. Before Liberation, our whole family never had a full meal. Then came Liberation. After Chairman Mao's troops came, we poor people began a new life, and I got, at last, the opportunity to go to school.

At seventeen, I began working, doing my little bit for the people. From the bottom of my heart, I was happy to be able to do something for the people. On the day that I joined the Party, I vowed that, if it cost my life, I would always remain loyal to the Communist Party and the revolution. At home, we would often talk about the old days and contrast them with the present. Before Liberation, Mama would get edible weeds for us children to eat. Of course, my former life is as different from my children's present life as Earth is from heaven. How fortunate they are!

But since the children aren't eating properly now, they are getting thin. Every time I ask the nanny or the service personnel for help, they refuse. When the people in charge of us see me, they either glare at me or lose their temper. From their attitude toward us, it seems that the organization has placed our whole family in the category of enemies.

This reminds me: Why are my Party dues rejected and returned every month? For eighteen years I have never been apart from the Party. For eighteen years, the Party has led me. But today, the Party has pushed me aside.

Sometimes I think this strange thought—if I'm apart from the Party, what meaning is there in life? But then I think to myself, a Communist should endure any investigation or trials that the Party undertakes.

Dear Premier Zhou: I am really very upset, and I can't find any dear one with whom to talk about what's on my mind. Mao Zedong teaches us, "We must struggle against selfishness and critique revisionism." I will follow Vice-Chairman Lin Biao's instructions, doing live study and live use of Chairman Mao's thought, emphasizing application. I will fight hard against selfish ideas and wayward thoughts.

Premier Zhou, I have a sincere request. Bring my mother to live with us. She's been living with us for a dozen years. Now she's gone to see my brother and sister in Shijiazhuang. I fear that she misses us, weeps every day, and has gotten thin and drawn. She once had a stroke because of shock, and I'm very worried about her health. I know she will listen to me, and if I can be with her and comfort her, she'll be okay. I hope the leadership will consider letting us, mother and daughter, live together.

Dear Premier Zhou, I hope the leadership can understand my troubles. I know you're very busy and I shouldn't disturb you. Also, this letter is chaotic, lengthy, and low quality. But I couldn't help myself—I was going to keep it short, but for some reason I couldn't stop. Please forgive me.

Salute!

Long life without end for Chairman Mao!

Eternal health for Vice Chairman Lin!

Good health to Jiang Qing, the comrade great standard bearer of the Great Proletarian Cultural Revolution!

Good health to Premier Zhou Enlai!

Long live Chairman Mao!

Long live the Communist Party of China!

Wang Yulin,
August 21, 1968

Chapter Twenty-Six

Release

To keep the children in good spirits, I would pretend to be full of life. I wouldn't let them see me looking sad and worried. I taught them to sing popular songs and Beijing opera arias from *The Legend of the Red Lantern* and *The White-Haired Girl*. When we sang, the service personnel in the courtyard below would listen and applaud our singing. The children enjoyed this, and they would deliberately sing for the audience below.

Standing at the window, Jenny and Toni would sing their favorite song, which they remember to this day:

I yearn for the stars, I yearn for the moon.
I yearn for the sun to come out, in this deep gorge.
I yearn for the day I can speak freely among the people!
I yearn for the day I can put on my pretty girl's clothing.
I yearn for the time I can take revenge for eight years of bloody mistreatment!
I hate that I cannot sprout wings, take up my gun, and hunt all those jackals.

This was from a revolutionary opera, approved by Jiang Qing herself. She could never know what meaning it would have for my daughters. When my girls finished singing, they would have tears in their eyes. "Mama, when will we be able to go out? When are we going to see Papa again?"

"One of these days, when we go out, we'll give three big roars of laughter!" said Toni. "I'm going to sing this song at the top of my lungs and laugh for all I'm worth!"

On the morning of October 18, the older Liberation Army man who had first brought us to this room suddenly appeared and said, "Wang Yulin, your behavior here has not been bad. You have been teaching the children the writings of

Chairman Mao. I hear that you sing 'The East is Red' every day, and then recite the Three Old Essays."

"Yes, I give them their lessons every day," I replied, nearly choking with hope.

"Things are in very good shape outside. We have decided to let you go back to your organization, to take part in the movement along with everyone else."

The children stared in wonder. "You mean that we can go out?" Jenny asked.

"Yes. Get ready, settle up the accounts, and you can leave this afternoon."

The children cheered and ran around in delight.

I heard the news with mixed emotions. I was happy that the kids would finally be able to go out and play. But I was apprehensive about what the future would hold. As long as Sidney was being held on spy charges, it would definitely not be good. As his wife, I would be linked to his spy case, and there was no getting away from this millstone around my neck.

Of course, they had already offered me a "way out"—to turn against my husband, expose his "crimes," and I would be a good citizen again, free from hassle. But there was nothing to expose. Of course, during the mob madness of the Cultural Revolution, making up things to expose, being "creative," was a common occurrence. But I am not built that way, and I never gave a thought to the idea of taking that easy road out of my troubles. No, I would see it through in honesty, or die in the attempt.

That afternoon, shortly after lunch, the same man returned and said, "Are you ready with your things packed?"

"We're all ready," I said.

"Let's go then."

We—the children, the nanny, and I—followed him out of the room, past the big screen, and down the corridor.

First, we turned and waved thanks to the three white-clad men who had been in charge of us all this time. The waiter, Mr. Cui, was there, too. They waved back at us.

We took the elevator down, then walked to the front door. This was when I turned around, took in the lobby and the reception desk, and realized that we had been living on the third floor of the Qianmen Hotel, just a few blocks from Tiananmen Square. Emptied of guests, the famous old hotel was being used as a detention house.

We climbed into an army jeep outside the front door. As I had done on the night when they first took us away, I paid careful attention to the direction in which the car was moving. If it headed for the Foreign Experts Building, where we used to live, it would mean that Sidney's case had been cleared up. If it went elsewhere, it would mean that the case still wasn't settled, and there was no telling what was in store for me and my children.

As harsh and unfair as my detention felt at the time, others suffered much worse during those violent years of the Great Proletarian Cultural Revolution. During my eight months of detention, gangs calling themselves Red Guards continued to fight one another, students continued to attack teachers, cultural treasures were destroyed, and religious sites were vandalized. Millions were persecuted, and untold thousands committed suicide after public humiliation and torture. Violence and lawlessness were rampant.

The Communist Party of China as I knew it had been destroyed and established anew to worship Mao Zedong and continuing revolution. Mao and his leading group were sacrosanct; almost all other Party officials were criticized and attacked. Liu Shaoqi, head of state and once one of the most powerful leaders of China, was beaten publicly, denounced as a traitor, denied medication, and left to die in prison.

Later, I learned that Premier Zhou Enlai had arranged for us to be held in that hotel room to protect us from the chaos and the vengeful spirit that raged outside. He probably arranged for our release, as well, in response to my letter.

It is now known that Premier Zhou used whatever power and prestige he wielded at that time to protect at least a few people and salvage precious cultural sites, including the Imperial Palace in Beijing and the Potala Palace in Lhasa. Unlike other high-level leaders, he managed to avoid removal from his official position by publicly siding with Chairman Mao, yet he was able to moderate some of the excesses of Mao's most radical policies. Many Chinese venerate Zhou Enlai for these reasons. Still, when we emerged onto the streets of Beijing in October 1968, I could not even imagine that our detention and suffering might have been a favor.

The Cultural Revolution was still raging. The soldiers who released us had not mentioned Sidney's name. I knew that was a bad sign. Furthermore, they came for us in a military jeep, not a passenger car. That seemed to be a clear indication, too, that I was still in trouble.

As I feared, the jeep pulled up to the gate of the Radio compound—not the Foreign Experts Building. Waiting out front for us was Zhang Wenxiu. He had worked in the English section answering letters, but he had finally come into a position of power now as Party branch secretary and seemed to enjoy lording it over those who had once been above him. He regarded me with pure hate; I suspected he would have liked to club me to the ground, if he had been allowed.

Without saying a word, but glaring balefully at me, he got in the jeep, which drove us to the cadre living quarters known as "New 302." The car stopped before Unit 38 of Building 5, and Zhang said, "You're on the fifth floor."

The children and I got out quietly and followed Zhang Wenxiu up five flights of stairs. On this floor, there were two apartments. Ours was a single room of fourteen square meters, about one hundred and fifty square feet, the size of a typical American bedroom; while the apartment next door, designed for two people, was only twelve square meters, a little over one hundred square feet. The occupants of the two apartments had to share a tiny kitchen.

In our room, there was one large bed and a bureau with two drawers. That was it—no other furniture. But even this left only a tiny open space in our little room. It made our hotel room seem huge. How could six people live in one tiny room?

In a voice full of self-importance, Zhang announced, "Wang Yulin. Starting at eight tomorrow, you must come to the office every morning. Whenever you leave this room, except for going to work, you must ask leave from the residents' committee. You are not permitted to go to your father's home, and your father is not allowed to come here." In other words, I was under house arrest.

"But we don't have bedclothes, and we don't have a stove!" I said. "What can we do?"

He said, "We'll let you go back to your old home just once, to fetch your bedclothes. As for a stove, daily necessities, and grain, we'll give you fifty yuan and some grain ration tickets. You must go buy them yourself."

Before Zhang left the room, Dong Decai, from the People's Liberation Army Management Group that was in charge of Radio, came in. In a strident voice, he announced, "Li Dunbai is an American spy. You must draw a clear line of demarcation from him!"

The children and I stared at him in silent defiance.

He softened only slightly for his next sentence, "Whether or not you need the nanny is up to you."

As soon as he left, I dismissed the nanny, at last. Oddly, after all those months of hostility, she begged me not to dismiss her. I guess she needed the money. But I sent her away anyway and never saw her again.

The children and I put our few possessions in the bureau, and the girls took their brother down to the courtyard to explore, their first moments in the fresh air. With no winter coats, I knew they wouldn't go far.

I collapsed on the bed, my mind overloaded. So the spying charges against Sidney had not been dropped. As his family, what kind of life would this be for us? We were no longer confined, but we were not free.

Later that day, I got a visit from Zhou Hong, a woman who had worked in the English section for some time and had been a member of the same Party group as Sidney. Zhou Hong knew the real Sidney and had often joked with him. Seeing her face gave me hope; she, at least, might be friendlier than others. She had come to take me to my office, the Europe/Americas Department of Radio Beijing, to answer to a special case group dealing with Sidney's case. People from an "outside unit," she said, had come to question me about Sidney.

I left Jenny in charge and told the children not to speak too freely with anyone they saw. I needed to figure out the political landscape at Radio before I could trust anyone. As Zhou Hong led me across the courtyard and down the street to the office, I found myself unsteady on my feet. After being shut up in one room all those months, my legs were wobbly, and I was blinded by the sunlight.

"Zhou Hong, take it a little slower," I said. "I can't keep up. I'm sorry, but my legs feel like cotton and I'm still shaky."

She shot me a cold glare over her shoulder and forged ahead, no slackening in her pace. This was really a bitter blow and I began tearing profusely. I beat on my legs and scolded them. "Why are you so worthless!"

Finally, I managed to hobble over to the office.

A group of stone-faced strangers waited for me there. I didn't know which "outside unit" these people were from, and they didn't tell me. As in the hotel, they sat in a row and I had to stand before them during the interrogation. They asked me similar questions about what organizations and individuals Sidney had been in touch with for his "espionage." They were not attacking me but looking for hard evidence about Sidney.

All I could say was, "I know nothing about what he was doing. I was living at the university for six years. I came home just one night a week."

They frowned with displeasure at my answers and criticized me for "not having drawn a line between Sidney and myself," and for a "bad class attitude."

After hours of interrogation, I returned to our room, feeling down and disparaged. But my girls had big smiles on their faces.

"Look, Mama! They let us go back to get our quilts!"

"And they promised to move over your sewing machine, too."

"You won't believe it! Look at this!" Sunny proudly held out a flowerpot with long green stems—our amaryllis plant. "No blossoms, but it's still alive!"

"And nobody watered it for eight months!"

None of us could believe it.

"But we have bigger news," said Jenny, with a joyful smile.

"We went to see Grandpa!" Sunny said, with a sparkle in her big round eyes.

"He's fine," added Jenny.

"And you'll never guess who is staying at his place!"

The girls were nearly jumping out of their skins. Even Little Ming was grinning.

"Grandma!" they shouted.

My heart lifted. "Really? Did you see her?" I asked.

"We did!" said Toni. "She came back from Shijiazhuang and has been asking about us. When she saw us, she wept and gave us big hugs. Do you believe it?"

This good news brought tears to my eyes. "How is her health?"

"She looked great!"

A burden was lifted from my shoulders. Mama was fine.

The next morning I asked permission to visit my mother and father, but my request was denied. However, no one stopped the children from slipping over there. I could imagine how delighted my mother was to gather them in, like a mama bear. I hoped she was feeding good food to Little Ming. With the image of them happy together, I decided I could handle whatever political rubbish was thrown at me.

Chapter Twenty-Seven

Into the Frying Pan

AFTER TWENTY YEARS of loyalty, I did not give up my Party membership. But according to Party rules, if you don't take part in activities for half a year, or pay your dues, you are no longer a member. Because I had not been able to attend Party functions after Sidney's arrest in 1968, I was no longer a member. Worse, I was treated as a traitor.

Over the next few weeks, I had to report to the office every morning for interrogation by some group or another. I can't remember how many units came to question me, but there were many. Every factory or office or school where Sidney had spoken or made any connection sent someone to question me. They all suspected that some of their people could be spies who had leaked internal secrets to Sidney. My job was to help them collect evidence to use against their own people. But I couldn't satisfy any of their demands.

Regardless of whether interrogations were scheduled, Radio leadership demanded that I arrive at the office every morning at eight. But with four children and no help, this was a problem. Initially, I explained that arrangements still hadn't been made for my three children to go to school, and there was no one to take care of my son.

The man in charge of the English section spoke gently at first, but was anxious to make himself look good to others. "What do you mean, 'problems with the children'?" he said. "Just send them to school and show up promptly at the office."

"But I have a two-year-old," I explained.

"Lock him up in the room," the man insisted.

"What? I live on the fifth floor. He isn't big enough to be alone all day. He doesn't know what to do. He can't take care of himself."

He scowled at me. "This isn't our problem. Just leave him in the room! I'm telling you, you must report to the office tomorrow morning at eight! That's a must!"

Then I lost my temper and shouted at him. "I can't do that! Suppose the baby falls from a window and dies! Are you going to take the responsibility? My baby can't even talk yet!"

Without another word, the man swept out of the room.

I went home in tears. As I walked along the street, passersby looked at me askance. I heard some of them say, "Look! That's Li Dunbai's wife." Some of them picked up little pebbles and threw them at me, snarling, "American spy's wife!"

One of them called me "dog-spy's wife!" This was the first I had heard this. In China, the word "dog" is often used in the sense of "dirty dog"—a generic insult. So this was to be my identity. Steeling myself against the hecklers, I went to a nearby school and enrolled the girls in their proper classes, as if they had not missed months of schooling. They would be day students this time, living at home in our tiny room. The next morning, after I saw the girls off, I took my son to work with me. Since my work pass had long ago been confiscated, I had to wait at the gate guardhouse for someone to take me to the office. Standing in the freezing rain, my little boy was miserable.

While I was waiting there, I burst into tears and told the guard my troubles with taking care of the children. It turned out that he had known my father, and—quite unexpectedly in those days—he was sympathetic. "You can't take the child to the office," he said. "But go talk to the military management group."

I took the baby home again, thinking hard. I needed Mama's help.

So I phoned the military management group and made two proposals. First, I asked them to accept my son into the Radio nursery school, which was low cost and close to home. And second, until my son was actually attending the nursery school, I asked that they allow me to take him to my mother, who would care for him.

They agreed to let Jenny take her little brother to my mother's temporary residence until he could start nursery school. But I was not allowed to see my father or mother; still less were they allowed to come to my home.

In this way, by fits and starts, we pieced together new routines as a family.

≈

At the office, I faced repeated interrogations by groups from different schools and factories. They weren't allowed to go to the prison to question Sidney—most of them didn't even know where he was—so they considered me their best hope for uncovering useful material. I studied their tactics, and my answers were more or less the same. I would explain that I didn't know what had been said at their factories or schools; I hadn't taken part in Sidney's conversations or even heard his speeches. I had been a Red Guard myself.

Sometimes people would come from a factory to ask about a specific worker. Often this person was a friend of Sidney's whom I remembered very well. But still I would answer that I didn't know or couldn't remember. How could I bring trouble down on somebody's family just because they had spoken with Sidney or heard one of his speeches? Why should I get anyone in trouble by colluding with these people? They could shout and curse all they liked, but I refused to fall into that trap. Implicating innocent people wasn't fair!

So my questioners failed every time. And every time they would roundly upbraid me. I tried to keep cool by reminding myself that they were gathering evidence for their own purposes. They were not attacking me personally. But the more they pushed, the more painful their taunts became.

Once, a group of rebels from the Number Two Machine-Building Plant, where Sidney had friends, questioned me, aiming to find out what secrets their workers might have told Sidney about their plant.

"You are Li Dunbai's wife?" one of them asked.

"Yes."

"Now, Li Dunbai is a spy, and you should draw a clear line between you and him. You can't fail to stand on the people's side just because he's your husband."

I was silent.

"Li Dunbai is a very slippery spy. He's been in China for such a long time, and he's been in contact with all kinds of people all over the place. Tell us, who has he talked to at our plant, and what did they talk about?"

"I don't know. He was in touch with so many people, and I didn't ask him who he contacted every time. That was his business, and I never meddled in it."

Someone called out, "You're not willing to talk, is that it?"

"It isn't a matter of whether I'm willing."

"Then why won't you tell us which of our Chinese secrets he got out of the people he talked with?"

"I have no way of knowing. I only poured tea for the guests. I didn't join in their conversations. I had my own work, and I had four children to take care of."

"We hear that you're a veteran cadre, too—a Party member for many years. You should be able to consider the interests of the Party and the people, to change your stance, to come over to the side of the people. Don't conceal anything for an American spy! What do you say, Comrade Wang Yulin, isn't that right?"

Zhou Hong, who was auditing this session, suddenly jumped in with vehemence. "Why do you call her 'Comrade'? She's a spy, too!"

My head spun. Tears came streaming down. I had never dreamed that I would be suspected of being an enemy agent!

"What are you crying about?" said Zhou Hong. "Huh? Do you think your tears can wash away your guilt?"

With the wind knocked out of me, I said, "I don't know what they're talking about." My brain was in such a state of confusion that I could no longer look into any of the faces; I didn't even hear any of the other questions that were thrown at me. As I stumbled home, I lost awareness of time. My heart was full of a terrible feeling of being wronged, and there was no one to help me carry this load, no one to tell my troubles to. They say wormwood has a bitter taste; I would rather have eaten wormwood than endure that kind of insult and humiliation.

At that time, anything or anyone related to the United States was judged as despicable—including my family. Even worse for us, Sidney was notorious because his case was a big one. He had, after all, been the chairman of the leading group at the Central Broadcast Administration. Add to this the fact that our children's faces are different from Chinese faces—especially my son's. He doesn't look Chinese at all. When he was a child, he looked like Sidney when Sidney was young—very handsome. So my kids were often targets of contempt. When people passed by in the street, they might shout at them or throw little stones. Of course, the neighborhood kids listened to their parents, who told them that Little Ming was the American spy's son. Having no understanding of their own, the kids just mimicked their parents, saying, "Look! It's the little American spy!"

One day Little Ming came home crying. He was not really talking enough yet to tell me what happened, but I could see some bruises. I was alarmed that he couldn't stop crying. I asked him, "What happened? Who beat you?" He could only say "sister," and he pointed up at the next building where the neighbor family lived.

Extremely upset, I marched over to the next building and found the bully before I got to their door. It was a little girl of seven or eight, who was much bigger than three-year-old Ming. I clutched both her arms and shouted at her, "You dare not beat my little son—not ever again! If you do, I'm going to beat you! You understand?" She was shocked and frightened. As soon as I let go of her, she ran home as fast as she could. You cannot blame the kids, but at least I scared her into leaving my son alone.

I picked up Little Ming and took him home, but I was so distraught that I couldn't stop my own tears. This boy was only three. I had never told him who his father was, hoping to prevent his little spirit from being hurt. Only two years old when Sidney had been arrested and taken to prison, Ming had no memory of what had happened; in fact, over time he lost any memory of his dad. Since my little boy had never known his father's love, I paid special attention to pouring loving care on him. I was constantly anxious about his health because he was undernourished and skinny. And now he was being beaten!

Meanwhile, the pressure at the office was getting to me. Often, during the interrogations, I would become enraged to the point of tears. How could a girl who'd been liberated by the PLA, who completely believed in the Communist Party and had conscientiously worked hard all those years, actually end up being vilified as a spy? Being cursed and bullied every day? It was outrageous! My head felt like it was exploding.

At home, I hid my tears. I would look at Chairman Mao's portrait and silently tell him my troubles. "Chairman Mao, Chairman Mao! Why do they treat me like this? When are you going to speak out, to speak justly on my behalf?"

Sometimes I would stand on the little fifth floor balcony and think about jumping to end it all. In the political movements of the past, there were many people who took that fatal leap to escape their suffering.

No! I told myself. *I cannot! What would become of my four children? Their father is accused of being a spy, and their mother would be labeled with the crime of "suicide brought on by guilt." The children's futures would be totally destroyed; they would be marked for life.*

I had to go on living! The only path I could take was to fight for survival, no matter how hard it got. In my mind's eye was the image of our amaryllis. During our eight months of detention, no one had been there to care for it. Yet once we started to water it again, it produced four brilliant red blossoms—like my four bright children. Like our amaryllis, I would survive. I would keep fighting, no matter what, for our exoneration, for our children's future, for the truth.

Chapter Twenty-Eight

Dog-Spy's Wife

EARLY ONE MORNING, as the winter winds blew, I was the target of a criticism and struggle meeting in the English section office. When I opened the door, those gathered at the meeting shouted in unison, "Down with Li Dunbai! American spy, Li Dunbai!"

Posters with slogans in huge characters were hung all around the room, saying "Down with American spy, Li Dunbai!" and "Lenience for confession, harshness for resistance!" Also, "The only way out is to confess!" The desks were pushed to the sides of the room, and people from other sections had brought in their chairs and teacups to crowd into the English section office. These were my coworkers, including people Sidney had patiently trained for many years. Zhang Wenxiu, in charge of the meeting, gleamed with pleasure in his role as tyrant. He harshly told me to stand facing the crowd and to bow my head like a criminal.

He announced to everyone, "Li Dunbai was already an American spy back in the Yan'an years. And not an ordinary spy, but a strategic spy!"

He and other speakers demanded that I confess that I had a "spy relationship" with Sidney. With my head bowed, I thought, *How am I going to confess to that? I don't even know what they mean. ? But if I don't do that, they won't let me pass.*

Mostly, they didn't give me a chance to respond, but I did answer one question.

"Is it true that Li Dunbai donated all your precious Ming Dynasty yellow rosewood furniture to the ancient Palace Museum—just before the Cultural Revolution began?"

"Yes," I said. "That is true."

"Did Li Dunbai have advance notice of the Cultural Revolution?" they asked.

"I don't know." Sidney had already been asked this question when he was under house arrest, before going to prison, so I knew that some people suspected him for this reason—although how it proved he was an American spy was a mystery to me. Aside from this, I had no answers to any of the other questions, which made them unhappy.

One woman shrieked at the top of her lungs, "Stinking wife of Li Dunbai! Confess!"

A lanky young man shouted, "Drop those 'Madam Foreign Expert' airs, and tell the truth!"

"Just tell us the facts. Stop lying!"

"Surely you helped him collect information that he passed along to the American imperialists!"

"Down with Wang Yulin!" one person shouted.

"I know nothing," I said. Perhaps my lifelong stubbornness helped me at that moment.

Then one woman yelled out, "Do you dare to write a statement, guaranteeing that what you have stated is all you know?"

I said, "Yes, I dare." With that, I picked up a pen.

Then they all shouted repeatedly, "Down with the dog-spy, Li Dunbai!"

Instead of being frightened, I was full of rage at this sort of meeting, where I wasn't allowed to speak on my own behalf. *I haven't committed any crime*, I told myself. *I haven't done anything against the people. I am not a counterrevolutionary. Why should I have to bow my head and accept their judgments? This is not Communist Party policy. They are defying discipline and authority.*

I don't know where the courage and the strength came from, but I jabbed my pen to the paper and began to write my guarantee.

This seemed to catch them by surprise and make them angrier. They screamed out their slogans again and again, "Down with the American spy, Li Dunbai! Lenience for confession, harshness for resistance! The path of resistance ends in death!"

I was then escorted back to my seat in the office. Defiance, I discovered, felt better than tears. But after several such sessions, even that small victory tasted bitter.

≈

Frankly, it hurt more to see my family punished than to go through it myself.

My dear father, now retired, lived in a little neighborhood of mud-brick huts, tucked away like a forgotten interlude among new office and apartment buildings. His landlord, who lived in the same compound, belonged to a little sect called

"Yi Guan Dao" who worshipped Guan Gong, the ancient god of war. The man's daughter was a factory worker and my father used to teach her to play chess.

When Sidney was accused of being a spy, some of the neighbors suspected that my father was a secret messenger for Sidney—since he frequently came over to our home in the Foreign Experts Building.

"He's old and retired; he has nothing to do," they said. "That's why he took up this work, delivering spy messages."

Actually, he used to come to our place every Saturday to bring the girls home from school and take them back again on Sunday. The three of them would sit on the seat, the rear fender, and the handlebars of his bicycle, while he pushed it to deliver them safely home. As they went, he would tell them stories from the ancient Chinese chronicles of heroes and heroines.

Many years later I found out that during the Cultural Revolution, the neighborhood committee from his little community organized struggle meetings against my father, demanding that he confess to the spy relationship with Sidney. My father took pride in his honesty. He could never bring himself to give in to pressure and say things that he knew were untrue. He would not say a word against his American son-in-law, no matter how hard they were on him. When his neighbors pressured him, all he would say was, "My son-in-law is a good man. He's not a spy!"

They smashed a bunch of bowls into sharp little pieces and made him kneel down on a washboard covered with the shards. After kneeling for a long time both legs were swollen and covered with blood. Even ordinary neighbors took part in torture in those days. At seventy-three, Papa already had chronic bronchitis, but the neighborhood committee forced him to move out of his little hut with its coal briquette stove. They shut him up in a dark room with no heat; he had to sleep on the cold earthen floor. His legs swelled up even more. Still, they forced him to sweep the streets every day, even in the winter.

My father was an unpretentious working man, proud of his skills but humble in his dealings with people. He carried himself with an air of simple nobility and was unfailingly kind to strangers. No matter how poor we were, no one asking for food was ever turned away empty-handed. This white-haired old man, as he swept the streets, was subjected to a steady stream of curses from passersby, who called him "Rotten!" and "Traitor!" and cast pebbles at him.

This lasted for almost six years, till 1974, when his area police outpost formally informed him that the criticism and struggle against him was mistaken.

His name was cleared. The conclusion drawn on his case read, "The charges that Wang Hanqing was a spy messenger were unsubstantiated, and neither is he a bad element."

After that, my father returned to Shijiazhuang to live with my elder brother. But his health was ruined. He could hardly walk after what he had been subjected to. Soon afterward, he passed away. After a lifetime of honest labor and good deeds, he came to that unhappy end. And there was nothing I could do about it. I wasn't even allowed to go to his funeral. In those days, tragic stories like this were common. But that didn't make them any easier to bear.

≈

As for me, the pressure kept growing, week by week. At first, each time an interrogating group would finish with me, some painful burden would be added to the growing pile weighing on my heart. Finally, I recognized that what was happening to me was mental torture. I knew I should just put my head down and power through it, but it was too hard. My nervous tension grew until I couldn't sleep and had no appetite. I became very irritable. I felt that I had no place to express my feelings; everything had to be held inside.

The more the pressure increased, the more I missed my husband. Dear Sidney! I didn't know where he was. I had no idea how he was. I yearned to have him at my side so I could tell him all my sorrows. When would these painful, seemingly endless days of suffering come to an end?

Now I knew how others felt when they had been wrongly accused during the Anti-Rightist Movement and other political campaigns. Driver Guan. Deputy Director Wen Jize. Marshal Chen Yi. How had we let our beloved Communist Party commit such outrages? And why were there no reasonable leaders who could straighten it out again? Surely Chairman Mao would be furious if he knew what wrongs were being done in his name! And where was Premier Zhou, who had helped me once? Couldn't someone stop the madness?

I could only tell my troubles, silently, to the skies.

Sometimes, after the children were asleep, I would lie in bed weeping silently. People say that if you miss someone really badly they will appear to you in a dream. How I hoped that I could catch sight of my husband when I closed my eyes! But heaven was without mercy.

I began to believe in what the old folks used to say, that some people were just destined for a "bitter fate." Had heaven put me on the bitter fate list? Was it because I didn't worship Buddha? Were the children of the Wang family doomed

174

to tragic outcomes?

My first sister was widowed at age nineteen, when her opium-addicted husband froze to death on the streets of Beijing.

My second sister died after being raped by a Japanese army officer.

My third sister's husband was imprisoned for three years soon after their wedding.

And now, me—the youngest daughter. Was I, too, about to become a widow?

My parents had never gotten along, from the day they were married—always quarreling. I hated that kind of family friction. I had made up my mind that I would find a man whom my heart loved, and we would live together in love and caring right into old age.

As a result, from our wedding right up to the time Sidney was arrested, my husband and I always found a way to smooth over any differences we had. Everyone called us a good couple. I had always felt fortunate about my marriage and my family. And I loved my husband dearly. Why was my sweetheart taken as a "spy," and why was I labeled a "spy's wife"—when these charges were patently untrue?

Every time I stood back, desperate for perspective and a sane place to stand, I wound up exhausted, in grief, and holding onto one last question: Why was life so unfair?

Our situation was a riddle, and no one knew when or how it could be solved.

Chapter Twenty-Nine

Bitter Winter

NOW THAT I had been labeled a "dog-spy's wife," I was deprived of all citizens' rights, stripped of my Party membership, and listed among the "enemies of China." Shortly afterwards, in December 1968, my case group placed me with people they called "counterrevolutionary elements." They demanded that I write self-criticisms because I was supposedly wrong not to expose Sidney's alleged anti-China activities. All my normal activity was suspended. I was not allowed to take part in any meetings, except for meetings to struggle against other counterrevolutionaries—where, presumably, I might learn something.

Every morning, before we began writing our statements, we were required to stand before a portrait of Chairman Mao to confess our crimes and beg for forgiveness. "I didn't listen to your teachings, Oh Ancient One! I believed in false rumors and, in fact, helped the enemy. . ." and so on. At the end, we had to say, "I admit my guilt, and I will correct myself in the future." Likewise, before going home every afternoon, we would have to stand before Chairman Mao's portrait and repeat the recitation.

Before long I was separated from the others and placed "on exhibition" in the corridor. At the door to the women's restroom, I was placed on a stool before a little square table. A long scroll ran horizontally on the wall behind me that said, "American Dog-Spy's Wife!" The verticals on either side read, "Lenience for confession; harshness for resistance!" and "Holding out to the end is the road to death!"

The bathroom door faced the staircase, and everyone who passed by glared at me with contempt. A number of the foreign experts came over to watch. Aside from Sidney, all the foreigners who worked for Radio Peking had been spared, no matter what their class backgrounds were. Most of them had stayed out of the factional infighting.

My heart was boiling with indignation. They were treating me like an animal, putting me on display for Chinese and foreigners to scorn! I would pretend to be reading—the only book I was allowed, *Quotations from Chairman Mao Zedong*—and kept my head down. But the corridor lights were so dim it was impossible to really read. I was sad. I was indignant. I was disappointed. But I knew in my heart that I had done nothing to let down my people or my ancestral homeland, nothing to deserve scorn. I would keep my dignity and let them get their fill of glaring at me! I would never again bow my head to them, nor would I shrink from their stares. I set my jaw, lifted my head, and looked around me when people walked by..

The disdain and disgrace, the shaming and shivering shone a different light on our eight months of confinement as a family. Crammed in that hotel room, I had at least been with my children, all day, every day. Now that we were "free," they could go to school and have a somewhat normal life. But I saw them only in the evening, and we were squeezed into an even smaller room. Before, we had not encountered public contempt, and now these slanderous spying charges were smeared in our faces daily. During the day, parked under that libelous label, "American Dog-Spy's Wife," I tried to direct my mind back to those days in the hotel room, when I had wept so often. I remembered with nostalgia how the kids giggled when they ran into each other, chased a bird, and sang revolutionary songs at the top of their lungs.

My seat in the corridor was subject to cold drafts from the icy winds outside. Lacking winter clothing to keep myself warm, I would sit there trembling; I was not permitted to return to my original home and get my heavy clothing.

Then I had an idea. I asked my case group to let me do some physical labor, like sweeping the corridors. I knew I needed to get up and move around to keep warm. Otherwise, sitting there, without moving, for eight hours a day would have ruined my health. Fortunately, they agreed.

While I was stationed in the corridor, two of the Foreign Broadcast Department's senior editors, Hu Ruomu and Lu Ye, were seated similarly in the doorways of their offices, which were along the same corridor. When they saw that I was allowed to get up and sweep the floor, they asked for the same rights, and they were able to get up and move around as well. Unlike me, the two of them were fortunate to have sufficient winter clothing.

With the three of us all sweeping away, to keep warm, we undoubtedly had the cleanest corridor in the entire State Broadcasting Administration. I was more agile than they were; I could sweep once every hour. When my feet would begin to freeze sitting at my table, I got up and swept the floor.

Aside from sitting on exhibition, I would frequently be taken away for interrogation. My case group would assign me questions about Sidney, and I was to write my answers as statements. I was also to write about how I saw Sidney's character, my estimate of him as a person.

Every time this happened, I felt severely troubled. I had no evidence of espionage to write about and I didn't know who his contacts were. I would think, *Oh, please, Sid! Can you tell me in a dream? What were you talking about when you met with those people?*

When I couldn't supply the information the interrogators were seeking, they would scold and curse me. "You turtle's egg!" they called me—an ugly Chinese insult equivalent to "bastard." "What a disgrace to the Chinese People! No shame! You can't even draw a line to separate yourself from an American secret agent!" they would say.

Zhang Wenxiu was especially harsh. "You know very well the answers to our questions. You just don't want to talk! Turtle's egg! Don't imagine you can get by like this. Change your stance! Come over to the side of the people, and give a clear account of Li Dunbai's crimes!"

Once, when my case group demanded that I give evidence, they waved a stack of papers in front of me, saying, "Look—Li Dunbai has already confessed to all this."

A surge of hope washed through me. Was this really Sidney's handwriting? Was he alive? But then my heart sank. Had he made a false confession, just to get more lenient treatment? Had they been torturing him?

My interrogators continued. "See? You'd better come clean! Don't try to play tricks on us. We know what you've been up to! We know it all. The question is whether you confess it yourself and take this opportunity to admit your guilt. But if you wait until we have to produce evidence against you, you'll regret it!"

I felt nothing but deep resentment in the face of their threats. I had participated in so many movements—although I had never been a victim before. That bunch of papers they brandished at me couldn't possibly be Sidney's confession of spy activities. If they had the evidence they needed, they wouldn't have to try to force me to talk. Instead, they would have used details from Sidney's so-called confessions to make me talk. But they could produce nothing. They were the ones playing tricks, but they were only deceiving themselves. My unsatisfying responses made them shout louder, and unfortunately, also caused them to make life harder for my family.

I told them, "You say that Sidney has confessed? I know nothing about his activities. You talk to him about that, not to me."

One day, as I walked home, after another miserable interrogation, I saw a commotion ahead. A man had jumped from the top floor of our building and killed himself. I rushed to see who it was: Hu Maode, from the Central News Department. Because of his earlier affiliation with the Democratic League, he had been labeled a class enemy.

"See!" Someone in the crowd said. "This is proof that he was a spy!"

"How?" I asked.

"Look! See how his body compressed into such a small spot? He must have jumped headfirst. That's why you can't see his whole body. That shows he was trained in how to commit suicide."

It was tragically ridiculous logic, but no one protested.

≈

The interrogations dragged on in the midst of Beijing's bitter cold winter, with the Northwest winds howling in from the Mongolian desert. I had no money to buy winter clothing for the children. My son, especially, was wearing his big sister's shoes, which were much too big for him. When I asked to return to our old home to get clothes for them, my former colleagues shouted at me angrily. "Why can't you draw the line against Li Dunbai! The things in your old home were all bought with his money. Are you really so poor that you can't afford shoes for your son? You want to go back to get those clothes? That's out of the question! You can't take anything from there."

I argued with them. "You can't say that everything in our home was bought with Li Dunbai's money. Though we never separated our incomes, I have been earning my own salary. It's shameful to say that all our property belongs to him!"

The injustice in this world! They wouldn't listen to my economic needs, wouldn't even let me get clothes for the children. And why? Did they think my children could be spies? At three years old, how guilty could my little boy be? If they were innocent, why did they have to suffer?

"Your money!" they sneered at me. "How much money could you have? We told you that you can't get those clothes, and that means *you can't get those clothes*. See how low your level of consciousness is!"

After repeated struggles like this, and after numerous letters to the Military

Control Committee, they finally consented to let Mama come to our place in the daytime. This relieved part of the heavy burden on me. But my monthly salary of 87.50 yuan was not nearly enough for the family's expenses.

One day, when I went to pick up the grain ration coupons for the family, they told me that the coupons for my little son had been canceled. I marched into the office of Zhang Wenxiu, the liaison for the English section. "What happened to my son's ration tickets?"

"You should know why he doesn't get any," he snarled back. "You conspired with the American spy Li Dunbai to have the child registered as a U.S. citizen! And you dare to ask about his grain coupons?"

"What? That's not true! All the children were properly registered at birth." After all four births, I had taken the hospital records to the Foreign Experts Office, which was supposed to issue birth certificates and keep them on file.

"Don't pretend. You must confess why you and Li Dunbai had your son registered as an American citizen. What were you plotting?"

"Plotting? That's a ridiculous story."

"It's not ridiculous. We have looked it up in the records. I tell you plainly: there'll be no coupons for him, and that's that. You should make an honest confession!"

I don't know where I got the courage from, but I snapped back at him.

"Why won't you listen to reason? There are no diplomatic relations between the United States and China! There isn't even an American embassy in Beijing. For years, my husband has not been allowed to correspond with his family. How could I possibly make my son an American citizen? That's impossible! Don't you even know that?"

"You watch your attitude, you! Don't forget what you are—the wife of an American spy! Spy's wife—understand?"

Our arguing had attracted a circle of spectators. Some of them were saying in low voices, "Wow, Wang Yulin is being so strident!" Others said, "Doesn't she see what will happen if she stands up to him at this point in time?" Still others gave me nasty looks and drifted away. There was not a friendly or even neutral face among them.

When I went home and told the children about this argument, the three girls were very angry. Our oldest, Jenny, said, "Mama, maybe they never really registered the birth of my little brother."

Could she be right? Could I have forgotten to do so? I didn't know what to do. It had been hard enough to get back the grain coupons for the three girls. This was because the police outpost that issues the coupons said that we had not been registered for over two years. I had sent the children to register with the outpost as soon as we got out of confinement at the hotel, but the police refused to accept their registration, saying that we had delayed too long.

Finally, I had asked for help from Sidney's case group in the Ministry of Public Security, and they made the outpost register the three girls. But they hadn't included our son. Perhaps the girls were right and the Foreign Experts Building had failed to register Little Ming. Perhaps they had lost his birth certificate.

The upshot was that there were grain rations for only five people, and six people had to live on those rations. That included Mama's rations, although I was never allowed to see her.

When the girls went out to buy vegetables, they couldn't afford anything on display but had to go for the bundles of the cheapest cabbage that was tied up and left on the floor, for ten fen each. The bundles contained lots of rotten cabbages together with the good, so that I'd have to sort through them at home. But at least there were some edible ones among them. Though it was better than the edible weeds I had eaten as a child, wasn't life supposed to be better after Liberation?

The children, raised in relative comfort, had to learn to separate the good cabbage from the bad. For the first time in their lives, they felt constant hunger pains. Since they weren't getting fat in their diet, they were eating more grain, which meant that Mama, like me, didn't dare eat her portion. Meat was out of the question, but I was able to use some leavings from rendered lard. I did sewing in the evenings for people who didn't know how to use a sewing machine, and in exchange, they gave me some of the leavings from the fat they rendered at home. I would mix some of this in with chopped cabbage and stuffed steamed buns for the children. The only time I had to chop the vegetables was in the evening, after I came home from work. The whole next day's food had to be prepared the night before. However, the sound of my chopping disturbed the neighbors. They were a good young couple from the technical department, but they complained when the noise kept them from sleeping. After that, I would chop as lightly as I could to keep the noise down. It took a long time, so it was often one in the morning before I could go to bed.

Then there was the problem of economizing on clothing. I could redo the older girls' clothes for a younger one. But my poor little son had nothing to wear except his sisters' hand-me-downs, so that he never had an item of boy's clothing.

On top of that, Mama had a weak heart and high blood pressure, and now I had to pay for all of her health care because we were no longer on the public health program. I had to pinch every penny in order to get by.

Short of grain rations and short of money, I took the only action I could think of: I stopped eating breakfast. As a result I often felt dizzy and unsteady on my feet when I took up my cold seat by the women's restroom and later swept the drafty corridor.

＝

Several months later, I was reassigned to clean the carpets that lined the long corridors of the Broadcast Administration. I was one of a group of five accused counterrevolutionaries assigned to this task: Yang Zhaoling, Hu Ruomu, Lu Ju, Lu Ye, and me. The others were older men, many of whom had joined the revolution when the Communist Party was still headquartered in the caves of Yan'an. Some had been born into wealthy families but gave up everything to join the Communists. At Radio they had risen to high positions, in charge of major departments in the Chinese-language national and international news. Now they were accused of being class enemies.

Installed ten years earlier, the carpets had never once been cleaned. We had to carry them out into the courtyard and beat the dust out of them. It was the coldest season of the year in Beijing. People who stuffed their feet into their cotton-padded winter shoes would stamp and complain of the cold. I couldn't afford to buy winter shoes, so I was working in ordinary cloth or bast summer shoes, which were no protection at all.

In the courtyard, we hung the heavy carpets on wooden poles suspended between big trees, with one of us sitting on the end of the carpet to keep it from sliding off, while the others pounded it with long sticks. The dust would rise in clouds and settle down on us, especially on the person who had to sit on one end. We would rotate that unsavory job, because whoever did it turned into a "Dust Man." I would come home with my hair full of dust. As I couldn't afford to use enough fuel to heat up water to wash my hair out every day, I contracted infections behind both of my ears.

One day, when it was my turn to sit on one end of the carpet, a member of the case team saw me and dragged me to the office. He accused me of slacking while others were doing the work. "You think you're still Madam Foreign Expert?" he said.

I was furious. "Do you think sitting on the carpet is easier than beating the carpet? Is that what you think?"

"Watch your attitude!" he warned me. "You're doing transformation-through-labor, so that you can understand your crimes!"

"I would much rather beat the carpets than sit there. That's the hardest job, and that's why we rotate it. If you don't believe me, go and try it yourself!"

I was trembling with rage, and the tears came pouring down.

"All right, go back to work. But I'm warning you, you're not to shirk your job."

That night, I unloaded my feelings to the girls, telling them about the incident and about how I suffered in the cold, wearing summer clothing and thin, lightweight cotton shoes. My good-hearted daughters told my mama about it. So from then on, without letting me know, Mama set about making me a pair of thick winter shoes. Little Ming was very small, but each day Mama took him out walking on the streets, picking up whatever rags they could find. They even searched through the garbage, looking for scraps of cloth. To make a pair of thick shoes, she added in some cotton padding, put small pieces of cloth on a wooden board, and glued them together with wheat flour mixed with water, like cornstarch. As Chinese have done for centuries, she laid down several layers of cloth, then let it dry. Then she took the board out and cut it into the shape of a foot, to make the sole of the shoe. It took days of careful work. My son learned how to spot and retrieve the smallest bits of rag, and he continued doing that for many years, whenever he went out on the streets. It reminded me of how I once picked things out of garbage cans in the Old Society. Who would have thought that my children would be doing the same thing?

The day my daughter brought me the padded shoes that my seventy-seven-year-old mother had made so painstakingly, I couldn't help weeping! This wasn't a pair of shoes; it was the sweat and blood of my mother. How I longed to see her! To see how many extra wrinkles had been added to her face, to notice how much hair she had lost! I hugged my little boy, kissing him again and again. These shoes embodied his work, too. They were the crystallization of love.

Chapter Thirty

Reform through Labor

ONE DAY IN April, just as the air was starting to warm and the buds were beginning to show on the trees, I was summoned before the secretary of the Party branch, who was in charge of everything at the Broadcast Administration at that time.

She said, "The leadership has decided to send you to the May Seventh Cadre School at Fangshan, to work hard and strengthen yourself. You will be there for one year."

These "schools" were named for a directive that military leader Lin Biao had issued on May 7, 1966, setting up camps in which office workers were supposed to be trained in the spirit of Communism. Their original purpose was to break up the capitalist division of labor, so that cadres could learn about working in a factory or on a farm. This way, they would understand and identify with workers and peasants, not with urban intellectuals and the bourgeoisie. At first, people would rotate by performing the tasks of workers, farmers, soldiers, students, and merchants. Through communal life, Marxist study, and manual labor, they were supposed to become well-rounded citizens of the new society. This was the stated objective; however, these collectives quickly turned into labor camps, including forced labor as punishment for "bad elements."

"When do I leave?" I asked, aware that as a class enemy, I had no choice. I had suspected this might happen and had been dreading it.

"Get ready to leave in one week—as soon as you make arrangements for the children."

Judging from the Party secretary's attitude toward me, I suspected they were planning to transfer me out of the State Broadcasting Administration and force me to labor on a farm, long term. Every person in China had a "residence permit" that allowed him to live and work in a certain neighborhood. Once a residence permit was transferred from the city to the countryside, it was almost impossible to get permission to move back to the city. This was a convenient way for an office to get rid of troublesome people. I dared to hope that a different arrangement might be made for me after Sidney's case was resolved. But I had no power to stop the transfer. They were watching me for signs of a bad class attitude. The best I could do was show them, by my loyal attitude and willingness to work hard, that I could learn from the workers and deserved better treatment.

I went home to prepare the children for this change. Not only did I have to explain to them about my new assignment, I had to guide them in how to stay safe without me. It was common in those days for children to be left to fend for themselves when both their parents were sent away—particularly in Beijing, where the jobs were most powerful and sensitive. The first thing I did was to patch all their torn clothing and talk to them about stepping up their studies.

Most important, though, I gave clear directions: if Radio leadership talked to them about going "down to the countryside," they should firmly resist. In December of 1968, Chairman Mao had announced this new initiative, and throughout the winter, thousands and thousands of high-school students had been sent away from their homes in the cities to live in rural villages. Sent "up to the mountains and down to the countryside," they were to learn from the workers and farmers, to better understand the struggles of the masses. Some, full of revolutionary fervor, were eager to go; others were reluctant but had no way out. I suspected it was a way to get troublesome, rebellious students out of the cities; of course, it also disrupted many families. From friends, I learned that the residence permits of these young people were transferred out of the city and to these villages, which would make a college education out of the question since it was unlikely they could return home. Although my children were too young to participate now, I suspected they might be sent anyway. I especially entrusted my eldest, Jenny, to make sure that all my children knew they should resist.

I put in a request to the Party branch asking them to let Mama come live full time with the children. Fortunately, they agreed. She would take excellent care of them while I was gone. That knowledge eased the pain of separation. I figured I could handle any kind of hard labor if I knew they were safe.

To help out, my second daughter Toni took Little Ming to nursery school every day and fetched him back in the evenings. A special bond grew between those two. Later, I found out, if the nursery school gave him two pieces of candy, he would bring one of them back for Sister Toni. If he got a piece of cake, he would bring her half.

Located in a rural area southwest of Beijing, the Fangshan May Seventh Cadre School was set up to benefit Broadcast Administration cadres who had been engaged in "mental labor," such as editors and translators. On a rotation basis, these people spent short stints at this camp where they performed physical labor, so they could better understand the typical life of Chinese workers and farmers. Sidney had once volunteered to plant apple trees on the same farm.

But as the Cultural Revolution continued, the Broadcast Administration began to use it also as a place for "labor reform" for "bad elements." I was in one of the first group of counterrevolutionaries, spies, and "persons in authority in the Party but taking the capitalist road" to be sent there for forced labor. In theory, we were supposed to learn a new attitude through hard labor, but in reality we were being punished. The regular cadres doing their stint in the camp were informed that we were class enemies, not to be addressed as "comrade," and that they were expected to keep their distance from us.

Even though I knew many of them personally, not one of them ever crossed that line to make the simplest gesture of friendship or goodwill toward me or any of my fellow counterrevolutionaries. Vastly different from our solemn ranks, the regular cadres were having a good time. So in effect, there were two very different camps being run there simultaneously.

The men in our group lived in a big shed near the headquarters. More than forty men slept side by side on the floor on heaps of straw rushes. I was quartered with six or seven other women in a peasant compound where we had a room to ourselves and a big kang to sleep on. Each person had enough space on the kang to put her bedroll. There was no stove in the room, so keeping warm depended on burning firewood, sometimes along with a bit of coal, in the kang. There was nothing else in the room, except for a square black table, the kind that peasants call an "eight immortals table" since it has room for two people on each side

Strict rules governed our lives. We were forbidden to make any contact with the peasants or to eat from their food supply. When we walked over to the "reform school" headquarters for our meals in the canteen, or to receive our work assignments, we had to go in groups of at least three; one or two people were not allowed to walk alone.

Even worse, I was not allowed to write letters to my children, and they were not allowed to write to me. I had no way of knowing if they were sick or healthy, sad or upset, or how Mama was holding up under the strain of my absence. Little

Ming's health especially worried me; he still wasn't growing as he should, and at age three he could say only a few words. I had never been separated from my children for so long, and on that first night and thereafter, I missed them like a severed limb.

The second day there, as we walked single file along the edge of the fields, carrying our bowls for food, one of my companions whispered, "Just look at us! We're like the exiles to Siberia in old Russia!"

"Right," I answered. And so we were—in ragged clothes, moving in long lines with rice bowls in hand, to get our rationed food. We spoke in whispers, lest someone hear us and report us. The snitch would be rewarded, and we would face struggle sessions.

On our first day of labor, we worked with unfired bricks, called "brick embryos." They were mud blocks, which would be sun dried and then baked in a kiln to become sturdy red bricks. I carried twelve brick embryos on my back, over a hundred pounds in weight—the same load carried by much stronger young men. I was the only woman singled out to do this heavy labor. I had no board to carry them on, no rope to hold them together. I had to steady the load by forming a platform with my arms beside my back and my two hands meeting behind my waist, straining my wrists.

Another job was to make adobe bricks, the first step in the process of brick-making. We would lay out wooden forms or molds on a piece of hard, level land. Two men, one on either side, would load the molds with a wet mixture of clay and sandy soil, sometimes containing grass. My job was to stoop in front of the mold and smooth the clay so the adobe bricks would be flat. When I finished smoothing down one set of molds, I would move backward to the next set of empty molds, sprinkle some dry earth on them, and start over again. I had to crouch in a frog-like stance and hop backward, never able to straighten up. The others making adobe bricks worked in teams, with one man shoveling the mix into the molds and the other smoothing it down. I was the only one who had to work two molds at once, with two men supplying the mix, one on each side.

I would smooth out the mix so the mold filled in evenly, and then move the double mold back one pace for a second filling. Stooping in this way, I would process over one hundred of these wet brick embryos in one hour. If I stood up to rest my back and legs, or to take a stretch, I was exposed to stern criticism, either from a supervisor or from one of the men in our work group, who wanted to earn favors by snitching on others—something that I could never bring myself to do.

After the molds were all filled, we would stack them up, about four and a half feet high, being careful to leave air space between them. We would leave them out to dry in the sun for three days until they were ready for the kiln. This was exhausting, back-breaking work, but it did help take my mind off my family during the day. Just not at night.

Chapter Thirty-One

Into the Fire

MY BACK ACHED from the constant stress of crouching over those molds. But several weeks later, I was assigned to a job that strained my body beyond its physical limits—loading bricks into the kiln. There were over 130 of us counterrevolutionaries, but only nine of us were assigned to the kilns and I was the only woman.

When I got the assignment, I had no idea what I was in for. In China's villages, sturdy young men usually performed this kind of work. It was heavy work, and they were paid more than other rural workers. No villager would give this job to a thirty-seven-year-old mother.

To fire up the kiln required a high level of skill, so older and more experienced peasants managed the kiln. Each of the unfired bricks had to be placed in exactly the right position, with exactly the right space between them so that the fire would bake them evenly. The herringbone pattern in which they were placed was like the diagonal lines in a woven bamboo mat; everything had to be just right.

The raw bricks had to be stacked in that pattern, layer by layer, leaving little twisting corridors, like so many dragons, where the kiln firer could pass among the bricks. When the bearers of the bricks climbed up to place or retrieve them, they had to pass, snakelike, through these tiny corridors. One false step, and you could be killed under an avalanche of falling bricks.

Outside the kiln, the unfired brick embryos would be stacked up on a raised platform, ten to a load. I had to go over and stand, with bent back, in front of the platform. Then I would reach back and pull a load of ten bricks onto my back. Each load weighed about 110 pounds.

Then I would walk at a sort of trot about one hundred yards to the kiln, where there was another raised platform. I would back up to the platform and unload the bricks. I would then divide the bricks into two halves, about fifty-five pounds each, and carry each load on my back into the kiln.

Threading our way through the narrow corridors, nine of us would fill the kiln from top to bottom with the bricks, waiting to be fired. My legs would tremble as I climbed down through the narrow, twisting corridors, placing each brick carefully as I went. I knew that the slightest slip could be fatal. When I finished, the firer would start the fire, and the bricks would bake for one week. The kiln was in constant use. Every seven days, a new batch of bricks needed to be removed, and our crew would unload it.

Normally after firing, a kiln full of bricks would cool down for another week. Then the top of the kiln would be removed to refresh the air, and the bricks would be unloaded. But for us counterrevolutionaries, the top of the kiln was removed on the fourth day, before the bricks had properly cooled. Then we "who had serious political problems" were required to unload them while they were still hot.

To do this, we had to clear out the kiln quickly. We would start with the bricks at the top of the kiln, about the height of a three-story building, and trot down the circular winding corridors, out of the door, and over to the stacking grounds. I carried the bricks on my bent back, spread from waist to neck, using my hands to support the bricks. We were desperate to get those baking-hot bricks off our bodies, so we moved as fast as we could.

This meant that, compared to the loading process, I now made twice the number of runs back and forth to the kiln before reaching my rest time. It was fortunate that I had been an athlete in middle school and kept up my exercises all these years. Otherwise, I would never have been able to bear up under such heavy loads.

Every night, my whole body would ache from the day's work. The constant stooping under heavy loads was bad enough. But worse than that, the need to twist my wrists back to hold those heavy bricks in place left me with a permanently sprained left wrist—and a damaged lower back as well. These disabilities stayed with me for life.

Each evening, no matter how tired we were, we had to sit through political meetings and offer self-criticisms. We also studied news reports about the Ninth Party Congress in April 1969. I was relieved to read that the leaders had shifted their focus to rebuilding the Communist Party and the structures of state, which had been suspended during the chaos. But other news made me uneasy. Several of the people named to power were people who supported "continuous revolution" and violent class struggle, rather than a return to stability. China's former head of state, Liu Shaoqi, was denounced as a "renegade, hidden traitor, and scab" who was "plotting to restore capitalism." Lin Biao was named as the official successor to Chairman Mao and called Mao's "closest comrade in arms." I knew little about Lin Biao, except that he was a military leader and one of the ten marshals who had won the revolution. However, I trusted the People's Liberation Army, which had always been a force for good. Still, I felt anxious when I read about fighting with the Soviet army along the border; the papers were full of war fever. The American army was fighting a bloody war in Vietnam, too. I felt so helpless, at the May Seventh camp, unable to protect and comfort my children in the midst of such turmoil.

Each night, in bed after the meeting, I would stretch my back and cradle my wrists. Whatever was happening at the national level didn't ease my suffering. To escape the pain, I thought of my children. How happy they had been when they were released, and when they found their grandma! I tried not to worry, and I hoped they were doing well in school, after all those lessons I had given them during our detention.

~

Unloading the kiln in summertime was a nightmare. In the oppressive heat, we were running back and forth from the kiln with over one hundred pounds on our bowed backs. The young guys worked in shorts and bare chests. I wasn't free to wear less clothing like the men. All day long, my clothes were drenched in sweat. Even if I could have worn less clothing, I had nothing to put under the bricks, which would have burned my skin and scraped my back.

The quantity and quality of the food we were given was not nearly adequate for people doing this heavy physical labor. We got about four ounces of pork a week, but otherwise ate mostly cabbage and turnips. Each person received grain according to an individual ration; for me, it was less than a pound a day, served with steamed bread or rice. Every day, it felt as if my body burned far more calories than I was consuming.

Sidney had once told me about a famous European book, by Dante, that described nine layers of hell, each one with greater suffering. Looking back on my eight months of detention, followed by the bitter winter of torment, I felt I had entered a third layer here at the camp in Fangshan. How could I have found the previous suffering unbearable? At least I had been with my children. Sweeping floors and cleaning carpets had been so much easier than making and carrying bricks! This, I hoped, would be the last, lowest layer of hell. Under the fiery sun, bearing searing bricks, it felt like it. I truly could not bear anything worse.

Surely, this political campaign would end. Most movements had lasted only six months or a year; even the Great Leap Forward had ended in less than four years. Now, in 1969, the Great Proletarian Cultural Revolution had been raging for three years. I hoped it would burn itself out—before my body gave out.

Among us counterrevolutionaries, there were two overseas Chinese. One was from England; his Chinese was not very good, and he was suspected of being a British spy. The other was from South Africa. He had sold all his possessions and brought the money with him to China, responding to the Chinese government's call for overseas Chinese to come back and help build the country. Despite his personal sacrifice, the Cultural Revolution rebels labeled him a "capitalist," and so he ended up being punished with us.

These two men had come from overseas to contribute to the new China. And in a gross betrayal of their trust and loyalty, they were now categorized as traitors. It was hard enough for them to adjust to work in the Chinese countryside, but they couldn't stand being treated as enemies. The man from South Africa told me, "Before I came to Fangshan, they said that my case had already been cleared up. So why are they treating me like an enemy?"

The man from England asked, "What grounds do they have for investigating me as a spy?"

Seeking to be reasonable in the situation, I said, "But what can we do? We're sent here to labor, and we have no choice."

One of them said, "We've talked about it. There is something we can do. We're going to make our way back to Beijing!"

"What? Back to Beijing? How can you? They'd catch you and bring you back before you got very far. You know that we have no rights in this place."

"Just watch us!" they said. "We're going to do it. Come with us!"

I was shocked at their plans—and at their invitation to join them. "Thank you," I said. "Thank you so much for trusting me. But my situation is different. I couldn't possibly leave."

These men were as good as their word. The next day at noon, a great hubbub erupted near the center of the camp. The political instructor was shouting, "You cannot go back to Beijing!"

But these two argued. "Why can't we? Before we came here, it was announced that our cases had been cleared up. Why should we be put together with these people whose cases have not been cleared up? Why should we be treated like enemies?"

"Who's treating you like enemies?"

"You people are! We have no freedom here. The other people, the ones who are here for labor reform, are allowed to go back home once a month. Why can't we get one single day off from labor? Not even on weekends! We're going back to Beijing to appeal our treatment. There's no justification for it!"

"You can't leave here without word from the State Broadcast Administration!"

The British man, in his broken Chinese, shouted, "Turtle's eggs! You have no right to stop us from going back to Beijing!"

"Who are you calling turtle's eggs? You're not being reasonable."

The South African said, "Who's not being reasonable? It's you, that's who! Why are you holding us in confinement? Huh? We're under guard day and night. Even the windows in our big room are nailed shut! What kind of living quarters do you call that? Thirty or forty men sleeping in the same room, on damp floors—everyone is going to get sick! Don't you see that? We're being treated like prisoners! Is that a dormitory or a prison? And where are you people living?"

The British man said, "I'm telling you straight. We're heading back for Beijing right now!"

And as they spoke, they headed for the entrance to the camp.

"Stop! Stop! That's illegal. You can't leave!" the political instructor yelled at them.

"Excuse us, we're gone. Good-bye!"

The crowd of forced laborers witnessing the showdown didn't dare say anything. Everyone was waiting to see what would happen. The two brave overseas Chinese marched out of the camp and down the road, while the political instructor yelled helplessly at their departing backs.

As for the rest of us, we went back to our labor. But I felt that what they did was awesome. They dared to fight back! They spoke up for their rights!

At the same time, I knew that I couldn't take the kind of daring stand that they did. For one thing, Sidney had been fingered by Jiang Qing personally as an American spy. It seemed that everyone in China, from top to bottom, knew his name, Li Dunbai, and my name was associated with his. Also, I had four children and my aged parents to think of. If the Broadcast Administration cut off my meager wages, they would all be thrown out on the streets as beggars with no one to take care of them.

Even more important, the more I suffered, the more I wanted to see justice. I felt that our family had been deeply wronged. As long as there was breath in my body, I was determined to see it righted. My goal was not just freedom but full exoneration. Trudging along, with bricks on my back, I dared to dream: I would persevere until I saw our detractors bow down and apologize. That image brought a secret smile to my face.

Chapter Thirty-Two

Suspected of Friendship

BETWEEN BOUTS OF brickwork, sometimes we were assigned the task of pulling up weeds in the rice fields. I knew nothing about farm work, and I couldn't tell the difference between the rice sprouts and the weed sprouts. At first, I would bend over to do the weeding; then I tried stooping down; finally, I knelt down in the fields, moving slowly forward on my knees as I pulled up row after row of weeds. Crawling in the dirt, I recalled how this same Central Broadcast Administration, now punishing me for wrongdoing I never committed, had also paid for my college education.

On my knees, I moved slowly and with difficulty. A man way up ahead of me saw that I was in trouble and was falling behind the others. When he finished weeding his row, he started back from the opposite direction to help me finish mine. How thankful my heart was for his help!

"Thank you," I said when we met in the middle. "Without your help, I never would have finished in time."

"I grew up in the countryside," he said. "I know something about farm work. You're worn out, aren't you?"

I nodded. "I can't figure out which way is best—stooping, squatting, or kneeling."

Then he said, "Let me know when you're having trouble, and I'll do my best to help you."

My heaven! What a good man! This was the first helping hand that had reached out to me since I had become a target of struggle. And he was a perfect stranger. Grateful as I was, we were forbidden to talk to each other. I found out later that his name was Zhang Yunlai, and that he worked in Radio's technical department.

Once, not long after the weed incident, I was sent to turn over the sweet potato vines so that their tendrils wouldn't take root in the ground along which they lay. I tried to use a wooden pole to turn them over from one side to the other. Seeing that it wasn't going well, Zhang Yunlai came over to help. He took the pole from me and sharpened one end. Then he taught me an easier and faster way of using the sharpened stick to turn the vines over.

Because of this brief contact and the exchange of a few words with this good man, I was followed wherever I went. Every evening after work, we had a meeting at which people were supposed to expose improper behavior, and we were expected to make self-criticisms. At that evening's meeting, someone "exposed" me as having illicitly spoken with that man for some "clandestine purpose."

I argued back, angrily, but our team leader sternly scolded me. Some of the others chimed in, saying that I was having "illicit relations" with Zhang Yunlai.

"Wang Yulin, look at you! Don't you know who you are?"

"You tell me! Who am I?" I replied angrily.

"You are in serious political trouble. Your husband is an American spy—an international spy! Understand?"

These criticisms and attacks usually came from fellow workers who were trying to win brownie points from the leadership to get relief from the hard labor. I looked them straight in the eyes. What makes some people turn on their colleagues, while others reach out to help? We all had a choice. I aspired to be like Zhang Yunlai.

～

Our manual labor was hard; our mental life was harder. They were always having meetings, demanding that we write depositions and make confessions. They continued to pressure me to denounce my husband and admit he was spying for the United States. I had run out of creative ways to tell them I knew nothing about it, but I still had to keep writing the same things, over and over.

Among the women on our team, I had two friends. One was an overseas Chinese from Vietnam, Zeng Hong, whose nickname was "Little Round Ball." She had returned to China at age five, had joined the military as an adult, and had become a talented Vietnamese language radio announcer. She was accused of having "complicated social contacts."

The other woman, Liu Xia, had grown up in the Soviet Union. When she returned to China at age thirteen, she became an outstanding broadcaster in Russian. But she had very little Chinese language ability. Her husband was a researcher at the Nonferrous Metals Institute, but since he had been trained in the Soviet Union, he was also suspected of being a Soviet spy.

The three of us would manage to get together sometimes and say what was in our hearts. Mostly we talked about how we missed our families; sometimes we complained of unfair treatment. But this soon attracted attention, and a meeting resulted in which we were required to confess to "plotting counterrevolution."

Liu Xia was a brave, outspoken, straight-from-the-shoulder girl who would take up for anyone she thought was being wronged. Though her Chinese wasn't great, she had learned lots of popular Chinese expressions. She scoffed at the accusations that she was a "Soviet revisionist spy." She would say, "I've done what's right. Why should I be afraid of those turtle's eggs!"

I would counsel her not to cross swords with our critics, since it would do no good. But that was part of her personality, and she wouldn't take my advice. The result was that every criticism meeting against us would turn into a hot debate between Liu Xia and our critics. The critics did everything they could to pressure us into admitting to wrongdoing and confessing our "counterrevolutionary liaison activities," but this didn't bother Liu Xia at all. She would stand up and argue with them, toe-to-toe. I didn't have her courage, but I admired it. Unfortunately, because of the friendship that had developed between the three of us, our chances to be together were restricted, and we were given different work tasks to keep us apart.

Chapter Thirty-Three

A Week at Home

ACCORDING TO THE plan for the May Seventh Cadre Schools, participants worked in the labor reform program for one year. But after the first six months, all of us were sent back to our homes for one week only—in October—to prepare winter clothes for our children. After this one week at home, I was told I would have to return to Fangshan for another half year of hard labor.

How hard it was to be away from my kids for those first six months! I had never left them that long. With no letters or phone calls, I was eager to see them and find out if they had been sick or healthy.

All of us from Radio took a big bus from Fangshan to Beijing. When it came to a stop in the Broadcast Administration compound, I saw Toni and Little Ming. He was yelling, "Mama! Mama!" The children embraced me in big hugs. I picked up Ming and carried him. How he had grown! Toni talked about Ming's school and all the things her little brother had done.

Little Ming looked wonderful, and he could talk in full sentences! Aside from a few one-word utterances, it was the first time I had ever heard him speak! I was really excited and surprised. As we walked to our little one-room home, they talked to me nonstop, all about their school and their classes. I was comforted to hear Toni tell me about her marks in school, and her sisters'. In spite of everything, they were all in first or second place in their classes.

Jenny and Sunny came home from school and danced around the room.

"Mama, Mama!" Sunny announced. "The teacher says that I can skip a grade! The lessons you taught us are way ahead of what they've been doing!"

"That's what my teacher says too," said Jenny.

I was overjoyed. I had succeeded in my objective of teaching them; it hadn't been wasted effort! This gave them some protection from the insults.

But to them, I said, "You may be a little ahead of the class, but I think you should stay in your class and get a solid foundation."

"But Mama," Sunny said, "my teacher insists that I skip a class!"

"Well, if that's the way it is, then let the teacher decide," I said. "But remember—none of you must quarrel with any of the other children. Otherwise, they'll say that I'm not raising you well, and they'll worsen the struggle against me. Do you understand?"

"We know! We know!" they said in chorus.

"We never tell people that Papa is not a spy," said Jenny.

What great kids! What lovable kids! They understood from early childhood how to handle those complicated relationships. It brought tears to my eyes.

"Mama, why are you crying again?" Sunny asked. "Are you sad?"

"No, no," I said, with a little laugh, "I'm happy!"

Everybody joined in the laughter. I asked them how the other students treated them.

"Some of them call me a 'little American spy,'" said Sunny.

"I get so sick of the words, 'daughter of the American spy, Li Dunbai,'" said Toni.

"Some of them just ignore me and don't speak to me," said Jenny. "But when they have trouble with their homework, they ask me for help."

I thought about the daily persecution each of these kids had to handle. All it took was for one member of a family to come under suspicion, and the entire family would be under a dark cloud. Not only would the spouse be implicated—even the little children.

I asked myself what difference there was between this reality and the old feudal system, under which the whole family was executed if one member was found guilty of a crime. In feudal China, the emperors would sometimes punish a man by executing not only him but nine sets of relatives, including parents, grandparents, children, grandchildren, wife, siblings, and uncles—a practice called "nine kinship exterminations." In the New China, hadn't we rejected such primitive customs?

What did my family's treatment have in common with the basic principles of socialism? Nothing! Where was the fairness and decency that had so moved me and my family during the Liberation of my hometown?

With the Cultural Revolution, the pendulum had swung hard in the opposite direction. Gone was the original spirit of caring for comrades. Now everyone was concerned for his own safety. There was no open discussion of different political views, because people never knew when they might be accused of something or have their private conversations exposed. If they expressed doubt once, they might be severely punished, or even dragged out for struggle sessions, on the pretext that they had attacked the socialist system. People who were once good friends could become bitter enemies in the twinkling of an eye.

Why should this be? How could my beloved Communist Party, founded on ideals of justice for the downtrodden, have become so warped? How could Chinese people, steeped in centuries of Confucian teachings about honorable behavior and respect for others, have lost all sense of basic decency?

Dark clouds covered the sky. When would we see the sun again?

But that day, reunited with my kids, I learned that not everyone in China had lost a sense of fairness and kindness. My children told me about a few good people who, at the height of our suffering, had reached out a helping hand.

The most amazing was "Uncle Zhang," who had become a special friend while I was away. A young company commander of the garrison troops at Radio—someone we had never known, and whose full name we don't know to this day—had run into Toni buying food at our co-op store.

"Little girl, that isn't good cabbage that you're buying. You should buy some of this," he said, pointing to the fresh vegetables on the stand.

"We can't afford that in my family," said Toni.

Later that night, when everyone was asleep, he came tiptoeing to our door in the darkness and left a basket full of good, fresh vegetables.

After that, he would stop Toni on the street and take her to a little local restaurant for a meal, after which she would bring home a meat dish for her little brother. Toni and Ming often went out and played with him and the other PLA guards.

"What's his name?" I asked Toni.

"I don't know. I just call him 'Uncle Zhang.'"

In China, children are taught to address adults as "Uncle" and "Auntie," or "Grandpa" and "Grandma," depending on the generation—and to call older boys "Elder Brother" and older girls "Elder Sister," even if they are not related.

"He's a political instructor of the garrison company at Radio," Toni continued. "When Papa was here, we used to go play at their barracks. They all know us."

I was deeply moved. What a fine man! Uncle Zhang reached out a helping hand at our time of greatest hardship, knowing full well who we were, not afraid of being implicated in my case. I cautioned Toni not to tell a living soul about his help. She understood.

"Just yesterday," Toni added, "he invited me to go play at his home. He said he has a three-year-old daughter. Is it all right if I go?"

Uncle Zhang had told Toni that his wife worked at the Number Two Machine-Building Plant. She had just been elected vice-chairman of the factory's ruling body, the Cultural Revolution Committee. Their family lived in the Air Force compound at Xidan crossing, which was about a mile away.

"Yes, you can go," I said. "But don't let anybody else know, or we might get him in trouble."

"I know, Mama, I know," she replied firmly. Smart girl.

When Toni returned from her visit, she shared that Uncle Zhang's family lived with his father in the Air Force officers' compound, and that his father was a high-ranking officer. Their house was big with many rooms, and he even had a horse.

"Auntie is really nice," Toni explained about Uncle Zhang's wife. "She heard Papa speak once, and she asked me to comfort you and tell you not to worry. Sooner or later, Papa's case will be cleared up. She said you're carrying a heavy burden, and you need to pay attention to your health."

Toni went on, chattering excitedly. "And the Little Sister in their family is really fun. She's just three. Auntie takes her to the nursery school and brings her back on weekends. They have a nanny who's from the villages. Oh, and listen to this! Yesterday Uncle Zhang sent the nanny to the bank for some money, and she was robbed by some ruffians on the way home. That's why Uncle Zhang couldn't buy clothes for me. But Uncle Zhang said not to worry. After a time he'll figure out a way to buy us some new clothes."

"You can't let him spend money on you," I cautioned.

"I said no," said Toni, "but Auntie insisted that he get me some clothes. She said that I was welcome to play with Little Sister, and that she would bring her to our home sometimes, for us to take care of her when they were all out."

"That would be fine," I said. "There's nothing else we can do for them, but we can certainly take care of the child."

"And Uncle Zhang told me that they will take Xiaoming and me to a restaurant once a week, so that we can eat a good meal! He has a meal ticket, so that we wouldn't need money."

"That should be okay," I said. "I wouldn't worry, as long as you're with an uncle from the PLA. But remember your manners."

Then I knuckled down to the work at hand, preparing the kids' winter clothes.

Within that one week, I had to complete an amazing amount of work. I didn't have money to buy new clothes, but I could buy cloth. This I used to alter old clothing and sew new clothes. I used a sewing machine with a treadle that you moved with your foot; we called it a "step machine." So, with hour by hour of focused effort, I made sure that each of my children had decent clothes for the coming winter.

The other major task was washing their quilts. With the needs of all four children, I was so busy! But all too soon the week was over. I had to obey orders. Anyone who didn't return to Fangshan to finish out the year was severely punished.

≈

Back at the May Seventh school, I again faced all the different kinds of hard labor I had learned to do in the previous six months. As before, I had to spend most of my time doing brickwork. While the bricks baked in the kiln, we were given other tasks. A team of four—myself and three men—would pull a heavy stone roller over the young shoots of winter wheat. This kept the shoots from growing too tall and being killed by the winter frost.

Another roller was pulled by a horse. We were told that this old horse had given meritorious service in wartime and furthermore, had once been ridden by a Central Committee leader. Therefore, the horse had to be given fifteen minutes of rest out of every hour.

There was no such rest period for us.

One of the men on my team said, "We are 'counterrevolutionaries,' and this is called 'exercising dictatorship over counterrevolutionaries.'"

Another one asked me, "Wang Yulin, all the walking we're doing should be enough to make several round trips to Beijing, don't you think?"

And so it was. That's how far we were dragging that heavy stone roller.

All this heavy pulling produced inflammation in the heels of both my feet so that walking became very painful. Our doctor at the cadre school wasn't trained in orthopedics and didn't know how to give injections properly. Each time she gave me shots, the needle would pierce the bone itself instead of the spaces between the bones! Often, it took her several tries before she could find the right spot for the needle.

The experience was excruciating I began to understand what I had read in novels about people in pain sweating big drops like soybeans. This wasn't literary exaggeration—this really happened!

I did learn a lot at the May Seventh Cadre School, but probably not what they expected. Instead, I learned about human nature, perseverance, endurance, and how troubles made some people mean and others kind.

As I pulled the roller or transported the bricks, I sometimes wondered why life was so hard—not just for me, but for people everywhere. Bricks have been made with hard labor for untold generations. For centuries, farmers have had to struggle with nature to produce food. In every time and place there are all sorts of unsavory people who treat others unfairly, from slave masters to capitalist oppressors, from abusive husbands to tyrannical rulers. Natural disasters like droughts and floods and hurricanes devastate all in their path. Even those who live in the relative comfort of modern cities have to wrestle with illness, accidents, family problems, and conflicts with people at work. None of it was fair.

On some days, these dark thoughts overwhelmed me. But then I would bring to mind my children's bright faces, one by one: Jenny, Toni, Sunny, Ming. I remembered their soft skin, their round eyes, their happy laughter. They were the reason I refused to give up. I would get through this. I would never adopt the slave mentality, accepting other people's view that I deserved this inhumane treatment. I didn't.

I could not leave the labor camp before my year was up. But I could show these people, by my attitude, that I was willing to work harder than anyone else. I could show them that I wouldn't be cowed into admitting charges that were not true. For the sake of my loved ones and the integrity of my whole extended family, I would make the choice to power through this tough time. When all other freedoms had been taken away from me, I still had the freedom to persevere. And to hope.

Chapter Thirty-Four

Unhappy Homecoming

FINALLY I FINISHED the full year of hard labor; my group returned to Beijing in the spring of 1970. I couldn't wait to see my children, and the idea of living with them again filled me to overflowing with joy. I expected heaven after the hell of the May Seventh school.

But the day of my return hit me with a rude reality.

When I opened the door to our tiny one-room apartment, I saw a familiar face: Mama! This was the first I had seen her in more than two years. I took her hands and wept with relief.

"Mama! Is your health okay?" I asked immediately. I had been worried about her weak heart, and she looked old and worn down. "Are the children obeying you?"

Instead of embracing me with joy, Mama looked away, her eyebrows twisted in anguish.

"Good. You're back," she said, pulling her hands away. "These children of yours! I can't take it anymore."

My heart sank. "What? What have they done?"

Mama launched into a litany of problems she had been facing, raising four children in one room on an extremely tight budget. By and large, the children had been very good, but sometimes they talked back. Living under a cloud, with a father accused of spying and a mother in labor camp, their lives overflowed with stress. I tried to explain how it would affect their behavior.

But Mama was vehement. "You don't understand. I've had it. I've made up my mind. Now that you're home, I'm going back to Shijiazhuang!"

This really shook me up. I had seen too many children whose parents had been pulled away from them during the Cultural Revolution, so that they had no one to take care of them. Many of them turned into desperate, wild kids that got into all sorts of trouble. Yes, I was home but there was a chance I would be sent away again. I desperately needed Mama to take care of our kids. I couldn't imagine coping without her. I pleaded with her not to leave, but she insisted that she was going. She packed up her few belongings but promised to wait till the next day, so she could say good-bye.

By the time the children came home from school, I was distraught. Instead of the warm homecoming I had been anticipating for so long, I lashed out at my precious children.

"Grandma says you're not obeying her. How could you be so bad? Now she wants to leave us."

They were shocked. "Mama, Mama," said Jenny. "What's wrong with you?"

"Grandma!" said Toni. "Please don't leave. We'll be good."

Caught between their distress and my need for Mama's help, I broke down in tears.

Fortunately, Mama relented. "Fine, fine, I'll stay. I'm not leaving. Not now anyway."

I hugged them all and said, "Mama's sorry! I'm so sorry I yelled at you!"

My own breakdown made me think hard. Of course, I was under tremendous stress. But if I let the pressure get between me and my children, my tormentors would win.

≈

Once again, I had to report to the office every morning at eight. Radio Peking continued to broadcast China's news in English, but my job was to sit in an office, write confessions, and undergo struggle sessions. No one called me a dog-spy's wife, but few of my colleagues spoke to me. The shadow remained.

Shortly after my release from the May Seventh school, I learned that Anna Louise Strong had died, in March 1970. This grand old American leftist had treated Sidney like a son, and Sidney had taken her out to lunch once a week for years. After his arrest, I had thought of writing to her, since I knew she would believe in his innocence. But in the end I decided not to, since I didn't want to put her in an awkward position. Besides, I doubted that the letter would reach her. Now, I felt very sad at her passing, sure that the sudden loss of her old friend Sidney had played a major part in her failing heart and death.

Suddenly one day, Zhang Wenxiu, the chief of my English section special case group, came to me holding a bank deposit book.

"We have taken into consideration the economic difficulties of your family, and have decided to return your bank deposit book. Your account has about one thousand yuan."

I didn't know what to say. It was my money, but I hadn't been allowed to touch it. Now, they were returning it because of our family difficulties. He acted as if he were doing me a favor. Did this mean that if it hadn't been for our difficulties, they would have confiscated the money that I had stowed away over long years of work—just because they suspected my husband was a spy? I dare not ask. Without a word, I accepted the bank deposit book. Maybe this was a sign that things would get better.

The first thing that came to mind was to buy some meat for the children, to improve their diet. Aside from the meals Uncle Zhang had treated Toni and Little Ming to, it had been years since they had eaten a real meat dish. Since I was still not permitted to leave the courtyard, I gave the bankbook to Toni and told her to withdraw twenty yuan.

At the time, I didn't comprehend what turmoil there was outside: ruffians and thugs roamed the city streets. On the way home from the bank, Toni was suddenly seized from behind by two men who took the twenty yuan and the deposit book.

Weeping, she ran home, shouting, "They took my money! They took my money!"

Two patrolling People's Liberation Army men from the garrison troops attached to Radio rushed over and asked what was the matter.

"Don't cry. We'll catch them!" They turned and sped after the two young thieves. They caught one, but the other got away with the money. The PLA men returned the bankbook to Toni, who ran home and told me what happened.

What a contrast with the 1950s, when Communist Liberation had made the streets safe for all! Still, we felt gratitude toward the PLA soldiers. How many times had they come to our rescue?

～

Before long, my nemesis Zhang Wenxiu again started organizing meetings, which I was forced to attend. The theme of the meetings was "struggle with selfishness, criticize revisionism," but what really happened was that my former colleagues found yet another way to revile and slander me.

They didn't let up on the old demands: "Change your class stance!" and "Give an honest account of Li Dunbai's spy activities!" and "You shouldn't stand with a spy!" But they added a new one: "Examine and expose the filthiest ideas in the depths of your soul."

This was a new movement, called "Breaking through Three Barriers." First, I was to break through the barrier against revealing bad ideas that I had already let slip in meetings. Second, I had to break through the barrier against bad things that I had thought of doing and confided to my closest family or friends. The third barrier was against evil thoughts that had crossed my mind but that I had never revealed to a single person. They seemed convinced that this fresh approach would finally get me to confess.

Every day at these meetings, more than forty people in the English section would point their fingers at me and berate me. Again, not one person said a word on my behalf. And again, I was not allowed to utter a word in my own defense.

Not only that, but Sidney's special case group joined with my case group for a whole week of "education" aimed at me. They shouted the same old stuff. "Correct your attitude!" "Look at the situation!" "Expose Li Dunbai!"

I had nothing new to report so I couldn't say anything to lessen my suffering. Some days, I thought that they just needed a target for their political struggle sessions, and by attacking me they deflected possible charges against themselves.

By then, I was just sick of the whole thing. China was full of smart people and badly needed to get moving again after years of chaos. Couldn't these people see what a waste of time it was to toss the same false charges at me? They should break through the barriers of their own bad ideas.

Instead of feeling confused or humiliated or defiant, I just gritted my teeth and endured it. It simply could not drag on forever. Yet it seemed to. And that got me down.

Every night, when the children were asleep, I would open the Little Red Book of *Quotations from Chairman Mao Zedong*, and say, without sound, "Chairman Mao, when are you going to say a just word for me? Sidney and I haven't done anything counterrevolutionary. Why are they calling us spies? You yourself admitted that Sidney was wrongfully imprisoned before. Why is he a victim again? Why? Why?"

I began writing letters to Chairman Mao, complaining about my treatment and asking these questions. Whenever I got to the end of my rope, I would write another letter. Using the most respectful language, I would sincerely express my appreciation for all that the Party had done in the past. I would remind Chairman Mao of our meeting in Shanghai in 1965 and respectfully request that the Party clear Sidney of these false charges of spying. I asked if he would please tell me where Sidney was and allow me to visit or write to him. I reminded him of how Sidney had contributed his hard work to the Party over the years. Each time, I would address the envelope to Chairman Mao, put a stamp on it, and drop it in a mailbox. I never heard back. I doubt he ever received my letters.

All it would take was one word from anyone with power in the Party, and the pressure would be off of me, an innocent woman. But the Party members at Radio wouldn't say a word. To defend me would be to open themselves to criticism and attack. The cost was too high.

From the window of my room, I could see a twelve-year-old girl, half-Chinese, half-Japanese, walking through the courtyard below. Accused of being Japanese spies, her parents had been hauled off to prison. A compassionate teacher had taken her in and was caring for her. But she didn't dare walk down the center of the path; she walked close to the wall on one side, hoping no one would notice her. What had she done wrong?

I thought about other children I knew who had turned into street ruffians after their parents had been carried off. I heard of one woman named "Big Sister Ma" who was trapping children into prostitution. I could not let this happen to my kids. If they had no mother, with their father in prison, that's what could happen to them. That gave me the courage to stick it out during the struggle sessions.

Before his arrest, Sidney had been making speeches all over Beijing, especially at universities, and writing articles for prominent newspapers. As a result, everyone knew his name. When he was accused of being an American spy, everyone naturally wanted to see what this spy's wife looked like.

Wherever I went, I heard comments. "Who would have thought it? He was so nice to everyone, and then he turns out to be a spy!" "In all the time he spent in China, how come no one discovered that he was a spy?" "Oh, look! That's his wife!"

Because of his notoriety, I became notorious too. Everyone was afraid to contact me or speak to me, lest they be implicated and struggled against.

Chapter Thirty-Five

Uncommon Kindness

NO ONE DARED to defend me publicly, but there were some kind-hearted colleagues at Radio who would privately say a few heartfelt words to me when no one else was listening.

"Wang Yulin, don't worry," one said. "Sooner or later everything will be cleared up."

"Take care of your health," another said. "Whatever you do, don't get wild thoughts!" That was a reference to the large numbers of people who committed suicide.

The former vice director of the State Broadcast Administration, Zuo Moye, and the chief of the Foreign Broadcast News Department, Zou Xiaoqing, would ask me, "How are you getting along? Do you have enough money for your living expenses?"

Before he was taken, Sidney had shared an office and worked closely with Zuo Moye, who had been an innocent victim of the witch hunt at the tail end of the Yan'an Rectification Movement in the early 1940s. His nerves had been shattered by the terrifying experience, and only great courage enabled him to keep working.

Sometimes, when no one was around, a colleague would quietly approach me and say, in a very low voice, "Any word from Li Dunbai? What's going on?"

Unfortunately, there was no word about Sidney. The authorities had never informed me that he had been arrested and was being held in prison. On bad days, my mind went to the darkest place: Was Sidney still alive? How could I find out? I wrote yet another letter to Chairman Mao, and one to Party Central, but got no response.

One day, the children's soldier friend, Uncle Zhang, said to Toni, "How are things in your family? Tell me what you lack, and we'll work it out."

Toni said, "I haven't heard Mama say that we lack anything."

"So many people in your family," he continued. "Do you have a big wok for cooking?"

Toni said we didn't have one.

"All right, we'll go buy a big wok. You can use it as a steamer, too."

When I came home from the office that afternoon, I found a big steamer wok on the table, along with a heap of candy and some cookies.

Just as I was looking at all this in amazement, Toni came bouncing into the room. "Mama! I ran into the PLA uncle from Radio today. He said he wanted to get us something, because he knew we were having a hard time. I said we didn't need anything, but he insisted on getting us this big pot!"

"Was this Uncle Zhang again? Did he say anything about Papa?"

"It was. Uncle said to comfort you and tell you not to be anxious. Papa's problem is sure to be cleared up. He told me that the candy and cookies were for me and my little brother."

I was deeply moved. This fine man reached out a helping hand at our time of greatest hardship, not afraid of being implicated in my case.

One day, Little Ming was playing at home, wearing a new blue playsuit. I asked Toni where the new clothes came from.

"Uncle Zhang bought it for him," she said.

Another day when I went home to fix supper, I discovered that our new wok was full of big white mantou. I stood there looking at them in wonderment, thinking, *The kids don't know how to fix mantou. Who did this? Did they buy them from a restaurant?* It didn't look like it, because they weren't uniform in size; they were obviously homemade. Then I noticed that the furniture had been moved around, too, and the room was squeaky clean. I was overjoyed, but who had done all this?

Then Toni came home from school. "Are the mantou ready, Mama?"

"Yes, I heated them. But who made them?"

"It was Uncle Zhang. He brought several squad leaders with him. They swept and cleaned the room, too. They said, 'We want your Mama to feel happy when she comes home! She should be able to rest and not have to cook.'"

"You must visit their home and thank him, and his loved ones, for me," I said. "But be careful not to mention to anyone else that they came to our home and helped us. Otherwise, they could be criticized for not drawing a line against a spy's family."

"I know," said Toni. "I always look first to make sure no one's around. Then I wave to them, and they slip into our room."

One day, Uncle Zhang told Toni that his company was being sent south, and another unit would be taking over. "The squad leaders have prepared some little gifts for you. How about giving them some gifts, too, as mementos?" he said to her. "They're all fond of you, and they will miss you and your little brother."

"I'll ask my Mama," Toni said.

"I have an idea," Zhang said. "They all love to read the *Selected Works of Chairman Mao*. What about giving them the four-volume edition? I'll pay for most of it, and you ask your mother to put in a little bit, maybe twenty yuan. But don't tell them that I helped pay for it."

"All right! I'll check with Mama," said Toni.

When Toni asked me, I did some figuring. It wasn't a lot of money, but in our family's circumstances, even a little was a lot. It amounted to one-fourth of our living expenses for a month. Usually, by the end of the month we couldn't even afford to buy the shredded pickled vegetables. But I gave twenty yuan out of my monthly salary to Toni and told her to ask her Uncle Zhang to buy the books for us, and to thank him for his help.

Later that month, we hit bottom. I had used up all my savings in the bank, and my monthly salary could not cover our expenses. With only one fen left, we had nothing to eat. For an American, that would be like trying to feed a family of six with one penny.

"One fen?" said Sunny. "What can you buy with that? A little bit of cabbage costs five fen!"

We all went without anything to eat on that day, aside from steamed bread. All I could do was to put some soy sauce in a bowl of water. The kids called it "High Grade Soup," which was slang for dishwater. But it was all we had.

Still, it was worth it to give these soldiers a thank-you gift. During all the trials we were going through, no one else dared draw near to us, let alone reach out to help us—only these lovable People's Army men. We had to give them something to remember us by!

Toni found out that after the PLA company left Radio, Uncle Zhang was transferred to Tianjin for a meeting in which PLA members introduced what they had learned from studying Chairman Mao's works. He was considered a pacesetter in the study program.

At the Lunar New Year festival of 1971, he was still in Tianjin, but he instructed his housekeeper to bring us several pounds of meat for our family dinner.

We were really moved at his thinking of us, even after he had left. In the midst of madness, he exemplified the Communist ideals I had learned in the early 1950s.

After that, we lost track of Uncle Zhang. Toni heard that he had been promoted to political instructor of his battalion. She looked for him everywhere in vain. I worried about the possibility that he might be investigated or persecuted because of getting close to our family.

To this day, I deeply regret that I was never able to thank him in person. I never saw him, and I don't even know his full name. But every time I got out that steamer, I thought of Uncle Zhang.

Chapter Thirty-Six

A Deeper Layer of Hell

IN JULY OF 1971, Radio Peking erupted with huge news: President Richard Nixon of the United States planned to visit China the following year! The staff members of the English section went into a tizzy, translating this news and trumpeting it. After years of diplomatic isolation, China's leaders were taking bold steps—reaching out to the very leader who had led the fight to quash Communism in Vietnam. Sidney would be amazed. If he were free, he would be leading the English language coverage of the event, scheduled for February of 1972.

This dynamite news filled me with hope. Each day, I waited to hear: Would they release Sidney now?

But nothing happened. Silence.

In September and October, I started noticing strange omissions in China's news coverage, and on National Day, October 1, the annual celebrations were abruptly canceled. I was mystified. We all read the papers carefully to try to figure out what was happening. A few months later, we found out that Mao's chosen successor, Lin Biao, had died in a plane crash in mid-September, in Mongolia. No explanation was given as to why or where he had been headed.

To me, this was a bad sign. I trusted the military to ensure stability; without Lin Biao's leadership, who would provide a counterweight to Jiang Qing and the other continuous-revolution radicals? Zhou Enlai was still premier, but we all wondered what kind of power he still had. Rumors swirled that he was in poor health—and that Chairman Mao was, too. No one knew for sure.

Nixon was coming to China, but the radicals were still in charge. Sidney was still incarcerated, and I was still being treated like a traitor.

≈

For months, the criticism and struggle at Radio continued, and I still couldn't satisfy my critics. I wouldn't "break through my own mental barriers" and do what they wanted: produce evidence that Sidney was a spy. I was unrepentant, uncooperative, and unreliable.

The Party branch secretary for the Europe/Americas Department was a full-time Party worker. Wife of an army officer, she was mean and tough. One day in January of 1972, she called me in and said, "Wang Yulin, we have decided to send you to a cadre training school in Henan Province."

My insides collapsed. This had been my worst fear. "For how long?" I asked.

"Probably for one year," she said.

"When do I leave?"

"Go back and get ready. You leave in one week."

"Can I take my little son with me?"

"Of course you can. Why don't you take your daughters too?"

Very firmly, I answered, "They're in school. They can't go."

"They can go to school there, too," she said. "You'd better take them all with you. Go back and think it over carefully."

I understood immediately what they were up to. They wanted to run our whole family off to the countryside, to settle us there as rural residents so that we would never be able to return to Beijing. I had heard through the grapevine that the Henan cadre training school was actually a holding ground for "problem people." A factory was being built there, where the children of these "problem people" could work. In other words, people whom the authorities considered troublesome were being transferred from city to countryside, just to get them out of the way—permanently. What else could they do with me? They didn't trust me to work on the news.

In effect, I was being sent to a prison camp—this time, far from home.

I made up my mind never to allow them to send my three daughters to the country. But I decided to take my five-year-old son with me, because he was small and weak, and he needed a mother's attention. Besides, my aging mother, with her weak heart, couldn't take care of four children. Also, it might make my burden easier, to have at least one of my children nearby.

With a heavy heart, I went back home that day and called them all together. "No matter who says so, if anyone from Radio asks you to go down to the country, you just say, 'My mother told me to stay here and go to school.' Don't leave Beijing, no matter what."

The girls nodded solemnly.

"In the villages," I said, "the peasants don't know what's going on, and they are not educated. If they should hear someone say that your father is an American spy, they could be very hard on you. There are no colleges there, hardly even senior high schools. If you go there, it means your education comes to an end, and you'll just be laboring alongside me."

Mama supported me on this. "You mustn't go. Once you go, you can't come back."

"Grandma will take care of you at home," I continued. "Put your energy into studying. Don't go out unless you have to. Read books besides what you're assigned in school. After supper at night, stay home and study. Things are too messy outside. If anything should happen, I won't be here and Grandma is up in years and couldn't handle it. You're big girls. Take good care of Grandma, help her with the housework, and listen to what she says."

They had heard it all before but nodded dutifully. "We know, Mama."

"When will you be back?" asked Sunny.

"Back? Heaven only knows! Maybe I won't ever get back. Henan is over a thousand miles from Beijing. I can't even get a train ticket without their approval."

They all started crying and hugged their little brother, showering him with kisses.

"Will you miss your sisters?" Toni asked him.

"I will!" said Little Ming, nodding vigorously.

I had seen all I could take. "All right, children. Everyone get ready, and we will have another good talk before I leave."

Jenny asked me what to do about getting the food money when I wasn't here.

I told her, "Every month, go to the front gate of Radio and call up to the English section for the money."

The next week of preparation at home exhausted me. Once again, I had to sew and alter clothes for the four children, to adjust each child's clothes for the younger one to wear. I had to prepare clothing for spring and summer as well. Every day for a week, I worked till one or two in the morning. They were telling me that I would be at the labor camp for one year, but who could say? They were transferring my residence permit to the villages, so if they decided to keep me there, they could do it. No one said anything about a home visit after six months, as had been permitted last time.

My heart was heavy. What miseries would befall the children while I was away? I felt as though the devil himself was threatening to carry off my kids. I uttered a silent wish that the Old Man in the Sky would protect them.

The three girls accompanied Little Ming and me to the big truck that pulled up in front of our living quarters to take us to the train station. Toni called out, "Ming-Ming! Get Mama to teach you to read and write, and send letters to your big sister."

Unaware of what was going on, he called back, with a big grin, "I draw pictures for you!"

I told the girls, "Pay attention to your studies! Keep out of trouble!"

"Bye-bye, Mama! Take care of your health!" The three girls called out repeatedly as the truck pulled away, taking us to the prison camp.

Chapter Thirty-Seven

Child in a Gulag

AFTER ARRIVING AT the Beijing train station on an icy January afternoon, we marched single file through the gate, onto the platform, and onto a train. We each lugged a bedroll and a small bag of clothing. The Broadcast Administration had bought the tickets in advance for about fifty of us. Aside from a few ordinary leading cadres sent to supervise and monitor us, we were all problem people from Radio, being sent down to labor.

Technically the camp in Henan was neither a gulag nor *laogai*, meaning "reform through labor," since we had not been sentenced by a court as criminals. Nonetheless, we were political prisoners sent there to do forced labor. My only "crime" was marrying a foreigner and standing up for him when he was falsely accused. It had been nearly four years since that night they took Sidney away.

For the seventeen-hour rail trip, we sat in a "hard seater" car, two or three on each wooden bench, facing another two or three. The seats couldn't lean back, so I had to sit straight-backed the whole way. Xiaoming curled up against me and tried to sleep. We made sure the windows were shut tight, which kept out not only the chilly winds but the thick black dust from the coal-burning steam locomotive.

Every hour of the long journey reminded me of how far I would be living away from my daughters. My first labor camp had been in a Beijing suburb, just an hour or so from the city. Now I would be in the middle of nowhere, unable to return if something went wrong at home.

As we sat there, staring out the windows at the featureless, frosty plains, we were all probably pondering our problems and worrying about our families and the ominous future, but not one dared to voice these thoughts. Everyone knew that there might be spies or someone looking to earn brownie points by snitching, who might report what we said in distorted form and get us in trouble.

After a night and day, sitting bolt upright in that cold car, we finally arrived at

Huaiyang County station in the eastern part of Henan Province—at the heart of the North China plain, south of the Yellow River. This region was the birthplace of Chinese civilization, with an ancient history dating back five thousand years, but over the centuries, it had been damaged by war and floods. By the time I got there, it was one of the most backward parts of China, an overpopulated, impoverished farm region with flat, featureless fields, barren in winter, stretching off to the horizon.

We got off the train and waited hours in the wintry wind for the Radio trucks to come pick us up. When the sun went down, there was still no sign of the trucks. I wrapped Ming-Ming in my overcoat to keep him warm, as we sat on the hard ground in front of the station, waiting and watching for a sign of the trucks that would carry us away.

My son and I munched on the ice-cold mantou bread and pickled vegetables that I had brought with us from home. Those who could afford it were eating sausage and white bread. In my little son's pockets, I discovered some biscuits and two apples. I knew that his sisters had put them there; they were always thinking of their little brother.

While we waited, a woman whom I couldn't see clearly in the gathering darkness sidled over to me and asked, "Wang Yulin, how could you bring such a little child? You know that we're going there to labor. Why didn't you leave him home?"

I had begun to wonder about that myself. "Nobody to take care of him at home," I replied. "My mother is nearly eighty, and she has heart trouble. It's enough to leave three little daughters with her. I couldn't ask her to take her of my son too. I had to bring him along."

"I see," she said, with a sigh. "You couldn't expect such an elderly one to handle four little children. But you'll have a hard time laboring with such a small child."

Looking around to ensure we were not being watched, she said, "You know, they say we have been sent here for transformation through labor, but I've heard that they're going to keep us here, long term."

She had given voice to my own worst fear. "Well," I said, "we just have to take whatever they give us. What can we do?"

It was my fate to swallow yet another bitter pill.

Soon we heard horns honking in the distance. We got up, dusted ourselves off, and got ready as several trucks pulled up. They were open sided, with only canvas to protect the people sitting on hard benches in the truck bed. I hugged

Little Ming tightly, fearing he would take sick if we rode in the open trucks on this bitterly cold and windy night.

As we lined up to board the trucks, a woman called out to the cadre in charge. "Wang Yulin and her little child should sit in the driver's cab." A chorus of voices spoke out in support. "That's right. Otherwise, it would be terrible for such a small child."

I deeply appreciated their support, and I tried to show it in my eyes. I saw that most of them sympathized with us. And sure enough, the cadre in charge seated us in the driver's cab of one of the trucks. This unexpected kindness moved me.

It was a rough road. The truck rocked wildly back and forth, and progress was slow. After two hours, we arrived at the camp close to midnight.

Our quarters were cramped: each room was small, about 150 square feet, with one bunk bed. My roommate was a woman from the English section, Cheng Jingyuan, and she yielded the lower berth to me and my little son. Ming and I would have to sleep together on a single bed.

What bothered me most was that the woman who was overseeing me lived in the room just opposite us, where she could keep an eye on me, twenty four hours a day, seven days a week. And the woman doing the surveillance? Wei Lin, Sidney's former wife. She was a deputy squad leader, in charge of a small group of six inmates, including me. Her job was to make sure we were truly "transformed through labor." Every day, after laboring, I had to report to her how my thinking had evolved.

Wei Lin could not have been happy about being sent to the labor camp to oversee us problem people. Recognized as one of the best English speakers in the section, she had been working as an announcer on Radio Peking. But her mind had also been distorted by the ugliness of repeated political campaigns. Over the years, she had denounced Sidney and accused him of spying three times! Yet once, when someone had called a mass meeting to criticize her, she had gone to Sidney and begged him to call it off, and he did. She told him she didn't think she could handle the mental pressure.

By 1972, Wei Lin had become a Party snitch, eavesdropping on conversations and providing ammunition for people to attack their colleagues. Nobody trusted her. She never smiled at anyone and always had a deadpan expression. I knew she envied me because I had a loving marriage and four children. She had adopted a child because she was unable to get pregnant; I had heard rumors that her relations with her husband and daughter were poor. Certainly she knew that I had criticized her for divorcing Sidney when he was in prison, saying that

I would have waited for him. Now I was doing just that. My example must have rankled her. I might have felt sorry for her, except that in Henan, she set about doing everything she could to make my life miserable.

≈

On our first full day at the camp, we received our official "Ideological Education on Entering the Camp." What it really amounted to was an announcement of the camp regulations.

No leaves or furloughs; no strolling around the camp or its exterior; no visiting the farmers' markets; no candy or other edibles received from home; no liaison among us or "little clique activity." It sounded depressingly similar to Fangshan. But at least we would be allowed to receive letters from home. I took solace in this.

That afternoon, we were taken to the camp exhibition. It was the story, in posters, of a young man and a young woman who had come to the camp and were caught making love. This showed, said the posters, that they were not really accepting ideological transformation, so they were both punished.

All this indoctrination was designed to make sure we would work hard, keep our mouths shut, obey the leaders, and abide by camp discipline. Otherwise, we would be severely punished. I was dreading that the experience here might be even worse than Fangshan.

On the way back to our quarters, we saw a crowd of people gathered around something stuck up on the wall. Curious, I went over to look. It turned out to be a container of facial cream and several sausages. A notice said, "Look! This is what bourgeois element Zhang Yanyan asked her family to send her!"

"Scary!" said a woman next to me. "A little face cream for the winter and a couple of sausages got her into all that trouble. Was it worth it?"

On the third day, our regular labor began.

My heart slumped when I heard my labor assignment: brickmaking again. We were assigned to make bricks the same backbreaking way Chinese have done for four thousand years.

This time, though, my task was to pull a wheelbarrow, loaded with over five hundred pounds of the yellow earth, from a field to the place where they were fashioning it into bricks. Like a beast of burden, I pulled the load with a rope around my shoulders and upper chest, the ends of the rope tied to the handles of the wheelbarrow.

I struggled to pull the heavy load up an incline. Whenever I got to the slope, my five-year-old son would get behind the wheelbarrow and push. Even though he was a weak little child, I would have had a really hard time walking up that slope without him.

Other people saw what was going on, and they would call out to him. "Xiaoming, help me with my load. Give Auntie a push up the hill!"

He became the pet of the laborers at the camp, and he called them all Auntie or Uncle. His little round face and lanky child's body were the only sight that made us smile. A man named Liang, in charge of the tool shed, found a tiny shovel for Xiaoming. From then on, Ming would bring his little shovel to work with me every day.

One thing that made our laboring more difficult was the weather, which struck me as strange. In the morning, I shivered in my cotton-quilted jacket; by noon I would be sweating in a short-sleeved shirt; by nightfall it was again unbelievably cold. A local saying captured this perfectly: The weather in Huaiyang is hard to guess; every day you go through three changes of dress.

It also frequently drizzled, and the slightest bit of rain would make the dirt roads almost impassable. Everyone would put on galoshes, but in the winter your feet could freeze. To keep this from happening to my son, I got him an oversized pair of galoshes and made him a pair of cotton-padded socks. But the galoshes were far too big, making them clumsy to walk in. He was always falling down and getting covered with mud. This was a child who was very particular about keeping himself clean. Every time he would fall down he would run back and change his clothes—sometimes two or three times a day. The aunties around him would say, "Xiaoming, you're making trouble for your mother again!"

When I came back from labor each day, my first task would be to take his clothes to the pump and scrub them clean. The water was bone-piercing cold. I would tell my son, "Ming-Ming, try to be a little careful and keep from falling down, okay?"

"I don't know why I'm always tripping and falling. Auntie says my galoshes are too big."

"Mama's worried about your feet freezing. That's why I made you the thick socks."

But my efforts were in vain. Before long, his two little feet were covered with purple marks from frostbite. I wrote home to Jenny and asked her to send us some frostbite ointment.

Eventually, all the women at the camp looked strange, with cheeks purple from the cold. They all smeared on frostbite ointment and covered it with white gauze. The men would poke fun at them. "Look at these women! Most people put up scrolls on their doors for New Year's, but they are putting the New Year scrolls on their faces!"

The women answered back, "Don't laugh at us. You'll be putting scrolls on your faces before long!"

"We never wash our faces with warm water," answered one man. "We always use cold water, so our faces are hardened to the cold."

One of the older women named Liu commented, "The men don't understand. The camp lets us use a little warm water to wash with during our periods, and the men think this is some kind of special treatment."

"What are you saying?" one of the men called out.

"We're saying that you men don't know what you're talking about," came the answer, and everyone cracked up.

The laughter surprised me. At a labor camp, could people laugh? Already, I could see the atmosphere was more lighthearted than in the previous camp, although the labor was just as hard. Perhaps having a child around made people kinder.

Jenny mailed us the frostbite ointment, but Little Ming's feet and cheeks suffered anyway, and soon he was wearing "scrolls" on his face like the others.

Once I heard him say to an auntie, "Mama says my skin is too tender."

Old Lady Liu said, "Yes, our Ming-Ming is still a little boy, right?"

Every day he went out to labor with us, helping people push their wheelbarrows and using his little spade to dig, like the grown-ups. He would work until he was drenched with perspiration, taking off his cotton-padded vest and sometimes even his jacket.

"Xiaoming! Put your jacket back on!" I would shout from a distance.

"No, I won't. It's too hot," he would reply, going on with his digging.

"Ming-Ming, you're too small—you can't work like that. Take it easy, okay?"

But then he would find someone's wheelbarrow to push. People admired his willingness to work hard, and they would encourage him. He would tell the uncles pushing the wheelbarrows, "Add a little to this load!"

It was taxing on his little body, but he seemed to love doing it. After years spent in a nursery school, where he was just one of many children, here he was doted upon by dozens of adults, praised for working like a grown-up. Years later, looking back on life in the camp, he said, "I remember it as mostly fun."

A few other prisoners had their children with them, too, but he was the youngest. Many of the adults were fond of him, and no one said he looked like a foreigner.

He yearned to push a load equal to what others were pushing. Once, when I saw him pulling a cart alone, I ran over and said, "Put it down, Ming-Ming! You can't do that by yourself."

But others in my group criticized me. "If the kid wants to do it, let him do it. He's learning how to be a worker."

But I was greatly agitated on the inside. How could such a little child do this kind of work? I worried that it would affect his growth. This was a constant worry, but I didn't know what to do about it. I was afraid to talk about it in the group, because he was supposed to be the son of a spy, so some people would feel that it was right for him to work hard and accuse me of spoiling him. But Ming-Ming, always helping others and making us smile, was anything but spoiled.

As Ming-Ming grew, I had to patch his well-worn pants and attach extra fabric to his stained pajamas, using whatever material I could find.

Chapter Thirty-Eight

_____

Punched in the Eye

EACH EVENING, WE would have a meeting to examine the day's work and criticize our own shortcomings. As our deputy squad leader, Wei Lin sometimes led these meetings. Worn out after the day's work, Ming would often fall asleep in my arms during the meetings, so I would ask for permission to put him to bed. As soon as I would put him down, he'd wake up and put his arms around my neck. "Mama, I'm afraid! Take me to the meeting with you!"

"What is there to fear, my good child?" I said. "Aren't you studying the heroic spirit of the PLA? They stand guard by themselves, and they're not afraid. You're not going to be afraid, are you?"

"Mama, I won't be afraid after today. But today, don't leave me!"

"Be a good boy! I had to ask for leave to bring you back to our room, and if I don't return I'll be criticized. I have to go back, don't I?"

"Well, leave the light on."

"All right, I'll leave the light on for you."

"All right, Mama. Go ahead, then."

He was a good boy, and he understood. He didn't want his mother to be criticized. I gave him a kiss and hurried back to the meeting.

After we'd been there a few months, I made up my mind not to let my son help with labor any more. The camp had set up a primary school for children who lived there with their parents, as well as some local village children. But it started in first grade, and Little Ming was still in kindergarten. When I asked if he could just sit in the first grade classroom and listen, I was told that he was too young. Refusing to take no for an answer, I appealed to a woman from the Radio Planning Department who was fond of my little boy. She knew the principal of the school, and she pulled strings for Xiaoming. The principal sympathized with me, although she couldn't show it. At first, she insisted on sticking to the rules, but eventually she gave permission for Xiaoming to attend school as an auditor. That ended my worries about the effect of hard labor on the health of this growing body.

Because the pupils at the school included children from local farm families, who didn't understand the unfairness of political labels, I was afraid that Ming-Ming would suffer harassment there, so I changed his name from Li Xiaoming to Wang Xiaoming, using my surname. I didn't want people at the school to know that he was Sidney's son, which could incite curses and discrimination.

Over and over, I trained him. "Your name is Wang Xiaoming. Understand?"

"Why am I not Li Xiaoming?" he would ask, fixing his eyes on me.

I didn't want to hurt him, so I just said, "You're here with Mama, and while you're here you have to use Mama's surname. Understand?"

"Well, are my big sisters going to change their names too?"

"Your big sisters are in Beijing, not here with Mama. They won't change their names."

He seemed to accept what I was saying. Like a real grown-up, he grunted, "Oh."

But ultimately I could not prevent him from being hurt by Sidney's reputation. The pupils found out very soon that he was the son of the notorious American spy, Li Dunbai.

One evening, Ming-Ming was playing hide-and-seek with several big kids in the yard outside. When it got too dark, Ming-Ming decided to quit and go home, since he didn't like playing in the dark.

One of the big kids, who was a bit of a roughneck, insisted that he stay and play with them. When he refused, the big kid knocked him flat. One of Ming-Ming's eyes swelled up and turned crimson, and he lay on the ground crying. Frightened, the big kid took Ming-Ming to the clinic. On the way, he threatened to kill him if he told anyone who had hit him.

When I came back from a meeting, I found Ming-Ming sitting in our room, crying. I took a close look at his eye, which frightened me. It was swollen shut.

"What happened, Ming-Ming? Who hit you?"

But he shook his head and wouldn't say a word.

"Tell Mama who beat you," I said, crying myself as I sat there hugging him and rocking back and forth.

The neighbors heard the crying and came to see what was happening. They were all shocked at the sight of his puffed-up eye.

"What happened?" they asked.

"I don't know," I said. "I just came back and found him like this. He almost lost an eye!"

But Ming-Ming wouldn't say a word about who did it.

The next day, I talked to him patiently, as did his teacher at the school, insisting he tell us who had hit him. His teacher admonished him to tell the truth. Finally, reluctantly, he did.

I was shocked at his answer.

The kid who hit him was fifteen years old and had a reputation for bullying. Word got out, and there was great indignation at how an innocent little child had suffered because of his father's issues. Mr. Xiao, a man from the French language section who was the cook at the camp, grabbed the roughneck teenager and boxed his ears soundly.

"Why are you beating me?" the boy shouted.

"Because you hit Little Ming," he said. "Look how much bigger you are! You're fifteen years old, and you hit a five-year-old child. Why did you do that? Tell me! Why?"

A little crowd gathered around them, and they all demanded that the teenager answer.

Hearing the commotion, his mother came over. It turned out that she was my friend, Liu Xia, my good buddy from the May Seventh Cadre School who had grown up in the Soviet Union. While at Fangshan together, she had confided in me how she struggled to raise her teenaged son in a rough labor camp, without his father.

Still angry, Mr. Xiao said, "I'm going to take care of this kid."

Liu Xia said, "You can't! You have no right to beat my child."

"I'll take care of this, right through to the end," answered the angry Xiao. "You shrew!"

Some of the group brought Xiaoming over and said, "Just look at him. Look at that eye!"

The noise attracted Cai Baozhu, former Party secretary in the Foreign Broadcast Department and now our political instructor at the camp. "No fussing! Everybody go home, and we'll take it up at the meeting tonight," she said,

That night, the whole group met together, and Liu Xia was criticized for raising such a rough, ill-mannered son. She stood up, weeping, and criticized herself, too, for not doing a good job of educating her child. As angry as I was about the beating, I couldn't help empathizing with her. When adults were tormenting each other, it was hard to teach a child that was wrong.

Liu Xia apologized to me and to Little Ming, and that was the end of that little tempest. But others in my group warned me against the possibility of Ming's tormentor taking revenge. From then on, friends watched over him at school. For the next few days, I accompanied him to and from school, along a little trail, over three miles each way. But after a while, I had to give that up because it was taking time from my labor. So Ming started walking by himself again.

One day I asked him, "Don't you feel tired, walking all that distance to school?"

"Of course I do," he said. "When I get to that little bridge I sit down and rest there for a while. Sometimes there will be an auntie or uncle who lets me sit on their handlebars."

Everyone wanted to take care of Little Ming, in part because of his helpful attitude, but I think deep down people at the camp also knew that their children were subject to persecution, whether here or back home. Perhaps they took extra care with Ming in the hopes that someone would do the same for their own little boys and girls.

~

Food at the camp certainly didn't make life any more tolerable. There was very little meat in our diet and what meat there was, was mostly fat. Before, my son had always refused to eat fatty meat, but when he realized there was no other meat at the camp, he would eat it with relish. He seemed to get hooked on it and would ask for it every day.

I told him to go talk to his friend, Auntie Cai Baozhu, to see whether she could get him some meat. When he asked her, she said, "Oh, Xiaoming wants some meat? All right. Pay attention to which company is having meat. Let me know, and I'll go get you some."One day, he came bouncing back to our section, singing, "Auntie Cai! The Vanguard Company has killed a pig, and they're getting ready to have meat!"

"All right. I'll go tell them to leave a little for our Xiaoming," said the kind-hearted woman.

She had friends in all the companies, and they would bring her jiaozi, Chinese dumplings stuffed with pork, when they had a feast. Once, she got three bowls of jiaozi for us, and as it happened I had one bowl too. Ming-Ming was overjoyed! We had no fridge, so I put the food outside on the windowsill so that it would last for three days. I wrote his three sisters in Beijing and told them about how shamelessly addicted to meat their little brother had become.

That year, Ming-Ming's birthday, February 15, fell on the same day as the Lunar New Year. To celebrate his sixth birthday, his sisters managed to mail him a little can of sausages and some confectioner's sugar. They knew we were not allowed such luxuries, so they put the powdered sugar in a plastic bag clearly labeled "wash powder." Inside, they hid a small can of sausages. They wrapped the whole thing in cotton cloth and mailed it to Little Ming.

Families often sent detergent to their relatives in the camp, since it was hard to find in Henan. Though it was lawful to receive detergent, it was against camp rules to receive food, such as sugar and sausages. When the package arrived, I opened it in private, and as soon as I figured out their trick, I told Ming that he was only to eat the sugar in our little room. Afraid that someone would expose us, and I would be the butt of another struggle session, I told him he was never to take it outside nor reveal it to anyone else.

Each day I put a little sugar on his bread, hoping it would last a long time. But one day he ran out into the courtyard with his mantou covered with powdered sugar, and Wei Lin spotted him.

"Xiaoming! What's that on your mantou?" she said, glaring fixedly at him.

"Sugar!" he announced. "My big sisters sent it to me for my birthday."

"What? Your big sisters sent you sugar?"

Wei Lin marched into my room like a grand inquisitor. Unfortunately, she discovered not only the bag of sugar but also the empty sausage can under our bed.

"Aha!" she said, triumphantly. "Wang Yulin. Did you put that can under there?"

"Yes, it was me." I was caught completely off guard.

"Who sent you the can?"

"Xiaoming's big sisters sent it as a birthday gift for him."

"And the powdered sugar?"

"That, too. His sisters sent it. I didn't ask them for it. It was their idea."

"Do you know that it is not permitted to eat sugar?"

"I know, but I didn't know they were going to mail it here. They sent it because they love their little brother. I can't criticize them for that."

"You think your family is above the rules? You must make a self-examination before the group," she ordered.

Wei Lin impounded the sausage can and the powdered sugar and displayed them triumphantly as evidence at the meeting that night. The next day she organized a special struggle session against me. She said I was training my son in capitalist ways. I had to make a self-examination before our group of eight or nine, admitting that what I had done was wrong. But in my heart I felt wronged. Why could other people's children eat what they pleased, but my son was wrong for having some sugar? Why couldn't my son have a happy birthday and enjoy the gifts his sisters sent him? It reminded me of the old saying: Like a deaf mute eating wormwood, you have to eat bitterness in silence.

Chapter Thirty-Nine

Pain

CAUGHT UP IN the drama over Ming's sausages and sugar, I barely noticed the big news out of Beijing: American President Richard Nixon's visit from February 21 to 28, 1972. The front page of the newspapers ran a photo of Chairman Mao shaking Nixon's hand: a sight I had never imagined. After all, Nixon was an outspoken anti-Communist and Mao was the head of the largest Communist nation on earth. After more than two decades of hostility, the leaders of the United States and China were at least talking.

But Nixon's visit had zero effect on my life. Sidney was still in prison, unable to write to us. I was working like a pack animal in a labor camp. Little Ming was being taunted as the son of an American spy. My daughters were growing up motherless and fatherless. The United States-China rapprochement was a cruel tease. My personal hell was not over. In fact, it got worse.

After a few months, as winter waned and the weather warmed up, I was assigned new tasks. Instead of digging and loading dirt, I joined the team making adobe brick, this time using a more modern method: a brick-making machine. I had been a technician, so they figured I would know how to handle any machine. Besides, they said, my movements were agile.

Four of us would mix the mud and straw and pour it into the crude machine, which would turn out the bricks. Unlike regular gray or red bricks, adobe bricks had straw in them, to make them sturdier.

This machine spewed out a long unbroken line of shaped adobe, and my job was to chop it into separate bricks. The chopper had been developed by men at the camp, a group headed by our engineer from Radio It could cut ten bricks at a time. But he had limited materials to work with, so the quality was poor. The steel blades on the chopper constantly needed replacement because they jumped out of their tracks. If the operator didn't change a defective blade within one minute, the machine would turn out lots of waste product. Plus, the leaping blade posed a constant danger of accidents.

One day the workers on the previous shift told me to be extra vigilant because the chopper blades were acting up particularly badly. After a few hours of repeatedly changing blades, I grew tired and my movements slowed down. Once, when I was changing a blade, I moved a little slowly and the blade cut a big gash in the middle finger of my right hand—right down to the bone. The blood spurted out, and I screamed in pain.

I rushed to the clinic. The doctor there was a woman who was working at the camp because she was suspected of being a secret agent. She was a fully trained physician, but she was overly cautious, afraid that giving too much treatment to any one patient might expose her to accusations of favoritism and severe criticism. When she saw my finger, she disinfected it, gave me a tetanus shot, and wrapped it tightly in a bandage. That was it. Fearful that she would be accused of "association with a female spy," the doctor didn't suggest sending me to the country hospital for examination, nor did she stitch me up or set the bone in a splint. She didn't even write a note recommending that I be allowed to rest from labor.

My finger hurt like mad, and I was dizzy from the sight of so much blood and bone. I now understood an old saying that I had heard from my mother: The ten fingers are connected directly to the heart.

Nevertheless, since the camp regulations required that everyone labor unless they had a doctor's orders, I had to go back to work at the brickmaking machine. My squad leader, Wei Lin, saw how much pain I was in, but instead of recommending I rest, she ordered me to pull the wheelbarrows instead, lugging bricks that weighed more than five hundred pounds. I burst out in tears. I had been wounded in the line of duty, and this leader didn't offer one word of sympathy or compassion.

"If you can't use your hand, you'll just have to use your shoulders," she said, as if relishing my pain.

After the shock of my injury, I could hardly walk. But I strapped the thick rope over my chest, set my teeth, and pulled that cart back and forth, determined not to show weakness before these heartless people. They were punishing me, but I wasn't going to bow down and beg them for mercy. Holding back the tears, I did my work.

Ming-Ming, who was always by my side when he wasn't in school, was the only one who showed any compassion. He kept asking me, "Mama, does your hand hurt?"

"It hurts a little. It doesn't matter."

Because that doctor didn't repair my wounded hand properly, the middle finger on my right hand became crooked. It remains that way to this day—a daily reminder of those bitter days of hard labor.

≈

In my brickwork, I learned the difference between red brick and gray brick. In those days, a red brick sold for 5.5 fen, while a gray brick cost 8.5 fen. Red brick broke more easily, and it was used for outdoor courtyard walls and cheap peasant homes. Gray brick was sturdier and more reliable, and it was sent to the cities for construction of strong buildings. That's why Beijing's cityscape in those days was unremittingly grey.

Originally, another group of laborers had been assigned to build housing for the labor camp—all made of cheap red brick, of course. But they were short-handed, so my group took on some of the work. Brick construction was very heavy labor in that fierce summer heat. I was assigned to the line that passed the hot bricks, hand to hand, to be tossed to workers on the roof.

The new bricks had rough edges that would cut your hands. We wore knit gloves, but they weren't much protection. You had to concentrate on what you were doing and move fast, catching the bricks and then flinging them up to people on the roof. If you missed the catcher, you would be criticized. My knit gloves quickly wore out from the rough bricks. I would reverse the gloves, back to front, and go on for a few hours until they had to be changed.

Every evening, we had to attend a meeting for "ideological transformation," so there was never time for me to repair the gloves. Seeing how torn they were, Xiaoming took my needle and thread and sat beside me at the meetings, sewing. He would sew up the holes and then hold up the gloves for me to see.

"Look, Mama! Now your fingers won't show through. Did I sew them up right?"

"Excellent, Ming-Ming! Mama is very thankful."

"This way, you won't hurt your hands tomorrow."

His little stitches were crooked and crude, and his sewing skills never improved, but his heart was in it. He repaired my gloves again and again, thank goodness, to protect my hands in those days. I was very proud of this child, this six-year-old boy who had learned to sew. And in spite of the calamity that had struck our family, I felt that all my kids were growing up very well. They all understood what was going on and knew how badly I was suffering—even this little boy, who did everything possible to help relieve his mother's distress.

The people in my group all praised him. "Little Ming helped his mom sew up her gloves. What a good boy!"

Auntie Liu especially loved him. "Ming-Ming," she said, "we'll put a stamp on you and mail you back home to Beijing!" The other aunties and uncles laughed and repeated this idea.

"No," he said, in all seriousness. "I'm not going back to Beijing by myself. I'll go back with my mama."

"They're just teasing you, Ming-Ming," I said. "How could you fit in the mailbox and be mailed off? We will need to take the train to go back to Beijing."

~

That summer was unusually hot, even for the flatlands of Henan. Every day was over ninety degrees, and often the temperature rose to well over one hundred.

As the heat rose, the population at the camp diminished. Some people's cases were cleared up, and they were sent back to Beijing to work. As a result, the kitchen lacked hands, so my fellow campers asked for me to help with the cooking. "She's a good cook," they said.

But cooking was not much easier than brickmaking. The cooks had to stand for hours in front of the hot ovens in the blistering summer heat. Sometimes they passed out. In order to prepare meals for 130 people, I had to start work at eight in the morning and keep moving all day. I steamed mantou, baked sesame seed cakes, stuffed pancakes, and made noodles, all day long. When we prepared mantou, it took over sixty pounds of flour to supply the whole camp. As I stood there kneading the dough, the sweat would flow down my sides in a steady stream.

One day, on the Chinese Moon Festival, we kitchen workers decided to improve the food. We built a brick oven and made mooncakes, stuffed with cabbage, sugar, red bean paste, and Chinese dates. We made enough so that each person could have two mooncakes, which meant making more than 260 of them. I got dizzy standing over the griddle in that ninety-seven degree weather. I told myself, *You can't faint! Stick it out for another little while, and you'll make it.*

People walking by smelled the aroma and came to look at what we were cooking.

"Wang Yulin, what is it that smells so good?"

"We're having mooncakes."

"Yum, mooncakes for lunch!"

"Hey, Wang Yulin," said my friend Liu Xia. "What's wrong with you? You look white as a ghost. Are you not well?"

"I'm okay," I managed to say.

"No, you're getting heat exhaustion. Quick. Go outside and get some air."

"I'm fine. I'll rest as soon as the cakes are done." Actually, I was already unsteady on my feet.

"Help! Wang Yulin has fainted!"

Somehow, I was taken back to my quarters. When I awoke, it was two o'clock the next afternoon. After that, I really understood the hard life of the cooks; it was tougher than working in the sun. Of course, there was no such thing as air conditioning anywhere in our camp.

Aside from the heat and humidity, another feature of Henan summer was what we called "the shakes"—malaria. There were clouds of mosquitoes. We took quinine as a preventive, but many people got the shakes anyway. An attack would last about a week, with the patient rotating between burning fever and freezing chills that no amount of bedclothes would drive away.

Our one and only stir-fry chef came down with the shakes. He sent for me and told me at his bedside, "Wang Yulin, you've been helping me out from time to time, and I know that you can do it. You have to take over from me now, and do the stir-frying."

Heavens! I now had full responsibility for feeding over 130 people. I had cooked for a few people: I fixed the halal food for our Muslim campmates, and I had prepared special diets for the sick. And I had prepared the mooncakes that one time. But I had never dreamed of cooking three meals a day for over 130 people. This man kept several giant woks going at the same time, using a cook-shovel to empty them into big steaming bowls.

"Shifu," I said tremulously, using the respectful term for a skilled master of any trade, "I have never done anything like that."

"It takes people to do anything," he replied. "If you haven't done it, you must learn by doing it. After the first few times, you'll know what to do."

So I began kneading sixty-pound mountains of dough and, together with a woman from the Russian language section at Radio, began cooking vegetables with a big shovel.

At mealtime, I watched as the others ate with gusto, but I was so exhausted that I couldn't eat a thing. Instead, I would sit there resting while sipping boiled water. How I longed for a cup of tea, but there was none.

As usual, Ming-Ming helped me to weather the burden of my new tasks as cook. When I made my daily trip to the vegetable garden to fetch the food, he would go with me—riding on the wheelbarrow when it was empty and helping to pull the load on the way back.

"Mama, I'll pull the cart myself!"

"No, Ming-Ming, you can't pull over a hundred pounds up the hill."

"I can, Mama! Remember how I used to push the dirt uphill?"

"But you're too small. You mustn't strain yourself, do you understand?"

"I know. I let it coast downhill, just holding on to the yoke. When you go uphill, I can help you push."

And that's the way we went to and from the vegetable patch every day, full of laughter and joking. He was very happy at his work.

Having my son with me made the labor camp bearable. Seeing his smiling face reminded me of what mattered most in my life: my children. If I could get through this horrible time, I could return to Beijing and see my precious daughters, too. Maybe someday, somehow, Sidney would be released and we'd be a family again.

≈

Even though I was now doing the cooking, I still had to go back to the kilns when it was time to remove the adobe bricks. Each kiln was a dome about three stories high, built to look like a small hill, with a round hole at the top. Inside, the bricks baked for a week, but during that time, we had to continually pour water on the bricks from that hole in the top of the kiln. The kiln needed steam to bake the bricks and turn them from red to gray. We each had to carry two big cans of water—each one weighing about seventy pounds—suspended from the ends of a long pole balanced on our shoulders up to the top of the kiln roof. To get to the top, we ascended the hill along a spiral path. If we spilled the water, it would freeze and we would be in danger of slipping off the mound.

Carrying two big cans of water suspended from a pole was not something that came naturally to everyone; it had to be learned. Some people staggered along as though they were drunk, and by the time they arrived at their destination they had lost half of the water. Others tried to support the weight with their hands, causing them to weave from side to side. But unlike my time in Fangshan, my workmates in Henan managed to make light of the situation.

"Look at Old Liang stagger. Where did he get the beer?" someone would shout.

"Old Liang! Get some beer for the rest of us!" The others in the line would roar with laughter.

I had started carrying water on my shoulders when I was still in middle school, so I was more experienced than most. But I still found it hard, since I hadn't done it for many years. My shoulders soon became red and swollen. The smart way was to use a shoulder pad. The Chinese had learned long ago to sew shoulder pads out of heavy cloth. I didn't have pads, and every night I would have to rub my shoulders to get some relief. If someone happened to slap me on the shoulder in fun, they would be startled at the response—it hurt! But I would grin anyway.

Gradually we discovered together that good humor and comradeship could make suffering tolerable.

Perhaps it was the occasional laughter with friends or the giggle of my little son, but eventually I began to rethink my earlier conclusion: that I was destined for a bitter fate. The traditional Chinese view is fatalism: life is unfair. If you have an unlucky fate, if the stars are aligned against you, you are destined for bitterness and you can do nothing about it, except endure. "To live means to suffer" is the first of the Buddhist noble truths. If you are suffering, the only response is either detachment or resignation. For centuries, millions of Chinese believed that it's a virtue to suffer in silence.

But during those days in Henan, looking at my little son, with his American-Chinese face, I made a decision to reject this fatalistic view. In the twentieth century, we did not have to simply accept our fate. Perhaps Sidney had influenced me, with his American individualism; he certainly had shaped his life in a way that was not preordained. I had always accepted whatever jobs the Party had assigned to me, and I had even accepted a wedding date I didn't choose. But now that the Party was not taking care of me, I had to learn to make decisions for myself. Even though I could not reverse the policies that had turned China upside down, even though I could not walk out of this labor camp, I could start to dream of a day when life would be different.

When facing an intractable problem, it often seems like there are only two choices: accept it or fight it. In my case, fighting it was not an option. But I refused to accept it either. At times, it's true, you can do nothing but endure. Day to day, in the camp, all I could do was work as hard as possible without complaining, so that no one could say I had a bad attitude.

But you don't have to wallow in misery and self-pity—or give up. If others are willing to laugh and lift your spirits, that friendship can help you get through each day. And if you are strong enough, and endure long enough, the time will come when you can make decisions about building a better life. If you give up hope somewhere along the way, when the moment comes you won't be ready to act.

I needed to hope that one day this suffering would end. What my life would be like afterward, I could barely imagine. Sidney might not even live through it. But whatever the condition of my life and my family, I would take control of my future, somehow, someway. The first Yulin, my second sister, may have been destined for a bitter fate. But I would not accept that. I would reshape my destiny.

Chapter Forty

A Shift in the Wind

BY THE TIME we had all been at the camp for six months or so, everyone actually had a pretty good idea of what was going on. Even the minders and squad leaders knew that the inmates at the camp had been implicated in unfair ways that had nothing to do with their basic value as human beings. In contrast to the mutual suspicion that pervaded the May Seventh school in Fangshan, where almost no one dared to make a gesture of goodwill, the atmosphere at the camp began to relax—especially when none of the known snitches was around. Friendships and comradeship grew and flourished, and there was much joking and laughter.

I knew all along that there were no real doubts about me. I was never asked probing questions about my life or activities, and no one ever accused me of wrongdoing. The reason I was there was because of the charges against Sidney. Until his case was resolved, my problem would never go away. With my new outlook, I was determined to take control, to find some other way. But how?

I thought a lot about the possibility of sending letters to someone influential, asking him to intervene on Sidney's behalf. Back in 1968, I had written to Premier Zhou Enlai, which had helped release us from our detention in the hotel. However, Premier Zhou had not been able to save even his adopted daughter, a brilliant stage director and actress who died in prison after seven months of torture. I sensed that even Zhou Enlai's position was insecure, although it was impossible to know what was going on inside the Chinese leadership.

But writing to Chairman Mao had not worked. One particularly disturbing thought nagged at me. Mao had personally admitted to me, in Shanghai in November 1965, that Sidney's first arrest had been a terrible mistake and that the Communist Party of China had erred. Such an admission of wrongdoing was very difficult to make. Could he possibly admit it a second time? That seemed highly unlikely. But if the Party could not admit it was mistaken, then—barring a miracle—Sidney would never get out of prison, and my issues would never be resolved either.

I forced myself to ponder two different outcomes.

First, it was possible that Sidney would die in prison. He had suffered from tuberculosis before, and twice had contracted infectious hepatitis. Upon his arrest, he had been thin and undernourished, his clothing sparse, and I had no idea how badly he was being persecuted. Judging from the fact that they were punishing me, and that they had not notified me as next of kin, I assumed that he was still alive. I clung to this hope, but I had no way of knowing for sure.

Second, by some miracle, Sidney might be released. After all, Nixon had come to China, and maybe someone was making inquiries about U.S. citizens. The Party would have to find some way of pinning a "mistake" on him, to justify imprisoning him. To save face for Chairman Mao, they probably would never explicitly clear Sidney of the charge of espionage. But maybe they would declare him guilty of some lesser charge and let him go free. That was my best hope.

Analyzing these possibilities helped me to imagine different futures for myself and my children.

～

Late in 1972, as the dreary winter weather chilled our bones, the character of the nightly criticism and self-criticism meetings underwent a change. All former Party members who were in the labor camp under suspicion were given an opportunity to demonstrate their loyalty and clarity by going through a self-examination process, known as *dou si pi xiu,* meaning "struggle with self and criticize revisionism."

The Party branch would decide which Party members would "pass" this self-examination and have their membership restored. Such a decision also had to be approved by the Radio Party committee in Beijing. But at least, it appeared, there was now a way out.

This policy shift blew a waft of hope into our camp. When my campmates were called to "struggle with self," we secretly cheered them on. Some of them passed and their cases were cleared. They packed up and headed home.

One day, our squad leader told me that I was to make a further examination of my issues at one of these meetings. This news spread, and a group of my campmates gathered around, congratulating me.

"Wang Yulin, it looks like the door's opening! You're going to struggle with self and criticize revisionism!"

That might not seem like good news, but, in that context, it was. Ordinarily, people under suspicion of having serious political problems would not be allowed to make an ordinary self-examination of their ideology. Since they were suspected enemies, no one was interested in hearing about their ideological issues. Only Party members got to talk about their beliefs. The fact that I was being put through this process now made it look as though I was being treated as an errant Party member, not an enemy of the state. Perhaps I was on my way out of the swamps of political suspicion and persecution, but I dared not get too hopeful.

"Humph!" I said. "It's just going through the formalities. There's no way they're going to let me pass. This is just another opportunity for them to attack me at the meeting. What else could possibly happen?"

But my friend Liu Xia said, "I tell you, things are changing. This is a good thing."

That afternoon, I ran into one of the most capable leaders, the former head of the Foreign Broadcast Department, Zou Xiaoqing. He said, "Good for you, Wang Yulin. I envy you. So far, I don't have a clue about my future."

"Don't kid me," I said. "You joined the Party before Liberation, and you rose to the position of a leader. But Old Zou, after you've been reinstated as an official, please remember your poor old comrades from labor camp!"

He smiled. "How could I forget? When that day comes, I'll invite you and Lao Li to be guests in my home."

"I'll hold you to your word," I responded with a smile. He had always been a good man and a friend to Sidney. In the camp, few people had ever dared to refer to my husband by that fond nickname.

For the first time, my campmates and I could begin to imagine working together again as colleagues at Radio Peking—even inviting each other to dinner. What small kindnesses would we remember? And what cruel words would be hard to forget?

Another member of my squad, Old Lady Liu, pulled me aside and whispered, "Wang Yulin, does this mean that there's been a change in Li Dunbai's case?"

"That's what I've been trying to figure out," I answered. "If he was really a spy, they wouldn't be giving me this opportunity. It must mean they don't have a scrap of spy evidence against him."

She nodded. "That makes sense."

"But," I went on, "I'm not holding out any hope whatsoever, at this point."

She said, "You shouldn't take that attitude. If they tell you to struggle and criticize, get yourself ready!"

With their encouragement, I sat up all night writing out my self-examination.

What usually happened was that whoever was making the self-examination would first write a report to the members of the Party branch, after which the members would criticize the person's statement. Generally speaking, the more profound the self-examination—the more you denounced your failings as representing serious incursions by the class enemy— the more biting the critique that rained down on you from the membership, but the more likely you were to get a pass in the end. If you passed this test, you could have your Party membership restored, and return to home and work. The stakes were enormous.

The basic demand of me, all along, had been to separate myself completely from Sidney—to "draw a clear line of distinction" between him and me. What I was supposed to focus on was why my political consciousness had kept me from seeing that Sidney was a bad person, and why I had lived with him for so many years without detecting that he was a spy.

But I realized I needed to draw my own line: I would not give in to any demands that I denounce Sidney. And I would never accept that I was disloyal to my motherland and my people. It still disturbed me that I had once been called a "disgrace to the Chinese nation." That was patently false and slanderous. Lately, no one had been saying that, and my friends all knew that was the one charge I could not tolerate.

But that left other areas for self-criticism. I could talk about my low political consciousness. I could say I had become accustomed to such "bourgeois luxuries" as music and theater performances. I could say I had lived a privileged life and took my perks for granted. I could say I failed to remember the dire poverty of my childhood and had lost touch with the daily sufferings of ordinary Chinese people. My time in labor camp, I could say, had reignited my understanding of the spirit of the working class. While sticking to my principles like a bulldog, I could be adaptable in other ways. It's good to be persistent, but sometimes you have to focus on what's most important and give in on the small stuff.

I had been through self-confession and struggle sessions many times before. But this time, there seemed to be a real chance that my self-examination would be accepted—and that I could be released from camp to go home to my children. That was the big prize. Here, at last, was an action I could take to change my destiny. So I took the task very seriously.

By the time I finished, my script for the self-examination was two or three inches thick. Finally, one night in a small shed with fifteen people gathered around me, I read aloud my self-examination. I put my whole heart into it and tried to show genuine remorse.

I was prepared when I heard the usual criticisms. "Your class consciousness is low." "You still don't get it. Your attitude is unrepentant." "You are stubbornly clinging to a position against the people's interests." Of course, they had to criticize something. Otherwise, the Party would have to admit that my time in the labor camp had been a huge mistake.

After making these required comments, most of the Party members nodded and seemed inclined to accept my self-confession as genuine.

But one woman would not: Wei Lin. "We can't let her pass," she said. "She is a disgrace to the Chinese nation."

In a rage, I walked out.

The next day, as we lined up to depart for the kiln, the platoon leader called to me.

"Wang Yulin, step out of the ranks!"

"What for?" I said, without moving.

"You must stay behind and work on your struggle with self-examination."

"I'm not going to do that again."

"Why not?"

"If I am a disgrace to the Chinese nation, I'm not qualified to struggle with self."

"Come with me. Company headquarters wants to talk with you."

All my campmates standing in line were drinking the whole thing in, probably wondering at my rigid attitude.

"If the leadership wants to talk with me, ask them to come to the brickyards," I said, and I set off to the kiln, marching in the ranks.

A young guy who was marching beside me said, "Wang Yulin, what's gotten into you? Where did you get the guts to stand up to the leadership like that?"

"I won't do that again, if it costs my life," I said. "They're calling me a national disgrace, treating me like an enemy of China. Once you're marked as an enemy, it doesn't do any good to try. From my attitude toward labor to the quantity and quality of my performance, I've been one of the best workers. Everybody sees this. But never once have I been commended—only criticized and attacked."

"Forget about it," he said. "This is not the moment to be stubborn."

I braced myself for a showdown with the Party leaders that evening. Quite unexpectedly, however, there was not a word of criticism. To the contrary, both the squad leader and the company commander apologized to me! I noticed that Wei Lin's usual seat was empty.

"Wang Yulin, certain individuals called you a national disgrace," the company commander said. "But that's not the view of the organization, nor is it a conclusion drawn on your case."

My attitude stiffened. I said, "I want to make my position clear: If I'm not considered at all qualified to be a Party member—if I'm a national disgrace—then I definitely do not intend to be a black mark on the Party. And there's no point in more struggle and criticism. That can wait until I'm qualified again."

The company commander said, "We have criticized that comrade. What she said was wrong. The organization has not reached a conclusion on you."

I raised my voice and repeated my stance. But the platoon leader emphasized, over and over, that this was the wrong attitude. I should go through the process for Party members right now. Just one more time.

I appreciated this new approach: friendly, warm, courteous. It was the first time in six years that the leadership had treated me like this! Ever since Sidney had been arrested, the Party leaders at Radio had treated me as if I were an enemy of China. They had shown me nothing but stern glares and harsh criticism.

At labor camp, my coworkers had often testified that my work was outstanding, and that I could endure more than others. But none of these small-minded leaders had ever acknowledged my efforts. I had thought to myself, *No matter what kind of hard labor they give me, I will never give up, and I will keep a clear conscience. I'm going to put 100 percent of my effort into it. I'll do such a good job that it will shut their mouths.* That's what I had done, and that was my moral victory.

Now, the leaders' attitude toward me had made a 180-degree turn.

This came as a great surprise. Why the sudden change? It must be that there were instructions from above. Who could it be? I had no way of knowing. Whatever the case, it was a welcome development.

Finally, I agreed to undergo one more struggle and criticism meeting. I read out my written self-examination, the exact same paper that I had read at the previous criticism meeting. In it, I never acknowledged that Sidney was a bad person, or a spy, but simply said that I had never detected any spy activity and admitted that my political consciousness was low.

This time, there was almost no criticism or commentary. Wei Lin said nothing. Nobody said whether I passed or not. They did not inform me whether they had "reached a conclusion on me." They did not restore my Party membership. But after a full year in the labor camp in Henan, they let me return to Beijing.

Chapter Forty-One

Hopes Dashed

WHEN I CAME home that winter, I was optimistic—still uncertain but hoping that life was about to change for the better. The leaders at Radio had said I could return to work, and they had even hinted they might allow my family to move to a bigger apartment, though not back to our previous home in the Foreign Experts Building. The political winds had shifted, and it seemed possible that all the ugly attacks would stop and life might return to normal. I planned to make discreet inquiries about Sidney; maybe I would be allowed to at least write to him or send him food.

Our train ride back to Beijing whizzed by quickly. Ming-Ming, once so silent, couldn't stop jabbering about his three sisters, quizzing me about them. In one year, he had adapted so completely to life in the labor camp that he had trouble remembering our family life in Beijing. For a six-year-old, one year can feel like a decade.

"Will the aunties and uncles be there?" he wanted to know.

Yes, I told him, many of my campmates had already returned to Beijing, and I would be seeing them daily at Radio. After the hard times we had weathered together, I wondered how our relationships would change once we were back at the office, But as the miles of wintry fields flowed by our train window, I worried most about how my girls had fared during my absence.

From the Beijing railway station, Ming-Ming and I rode home in the Radio shuttle bus that normally picked up cadres at their apartment buildings and brought them to work every day. As we drove into the residential courtyard, Toni raced over to meet us. "Mama! Mama! Xiaoming! Xiaoming!" she shouted.

Xiaoming called back excitedly, "Er Jie-jie!"—meaning Second Sister.

Outside the bus door, Toni was jumping up and down with excitement. When we emerged, she ran over and hugged both of us tightly. "I've been waiting here forever!" she said. She was fourteen years old now, as tall as I was—but too thin.

"How are things at home?" I asked.

"Everything's okay," she said, "except that we all really miss you!"

"I've missed my sisters and my grandma!" Ming-Ming said.

Toni hugged him again. "Look how big you are! I hear you're learning to read!"

My mother and the three girls were still living in the same tiny room on the fifth floor, all sleeping in the same bed, sharing a bathroom with the neighbors. Still, my heart swelled with joy now that we were reunited. Mama boiled a big pot of jiaozi dumplings to welcome us back.

Soon after I got home, though, I discovered that Jenny and Sunny seemed out of sorts each day when they returned from school. I asked them if they were being harassed, but I didn't get the whole story until one night when I discovered that Jenny was crying to herself under her quilt.

"What's wrong?" I asked, both startled and alarmed. I had worried about the children being bullied at school, because of their father's case. "Tell me, who's giving you a hard time?"

"Nobody," Jenny replied, trying to be stoic. Sunny started to cry, too.

"Then why are you crying? Tell me why?" By now, I was shouting.

Finally, Sunny came out with it. "They don't let us attend political studies class."

"What?" I said. "What kind of political studies?"

The girls looked at each other, as if they were reluctant to break their secret pact not to disturb me with their troubles.

Finally Jenny explained. "They're studying about the Lin Biao anti-Party clique. They won't let us read the internal materials or take part in political studies. They say that we're Americans."

My little girls, born and raised in Beijing, who had never been to the United States and couldn't even speak English, were being punished for being "American."

Toni angrily said, "At my school, it's different. But at their school, if they don't pass the political studies course, they won't get promoted at the end of the term!"

Jenny wiped her eyes. "The political class is during third period. We have another class after it, so we can't go home early. Xiaoxiang and I just have to wander around in the school yard till it's time for fourth period. And we don't have a watch to tell us the time. We have to stay by the school door."

"It's so unfair!" Sunny added. "We don't know why they treat us like that. Some of the teachers don't know that we're not allowed in political studies, and they ask us why we're out in the school yard instead of going to class."

At the time, I didn't stop to consider the irony of this situation. An American student might think it a good thing to be allowed to skip a one-hour class examining the twisted logic of the latest Communist political movement. But my daughters wanted badly to be treated the same as their classmates. And the rules were against them: if they failed political studies, they would have to repeat the whole year.

"Okay, don't worry," I said. "I'll write to the central leaders about this."

"Oh, no!" said Jenny. "Mama, whatever you do, don't write the central leaders. It may make more trouble for you at Radio!"

"We can handle it," added Sunny.

"I don't care if they never let me back into the Party," I said. "Your father's case must not interfere with your education! I won't stand for discrimination against you at school."

My mind was made up. Whatever calamity befell, I would let it all land on me. If I could prevent it, the children weren't going to be traumatized. But of course, I knew that they were already traumatized because of the overall social and political pressure, but there was little that I could do about that. Getting Jenny and Sunny admitted to political studies class was one concrete step I could take. And I had vowed I would not just sit back and accept our bitter fate.

That very night, I wrote a two-page letter to Premier Zhou Enlai.

≈

I know how terribly busy you are, but I am writing you in desperation. The school that two of my daughters attend doesn't allow them to attend political studies class, which means that they can't be promoted. The reason given is that the girls are American. Actually, their father, Li Dunbai, is American, but our children were all born in China, registered in China. Our country doesn't even have diplomatic relations with the American government, so how could they be citizens of the United States? We have raised them as Chinese citizens, loyal to the Party. Children don't get to pick their parents. When the parents get into trouble, what attitude should the government take toward the children? Should the children grow up hostile to the government? Or should the government educate them to love China and to have a positive attitude toward our society? I earnestly hope

that the premier will intervene in this instance. I realize that it is a big issue
for our family but a small matter for the country. Nevertheless, it is a matter
of fundamental policy.

≈

So many times I had written letters to Chairman Mao, and I was sure that
none of them had reached him. Mailing this letter or submitting it through the
Party branch people at my workplace, I knew, would not work. Afraid of attracting attention and getting criticized, they would never pass my letter along to the
premier.

So I found another way. The next day, I took the letter to Radio's Military
Administrative Group. I opened the letter for Vice-Director Liu to read. He made
no comment, but his secretary walked over at this point, so I said, "Shall we have
your secretary send the letter out?"

He grunted, half under his breath, "Okay. Send the letter out."

"Can you send it right away?" I asked the secretary, handing her the letter.

Previous appeals to them about discrimination against the children had fallen
on deaf ears, so I was anxious to get this letter taken care of right there, on the
spot. I didn't leave until I saw Vice-Director Liu give the letter to the messenger
who carried secret documents to the central Party headquarters at Zhongnanhai.

A little over a month later, my Party branch secretary summoned me. "We
hear that you sent a letter to Premier Zhou," she said. "Is that true?"

"True."

"How is it that we didn't know that?"

"I took it to the Military Administrative Group, and they sent it off."

"Oh, it went out through them. Premier Zhou sent your letter back with handwritten instructions on it." She waved the letter in front of me, so that I glimpsed
the premier's lines.

Hands shaking, I took the letter in my hands. In the margins, Premier Zhou
Enlai had written, "The children of Li Dunbai and Wang Yulin must be treated
exactly the same as other children. They must enjoy equal treatment and suffer
no discrimination." The premier used an ancient Confucian expression for equal
treatment—*yi shi tong ren*—meaning "regarded with equal humanity."

The branch secretary seemed annoyed at me but did not dare contradict the
orders of China's premier. "The Party branch will send someone to the school to
make sure that this is carried out. But let me remind you that in the future you
must not jump levels to send messages to the Party leaders. Every request must

go through this branch."

I was beside myself with joy at the premier's response. This was the first letter to the top leaders that had elicited a written response. Not only would his letter solve the children's problem, but it also showed that the premier had nothing bad to say about Sidney. He did not call Sidney a spy or a counterrevolutionary or a revisionist. This was a great comfort to me.

When I got home and told the children about Premier Zhou's response, they all jumped up and down for joy. And when Jenny and Sunny came home from school the next day, they had more good news.

"Mama, our head teacher apologized to us, and said that it was wrong not to allow us to take political study!" Jenny said. "The teacher gave us heaps of stuff to read about the Lin Biao anti-Party clique. She said that we should read those to get caught up, since we hadn't listened to the reports. She said to ask her if there were any questions."

The discrimination against my children stopped—one ray of joy in an otherwise joyless time. Some things are out of our control, like the wind and the rain. But you can always find some way to struggle against the elements. You just keep trying, whatever you can think of, even if your letters never get through. Then one day, perhaps unexpectedly, your persistence will pay off.

Later, I learned that Premier Zhou, in March 1973, commented on Sidney's case to a gathering of foreign experts who had been attacked during the early phases of the Cultural Revolution. Premier Zhou criticized Sidney for making speeches and supporting the rebels, stating that Sidney had been involved with a reactionary clique in the Party. Actually, some of his foreign friends thought he had been plotting to unseat the premier. This was not true.

But the news uplifted me anyway. Why? Because Premier Zhou made no mention of the main accusation against Sidney: spying. A man accused of being a "reactionary" might be released, if the Party's policy changed; a "spy" could be held forever. Some foreign friends who were present told me that Jiang Qing expressed anger at Zhou's comments. That bolstered my belief that it was Chairman Mao's wife who had ordered Sidney's arrest. She was still powerful, but apparently she didn't always get her way. Maybe her clout was waning.

⁓

Soon after we received the premier's response, we were moved to different quarters, where the five of us lived in two rooms instead of one. Instead of fourteen square meters, we now had sixteen. In the old place, the four children and

I all had to sleep on one bed. Now that the girls had grown bigger, that bed was impossibly crowded. Sometimes Jenny would sleep on the cold, damp cement floor, with just a blanket, which I hated.

In the new quarters, we got a second bed for the living room. The three teen-aged girls slept together on that bed, while Ming and I slept in the bedroom. Mama went back to Shijiazhuang to stay with my brother. This time, I felt confident letting her go. She had held our family together for a full year. For that, I was grateful and it was time she had a break.

Small as it was, this new apartment symbolized for me a new start on life. But things would get worse before they got better. These little apartments were set up so that two families shared a kitchen and bathroom. We had never met the other family, a husband and wife who were service workers.

But soon I "met" them: one night when I went home, the husband and wife were waiting for me in the hallway. They pushed me into a corner and began to beat me unmercifully. "You shameless traitor!" they cursed. "You wanted to live the good life by marrying an American, did you?" The man, especially, pounded on my ribs until I collapsed on the floor in great pain.

I called out for Sunny, who was in the bathroom, but by the time Sunny emerged, the couple had disappeared into their room, and I was lying on the floor, unable to move. My twelve-year-old daughter was shocked to see me, bruised and beaten, and so was I. In five years of humiliation and hard labor, I had never been physically punched or pounded. And these were neighbors I would have to share a bathroom and kitchen with, every day!

I was sure my ribs were broken. These neighbors had punched all the hope out of me. Even a handwritten note from the premier could not protect me as long as my husband was still imprisoned on charges of spying.

But after a few days, I appealed to my old friend, Li Xianhou, who was now chief of the Radio Security Department. Li was an upright man who had the guts to stick up for the truth. He was an old revolutionary who had known Sidney before 1949.

"Wang Yulin, I know you," he said. "Your work has always been good. Your problem is now that your husband isn't here and those people take advantage of you. Here's what you do. Go to the neighborhood clinic, and Radio will be responsible for all medical costs. I will talk to that man's leaders, because what they did to you was wrong."

I was fortunate to know Li Xianhou—the kind of cadre who was true to the original values of the Communist Party, as I had learned them. He worked honestly to serve the people, as well as he could.

At the clinic, I got treated for two bruised ribs. And, though I never had trouble with those neighbors again, I realized in the eyes of most people, I was still a foreign spy's wife—and a disgrace to the nation.

Chapter Forty-Two

Muddling Through

WHEN I RETURNED from labor camp, I was assigned to work at Radio Peking in the English section's Letters from Listeners Office. That was where they put people whose English skills were not great. Soon afterward, though, it was decided that it wasn't proper for me to work in that office, as it was considered a sensitive department, and I was a "politically dubious" person. Most of the listeners to our English-language broadcasts were foreigners. What if I misinterpreted Party policy or divulged secrets? Or worse, told them about my husband's case and appealed to them for help?

So I was transferred to the English section's news group, to edit Xinhua News Agency's English language news stories for voicecast. I hadn't written English in at least five years, but I could remember it reasonably well from my college training.

Life settled into a routine. Every day, I went to the office, and my colleagues let me work in peace. No more dazibaos, no struggle sessions, no labor camp, no beatings. But rogues and rebels still controlled the Party, and good folks who had been criticized still labored under a cloud of suspicion. Some of my colleagues barked orders at me, telling me to do this or that. Many of them refused to smile at me. There were no apologies for bad treatment. No reversal of false accusations. And worst of all, no news about Sidney.

Yet we still had good times. Year after year, the children grew up, and I delighted in seeing them every evening. The girls were turning into beautiful young women, and I loved hearing them laugh and chat together. They doted on their little brother, who was at last flourishing. Mama sometimes came back to visit us. The happiness I felt at home more than made up for the hard faces at work.

Eventually, we all learned to take most mistreatment in stride, even Xiaoming. When he first started primary school, his classmates taunted him, calling him a "little foreigner" and "a little American spy." When he came home in tears, I kept repeating, "You can't talk back to those kids. But just remember, your father is a good man."

The girls helped him through this too; they had already developed thick skins and had learned to ignore these taunts. At school and at work, they faced gibes and sneers but turned their backs on them. Years later I found out that they wept quietly at night under the covers, so as not to worry me.

During these years, my three daughters advanced through middle and high school. Like her father, Jenny was a good writer, and one of her essays was posted as a model on the high school bulletin board. She was asked to draft the regular annual summary of school activities. Sunny took after me and developed an aptitude for chemistry and physics. And Toni continued her interest in healing. Once, when Mama suddenly got a bad case of stomach cramps, I was amazed to see Toni take out a long needle and prepare to treat her grandmother.

"What are you doing?" I asked.

"Don't worry, I know what I'm doing. When our class went to the village to help with the harvest, I was the medical aid person."

I began to imagine Toni growing up to be an outstanding acupuncturist. She had always admired her grandfather when he treated his elderly neighbors, and she was impressed with the way the long needles could relieve human suffering. I just hoped she would have the opportunity to study medicine. College entrance exams had been abolished after 1966, so admissions were no longer based on merit. Students with a "bad class background" or "family difficulties" were routinely denied a college education.

At work, a few people asked me privately, "Do you know where Li Dunbai is? It must be hard to have to worry about four children by yourself."

Yes, I thought, it is hard. But we have to learn from hardship how to deal with hardship. I went without breakfast so that the children could have breakfast. I suffered taunts from all the people around me who didn't understand me. I too learned to disregard all this. I had four lovable children, and I couldn't let outside matters divert my attention from their well-being. But if anyone bullied or struck my children, I would spring to their defense. In that way, we were mother and children, and we were also the closest of friends. They all understood the hardships I was going through, and they all were careful not to add to my burdens.

〰

One evening, on my way home, I ran into the leader of the Spanish language section He asked me to go home with him, saying he had something to discuss with me. I was surprised, but I went with him. What happened there was totally unexpected: He locked the door behind us and grabbed me in a tight embrace.

"You scoundrel! What are you trying to do!" I shouted, trying to fight him off. Furious, I managed to slide open the lock and escape through the door. Then I rushed home to my children.

Another time, an overseas Chinese man who was supposed to have been a friend of Sidney's met me on the way home. He asked to come over to a clump of trees by a little restaurant and said, "Your husband's been gone for a long time, and you're all by yourself. That's no kind of life. Why don't we have some fun together?"

I pushed him away, saying, "You call yourself a friend?"

At age forty, with four children, I had thought I was safe from such advances. But apparently some men saw me as available. This incident made me miss my husband even more. How long could they keep him away from us?

All this did not escape the view of Bill Guo. Bill was a misfit in Beijing; he was a Chinese citizen but his father was a Bank of China official in London, where he grew up and went to school. He was a diminutive, cocky character who spoke halting Chinese with an Oxford accent and was generally looked at as strange, if not suspicious.

But Bill was honest and caring. From time to time, he would see me in the office and say, "Pay no attention to what they say. It's all nonsense."

≈

In the mid-1970s, during another wave in the campaign to get all educated youth to move to the villages, our family narrowly averted another misfortune. One day, the Party branch secretary came to see me. "Your daughter, Xiaoqin, has applied to go to the countryside, and we're preparing to send her."

Jenny had not mentioned this to me, but I had been tipped off by one of Jenny's schoolmates, so I was prepared. "That's impossible!" I said. "I won't agree to it."

"Li Dunbai has written a letter, asking that his children be allowed to go to the countryside," she said.

I didn't believe her. "I don't care about that," I replied. "I'm in charge here, and I won't allow her to go. The regulations state very clearly that all such decisions are up to the head of the family. Right now, that's me. I won't permit it."

Jenny begged me to change my mind. "All the other kids are going," she said. "Why should I be different?"

"Because you are different," I explained. "When the local peasants find out about the charges against your father, your life will be in danger. You may be raped or killed. I forbid it!"

And so she didn't go. A disaster was averted.

The daughter of an old Long March veteran named Yang Chaojun, who had been a friend of Sidney's, was the one who had told me about Jenny's application. Yang Chaojun was another example of a heroic, upright revolutionary who practiced what he preached. He never rose high in the ranks because he was incapable of flattery. But he was in a key position to help us more than once.

The next time was in 1975. Jenny was sitting at home, out of high school but not allowed to go to college. She badly needed work, but how could she find a decent job when her father's case was in her personnel files? Yang Chaojun's daughter-in-law, who worked in the personnel department of a big factory, took care of that. She erased all mention of Sidney's problem from Jenny's files, so Jenny was able to find work.

The job she found was as an apprentice to a master lathe operator in a suburban factory. This was considered a good job, since experience as a common worker would raise her consciousness and make her a better citizen. Bright girl that she was, she learned the trade in half the usual time and was able to operate the lathe on her own after the first few months. Still, Jenny felt vulnerable with that rough bunch of men at the factory, and she chose to take the two-hour bus ride home every day rather than to spend the night at the plant.

≈

My four children were thriving, and for that I felt lucky. But Mama told me that my brother and sister in Shijiazhuang had not fared as well. Although they had barely met Sidney—only once or twice, briefly—they suffered because of their connection with him.

When the Cultural Revolution broke out, my sister, Wang Guilin, had risen to chief pharmacist at Shijiazhuang's Number One Hospital. She was subjected to struggle sessions, where her colleagues demanded that she confess her spy connection with Sidney. Fortunately, she was well liked at the hospital, so the struggle sessions were not too bad. But then they took her out to a village where the peasants didn't know her, and the struggle became brutal. She was beaten and severely criticized. When she returned home, she was confined in a building belonging to the hospital for two years. After being released, she had to do construction work at the hospital, and her children were not allowed to go to college. Despite her troubles, my sister knew that I was having an even harder time than she was, and every month she sent me ten yuan to help us through.

My brother, Wang Weilin, eighteen years my senior, was dragged off to struggle meetings in his watchmakers' group. A quiet, honest man, and an accomplished watchmaker, he told his accusers he had nothing to say about me, that we had barely spoken in years. He was accused of withholding evidence, so as punishment he was confined for two years in a primary school building.

My brother's only son, Wang Xukuan, was working in a factory in northeast China when Sidney was arrested. The entire factory held struggle meetings to fight against this "accomplice of a big-time American spy." Xukuan was an awkward youth, not a good talker. Whenever he felt pressured, he would stutter. His tormentors proclaimed that that was a sign of guilt. He admitted having frequently been at our home in Beijing, and this laid him open to further demands that he report what "spy messages" he had carried for Sidney. They pressed him to confess what he knew about our alleged espionage. Of course, he knew nothing. They fired him from his factory job.

It happened that my mother was staying with Xukuan at the time. She was also humiliated and labeled as the "American spy's mother-in-law." Even some of my college friends were forced to go through struggle meetings and were paraded through the streets in disgrace. Wang Fengzhen suffered especially badly. The soul of integrity, she faced her tormentors unafraid and declared defiantly that she was my friend. None of my friends or relatives had ever done anything wrong. They were attacked simply because Sidney was in trouble.

This hideous injustice disturbed me—and haunted me. I had chosen to marry a foreigner. Why should my choice affect the way others treated my family and friends? Yet to many Chinese this made sense. If Sidney was guilty of disloyalty, so were my relatives.

~

I still had no word about Sidney. After years of wracking my brain to think of a way to get news about him, I decided to try an extraordinary measure—writing the Party Central Committee, explaining that in order to "draw the line" between Sidney and me, I wanted a divorce. In truth, I didn't want a divorce. I had promised Sidney I would stand by him, and I was determined to do that. But from my experience in personnel work, I knew that asking for a divorce was the only way that I could find out Sidney's status. According to regulations, I would not be allowed to divorce someone under investigation unless he had died or unless there was a verdict in his case.

To send the letters out, I went through a friend of Sidney's and mine—confidential documents courier Zhang Xinyou. He was a swashbuckling motorcycle rider with a daughter who had a leg paralyzed from polio. Her schoolmates generally ignored her, because of her disability, but sixteen-year-old Toni was in her class and her heart went out to this handicapped girl. Toni went out of her way to make friends with her, and she used to accompany her to the clinic for her acupuncture treatments.

Because of his job, Zhang Xinyou had access to high-level offices all around Beijing. Out of friendship for me and my daughter, he probed everywhere to try to find out where Sidney was being held. Once, he thought he had located Sidney, because he had seen a foreigner smoking a pipe in a prison near Taoranting Park. But it turned out to be Israel Epstein, a Polish Jew who had grown up in China. Epstein, a magazine editor and Chinese Communist Party member who was imprisoned on false charges in 1968, was released in 1973, with an apology. I dared to hope for the same for Sidney. Ignoring the danger to himself if he were caught violating regulations by delivering personal messages, Zhang Xinyou ensured my request for a divorce reached the Party Central Committee.

One day in the fall of 1974, the Party branch secretary came to tell me that the "leaders" were summoning me for a talk. When I entered the little office, there were three middle-aged cadres whom I didn't know – two men and one woman.

"Are you Wang Yulin?"

"Yes."

"We're from the Beijing Intermediate Court."

What does the court have to do with me? I wondered.

"You wrote many letters demanding a divorce from Li Dunbai. That's what we're here to discuss with you."

Now that I had a response from the court, I knew that my letters had gone through. Eager to find out news about Sidney, I stood my ground and insisted on demanding a divorce.

One of the men asked me, "Why do you want a divorce?"

"Because they say Sidney is a secret agent. I ought to draw the line. How can I live with an American spy?"

The woman asked, "Who said he's a secret agent?"

"People all over are saying that. He's been arrested. It's in the papers. Isn't that why they keep having struggle meetings, demanding that I draw a line between Li Dunbai and myself?"

The first man said, "But who specifically told you that he's an agent?"

"You people said it!"

The other man responded, "You can't put this on us! We never said that."

"Anyway, it's the government that said it, and because of that our whole family has been under investigation, my brother and sister in Shijiazhuang have been imprisoned . . ."

The first man, who seemed to be in charge, saw that my attitude was stubborn and we were in a stalemate. "Wang Yulin," he said, "let's not talk like that. Let's not talk about divorce. Only see what good times we're in now."

"No, I have to have a divorce. My contradiction with him is with an enemy of the people, not a contradiction among the people."

For nearly two hours, we went back and forth like this. Actually, I felt very happy all the time we were arguing, because I had found out what I had been fishing for—and the news was good. They were denying that Sidney had been classified as a secret agent! That must mean that his case was heading for a settlement.

Finally, the man said, "You should drop this demand for a divorce."

The woman chimed in, "That's right. Problems between husband and wife can be settled privately. Why insist on a divorce?"

Finally, the man in charge said, "You're very determined, but you'll find out later on that you may not need a divorce at all. Go back and think it over carefully."

Even more surprising—and heartening—was that when I stood up to leave, they all three rose to their feet and shook hands with me.

I ran home, shut the door, and exploded to the children. "Good news! Good news!"

"What news, Mama?"

"Your papa will be home soon!"

"Who told you that?" they wanted to know.

I told them the whole story. "I wrote letters to the leaders. I never contacted any court. So why would the court seek me out? Something has changed."

"Mama," the children said, "you asked for a divorce from Papa?"

"Silly kids!" I said. "That was the only way I had of finding out whether your father was still alive, and what was happening to him."

They stuck their little thumbs up and said, "Smart Mama!"

We all danced around the room. They sang out, "Papa's coming home! Papa's coming home!" But I shushed them immediately, lest someone should hear us.

Though he actually had no memory of his father, our nine-year-old son jumped up and down with his sisters. Then he asked me for one yuan.

"Why do you want money?"

"I'm going to buy some candy to give to my friends, to celebrate."

It is the Chinese custom to hand out candy when someone is engaged, or has a new child, or something else good happens. But I told him not to. For now, this had to stay our family secret.

But my hopes were dashed. For days, weeks, months, I heard nothing more. When I inquired, I found out nothing. It would be another three years before Sidney finally was released. Those were three hard years, struggling to keep the family going. Altogether, my children and I spent ten years without Sidney. During that time, I learned how tough life can be. Your parents give you your body, but what you make of your life is up to you. You have to be careful not to get carried away when everything is going smoothly, or you may collapse if things suddenly turn bad. When things got really bad for us, I learned to focus all my strength and resources on the simple issue of survival. Every step forward went through a bitter struggle. None of it was easy.

When the outside pressure got very heavy, I had to fight to keep a clear head. They were saying that Sidney was a major spy—a spy master—and they were accusing me, too, of being a secret agent. I couldn't let myself be swayed by their denouncements and accept charges that were not true, nor could I allow myself to abandon the struggle and, as we say in Chinese, "take the short way out"— commit suicide in order to escape from the suffering. I believed that I must never give up, no matter how hard life was.

I realized that everyone in this world, from the highest ranking leader to a simple housewife and mother, has to face all sorts of vicissitudes, confront all sorts of challenges, go through all sorts of struggles. Nobody but you can solve your problems. It doesn't do to shut your eyes to these problems, to try to beg your way out, or to try to evade the struggle that it takes to resolve them. Some of life's most profound joy comes from waging, and succeeding in, these struggles. I can sum it up in these words: Happiness comes from the struggle with unhappiness.

Chapter Forty-Three

Earth-Shattering Changes

ON JANUARY 8, 1976, a bone-chilling bulletin was released announcing that Premier Zhou Enlai was dead. At work when I heard the news, I felt as though the sky was falling in. My tears flowed down both cheeks. When I went home that evening, I found all four of our children crying.

As small as our family affairs were compared to the overall picture, this great friend had taken time out, twice, to protect us and to ensure us equal treatment to the best of his ability. Premier Zhou had not been able to arrange Sidney's release, but he had mentioned his name publicly and had avoided mentioning any suspicion of espionage. To me, it I felt like our country had lost its firmest pillar of strength and stability.

When I joined the Communist Party as a girl, it was truly a part of the people, "as close as lips and teeth." Party members lived and worked among the poor, listening to their needs, fighting and working on their behalf. The Communist Party of China stood for fair treatment and social justice.

Though the Party had changed, Zhou Enlai had managed to stay true to his core values over the years. He had kept his footing during the new storms that devastated China, doing whatever it took to stay in power to protect people under attack and to protect many relics of China's ancient culture. And now, he was gone. Who would protect the innocents? Like multitudes of Chinese on that day, I wept not just for Zhou Enlai but for myself and for China. What would our country do without him?

The people in power did their best to discourage pubic mourning for Premier Zhou and kept the day of his funeral secret. Hearing rumors about when it would be, our eldest daughter went down to the street crossing where the funeral cortege was expected to pass. Jenny stood on the street from noon until dusk, along with large numbers of people, waiting in silence.

Finally, after nightfall, she came home.

"Mama, I saw Premier Zhou's funeral procession," she said, between tears.

A curtain of darkness fell over China that day.

～

The following summer, in the wee hours of July 28, 1976, tragedy struck at the coal-mining city of Tangshan, east of Beijing. A tremendous earthquake destroyed the lives of hundreds of thousands of people and shook the neighboring cities of Beijing and Tianjin.

Xiaoming was the first to wake up. "Mama, Mama. The building's shaking!"

Still in our nightclothes, we all got up and raced down the stairs, The courtyard was full of people. Most of us had never experienced an earthquake before.

"What can we do?" a neighbor asked.

"When there's an earthquake, there won't be another one right away," someone reassured us. None of us knew about aftershocks. Everyone went home, got dressed, and fixed breakfast. When we felt the first aftershock, we all rushed back outside.

In the news business, an earthquake is no reason to stay home. When I went to the office that morning, I found a bulletin from Radio leadership, advising people to stay out of their homes. We were told to pitch tents outside.

I went to our little neighborhood co-op store, which carried food and basic daily necessities. The city earthquake defense authorities had already provided emergency supplies, so I was able to get a yurt-like tent for our family, similar to the tents that hikers use. We all moved into the tent during the daytime, which we pitched on the sidewalk leading from our home to the Radio building. We couldn't afford to buy folding cots to put in the tent, so at night we went back to our apartment to sleep and to cook.

During this time, aftershocks repeatedly rocked us. Then suddenly, around twilight one evening, Xiaoming disappeared. The girls and I ran around everywhere looking for him. Finally, I found him playing with a bunch of kids in the tunnel that was being dug for the Beijing subway system—the last place you should be during an earthquake! But at ten years old, he didn't know any better.

After three or four days, a national bulletin announced that no more major quakes were expected. With that, we all moved back home. What soon followed was a political earthquake, which plunged the whole country into greater shocks than the Tangshan temblor: Chairman Mao Zedong died on September 9, 1976.

It was a tremendous loss for our country, but I didn't feel the same level of grievous personal loss that I had experienced when Premier Zhou passed away. This time, I was most concerned about where China's new leader would come from and what policies he would pursue, choices that could make a huge difference for Sidney and for us. Of course, ordinary Chinese citizens, even Party members, had no say in the choice of Mao's successor.

Years later, Sidney told me his reactions when he'd heard the news in prison. When Premier Zhou died, Sidney had wept inconsolably for days. When Mao Zedong passed, he had felt that the loss was much more significant for China and for the world, but he did not shed not a single tear. And he couldn't understand why he hadn't!

For me, like many others, a big unspoken question festered in my heart: Why had Chairman Mao allowed the brutalization of so many people for ten long years? Without his support, what could his wife, Jiang Qing, and her radical allies have accomplished?

We heard in the English section that Chairman Mao had anointed Hua Guofeng as his successor. On his death bed, Mao had handed him a sheet of paper with six large Chinese characters on it: *Ni ban shi, wo fang xin*—literally, "With you at work, my mind is at ease."

But who was this Hua Guofeng? Mao had surprised everyone by naming Hua, a relative unknown, to succeed Zhou Enlai as premier. The general impression was that Hua Guofeng was an Honest John type, more cautious than bold.

Yet on October 6, less than a month after Mao's death, Hua Guofeng cracked down on Mao's widow, Jiang Qing, and three of her close allies. Labeling them the "Gang of Four," he arrested them all in one fell swoop. From then on, the excesses of the Cultural Revolution were blamed on those four individuals—and no one else. This arrest, finally, marked the end of the Great Proletarian Cultural Revolution.

People celebrated in the streets. Joy spread throughout the land.

Though the nightmare was over, so much had been lost. During those ten years of turmoil, from 1966 to 1976, the Communist Party, as we had known it, ceased to exist. School education came to a halt. Educated and experienced people were sent to work in the stables. Professors and Party leaders alike were paraded around with dunce caps and forced to endure humiliating struggle sessions. Mob violence ran rampant. Worst of all, the spirits of the people were shattered. There was a complete negation of leadership, a discrediting of all educated people, and a suppression of science and engineering.

Especially noxious was the influence of the "theory of class struggle," which stirred up strife among the people. Many who had committed no wrong worse than being born into an educated or upper-class family were viciously attacked—sometimes beyond the limits of their endurance. Factional infighting caused rifts that were sometimes irreparable. Husbands and wives refused to speak to each other for years. Children denounced their parents, who could not forgive them. Classmates and colleagues could not look each other in the face without remembering hideous insults spoken in revolutionary fervor. Instead of serving the people, Maoist slogans had been used to advance personal ambitions and to settle scores.

No one knows how many tens of thousands of people died during the Cultural Revolution. Many of the deaths were from suicide—or at least reported as such. Hundreds of thousands were imprisoned for political crimes. Millions, like me, were sent to do forced labor. Around seventeen million teenagers were sent down to the countryside, deprived of further education, and not allowed to return home for years.

Even before the arrest, I had heard that the power of Jiang Qing and her cronies was waning. It seemed that Chairman Mao had deliberately passed them over when he chose a relative unknown to be premier. Some top military leaders opposed the Gang of Four, too. That is why Hua was able to arrest them with relative ease. While the reign of chaos and terror had been quashed, the economy was in shambles. How was it ever to recover? Most of us could not even imagine a solution.

~

After the fall of the Gang of Four, people at Radio began speaking to me again. Now, when they wanted me to do something, they asked me and talked it over with me. Smiles began to reappear on people's faces when they looked at me, instead of the frozen expressions that had confronted me all those years.

At home, the children chattered excitedly. "The Gang of Four has been caught! Maybe Papa will be coming home now!" "It was Jiang Qing who put Papa in prison. Now that she's been overthrown, Papa should be freed."

Once again, days and weeks went by, with no news of him. What was going on? *They haven't decided on a conclusion to his case yet,* I thought. After ten years of turmoil and false accusations, the Party had thousands of cases to clear up. They couldn't just open the prison doors and let everyone out. It would take time. But I was impatient.

"When will he come home?" That was the question that was on all our minds.

The thought of welcoming my husband home filled me with both joy and trepidation. My deepest fear was that Sidney might have broken under harsh persecution in prison. I had seen and heard of this happening to other people. I myself had nearly cracked under the mental torment of public humiliation. Ten years in prison, especially in solitary confinement, seemed like more than the human mind could possibly stand. If Sidney came home, he might be mentally crippled. I tried to prepare myself for this worst-case scenario.

≈

Amid my fears about Sidney, I felt proud of the way my parents and siblings had stood up under pressure. My family was old fashioned and straight as a die. We believed implicitly in each other. We knew that none of us would do anything disgraceful. We had been trained in the old Confucian standards of honesty and charity toward those more unfortunate than ourselves. My father often said, "Do nothing shameful and you will not be afraid that the devil will knock on your door at midnight."

During the hard days of the Cultural Revolution, we had been scattered all over, from central Hebei to the far Northeast, and even those in the same city had not been allowed to see each other. But we had stuck together and had stuck to the truth. The result was that we came through as stronger people than we had been, not weaker.

At Radio, some people began asking if I had heard any news about Sidney. Old leaders of the Foreign Broadcast Department, including Vice Director Zuo Moye, Department Chief Zou Xiaoqing, and the motorcycle courier, Zhang Xinyou, asked for news about Sidney.

It was frustrating to tell them, again and again, that I had none.

Chapter Forty-Four

_____

Reunion

ONE FRIDAY MORNING, November 18, 1977, the Party branch secretary summoned me to her office. *What have I done now?* I wondered, ready to receive criticism for whatever it was.

When I knocked on her door, she said, "Wang Yulin, take a seat."

I sat down, waiting.

"Get some clothes ready for Li Dunbai. You're picking him up tomorrow. We'll have a car for you."

Instead of delight, I reacted with confusion. "Has his case been settled? Is there a conclusion?" A conclusion would be the final judgment about him: Was he a spy or not? Only a definitive resolution could free my children from the black cloud that had darkened our lives.

"It's basically resolved. He'll get the conclusion after he comes back here," she said.

My head spun. Sidney would be coming home! "I don't have any of his clothes," I said. "I have to go get them from our old home," meaning the Foreign Experts Building.

A slight frown flickered across her brow. "Let's do it this way. Tell us what clothes you need and we'll send someone to fetch them."

My mind was still muddled: If we were to return home, why wouldn't they even let me go back and get Sidney's clothes? Later, I found out it was because there wasn't a home to go back to. Our things had been tossed into cardboard boxes and stacked in a leaky storeroom, where a lot of it had gone moldy. Sidney told me later that the red covers of his two-volume version of *Hegel's Logic* had been half eaten away by the rats. As a philosophy major, he found that richly symbolic.

"He'll need a pair of leather shoes, a pair of black socks, a white shirt, underclothes, and his new dark brown suit. Also, a necktie." Sidney had always liked wearing Western clothes, and he would want to come out with his dignity intact. Who knew what he had been wearing all these years in detention.

"All right. We'll send someone after these things right away. If we can't find the dark brown suit, will another color do?"

"Yes," I said, curious to hear her tone of accommodation. Would she start being respectful toward me now?

"The things will be brought here, and then the car will take you to get him. Be here at eight tomorrow morning."

As I left her office, my thoughts swirled. Sidney was coming home! This was the moment I had been waiting for. But I wasn't prepared for it. What would he be like, after all this time? I had seen other men emerge from prison as mental cripples or catatonic. *Would he be like that? Would he be worn down by disease? Had he turned into a nervous wreck?* I didn't know yet that he'd been in solitary all those years, but I accepted that he was bound to have problems. I just didn't know what problems or how serious.

That evening at the supper table, I made the announcement in a serious voice. "Good news—your father will be home tomorrow."

The four children all leaped to their feet. "Really? Is it true? Papa's really coming home tomorrow?"

"Your papa may not be the same as he was," I cautioned them. "Don't expect him to be normal. Whatever he's like, just love him."

As usual, my three daughters chorused, "We know, Mama!" The oldest two, age nineteen and twenty, had already finished high school, and Jenny was working at a factory.

"Don't complain to him," I continued. "Don't say anything that he might not like to hear. Many people come out of prison with damaged nerves. We all have to take care of him, to keep him happy, and not aggravate him."

The girls begged to go with me the next day, but I explained that the arrangements were only for me to go. I didn't even know where their father would be. I told them they would have to wait at home.

My son looked pensive. Not yet twelve, he had no memory of his father. Under pressure, I had thrown out all photos of Sidney, so he didn't even know what his father looked like.

"My papa is a good man," he said to me, repeating a line I had often said to the children. His eager eyes contained a question.

"Yes, Xiaoming. Your papa is a good man. Now everyone will know that."

⁓

The next day, November 19, right after preparing the family breakfast, I got in a car that was waiting at the main gate and set off to bring my husband home. A package containing Sidney's clothes was waiting for me on the backseat.

It took more than two hours to drive to the prison. I kept my peace, but my thoughts were whirling in my head as the car made its way through the Beijing streets and out into the countryside, heading north.

What would Sidney look like? How was his health? Where had he been these past ten years? How badly had they treated him?

The man who came with me from Radio thought my silence was strange.

"Wang Yulin, what's the matter? You should be happy that Li Dunbai is coming back after all these years."

"I'm afraid of what kind of shape he'll be in—seriously ill, ruined nerves, or what?"

"Anyway, it's better for him to be out of prison than in."

Strange as it seemed, after ten years of separation, that was the first time I had been told that he was in prison.

"What prison?"

The man didn't know.

I dozed off and woke with a shock, startled to find myself sitting in the car under the highest wall I had ever seen, except for the Great Wall. On a guided tour, I had once visited a prison, where through an iron gate, there were prisoners in a courtyard, tending a garden, making various things, talking, singing, and laughing. By contrast, this prison had armed guards around the perimeter and a grim gray brick wall that blocked the outside world from the inside eyes, and the inside world from the outside eyes.

We entered a small reception room, where two middle-aged cadres in plain clothes received us.

"Li Dunbai will be out in a little while," one of them said, taking the package of clothing.

"I'll go inside to fetch him," I said.

"No, that's not permitted. Someone will bring him out. Wait here."

⁓

About half an hour later, Sidney, decked out in a brand new woolen suit and silk tie, slowly walked toward me. He looked sallow and dazed. I rushed over and threw my arms around him, tears streaming down. Sidney patted me gently on the back and said, in a low, husky voice, "Hao. Hao," which means "It's okay."

His stiffness came as a further shock. He didn't smile or weep. He didn't even hug me back. Had he lost all sentiment, all emotion? How could he be so cool?

I cried harder than ever. *He's turned into wood*, I thought to myself.

"Okay, let's go home now," I said, comforting him.

He nodded, but said nothing, his eyes staring blankly. I took his arm and he walked with a stumbling gait. All this reinforced my fears. Yes, his nerves were shot. Would he ever recover? As we got into the backseat of the car, I asked the driver, "What prison is this?"

"This is Qincheng, where the big shots are held."

Sidney said little on the way home. We just sat there, hugging each other.

"How are you, really?" I asked, anxiously.

"Okay," he said flatly.

"Are you sick?"

"Not sick."

His words came out one by one, as though he wasn't sure how to carry on a conversation. He had difficulty following what I said if I talked fast.

Suddenly, I noticed that the car was not headed back toward the Radio compound. I asked the driver where we were going.

"You're going to stay at the Friendship Hotel," he said.

"The Friendship Hotel? Why?" I asked the man from Radio. That was, I knew, a hotel northwest of the city center, where most foreign experts lived, in comparative luxury.

"We've arranged for you to live there," he said. "A very good place."

"But my children are waiting for us at home!"

"It's all been arranged. Your children will be waiting for you there."

All the way there in the car I held Sidney's hand.

"Tell me the truth. How's your health been?" I repeated.

"Not bad."

But his face was ashen, he was overweight, and he spoke slowly in an unnaturally husky voice. In ten years, he had barely spoken a word.

"How was the food in prison?"

"Later on, good. In the last few years."

His train of thought seemed to move slowly, and he struggled to comprehend my words. Clearly, he was not accustomed to his new environment. Giving him a chance to rest and recover, I fell silent. I was eager to find out how he had been treated and what kind of mental torment he had faced, but this was not the moment to ask such questions.

As he stared out the window, I was reminded of the fresh-faced innocent I had been when I first laid eyes on him, in May 1955.

"If I were his wife," I had boldly declared that day, "I would have waited until his case was cleared up! I wouldn't pay any attention to what people were saying." And before he was arrested in 1968, at the height of the craziness of the Cultural Revolution, I had promised him, "I'll stick with you, whatever comes."

I had been true to my word. So I could now look Sidney in the eyes with no regrets. I had protected the children as best I could. I had kept the family together. And I had survived. So had he. We had all made it through. But at what cost? That remained to be seen.

⁓

We pulled up in front of a four-story hotel building, and our three daughters rushed out to meet us. Our son stood behind the door, watching for the father he couldn't remember.

As we got out of the car, the three girls hopped and skipped, shouting, "Papa! Papa!" They formed a circle and danced around him, chanting, "Which of us is the eldest? Who is the eldest?" They were all fully grown now, so it wasn't easy to tell.

Sidney guessed twice, and both times he was wrong. The girls laughed and reported which daughter was which. I thought I detected a smile on Sidney's face.

"Where's Xiaoming?" I asked. My son came over and stood half hidden behind me, still a little nonplussed by the sudden appearance of his father.

"Papa," was all he could say.

Sidney didn't know what to say to him, either.

As we walked into the Friendship Hotel, I thought, *My heaven! The six of us are all together again. How hard, how trying these ten years have been! Suffering, tears, struggle . . . but it all led up to our reunion today.* At that moment, it seemed worth it.

⁓

The Friendship Hotel had arranged a very special setup for us: three suites taking up an entire section of the first floor. Moreover, the hotel had furnished it with a real upholstered sofa—something no one else at the Friendship Hotel had. After years of crowding into one or two rooms, it seemed like paradise. Or a bourgeois luxury, I couldn't help thinking. But I had not asked for it.

Our private reunion was awkward. When the girls asked him questions, Sidney responded very slowly, one word at a time, in that low, gravelly voice. He acted like a zombie, with no feelings. The girls tried to fill the silence with chatter. Little Ming hung back and observed.

We took Sidney to the hotel dining room for our first family meal in ten years. He ate hungrily. He watched us as if we were actors in a movie, speaking some foreign language.

After dinner, Ming-Ming went into our bedroom, where Sidney was reading the paper, and asked him a question that had been on his mind. "Papa, in English, how do you say *xingfu*?"

"Happy," Sidney said.

"That will be my name!"

He went by the English name Happy Rittenberg for several years.

~

The evening of Sidney's homecoming, the head of the Foreign Experts Bureau, who was in charge of the hotel, visited us. His name was Yang Fangzhi. During the Cultural Revolution, he had spent years cleaning out public latrines in far-off Ningxia. During that time he'd been uncomplaining, confident in final victory for the Chinese revolution, in spite of everything.

He did the talking. Sidney listened.

"I hope you realize what a wonderful job your wife has done," he said. "She kept this family together under the worst conditions. She taught the children when they couldn't go to school. She waited for you and endured persecution and hardship without bowing her head."

Sidney was deeply moved. "I understand," he managed to say.

In fact, it hadn't just been me. Our whole family had stuck together, and together we had preserved this family. The children had gone through all sorts of humiliation and unfair treatment, but none of them ever blamed their parents.

That night after the children went to bed, I poured out my heart to my husband. The pent-up tension inside me burst forth like water from a broken dam. I told him about the eight months of confinement in a hotel room, with no fresh air, under twenty-four-hour surveillance. I told him how our colleagues at Radio had forced me to sit in the cold outside a bathroom under a sign saying "Dog-Spy's Wife." I told him about the interrogations and the struggle sessions. I showed him my sprained hand and explained how I had been pushed beyond the limits of my physical strength at the two labor camps. I told him how our neighbors had beaten me. I told him how Premier Zhou had stepped up to help our family, twice.

But as the details poured out of my mouth, so did my bitterness, long bottled up. I was a worker's daughter, loyal to the Communist Party. How could they have put me through so many years of persecution? What had I done wrong? They had trained me in English, but I hadn't been allowed to use my language skills at all, for so many years. Now that it was over, what was the point?

Again and again, I collapsed into tears.

Fresh from prison, Sidney had no answers. In fact, he didn't seem to comprehend most of what I was saying. But he saw that it upset me to talk about these wrongs. In his awkward, halting voice, he tried to coax me into forgetting.

"That's behind us," he said. "Now we're fine."

But for ten years, I had had so much to say, and no one to say it to. I wasn't the only one who had suffered from Sidney's case. My whole family had suffered, too. I told him about how Little Ming had pushed wheelbarrows at the labor camp, how the girls had been excluded from political classes, how they had all cried at night because of the taunts of their classmates. I told him how hard I had fought to keep our daughters from being sent to the countryside. I told him how my brother and sister had been locked up and that my father had been forced to kneel on broken shards.

"Don't think about it," Sidney kept repeating. "That's all over."

I've been silent for ten years, I wanted to say. *If I can't talk about it to my own husband, who can I talk to?*

But I could see that it was too much for him. So I put him to bed.

≈

A few days later, we were taking a walk through the hotel grounds when I mentioned that Kang Sheng was a terrible person, one of those leaders who had denounced Sidney. Sidney was shocked. Kang Sheng had not yet been publicly exposed as a bad person. "How can you say that about an honored leader of the Central Committee!" he exclaimed. "He's a good man!"

I was surprised. But Yang Fangzhi, who was walking with us, was not. "Lao Li, don't get excited. Just listen to your wife and you'll gradually understand what's going on." In prison, Sidney's only source of information had been the newspaper, and he had trusted the official version.

After Mao's death, nobody worried about criticizing the hooligans who had promoted the Cultural Revolution. Almost every Chinese citizen had suffered from it, no matter which side they had taken in the beginning. If there was one thing we Chinese finally agreed on, it was that the Cultural Revolution had been a disaster. Sidney was one of the few who didn't know. He still thought it was right to rebel and that continuous revolution was needed to shake up the bureaucracy and root out the capitalist roaders.

When we got back to our quarters, Sidney was still talking like that, telling us we needed to speak with respect about the Cultural Revolution leading group. Finally, our twelve-year-old son said, "Papa, you sound just like the Gang of Four!"

Sidney's going to need quite a long time to catch up, I thought.

≈

Eventually, Sidney was able to tell me a little about his ten years in prison. He assured me that he had never been a spy, and in prison he had consistently denied those charges. Remembering my advice, he had not engaged in "wild talk"—confessing to wrongs he had not committed. During countless hours of interrogation, he had not gotten anyone else into trouble. Unlike other prisoners, whose screams he had heard, he had not been tortured physically—only mentally. He had spent the entire time in solitary confinement, and though he had suffered from malnutrition, dizziness, sleep deprivation, and blinding headaches—unlike his first stint in prison—he had not had a mental breakdown. By focusing on the power of his own human mind, he had fought against bitterness, self-pity, and depression.

As in his first stint, he had studied Chairman Mao's writings and those of other Communist leaders, trying hard to understand his personal failings as a Communist. He re-examined his actions during the early years of the Cultural Revolution: the speeches he gave, his support for the rebel group that seized power, the leadership role he had accepted at Radio. He regretted his involvement in the factional struggle at Radio. But he did not regret his loyalty to the Chinese Communist Party, which had improved the welfare of the Chinese workers and peasants. And he still believed in the Maoist ideals of the Cultural Revolution, which he thought would create a truly democratic and prosperous form of socialism. In prison, his biggest fear was that he might find out, after his release, that socialism had failed. He still wanted to contribute to the "freedom and happiness of the human race" and he believed that the best way to achieve that was through Communism.

No wonder he was puzzled by the cynicism he saw everywhere around him.

≈

As for me, if I had to summarize what I learned in those ten years, it would come down to two words: Persevere! Struggle! Perseverance, you could say, is another word for stubbornness. Perhaps that old flaw of mine helped me get through. I just plain refused to give up. And struggle, you might say, is another word for hard work. I had learned that from my earliest childhood days, picking up half-burned embers of coal.

During those tough ten years, I was confined and then forced to do labor that was beyond my strength. At first, I railed against the injustice. But I learned that no matter how hard life was, no matter what physical trials and mental torments might come, I could not allow my will to falter. After each exhausting day of hard labor, when I lay down to sleep, I could only use silent tears to deal with the pain in my back. But even then, I knew that I had to hold on. I could not allow myself to weaken. When my tormenters tried to break my spirit, I doubled my efforts to show no fear. The hardest struggle was against my own negative thoughts.

My kids were what made it possible for me to keep going. I knew that the children of some cadres had been cast out into the streets and had become ruffians or prostitutes. I had to let my children know that no matter what happened, no matter what sorts of derision and persecution they met with, their mother was with them.

Human life is a long chain of contradictions and struggles. When facing hardship or injustice, you can train yourself to use your rational mind to deal with it, step-by-step, instead of indulging in blame and self-pity. Each of us runs into unexpected troubles and challenges in this world. If we lose our ability to reason calmly, we will destroy our own health and turn into cringing cowards or bitter cripples. But if we maintain a strong will and improvise ways of dealing with hardship, we will come through as strong and clearheaded people. This is true of everyone in the world.

Maybe it's not so bad to be stubborn—like a block of granite.

Chapter Forty-Five

Vindication

AFTER SIDNEY EMERGED from prison, people treated him as if nothing had happened. But I knew better. Fortunately, my office let me take several months off from work to care for him. As soon as I could, I took him to the doctor for a checkup. He had high blood pressure and cardiac arrhythmia—conditions that were worrisome but treatable. It could have been much worse. But his movements and speech remained sluggish. Sometimes he had attacks of dizziness. The doctor said he might or might not recover from those conditions.

When I first took Sidney out to the street, he would shake and startle easily. He had not seen so many people in ten years. I held his arm firmly as we walked together. Whenever he saw a policeman in uniform, he flinched.

The whole family focused on taking care of him. A few months later, at Chinese New Year, people set off firecrackers. Toni raced over to her father's side and said, "Papa, are you okay?" She worried that the noise would frighten him.

For months, Sidney shuffled slowly, as if in a fog. Sometimes, his heart would start beating wildly. During a conversation, he would hear one sentence and understand it, but then he couldn't process subsequent sentences. He often looked confused. Sidney told me he found his condition to be scary. His mind was full of anxiety, which always hung over him like a suspended sword.

"Aloneness—it doesn't go away," he told me.

It took about three years for Sidney to recover completely and return to normal. Many times, I was afraid that he wouldn't make it. The children and I were very important in his recovery. We warmed up to him and tried to make him laugh. After a while, he was able to feel safe and to relax at home. Also, he had regular injections of vitamin B-12, which relaxed him and gave him energy.

~

Several months after Sidney's release, we both went back to work. I returned to my old job at Radio, but the personnel department did not want Sidney to face those ghosts and painful memories. So he took a job as a foreign expert editor at the Xinhua News Agency, the wire service that provided news dispatches to all of China's media. Sidney was allocated a car and driver, but both of us rode our bicycles to work instead. The commute from the Friendship Hotel took forty-five minutes to an hour each way, so we had to leave home around six thirty each morning. The wind always shifted at midday, so that we had to ride our bikes into the wind, on both our morning and evening commutes. That was hard in the winter, but I didn't want any more accusations of living in bourgeois luxury. Xinhua treated him well and even sent the two of us on a vacation in the summer of 1978—we travelled to famous sites all around China.

Things were looking up for our children as well. At last, the girls were allowed to attend college. Jenny entered Beijing Number One Medical College, and Toni studied at Capital College of Medicine. Sunny was accepted into the prestigious Beijing University and became a member of the first computer science class. Our son attended the middle school attached to People's University and learned to play basketball and football with the other children of foreign experts living at the Friendship Hotel. The children's lives were on track.

But that wasn't enough for me. I dared to dream of something bigger: full exoneration. Sidney had never been a spy. He had been wrongly imprisoned for ten years. My children and I had suffered under the cloud of these false accusations. It was time to clear the air.

Soon after Sidney's release, he received an official document from the government of China. It was handwritten, with a big red stamp that marked it as official: the government's conclusion about Sidney's case. His *jielun*.

I grabbed it and read it eagerly. The spy charges against Sidney had been dismissed. He was a good comrade. Restitution would be made. Everything was fine except one sentence, which said he had made "serious political mistakes in the Cultural Revolution."

When I saw this, I thumped the table. "Nonsense!" I said. "Serious political mistakes? What mistakes? Who said you made mistakes?"

Sidney was appalled at my reaction. "Calm down. It's fine. Clearly I did make serious mistakes, or they wouldn't have put me in prison."

"No way. I cannot accept this conclusion."

"They have to state some reason. I'm free now. What more can we ask? Let's leave well enough alone."

"No," I said. "You don't understand. Think of the children!"

In China, everyone's opportunities for study and work depended on the situation of their parents. A person's "blood" inheritance was what mattered most. If the father was a hero, the son was honored, too. If you were born with a "good class background," to the family of a worker or a peasant, you had a chance in life. If your parents came from a "bad class background"—and especially if your parents were labeled as having a political problem—you could be denied the right to an education or a good job. In 1977, the government formally abolished the class background system and reinstated college entrance exams; that was how our daughters had been accepted into college, by proving their own merit. But after all I had been through, I didn't believe that family background didn't matter.

My children had suffered discrimination long enough. If something was still hanging over their heads, a judgment that their father had made "serious political mistakes," all their classmates would talk about it. Another power shift or a new political campaign could resurrect the ugly old charges: bourgeois, reactionary, counterrevolutionary.

"Lao Li," I said to Sidney, "maybe you can accept this conclusion. But I can't. For the sake of the children. I insist."

Sidney refused to demand a correction of the conclusion on his case. So I did it myself. I wrote a long letter about Sidney's case to Hu Yaobang, who was then the director of the Party's Organization Department and a close protégé of the newly reinstated leader, Deng Xiaoping. Hu Yaobang himself had twice been purged and he was in charge of rehabilitating long-time Party leaders who had been wrongly accused during the Cultural Revolution. He was the new Party spokesperson and a solid reformer, and he had already "liberated" many cadres who had been wronged.

As I wrote the letter, my own blood pressure rose. *Serious political mistakes?* I thought. Whatever Sidney might have done during the Cultural Revolution paled next to the mistake of jailing an innocent man for ten years. Sidney had been terribly wronged, and the conclusion needed to be clear and unequivocal, leaving no guilt hanging over his head. After all, in the Cultural Revolution who hadn't made mistakes? This murky conclusion wouldn't do: I stated that I could not accept the Party's conclusion about Sidney and requested a new judgment.

The letter expanded to two pages, then three. Sidney had lived in China for more than thirty years. He had made great contributions to our country. Back in the 1940s, Sidney had voluntarily chosen to stay in China and join the Communist movement rather than going home. Starting in Yan'an, he had taken part in establishing the English language broadcasting for Radio Peking. He had trained a whole generation of Chinese broadcasters on how to translate and pronounce English. He could even take a Chinese proclamation he had never read before and translate it instantaneously into spoken English, for broadcast, live on air. Flawlessly. He was the only person at Radio who could do that. He had worked tirelessly, long hours, without complaining, because he wanted to see socialism succeed here, to improve the welfare of the Chinese people. Any time he had been asked to do extra things, to meet with a group from abroad on a weekend, to edit a special bulletin late at night, he never refused. He was a good person who never opposed China. Not only did he not deserve the years in prison, he deserved the gratitude of the Chinese Communist Party and the people of New China.

Sidney shook his head when he read my letter. As usual, it was long and rambling. But I insisted on mailing it, just the way it was.

"I won't give in on this," I said.

Our Chinese friends, including Ding Yilan, the widow of Deng Tuo, one of the first victims of the Cultural Revolution, vigorously supported me. So did our kids.

After two weeks, we got a response, a letter from Hu Yaobang, dated March 13, 1979. At the bottom was the official red stamp. The new conclusion contained exactly what I had asked for. Gone was the reference to "serious political mistakes." It included all the major points of my letter, including some of my own wording, such as "more than thirty years of important contributions to the Chinese people." At the bottom was Hu Yaobang's signature and an official red stamp. Sidney was completely exonerated.

It was the happiest moment of my life. I had taken control and made this happen. I had rejected bitter fatalism, resignation, and blind obedience. I had acted to change our fate for the better.

My suffering had not been in vain.

My understanding of who Sidney was had been validated.

At last, the cloud over our heads dissipated, and we had a solid ground from which to build our future.

Around the same time, Deng Yingchao, widow of Premier Zhou, spoke at a reception for foreign experts at the Xinhua News Agency. She went out of her way to emphasize that Premier Zhou had thought very highly of Sidney Rittenberg and valued his friendship. To Sidney, this statement mattered even more than the written conclusion. Zhou Enlai had been one of the thirteen leaders who signed the orders to arrest Sidney. But more than once, Zhou Enlai had intervened to help me and the children. Premier Zhou's high opinion was priceless. Any misunderstanding with him had been healed.

PART III

Chapter Forty-Six

Through the Looking Glass

AFTER THE FALL of the Gang of Four, things changed quickly in China. Deng Xiaoping, now in control of the Party and the government, was determined to utilize market forces—domestic and international—to grow the economy and satisfy the people's demand for a better life. Without satisfying that demand, Deng later said to American TV reporter Mike Wallace, no Chinese regime could survive.

Deng had learned some important lessons from the Cultural Revolution and his own suffering. He realized the need to reassure the badly shaken functionaries of the Party and the government that they would never again face the constant investigation and harassment in Mao's thunderous mass movements—the "class struggle" dramas that Mao believed were the central driving force in Chinese socialism.

Revenge was not an option. Deng prohibited seeking retribution by those who had been wronged in the Cultural Revolution. Aside from criminal procedures relating to such charges as murder, rape, and arson, all participants were to sit down together for one set of meetings, in which each person was encouraged (but not forced) to tell of the wrongs that he had done to others, after which all was to be forgiven and forgotten. This was much like the "Truth and Reconciliation Movement" that Nelson Mandela carried out later in South Africa, and it worked—although factional feelings and personal animosities persisted for a long time, naturally.

To clear the air after the wild demagogy of the Cultural Revolution, Deng used Mao's old motto, "seek truth from facts," and took it a step further, declaring that "Practice is the sole criterion of truth." Pointedly, that meant that the truth was not verified by books (the Marxist classics) or by great authorities (conspicuously meaning Mao Zedong) but only by what had been tested and found true

281

in practice. "Practice" actually meant "experience," but Maoist thinkers avoided that term since it was philosophically unclear.

Deng allowed greater freedom of expression, including public criticisms of the Cultural Revolution posted on "Democracy Wall," a long brick wall along a familiar street in Beijing. At a Party plenum in December 1978, Deng gained full control of the country, although he never took a title higher than vice-premier; wisely, he chose to avoid a Mao-like personality cult.

That same month, the People's Republic of China and the United States of America announced plans to reestablish diplomatic relations. Deng Xiaoping visited the United States in January 1979 in a memorable tour, heavily covered by reporters. Americans were enthralled with Deng and the way he was transforming China. On March 1, 1979, we joined the little crowd at the U.S. "liaison office" in Beijing, as it formally converted to an embassy.

As the country transformed itself, so our lives changed as well. The Broadcast Administration gave Sidney ten years of back pay, amounting to more than ten thousand dollars, so we decided to use the money to buy two round-trip tickets to the United States. His mother in poor health, Sidney wanted to see his family, and he was curious about how his homeland had changed in the thirty-four years since he had left it. He insisted that I go with him.

I was not eager to visit America. My children were just settling in to their new schools, and Sidney's health was still delicate. Our son was just twelve, and I was relishing the process of building a stable life together as a family of six. But Sidney wanted to visit his homeland, and I could understand why. If I had left China in my youth, I'd want to go back, too. He argued that I needed to see America and experience the land and the people. I wanted to be by his side in case the pressure got to him. At that time, it never entered either of our heads that we might move to America.

After Sidney's release, we had become good friends of Leonard Woodcock, director of the U.S. liaison office and later the U.S. ambassador to China. Like Sidney, Woodcock had started out as a labor union organizer in the United States. Naturally, he had reached out to Sidney and asked him many questions about China's Communist leaders and system.

Over dinner one night, Sidney asked Woodcock if he could help me get a U.S. entry visa. Pleased, Woodcock responded immediately. The next day, Sidney and I went to see the consular officer; the process was quick and easy. The standard question for applicants was, "Do you plan to return to China?" Those suspected of emigrating would be denied.

"Are you sure you're going to come back?" the American officer asked me. Then he placed both hands over his ears and shouted, "Don't tell me. Don't tell me!" Obviously, none of these Americans expected us to return to China after what we had been through. But actually, neither of us had the slightest intention of moving to America.

So I raised my right hand, in the manner of taking an oath, and said with full confidence, "Yes, I definitely will come back. My four children and my mother are all here!"

One of the questions on the application asked if I was or had ever been, a member of the Communist Party or any affiliated organization. The U.S. government had long had a policy of denying entry to Communists, whom they equated with terrorists.

"How should I answer?" I asked Sidney.

"Put yes," he said. And I did, although I was no longer an active Party member.

Later, we found out that even official Communist Party delegations to the United States never answered yes out of fear they would be denied entry. However, my admission didn't seem to cause a problem.

With a stack of cash from Sidney's back pay, we went down to the Air France office and bought two economy class tickets to New York. We picked our return date based on our plan to stay for three months.

On March 17, Saint Patrick's Day, we took off, flying through Karachi and Athens to Paris, where we stayed with French friends for a few days before flying on to New York City. I was nervous about the long flights, since I had only flown once before—that choppy flight from Beijing to Shanghai to meet with Chairman Mao, in November 1965. This time, in economy, my seat would only tip back a little, and I couldn't stretch my legs out comfortably. I finally dozed off, but I remained half asleep, half awake.

I worried about how Sidney might be received in his homeland. Ambassador Woodcock had told us enough to know that Sidney would not be in trouble when he went home—the warm welcome he received at the U.S. embassy and from the Western media assured us of that—although he might have if he had returned during the height of the anti-Communist hysteria in the early 1950s. Still, he seemed prone to disaster, so I tried to swallow my fears. I had heard years of propaganda about the evils of "American imperialism."

Flying across the Atlantic, Sidney told the flight attendant that I was his wife, going to America for the first time. The attendant brought us the wine cart and invited us to take as many of the little bottles of spirits and wines as we could carry. Neither of us are drinkers, but we thanked him and took some as gifts.

When we went through U.S. customs in New York, a large-framed African-American inspector asked if we were bringing in more than the allowed two bottles. When Sidney showed him the stash of little bottles we were carrying, he explained that he was returning to the U.S. after an absence of thirty-four years. The inspector thought for a minute and then said, "Well, it's against the rules, but thirty-four years is a long time. Pass!"

In New York, Sidney's sister and brother-in-law met us at the airport and took us to their condo in a tower across from Lincoln Center. Sidney pointed out huge Chagall paintings we could see from their window. I was amazed to see so many skyscrapers. In Beijing, the tallest building I had ever seen was the Beijing Hotel, less than twenty stories high. I could not even dream that in thirty years Shanghai would have four times as many skyscrapers as Manhattan!

Sidney's sister arranged for us to have lunch with my eighty-three-year-old mother-in-law, who suffered from advanced Parkinson's disease. She didn't say much, but she was obviously very pleased to see Sidney again. I gave her some silk fabric that I had brought especially for her and showed her photos of her four grandchildren, which made her smile.

My mother-in-law told us that she had paid fifty thousand dollars to a "rescue company" in San Francisco, who claimed they could get her son out of prison and bring him home. Both the company and the money disappeared. I knew she and Sidney had had a troubled relationship, so I was moved that she had tried so hard to find him.

Most clearly, I remember one thing she said to Sidney. "I thought you were dead."

Sidney responded, "There were times when I thought so, too."

⤳

As for Sidney's public reception, my worries were unfounded. Instead of being treated with suspicion, he faced a barrage of intense curiosity and friendly interest. After three decades of almost no contact with China, Americans were eager to know what was going on "behind the bamboo curtain."

The morning after we landed in New York, Sidney was interviewed on national television, on NBC's *Today* show, viewed by millions. A few days later, America's top newspaper, the *New York Times*, ran a large feature article about

Sidney that took up most of page two. The headline said that Sidney was a "native son" who had come home to tell his family about his "Chinese in-laws." I thought that was exactly right: true on the surface but also a good analogy for his desire to explain his adopted country, China, to his fellow Americans.

Reporters wanted to know why Sidney had stayed behind after the Communist takeover had driven away almost all Americans in China—especially after his first imprisonment. Why on earth had he joined the Communist Party of China? Did he really believe all that stuff? Had he really met Mao Zedong and befriended Zhou Enlai? They pronounced Mao's name "Mayo" and Zhou's as "Chow." Now that Sidney had suffered sixteen years in Chinese prisons, surely he was ready to expose the evils of the Communist Party of China.

Sidney answered their questions from the heart. He had stayed in China because he believed in the ideals of Communism, and he had seen many positive changes during the 1950s. The Party had exonerated him and apologized for imprisoning him. He tried to focus on the good it had done. More interview requests flooded in. Only sixteen months after emerging from solitary confinement, Sidney thrived on the attention and what seemed like adoration.

As for me, my head was spinning. The streets of New York were impossibly crowded with speeding, honking cars. I often grabbed onto Sidney's arm to steady myself, although he was also disoriented. New York's skyscrapers cast shadows on the narrow caverns of streets; elevators zipped us up to dizzying heights. The subways rushed through underground mazes, where we saw rats and graffiti. Neon signs blinked and advertisements blared commercial messages everywhere, even from the sides of buildings. I discovered that Americans came in all shapes and colors. Their clothing was colorful and varied, a contrast to the solid mass of blue and gray clothing on Beijing's streets. Some women wore shockingly short miniskirts and high heels. Ordinary people owned and drove cars; in China, all drivers were professional. Someone took me into a supermarket, and I marveled at the long aisles with different brands of canned foods and colorful boxes of cereal and acres of plastic bottles.

Even though I had spent six years getting a degree in English, the clipped American voices speaking in long sentences might as well have been clashing cymbals. Their accents and pronunciation played tricks on my ears. I could follow the gist of personal conversations, but the television newscasts might as well have been in Russian. They used words I had never learned: embargo, abuse, hostage, filibuster.

Each night, dinner often included a huge hunk of undercooked meat. Americans liked to eat a big plate of raw vegetables, called "salad"—unheard of in China, where everyone knew that eating raw vegetables was likely to make you sick. Frequently, Americans would offer me an alcoholic drink, usually grape wine. Hamburger restaurants and sugary, bubbly drinks were everywhere. I had never heard of McDonald's or Coca-Cola.

I felt like Alice after she stepped through the looking glass. In America, everything I had once learned as true was backwards or distorted.

Communists, lauded at home as selfless, dedicated civil servants, might as well have had forked tongues and horns on their heads.

Capitalism, a system of oppression and unfairness, was assumed to be the most effective economic system in the world, bringing prosperity to all.

The Communist Party of China, which I had learned in my teenaged years to be the savior of China, was portrayed as an oppressive dictatorship.

Capitalists, greedy bosses who made fortunes by underpaying their workers, were worshipped as innovative, enterprising role models.

America, an aggressive imperialist nation whose workers had not yet been liberated, was the leader of the "free world," a model of democracy, and a beacon for human rights.

The Kuomintang government, a corrupt regime we had overthrown in 1949, was known as "Free China" and proudly flew an old flag we had burned and spit upon.

My country was called "Red China." Americans were still learning details about the excesses and torments of the Cultural Revolution, and they pitied us "Red Chinese" who had suffered through it, including Sidney and me. Some mocked us because we had worshipped Mao Zedong, raised high his Little Red Book of quotations, and memorized his writings. Some Americans students had been taught that a central tenet of Communism was denouncing your parents.

Still, Sidney told me he was pleased with the press coverage of him and his life. "In America," he told me, "if the media says you're okay, you're okay. If they say you're no good, you're no good."

Perhaps most stark was the difference in wealth between the two countries. I could see, clearly, that China was poor by comparison. China had almost no rich people at all. Even the "bourgeois" privileges Sidney and I had enjoyed in Beijing were minimal compared to what everyday middle-class Americans had in their homes.

But that didn't mean I was ready to denounce my country as backward and full of self-deluded fools. It bothered me to hear Americans belittling China and its Communist Party. They didn't understand how hard it had been to unify the country, how much we had suffered under nearly one hundred years of war and chaos and weak government. They couldn't see the good that Chairman Mao had done, stopping opium abuse and prostitution and raising up the workers and peasants. In China, we breathed the ideal of equality.

My sister-in-law had a friend who worked with the American author and journalist Theodore White. "Teddy" had studied Chinese at Harvard and had covered China during World War II for *Time* magazine, after which he wrote a famous book, *Thunder Out of China*. When he found out about Sidney's arrival, he honored us with an afternoon reception at his Manhattan home. It turned out to be a fateful one for our future.

When we entered his beautiful home, Teddy met us in the foyer and sat down to chat before taking us in to meet the guests. After asking a few questions, he picked up the phone and called his literary agent, Julian Bach.

"There's a man here with a terrific story about China," Teddy said. "If you don't get him to write a book about it, someone else will."

That night, we found ourselves having dinner with Julian Bach, and in his office the next morning Sidney signed a contract, agreeing to produce a book about his experiences. Could an American publisher really pay Sidney to write a book about his life in China? After my salary of 87.50 yuan a month and Sidney's 600 yuan a month, the dollar numbers Teddy White quoted seemed like a small fortune. But then again, the price of a hotel room, a taxi, a cup of tea, a bowl of noodles all seemed absurdly high in America.

Next, Assistant Secretary of State Richard Holbrooke invited Sidney to Washington, D.C., where he was formally received at the State Department. Sidney told me that the liberal Secretary Holbrooke said, as they shook hands, "Some of my predecessors would not have received you like this."

Sidney replied, "If some of your predecessors had invited me, I probably wouldn't have come."

They had a good talk. I was not invited, and it made me wonder. If Sidney had worked as an American spy in China, they would want to debrief him in Washington. But I saw no signs of that. Sidney had a lot to say about China, but no secrets to pass on.

Together, we visited Mike Oksenberg, the president's national security advisor on China and distinguished China expert, in the Executive Office Building next to the White House. He was one of the officials who had worked behind the scenes to smooth the way for diplomatic relations. He asked us about the mysterious demise of Mao's anointed successor, Marshal Lin Biao, in 1971. Lin Biao had been planning to defect to the Soviet Union when his plane crashed.

Sidney explained our understanding of what had happened and reminded Oksenberg of the published report that a second plane, following Lin Biao, had been carrying secret Chinese documents. When the air force pilot refused to leave China, it had been forced to land. One passenger had been captured, along with the documents. Oksenberg was astonished to hear this story.

"But it was published in *People's Daily*," I said.

Oksenberg pointed to the stacks of files on a ledge behind his desk. "I get all these intelligence reports, every day. Do you think I have time to read through and pay attention to all of them?"

I thought to myself, *Such an important official in the American government, a leading expert on China, and you don't know these crucial details?* Washington's knowledge of Chinese affairs was shockingly poor. Didn't they take China seriously? China's experts on the U.S. would never have overlooked such an important story. Of course, these American experts on China had to review masses of reports every day. But why couldn't they separate the vitally important happenings from the insignificant?

I found this upsetting. It seemed to be proof that it would took a long time for these two countries to understand each other. This would require the efforts of many ordinary people, not just government officials. At that moment, I also got my first inkling of what role Sidney and I might play in the future: explaining China to Americans. Clearly, there was a lot about China that Americans didn't understand.

≈

Through a mutual friend, Sidney had been introduced to Howard Simons, managing editor of the *Washington Post* during a trip he had made to Beijing several years ago. He asked us to call him "Howie." When we arrived in Washington, Howie arranged an in-depth interview with his Style section writer. He told Sidney on the phone, "We're going to publish that interview, and you'll be a famous man."

Howie also invited us to sit in on an editorial meeting of the *Washington*

Post editorial board, followed by lunch with the newspaper's owner, the much-admired Katherine Graham. In those days, the *Washington Post* was lionized as the newspaper that had uncovered evidence that President Nixon had flouted the law, forcing him to resign. Such press freedom was hard for me to imagine.

The editorial meeting was run by Ben Bradlee, the executive editor. Each of the page editors and major writers reported on what they planned to write for that day. After they spoke, Bradlee either agreed with their proposals or vetoed them and told them to write something else.

I whispered to Sidney, "Just like an editorial meeting of the Communist Party."

He grinned at me. I wondered, *If an editor vetoes a story idea in a "free" country, is that censorship?*

≈

One of my deepest impressions was from our visit to the White House. On a guided tour, we saw President Carter's Oval Office. I was surprised to see how small it was. Also, I was amazed at the fact that it was open to the public when the president wasn't there. No one in China could imagine going through the Communist Party leaders' offices in Beijing. The whole White House, with its grounds, was much smaller than Zhongnanhai, which was originally just one corner of the emperor's palace.

When I was working at Radio in the early 1950s, I was sent to Zhongnanhai about once a week, to deliver data to an office of the central government. After being admitted through a side gate, as I walked through the compound to the office, uniformed guards often would appear out of nowhere and challenge me. "What are you here for? Who are you going to see?" I would show them my pass, and they would let me through. At the White House, I was a foreigner. Yet once we were admitted through the gate, no one interfered or questioned us, wherever we went. And this was the home of the president of the United States!

I was also struck by the protesters I saw in both New York and Washington, D.C. A lone individual could walk up and down across the street from the White House, carrying a big placard stating his grievances or demands. Large numbers of workers could strike and form a picket line, with signs showing their issues. Americans considered this natural and normal. It attracted no special attention, and I saw no interference from the police. A protestor outside the massive gates of Zhongnanhai would be detained immediately.

Driving past rows and rows of middle-class houses, I recalled the standard teaching in Chinese textbooks about the oppressed workers of America and the importance of liberating them. Had we all been duped? It was too much to take in at once. Sidney and I talked late into the night about what was good about America and what was good about China.

≈

Later in the trip, a professor hosted a heart-warming reunion for Sidney with his old comrades and classmates from University of North Carolina at Chapel Hill. Sidney's old college friend Moe Malkin and his wife, Hannah, were there, and so were Hannah's sister, Vera, and her husband, Dr. Abe Buchberg.

Relaxing among friends, Sidney told the story of how he had developed a sore throat and a high fever shortly after our arrival in the United States. There was such a long line to see the doctor, Sidney's brother-in-law gave up his own appointment so that Sidney could get in right away. At the professor's dinner table, Sidney told how he had paid sixty-four dollars for a four-minute session with the doctor in New York, followed by a penicillin shot from a technician.

"I have lived in China for more than thirty years, including three stays in hospitals and one operation. All told, it didn't cost me sixty-four dollars. And for four minutes!"

Dr. Buchberg, for whom medicine was a healing profession not a profit-making business, immediately said, "From now on, I'll take care of your whole family's needs, and you won't pay me a penny!"

Here in America, I thought, *there are two different worlds: the ordinary folk and the privileged.* Behind the gleaming façade hid another, less visible reality.

Chapter Forty-Seven

Curiouser and Curiouser

AFTER THE *TODAY* show appearance and the *New York Times* story, Sidney and I were invited to visit Hollywood by a Columbia Pictures producer named Gary Allison. From the powerful Allison Engine family, he had jumped into the movie business after years of studying international relations and philosophy and working in the White House under President Lyndon B. Johnson. Gary Allison paid for us to fly to Los Angeles in first class and met us at the airport.

An affable man, he greeted us warmly. "You should know that everyone in Hollywood is insane. I myself belong in an institution, but I'm too busy right now to go there."

He spoke so quickly that I had to ask Sidney to translate. Sidney was laughing, so I decided not to be alarmed. But from the first moment, Hollywood felt like a movie-screen world where everything was polished and warped.

Gary Allison took us to his Beverly Hills mansion, where we stayed about a week. Gary found Sidney's personal story fascinating and wanted to make a movie about him. Sidney laughed and told him he'd have to wait for the book.

Gary's business partner asked Sidney to advise him on a film they were making on the "Hanoi Hilton," the notorious jail where the Vietcong imprisoned American soldiers. It turned out, however, that it was such a right-wing production that Sidney wasn't any help to them at all. Sidney tried to explain the Communist point of view, but they weren't interested. They had already cast the Vietcong as the bad guys. Still, Sidney found that week in Hollywood to be a lark. He was wined and dined and lionized as a man who had survived against the odds. I felt like I had landed on another planet.

At his home, Gary spent quite a while showing us some of the biggest American box-office hits, none of which we had seen— including *Gone with the Wind*, *Lawrence of Arabia*, and *Doctor Zhivago*, as well as some of Gary's own productions, including his hit, *Fraternity Row*. I saw more movies in one week than I had seen in years.

Gary's two young assistants, Bob and Stanley, who hoped to break into the movie business, drove us around, showing us the sights of Hollywood and Los Angeles. When we were alone with them, they complained vehemently about how they worked for very little compensation and had only managed to shoot a few commercials. For the first time since arriving in this country, I felt comfortable enough with these young Americans that I could relax.

"I can hardly believe Yulin is from Red China!" Bob said. "She's full of humor and laughs and jokes and cuffs us around." The way they had been educated, they were surprised to find that "Red Chinese" were human. Apparently Americans thought we Chinese, dressed in what they called "Mao suits," must all be stiff and robotic. It turned out I wasn't the only one with stereotypes and preconceived notions.

～

Though I could hardly believe it, our trip to Hollywood got even weirder. Hugh Hefner invited us to visit the Playboy Mansion. Sidney told me about *Playboy* magazine, and it fit with the stereotypes I had heard in China about America—how television shows and magazines shamelessly featured "leggy" and "clothesless" women. Those were the words commonly used in China to evoke the depraved, self-indulgent American culture. I had seen nothing of the sort in New York or Washington, but I braced myself for an onslaught of it in Hollywood.

The Playboy Mansion had never before hosted a guest from the People's Republic of China, so Hefner ordered the place to be cleaned up in advance. All the girls were fully clothed, and the more daring art work and nude photos were removed from sight. Sidney noticed a lot of guest rooms with double beds in them and told me they were probably for quick sex, but there were no lavish parties while we were there.

Instead, what really struck me was that this rich man kept zoo animals on his property: peacocks, parrots, an African crane, turtles, and many types of monkeys in cages. The mansion itself was an ivy-covered Gothic stone building, and it had a wine cellar, a game room, a swimming pool, a waterfall, a grotto, and a wishing well.

Overwhelmed, I admired the beautiful, uniformly close-clipped green lawns that surrounded the mansion. Then we turned a corner and saw what kept the lawns so manicured: long lines of brown-skinned workers, dozens of them, crawling slowly up the slope on their hands and knees, trimming the grass and weeding by hand under the hot sun.

"This man is a big landlord!" I whispered to Sidney.

If he had lived in China, he would have been treated like a class enemy. Before Liberation, the rich landlords owned big houses and servants, ate well and dressed well, and they hired farm workers to till their fields. Our teachers told horror stories about how they cheated their workers, and we condemned them as decadent and exploitative. But I had never heard of a wealthy Chinese who owned monkeys and peacocks and hired people just to trim the grass.

Hugh Hefner's son Andy planned to interview us for his magazine, and that was set to be at the Hearst Castle in San Simeon. It didn't happen, because the DC-10 in which Hefner's son was supposed to be traveling crashed, and he was believed lost. As it happened, fortunately, his son had not taken the flight. But I could see that even a huge fortune cannot protect you from ugly twists of fate.

Instead of the interview, Hefner's editor asked Sidney to write an article about love and marriage in China. Sidney agreed, but after decades as a committed Communist, he couldn't bring himself to write for *Playboy*.

During our time in Hollywood, we were also invited to a banquet hosted by the publisher of the *Hollywood Reporter*, a well-known woman named Tichi Wilkerson. She introduced Sidney to some Hollywood bigwigs and asked him to act as her publication's correspondent in China. Again, he agreed but he didn't send them anything. This was a sharp contrast to the enthusiastic articles he had written three decades earlier for the *Daily Worker*, a newspaper published in New York City by the U.S. Communist Party.

I was pleased to see that Americans were fascinated by China and eager for news about my country, but it seemed obvious that the U.S. press had its own slant. They criticized the government-controlled press in China as one-sided, but Sidney noticed that American media coverage of China was also affected by biases. Even I noticed that all the TV channels broadcasted essentially the same news, although there weren't as many "clothesless" women on television as I had expected. What Hollywood considered important—celebrities and scandal and bare breasts—seemed trivial to me.

In California, we also saw a deeper, more appealing side of the United States. We met the gentle, scholarly George O. Totten III, a political science professor at the University of Southern California, founder of USC's East Asian Studies

Center, and an outspoken proponent of peace in the Pacific Rim. Fluent in Chinese as well as many other languages, he had some useful advice on book writing. Later, we met the distinguished USC vice provost, Professor Richard Drobnick and his lovely wife, Cheryl. He got us to do numerous seminar programs at USC, and we became close friends.

Also, Sidney was invited to speak at Stanford, where he had first studied Chinese. The Stanford students and professors seemed eager to listen to Sidney. Afterward, we visited Sidney's old professor of Chinese, Dr. Shau Wing Chan, at his Menlo Park home. Dr. Chan had earned a PhD in English from Stanford before helping to set up its department of Asian languages. After nonstop English, it was a relief for me to have a wide-ranging discussion in Mandarin. He told me that Sidney had been his best student.

≈

Wherever we went, newspaper and TV reporters clamored to interview Sidney Rittenberg, instant celebrity. In 1979, the "opening of Red China" was big news, and he was a rare American who had seen it from the inside. Often I went with him, but I was too uncertain of my English to say much. Instead, I was a prop, dressed in my sensible Chinese clothes, a visual reminder of the socialist world where Sidney had spent thirty-four years. If a reporter asked me a question, Sidney would translate my answer.

Back in New York, we did a long interview for *People* magazine. The reporter traveled with us to Sidney's old home in Charleston, and I got to see the house where he grew up. She produced the longest bio *People* had ever done—and then resigned over her displeasure with the way her editors handled the piece. Getting the truth out in America was going to be hard, especially if it was nuanced and messy, like Sidney's and mine.

As much as I had suffered during the Cultural Revolution, it bothered me to hear Americans criticize my country, especially those who had no clue about the complexities of modern China. Every country has its strengths and weaknesses, and none is all evil or all glorious. Eventually, I realized that it was possible to love China, my homeland, without endorsing every policy of the Communist Party. Thoughtful Americans told us they, too, loved their country but disagreed with many of its policies.

In late August, we went home to Beijing. I was exhausted and relieved to return to reality. The Friendship Hotel, which had once seemed luxurious, now seemed familiar and homey. My kids could not believe the stories we told them about America.

One day, Sidney answered a strange phone call. "Everybody else is willing to meet me and talk with me. Why is it that you don't?" a male voice said.

"Well, who are you?" Sidney asked.

"Jerry Mann!"

Sidney had never heard of Jerry Mann, but agreed to meet him. He turned out to be a wealthy Los Angeles garment manufacturer, owner of the company Jerry Mann of California. We found him to be gruff and genial, straightforward and trustworthy, a man who had left Flatbush, New York, as a left-wing youth. Though he had made his fortune in California, he continued to sympathize with progressive causes. He and Sidney became fast friends.

Sidney was struggling with the task of beginning to write his memoir, so Jerry encouraged him to stay in a condo he owned in Beverly Hills. "You can just sit there and write," he said. "I'll cover all your expenses, including airfare." Sidney thought this was a terrific offer, and we started to think about traveling to the United States again.

≈

Ever since his days at Stanford, Sidney had cherished the dream of working to build bridges between Chinese and Americans. In 1978 and 1979, it seemed he could do that from Beijing. Public discussions had led him to believe that the new era of openness and debate had arrived. He was particularly encouraged by a 1978 interview that Deng Xiaoping gave to American journalist Robert Novak, in which Deng expressed approval of the free democratic discussion taking place at the Democracy Wall. Sidney enthusiastically embraced these outspoken workers and students and invited some of them to our home at the Friendship Hotel, which became a center for open discussion about the path to democracy in China.

Sidney had long hoped that Communism could flourish in China along with freedom of expression; in fact, he had imagined that the Cultural Revolution was turning China into an open democracy. That had proved wrong, but still, China's leaders needed a way to know what the people were thinking, and Chinese people needed legal outlets to provide their ideas about national policies. The Democracy Wall seemed like a step in the right direction. Sidney hoped to see the rebirth of the Chinese Communist Party as he had once dreamed it could be: a promoter of social fairness based on the best ideas that percolated up from below. Democracy and socialism, he believed, could—and should—coexist.

But in January of 1980 that hope died. Suddenly, the same Deng Xiaoping, having consolidated his position as new paramount leader, gave orders that the Democracy Wall was to be shut down, and that all media outlets would only be allowed to reflect Party policy. No free opinion or debate was to be permitted. A number of outspoken advocates of democratization were arrested.

Aside from this personal disappointment, Sidney was concerned that Deng's crackdown would endanger the students and workers we had befriended, although we did not feel that there was any danger to us. Sidney was also shocked by the corruption he observed after he came home from prison. He worried that Deng Xiaoping was protecting corrupt cadres and that the crackdown might spark more mass protests, which could bring down Deng's entire ruling structure and plunge China back into deadly chaos.

After we read about Deng's policy shift, Sidney said, "That's it. We'll go live in America and work on that side of the bridge. There's nothing I can do here."

I agreed. Not that I wanted to leave China, but I felt that I had to go with him and help him bear up under all the different pressures. For me, the decision came down to one main thing: No one could keep Sidney from speaking his mind. China is not the kind of country where you can say and write whatever you want. It never has been, under any government. If Sidney was sent to prison a third time, I knew it would kill him. It might kill me, too. Our family had suffered enough. Moving to America was the only solution.

Even so, it was a big decision, especially for me. I could not imagine being separated from my children for a long time. But our children didn't even speak English. Though they had been labeled "American," there was nothing American about them. What's more, we didn't have enough money to support them in the United States. We were not sure how long we would be able to stay or whether we could adjust to life in America.

Sidney and I arranged for the wife of a friend to care for our children, especially our son, who was still in middle school. I hugged my kids and told them we would come back to see them within a year. I told them we were going to give life in America a try, and we might change our minds.

But in my heart, I felt certain that I was leaving China, my homeland. For good.

As the plane rose over Beijing's airport, I wept.

〜

Chapter Forty-Eight

Strangers in a Strange Land

ALTHOUGH JERRY MANN offered to let us live in his Los Angeles mansion, we decided we would be better off living on the East Coast. We accepted an invitation to live with our warmhearted, liberal-minded friend, Shirley Samberg, on Long Island. Shortly afterward, in order to focus on the book, we went to live with Sidney's old schoolmates, Moe Malkin and his wife Hannah, in Woodbridge, Connecticut, an affluent suburb of New Haven.

Moe, who had spent his career as an investment adviser, took care of everything. Even back in college in Chapel Hill, forty years earlier, Moe had been like an older brother to Sidney, and he quickly took up that role again. He and Hannah gave us the second floor of their home to live in. Moe let Sidney drive his diesel-powered Peugeot. And on top of that he gave us five hundred dollars a month for spending money. He said we could live there until Sidney finished his book and we got settled in this country.

Hannah was warm and welcoming and loved sharing her house with us. But I was not comfortable with the feeling that we were living off of other people. I did everything possible to earn our keep—cooking, cleaning, shopping, and helping Hannah however I could. But I still felt it wasn't enough. I realized that Sidney needed the quiet stability to recover and reflect on his past, but living off the kindness of others went against one of my core values: self-reliance.

The publisher who had bought the rights to Sidney's book, gave him an advance that seemed to us a princely sum: twenty-seven thousand dollars. We deposited it in a bank and got our first checkbook. Then we went to the Yale Co-op and bought our first computer—an Apple II Plus—and a daisy-wheel printer. Sidney also bought a secondhand, reconditioned IBM Selectric typewriter—the kind with upraised letters on a "golf ball." We felt very modern.

Chapter after chapter, we worked together, up there on the Malkins' second floor. Throughout his life, Sidney had developed a daily habit of taking notes on each day's activities and analyzing his thoughts. Some of those notes were lost or destroyed, but others had survived, especially from the 1950s. Before leaving China, he had already begun writing down his memories. Now in Connecticut, he spent long days typing up everything he could remember.

The words flowed out in torrents. As he tried to make sense of his life, he shared with me some of his darkest thoughts during his prison years. We talked late into the night, sometimes laughing and clear-eyed, sometimes tearful and tormented. I learned about his childhood and youth in America, his reasons for staying in China, his early impressions of Chairman Mao and Zhou Enlai. I was shocked to find out just how close he had come to madness during his first year in prison, when he had been drugged. Holding his hands, hugging him when he needed it, I had never felt closer to him.

That summer, Moe flew us to their Martha's Vineyard home in his little plane. He told me that I had a technical mind and that if I stayed long enough he would teach me to fly. It was unimaginable to me, that a private citizen could own an airplane, let alone two huge, beautiful homes.

"How different America is for the rich and the poor!" I thought. The contrast between penniless people like us and these affluent upper middle-class Americans was particularly striking.

As we worked on Sidney's book, both of us had to deeply analyze our beliefs and attitudes toward Communism and the Communist Party. He was writing for an American audience, yet in America, those very words evoked fear and loathing. Most Americans were mystified about why Sidney chose to stay after "the Reds" took over China. The American Communist Party had been outlawed and some of its members had been jailed on false charges of plotting the violent overthrow of the government. In China, they would have been lauded as revolutionary heroes and martyrs.

When I had first learned the term, "Communism," it meant fairness and social justice. However, to most Americans, "Communism" meant tyranny and oppression. Sidney and I had witnessed both aspects. Without the Communist victory, China might have remained weak and corrupt and ravaged by civil wars, as it had been in the 1920s and 1930s, when it could not defend itself against invasion. Sidney remembered his first impression of China in the 1940s. He recalled a rickshaw driver whose little daughter was killed by an army truck, and how the man was paid only twenty-six dollars to compensate for the loss of his only child.

He recalled starving girls on the streets of Shanghai, selling their bodies for one night's supper, and landlords who hoarded barn loads of grain while nearby villagers starved.

After 1949, both of us knew that the Communists had righted many of these injustices, which they blamed on "capitalism"—a word they defined as meaning tyranny and oppression. My own life and family were evidence of the crushing poverty before Liberation and the sudden blooming of opportunities afterward. But how could Sidney explain the good the Communists had done, as well as the bad? How could an American man, imprisoned for sixteen years by the Communist Party of China, explain why he had become a true believer—and still believed in the ideals of Karl Marx? Or did he?

After eight months of long days at the typewriter, Sidney had written hundreds and hundreds of pages. He had wracked his brain and resurrected every buried memory. He had progressed far on the road to healing his shattered psyche. But he had not finished his book. He could not. It was too soon.

When Sidney told the publisher the bad news, we had to return the entire advance. However, we had already spent most of the money. How would we pay back the debt? It felt like total failure.

Our kids begged us to come home to China. My heart ached every time I received a letter from them. Phone connections to Beijing were impossible, so I couldn't even hear their voices. Scrutinizing their letters, I tried to read between the lines: Were they really okay? Or were they just trying to reassure us?

Sidney did not want to move back to China. He said we needed to stay in America and earn enough money to pay our debts. My heart ruptured. I had worked so many years to keep our family together, and now we were half a world away from our children, too poor to afford the airfare to return home.

The glamour of America, so alluring during our first visit, faded. Sidney, a celebrity in 1979, became a nobody in 1980. Reporters didn't call. Hollywood had lost interest. Washington had moved on. Our friends stuck by us, but we could not live off their generosity forever. Who were we? Where should we live? What work could we do? Outside the cocoon of the Malkins' home was the unforgiving world of capitalism. In China, the state had paid us a salary. In America, we had to figure out how to support ourselves and our children back in China. But how could we earn a living?

In China, Sidney had relied on his fluency in Chinese and English and his ability to explain China to the world. I had technical expertise in outdated broadcast equipment and a college degree in English, which I spoke with such a strong accent few people could understand. That job experience wouldn't get us far in the modern U.S. economy of 1980. What other skills did we have that any American would pay us for?

After nine months with the Malkins, I decided that I had had enough of living in someone else's home and depending on them.

"I'm going back to Beijing," I said to Sidney. "I want to make sure the children are all right. I'll come back to live in America only on two conditions: I have my own kitchen and my own job. That's it."

Sidney promised we would find a way. He stayed in the United States, checking out various possibilities for where we might live and how we might earn money.

I flew back to China alone, with plans for Sidney to join me later. Back at our home in the Friendship Hotel, the children all gathered around me, hopping with excitement.

"Mama, Mama! Tell us all about America, everything!" The kids seemed to be all speaking at once.

They grabbed for the presents I had brought them—clothes, Hershey's bars, cashew nuts. There wasn't much, because we didn't have much money, but they were things the children had never seen before.

"Mama, what is it like, living in America?" Ming wanted to know.

"You can't get along without money. But if you're willing to work hard, you can make money."

"What else?" asked Sunny.

"Well, our friends all tell us not to carry valuable things with us, because there are so many thieves. They may hold a knife to you and take everything you have. We haven't run into anything like that, so far." That was not a side of America they had read about.

"There are lots of restaurants, but your father and I never venture into any of them," I continued. The food is expensive, and you're expected to give 10 percent to 20 percent additional for tips. If we have to go somewhere, we take the subway or the bus, because taxis are too expensive."

"Is it true that all you see on TV is half-naked dancing?" Toni blushed.

I smiled. "Not true! There is some of that, but there are lots of other programs too."

"Is it true that most Americans are rich? You wrote that they waste a lot," said Jenny.

"In New York City, people put their old furniture out on the sidewalk for the dump trucks to pick up. You can find tables, chairs, sofas, even beds out on the streets, there for the taking. We would never see that in China!"

I went in our son's room and saw that he had pasted a picture of a handsome red Porsche on the wall.

"Why did you put that up?" I asked him.

"I've made up my mind. I'm going to buy a Porsche," he said, with a straight face.

"My goodness! Where would we get the money to buy an expensive car like that?" I exclaimed.

He was a little taken aback. "Well, that's what I want, anyway."

The children were getting along fine, but I wanted to make a plan to bring us together again. Unfortunately, we didn't have enough money to bring them all over at once. Also, two of the girls were still in college and needed to graduate first.

"It's very hard to make a living in America, let alone get rich," I told them. "But your father and I have decided to give it a go. We will bring you over, one by one."

A few days later, I took all the kids to the U.S. embassy and met with the deputy chief of mission, Chas Freeman. I explained that Sidney and I had decided to live permanently in the United States. We wanted our children to have American passports so that it would be easy for them to join us if there was any trouble and they needed to get out of China. Having just gone through the ten years of Cultural Revolution chaos, I wasn't certain what was going to happen next.

Mr. Freeman knew Sidney and understood our problems. He had our kids fill out application forms, and before long they each received their first American passport. As children of a U.S. citizen, they were entitled to citizenship right away, while I had to apply and wait.

While they processed my application, I took the train to visit my family in Shijiazhuang—my mother, Third Sister, and my elder brother. I told them that Sidney had decided we should live in America. My mother worried about our livelihood there. "It's so expensive, and you don't have work. Nobody's going to support you there. How will you get along?"

"As long as we both have our health, and we each have two hands, we can work and we can get along in America. But we have to go and make our way first, before we can bring the children over—especially Xiaoming, who's still a little boy."

After staying with them about a week, I had a tearful parting with my mother. "You'll be living so far away. How will we ever see you?" Mama asked.

"We'll come back and forth," I promised.

Third Sister said, "If you're going to move to America, take your family flower with you." The amaryllis was still blooming, in her home.

"I will have to wait till we have our own home in America," I said, smiling.

The red blossoms, and my sister's confidence, reminded me: We would survive this separation and thrive again.

≈

If we were seriously considering staying in America, I needed to see some other people who were important to me. First stop: my old hometown of Shijiazhuang. Using the cheapest train ticket, it took me eight hours to travel from Shijiazhuang to Beijing—a journey that takes two hours in 2014. Back in Beijing, I looked up my old classmate Wang Fengzhen, one of my best buddies. In the early days of the Cultural Revolution, we had shared many of the same views.

Since college, Wang Fengzhen had been working as an English translator at a factory. She had suffered through serious struggle meetings because it had come to light that she had visited us several times. Her colleagues had demanded that she reveal her "connections with the imperialist spy, Li Dunbai."

After the Cultural Revolution, she was cleared of all suspicion. But the experience had filled her with righteous anger. Recently, she had taken her son to the factory with her, and they marched all over the place, shouting at the top of their lungs, "See—this is the secret agent suspect Wang Fengzhen! I'm free now, and what are you going to say? When someone's in trouble, there are some people that make up stories in order to gain some advantage for themselves. These are the really bad people!"

Wang Fengzhen told me that there were bad people like that among our own classmates, including some that knew us well. "Stay away from them," she said. "They have no character."

Later, she went to work at the Foreign Ministry and was sent to America as a visa consul. She was conscientious, straightforward, and upright, one of my best friends to this day. She could never forgive those who had attacked their classmates and colleagues during the chaos. At some level, I agreed with her. But I decided to let it go. There were just too many people who had said too many terrible things during those years. I didn't want to carry that burden the rest of my life. Of course, it helps when you live far away and don't have to see those people every day.

∼

When I returned to the United States, Sidney had arranged for us to live with our friend Shirley Samberg. Shirley was a widow who lived by herself in a lovely little Levitt home in Roslyn, New York, on Long Island. Her grown son and daughter had gone off on their own. Shirley was a lover of the arts, an avant-garde sculptor who welded figures out of automobile bumpers. Later, she began doing burlap wraps, which earned her considerable fame, but not fortune. Much later, we enjoyed seeing a prizewinning exhibit of hers at a Seattle museum.

For Shirley, friends were family. She herself was careful to live economically. She seldom used the dryer for things like towels, or the dishwasher, saying that they used too much electricity. Her diet was simple, too—nothing showy. But Shirley was always generous to her friends. She treated us like her brother and sister. She was interested in China, and she supported leftist causes. I liked her values.

Shirley understood our need to find ways to earn a living, so she helped us brainstorm. Sidney approached a local college that hired him to give occasional lectures on China in their continuing education program. I answered an ad for Chinese-language teachers and was hired to teach American businessmen at a foreign language school in Manhattan—for seven dollars an hour, fourteen dollars a week.

Our first big break, though, came with Norval Welch, who owned the company Special Tours for Special People. We had met Norval when he came to Beijing in the late 1970s. A former merchant seaman and National Maritime Union activist, he had gone into the travel business with professional tours to China in the pioneering days when few Americans could even imagine travelling there.

Norval hired Sidney and me to lead tours to China. So we made the plunge and accepted our first regular paying jobs in America. I liked the fact that this work would ensure I could get back to Beijing to see my kids.

For a short time, we lived at Norval Welch's home. A funny thing happened on the first evening we spent there. Marianne, his wife, invited me to fix a big Chinese meal for the whole family, which included the couple and their son and daughter.

"We'll do it tomorrow," Marianne said. "There's nothing in my fridge right now."

I went into her kitchen and came back after a while with four big plates heaped with Chinese food.

"Did that come out of my kitchen?" Marianne exclaimed.

It doesn't take a lot of special stuff to cook good Chinese food. She had far more in her half-empty refrigerator than our family had scraped by on in the early 1970s.

Working for this China tour company, we earned very little, but Shirley charged us nothing, so we had spending money. All those years that Sidney was in prison, I had learned how to make do with very little, and those skills came in handy in New York. It never entered our heads to eat out, even to have a hamburger in a restaurant. We never took a bus if our destination was within walking distance. Any new clothes came from friends or from special bargains discovered at flea markets.

In spite of our penury, Sidney and I would constantly tell each other how proud we were that we could get along by our own hard work, that we never borrowed money. We continued to put every spare penny into our savings account, until we finally accumulated enough to repay the book advance. Two affluent New York friends, Bob Schwartz and Bob Wechsler, offered to put up twenty thousand dollars to finance the book, saying that we did not have to repay it if we didn't have the money. We thanked them and asked them to hold the offer till later, in case we might need it. In the end we didn't need the loan. Later, Werner Erhard's foundation heard our story and gave us an outright grant of twenty thousand dollars with no strings attached. That helped tide us over.

Warmed by Shirley's friendship and encouraged by our first efforts at earning money, we got through the winter.

The following summer, I returned to China as a tour guide and was able to spent time with the children again. One evening, Sidney phoned me from New York with a surprise. Mike Wallace of CBS's *60 Minutes* would be coming to Beijing to do a piece on China—and he wanted to interview us! More than eighty million Americans watched this show every Sunday night, he explained; Mike Wallace was one of the most famous TV reporters in the world. Mike wanted to interview me, too, and bring a camera crew to Beijing to shoot videos of our home and children.

I was cautious, wanting to protect our family privacy, but Sidney's enthusiasm was unquenchable. He told me that our friends in New York—including a well-known entertainment lawyer—warned him not to accept Mike's invitation.

"He's too tough," one friend had said, "too skillful. He'll make you say things that you don't want to say." That was the reputation Mike Wallace had.

But Sidney told me he didn't believe this. From watching *60 Minutes*, he decided that Mike was tough only with people who were trying to conceal things that the public had a right to know. When Sidney went to Martha's Vineyard to talk with Mike before their trip, he told me he found him to be a straight shooter and a good-hearted man.

Sidney offered to work as a CBS consultant during the trip, but Mike replied that CBS hired the best consultants in the world; they didn't need Sidney for that—he need only sit for the interview and serve as interpreter. Still, Sidney accepted, and he traveled with Mike Wallace and his crew.

In August, Mike Wallace and the *60 Minutes* team arrived in Beijing with an American producer, a German cameraman, and an Italian soundman. Sidney flew in on the same plane. Still hesitant, I took the four children to the airport to meet them.

This tough, hard-nosed reporter struck me as kind and amiable. The team set up their equipment in our main apartment at the Friendship Hotel. Before beginning the interviews, Mike Wallace warned us. "Remember, there's no such thing as an embarrassing question. There are only embarrassing answers."

With the video cameras running, he put me at ease and had me go on and on about China, about Sidney, about our family. During the long taping, he did his best to keep the atmosphere relaxed. When he was questioning me, I felt as though I was just chatting with a friend—not being interviewed by the media. Twice, he stopped the camera and sound to look at me with a wry smile and say, "But you really married this man?" That made me laugh.

Over a two-day period, the crew shot all kinds of scenes on the hotel grounds, videos of Sidney and me jogging, shopping, and walking with the children. And Sidney had been right. Mike treated us well. He became a fast friend for life.

That was Mike Wallace's first trip to China. Knowing nothing about the country, he had originally planned a story that stressed a rising China as a potential threat to America. But what he saw and experienced in China changed his understanding. Instead, he produced a truly seminal story: "To Get Rich Is Glorious." It was about the new "opening and reform" program of Deng Xiaoping and the difference it was making for life in China— and in the global economy. Deng never actually said, "To get rich is glorious," but Mike caught the spirit of the reforms—to encourage people to produce, to learn, to innovate, and thereby to grow well-to-do in the process of growing the Chinese economy.

Sidney later told me about his experience in Nanjing, which had had a big impact on both of us. As Mike Wallace and his crew rode from the airport to the hotel, they passed big billboards, advertising a performance that night by the army song and dance ensemble that belonged to the infantry division we were to visit the next day. Immediately, they decided to tape the performance that night.

When they got to the hotel, the TV crew set out for the theater. They told Sidney there was no need for him to go. Half an hour later, they came back to the hotel, crestfallen: the young political director of the troupe had instructed them that they were only allowed to tape a specific five-minute segment of the performance and that it would cost eighty thousand dollars.

Sidney heard their story and said, "Don't get excited. Let me talk to them." He went to the theater and explained to the director that this could be an excellent opportunity for the troupe to make itself known abroad and to receive an invitation to perform in America. The result was that the troupe invited the TV crew to film as much as they liked, at no charge, as long as they could repeat any number that didn't come out well. That night, Mike phoned CBS in New York, and Sidney was retained as a consultant—his first gig for substantial fees.

For us, this was a lesson. Sidney had been toying with the idea of earning money through consulting, but I had argued that neither of us was qualified. In Nanjing, Sidney found out that consulting in China did not require any complicated skills or business genius; it was mainly about knowing how to talk to people on both sides, how to eliminate misunderstandings and ensure that the two sides were communicating clearly with each other. "You could have done it, too, Yulin," Sidney said. "You just figure out what each side wants and explain it."

While he was in China, Mike Wallace told us that he was going to refer Sidney to the prestigious Harry Walker Agency Speakers Bureau in New York, so that Sidney could earn money from lectures. I thought to myself, *Mike means well, but a busy man like that is never going to remember this promise.* But when we returned to New York, Sidney got a phone call from Harry Walker himself, asking Sidney to send him a resumé and to come in for an interview. When he went for the interview, Mr. Walker told Sidney that ordinarily he would not even look at his resumé. But Mike Wallace had been a client of his for thirteen years, and several times he had asked Mike for references about a potential client, and he had never even responded. But in the past week Mike had called twice, to insist that he see Sidney.

That afternoon, Sidney signed a contract to give lectures under their sponsorship. This kindness on the part of Mike Wallace gave us an entree into the corporate world. It also opened our eyes to the value of what Americans call "networking." In China, we call this *guanxi*, or "connections." In both places, it matters who you know—and what they think of you.

After that August interview in Beijing, Sidney and I returned to New York. We still did not have a steady enough income to afford our own home, so we could still only dream of bringing the children over. But we had reason to hope. That autumn, two *60 Minutes* specials aired—both on China, both quoting us. After that, sometimes people recognized us on the streets of Manhattan. Before Mike's death, Sidney did five special programs with him—more than anyone else had done on *60 Minutes*. We were deeply impressed with Mike—a warm friend and a journalist of strong integrity. We miss him terribly.

Chapter Forty-Nine

On Our Own, Scraping By

AT FIRST, I felt that our chances of making a decent living in America were pretty slim. I was forty-seven, Sidney was nearly sixty, and we had arrived in New York empty-handed. My English was rough. Although Sidney was American, he had been away for so long that he sometimes felt as much like a stranger in this land as I did. We were naïve, with no clue about how to be entrepreneurial and live off our wits.

Daily, we faced a reality about life in America that few Chinese back home understood: There's no "Mama" to take care of you here. Everything costs money: rent, food, college education, health care. You get nothing unless you can earn enough to afford it. No one else will take care of you, think about your interests, guarantee your family's basic needs, or plan for your future. The American government does not guarantee jobs. Even Sidney, who grew up in America but had spent decades in China, had the same feeling. It was scary to imagine living in a place with no "Mama."

Starting at age seventeen, I had received a salary from the state. Though small, it had allowed me to buy everything I felt I needed: food, clothing, and shelter. Even while Sidney was in prison, I had continued to receive my small monthly salary, which had remained the same, regardless of how much or how well I worked—or even if I worked at all.

Now, at an age when most Americans were preparing for retirement, Sidney and I had to learn how to "make a living." This was an entirely new concept, a new phrase in my vocabulary. As naïve as two kids just out of college, Sidney and I had to figure out how to support ourselves. We had no business experience and were not familiar with the American way of life.

One of our new American friends (Arthur Miller's nephew) told us, in all candor, that we would never be able to make it on our own in the highly competitive, even cutthroat American job market. "Better go back to China," he said, "where you'll be taken care of."

Despite our slim chances of success, we wanted to give it a try. Oddly, I had no fear. During those years of backbreaking labor, humiliation, separation, and imprisonment, I had developed a sense that I had the strength to handle whatever adversities life threw at me. I wasn't afraid of hard work or long hours. I knew how to scrimp and save. Our kids were okay for the time being. With Sidney free and safe at my side, how tough could it be to "make a living"?

~

At first, we tried what we had done before. I taught Chinese classes in Manhattan twice a week and Sidney did occasional lectures about China. We led tours. We were earning money, but not nearly enough to afford the New York's high rent, even for a small place of our own.

One day, out of the blue, a Japanese lady who was an executive at Japan Airlines in New York called us at Shirley's home. She said she had an empty studio apartment on East Thirty-Seventh Street between Park Avenue and Lexington that we were welcome to live in, at very low rent. It happened that she had been a bridge partner of Sidney's late mother, and she was president of the New York chapter of the American Association of University Women (AAUW). The AAUW owned a brownstone on Thirty-Seventh Street, which had been divided into several apartments.

We were delighted to accept her kind invitation. It was a large one-room apartment, with a tiny bath and an alcove kitchen, about the same size as the tiny room our whole family had shared after Sidney's arrest. But it was plenty big enough for the two of us. I was happier than I could say! We lived in rented space, but at last I didn't have to share a kitchen. And we had a bed of our own to sleep in.

After we led our first tour, Norval Welch hired Sidney as vice president, at fifteen thousand dollars a year and paid me on a commission basis, as director of China tours. It wasn't much, but it was steady income, and it gave us confidence. It was time to start bringing our children to live with us.

We first brought our son to the States, since he was the youngest and had always been with me. Now fifteen, Xiaoming was eager to join us. Many of his friends in Beijing were Americans, and he enjoyed playing basketball and football with them. They had given him a rosy image of what it was like to live in America.

But I was worried about the bad influences he might face here. Before I agreed to let him come, I wrote him a letter, telling him that our lives in New York City were not ideal, and that life in America was both good and bad. I warned him that he had to prepare himself to deal with all the drink, dope, vice, street crime, and other problems that he was not accustomed to, growing up in the China of that day. He wrote his own pledge, promising what he called "The Three Nos": No drinking, no smoking, no running wild. That was what I wanted to hear.

While waiting to pick Xiaoming up at the airport, we overheard two men talking as they came out of immigration. "I couldn't believe it! There was this American kid who looked Chinese and couldn't speak much English, but he got past the immigration officer."

Then, out came Xiaoming. But before we left the airport, a band of men crossed our path wearing T-shirts with a big Taiwan flag on it.

Ming said, "Mama, I'm going to get a T-shirt with a big Chinese flag. I'll show them!"

"Don't look for trouble," I cautioned him.

We enrolled him in a public high school in Manhattan.

Not long after Ming's arrival, we heard that Jenny had been diagnosed with possible leukemia and would not recover unless she had a full-body blood transfusion. In a panic, Sidney and I flew her to New York immediately, so that our friend Dr. Buchberg could examine her and she could get the best treatment in the world. So Jenny arrived in January 1982. Abe examined her right away, and we all breathed a great sigh of relief. It was a false alarm! Jenny had been misdiagnosed—she was in good health.

Although Jenny hadn't finished her medical studies at college, she decided to stay. The four of us set up housekeeping in that one-room studio. But four people living in one room was too much. Our two children were sleeping on futons on the floor. We had to find a new home.

Before long, we found a three-bedroom flat in Woodside, Queens, that seemed suitable and affordable. Curiously enough, the owner specified that he wanted "Chinese tenants."

When Sidney called the owner, the man said, "But you're not Chinese."

Sidney said, "You're not Chinese either. My wife and children are Chinese. Will that do?"

The next day, we moved to the new flat, just a block from the Roosevelt Avenue elevated railroad line, on which ran the number seven train to Manhattan.

We discovered that the owner of our flat was a Greek merchant marine captain, who found that Chinese tenants were generally quiet, hardworking, and paid the rent on time. He turned out to be an amiable man whose one request was that every time we went to China we brought him back some Tiger Balm, which he used to treat his headaches at sea.

Soon we set out to furnish our new home. Our friend Shirley drove us around Queens, picking up furniture from the sidewalk. We found everything we needed—sofas, tables, chairs, chests—everything except for a big bed, which was supplied by a friend of Shirley's.

There was an unanticipated downside to our Woodside flat that we discovered shortly after moving there. At night, we heard slithering sounds everywhere. As our eyes accustomed to the light, we saw cockroaches all over the floor. I had never seen such big roaches—and they had wings! When I went to the bathroom, they flew all over. There was no way we could get rid of them, because if one flat wiped them out they would cross over from the other flats. This was the worst experience that we had in America.

In Woodside, I found I had another skill that could help me earn money: teaching cooking. I never considered myself a good cook. We had to eat, and my mother had taught me how to fix some Chinese dishes, so I just cooked. That's it. But in America, I found that I had the skills needed to teach Chinese cooking. Who would have thought it, me being a cooking teacher!

I began teaching one night a week at the Roslyn School. Each class, I would demonstrate how to prepare four different Chinese dishes. Then the students would fix the same four dishes, and we would all sit down and enjoy what we had cooked. There were only twenty burners in the classroom, and lots of people wanted to take this class but couldn't get in. Finally, the school asked me to start a second class, so I started teaching two nights a week.

A huge success, it was the only class that the superintendent of education "inspected" every week. He loved Chinese food. One old gentleman took the class two semesters in a row. He became famous in his neighborhood for his Sichuan-style hot and sour soup.

If the students had seen how I prepared for the class at home, they would have been amused. I had learned how to cook mainly from watching Mama, who was, as Sidney wrote in his book, "a cook like Schubert was a composer." But I had no idea how much of what spices and ingredients to put in the pot, so I couldn't write out recipes for the students. Before class every week, I would rehearse the dishes in our home kitchen while Sidney watched me and put the recipe into the computer, line by line.

I would say, "Now you add some dill."

He would say, "How much is 'some dill'?"

Then we would measure it out, and he would write down the exact amount. I had to buy a small scale to measure meat and vegetables. Sidney also became my guinea pig. I would feed him first and only settle on a recipe when he tasted it and exclaimed, "Wow, that's really good!" If he thought it tasted good, I figured my American students would like it, too.

When the recipes were done, we would gather the pots and pans, spices and ingredients, meat and vegetables, and head for the subway. Then we would take the Long Island Railroad to Roslyn. We looked like a couple of peddlers, with, pots, pans, and bags of food dangling from our arms, waist, shoulders, back, wherever they could find a perch.

It was fun. After all the months I had helped him write his book, it felt good to have Sidney helping me with my project to support the family. He had a way of making me laugh, and we made a good team. I was also proud of the joy that the students got out of learning to cook Chinese food.

I taught them that Chinese cooking was not just a matter of filling the stomach. It was also about stimulating the appetite. When you place a dish on the table, its color, arrangement, aroma, texture, everything about it should excite the taste buds and fire the imagination. I came to understand that it was not just a skill; it was an art!

I told the students that they needn't think the materials for Chinese dishes could only be found at Chinese groceries. Plenty of the ingredients could be found at ordinary supermarkets. Of course, there were special items, such as Sichuan peppers, that could only be found in Chinatown. I showed them these ingredients and taught them where to buy them and how to cook them. The students felt they were being initiated into a secret club.

I only earned sixteen dollars an hour for my cooking lessons, but I felt proud of my earnings. Both Sidney and I earned very little, but we didn't drink or smoke, so we got by. The food we bought with the money we earned tasted better than any food I had ever eaten, because now I was eating from what I had earned. I began to get the taste for productive labor, to see what the old slogan "He who does not work, neither shall he eat," really meant. Within my circle of experience in America, this country seemed closer to carrying out "From each according to his ability, to each according to his work" than did China.

~

About that same time, I discovered another way I could make money. Shirley's friend Pat Penn, who lived in Glen Cove, Long Island, called us one day to suggest that we let our son live with her family and go to Glen Cove High School. Pat was a kind-hearted woman, married to a Manhattan attorney, and we knew that Xiaoming would be in good hands. Glen Cove High was a better school than the one he had been attending. But the main idea would be that he would be forced to learn English in that family who knew no Chinese. So our son went off to live in Glen Cove, coming home on the weekends.

Sidney and I took him to meet with the guidance counselor at the new school. We suggested that he be put back one grade, so that he could catch up with his English. After talking with him, however, and examining the list of courses he had taken in Beijing—far advanced compared to what his American peers were taking at that time—she recommended that he skip ahead one grade.

"He'll learn English in no time," she said.

That came as a big surprise to us, but there was a bigger one in store. When the guidance counselor asked Xiaoming what his name was, he answered, "Sidney Rittenberg, Junior."

No one had ever called him that before. His English name had been "Happy," ever since his father had returned home from prison. Xiaoming had picked a new name for himself after coming to America, naming himself after his father and his grandfather. After years of worrying how he would be able to relate to his father after such a long separation during his childhood, I was relieved and glad to see him make this choice.

Pat Penn introduced us to her friend, Nan Brown, who was a New York schoolteacher—and very talented at crochet work. Nan and I soon became good friends. When she found out that I was a knitter who had always produced warm, colorful sweaters for everyone in our family, she got me to teach her to knit while she taught me to crochet. I found it easy. I didn't let my broken finger slow me down. But I still stuck to my knitting, saving crochet work for occasional collars and trimmings.

Nan introduced me to *Woman's Day* magazine, which published patterns for designer sweaters. I designed two sweaters for the magazine, and they published photos of both, drawing attention to them on their cover. They paid me five hundred dollars apiece! This was more money than either Sidney or I had ever made from a single project at that time. Imagine how I felt!

Listed as "creator of designer sweaters" in New York, I was invited to designers' conferences, and I was supplied with high-quality yarn at wholesale prices. Yarn makers began to ask that I use their yarn, which they supplied free of charge, so that they could list me in their advertising. It was nice to see them boasting that I was an expert designer. This was a new image of myself, one that I could never have imagined back when I was making bricks.

That experience was my first insight into how commercial relations work—the ties between designers, manufacturers, jobbers, wholesalers, and retailers. I used to be what the Chinese called a "three doors cadre"—a person who went straight from the door of my childhood home to the door of my school to the door of the government office where I worked. Now, everything was changing.

One day, Jenny ran into a Chinese friend, who told us that former President Liu Shaoqi's daughter was earning money by knitting sweaters for the Bronxville company called Madame Defarge. So I wasn't the only Chinese woman who went from a privileged life in Beijing to knitting for a living in New York.

Sidney and I took the bus to Bronxville—more than two hours from our home—and talked to the supervisor at Madame Defarge. We discovered it wasn't a factory at all—just a big room, where they gave out the yarn and inspected the finished sweaters when the knitters brought them back.

The supervisor first tested my skills at knitting and then gave me a pattern and a batch of yarn, for which I signed out. To complete a long-sleeved sweater, according to the pattern they gave you, the knitter was allowed one week.

Though I was teaching classes in Chinese language and cooking, I spent most of my time knitting—till one o'clock in the morning—so I finished the sweater in two days. Sidney and I took the completed sweater back to the supervisor, who examined it carefully.

"Did you sew on the sleeves, or knit them on?" she asked.

"I knit them on," I answered.

"Well, we can't accept that," she said. "They have to be sewn on, tight." As she spoke, she was looking at where the sleeves connected with the body, and a puzzled expression came over her face. "Waaaaait a minute," she said, and she took the sweater over to her boss, who examined it in the same way.

When the supervisor came back, she said, "Okay, this one is all right. You really knit it tight!"

I passed my first test and became a regular knitter for Madame Defarge. It amazed me how ordinary life skills, like knitting and cooking, could earn a living in America. In China, I didn't know anyone who was paid for such work.

Since we lived so far away, I asked for yarn for more than one sweater. But the supervisor said it was against the rules and wouldn't agree, so I would knit a small sweater in one day, or a regular size sweater in two days, using all my spare time, adding sorely needed money to the family income.

Then, I began to get the picture of how this business worked. Madame Defarge paid me $36 for each sweater, and then sold them to Bloomingdale's for $150 apiece. Bloomingdale's in turn retailed them for $450 to $550 each. In other words, the consumer paid fifteen times what I was getting for creating the sweater. Even after subtracting the cost of materials and overhead, that was still a huge profit on my labor—a vivid lesson in the exploitation of the worker!

But in America in 1980, workers had other opportunities besides revolution. It was possible to work around the capitalist middlemen. As it happened, several people saw my designs in *Woman's Day* and asked me to provide them with specially designed fancy sweaters with my monogram, for which they directly paid me $450 to $500 apiece. I was beginning to understand what was known as the "market economy"—which was just getting started in China.

≈

Fortunately, I knew how to work hard and did not fear the long hours of my new business ventures. Knitting sweaters was simple compared to carrying burning bricks from a kiln or cooking for 130 people over a hot wok at labor camp. I had never been a teacher, but teaching Chinese language and cooking was easy to learn, especially given the eagerness of my American students.

However, despite the enthusiasm I felt about our new way of life, others found it unsettling. Gao Luduan, an old friend from the Foreign Experts Bureau in Beijing, came to New York on business and visited us in Woodside. Our simple, crowded lodgings and our frugal existence almost moved him to tears. He urged us to stop suffering hardship in America and return to Beijing. When he went back to Beijing he even wrote up a report about the tough time that we were having.

Still I felt empowered by the new life that Sidney and I were creating for ourselves in America. When I wrote to my mother and sister, I told them that life in America was much easier than life in China. Nobody pressured us about our political beliefs. Nobody humiliated us. Our family and class backgrounds were irrelevant. The harder we worked, the more money we earned. Opportunities were everywhere, beckoning us to try new things. It was true that we led simple lives, but we were very happy.

Woman's Day published photos of two sweaters I designed.

Both Chinese and Americans had told us that, at our ages, we would never make it in the United States. But we were proving them wrong. In bed at night, we would count up our money and figure out how much was left to spend on food after paying for rent, travel, and other expenses. Sometimes, not knowing where the money for next week's food would come from, we would look at each other and burst out laughing—what a strange new life we were leading. We felt that we were pioneering, doing things that we had never dreamed of before. Just imagine! I was now a designer sweater creator, and Sidney was a lecturer in schools.

Looking back, I'm amazed to recall how Sidney and I, both in a fragile state after our Cultural Revolution suffering, managed to move to a different country and figure out how to make a living there. Young people from China today have little trouble adapting to U.S. life, but at midcareer and older, it can be a tough transition.

For me, it helped that I was stubborn. All those years in the labor camp, I was determined not to let the experience break me, to prove to my tormenters that I could do any kind of hard work. Even with a bloody hand, I could pull that wheelbarrow. I could adjust to anything. Maybe it helped to have a new challenge to occupy my mind, so that I did not have time to dwell on old feelings of bitterness.

I do believe that all of us can do anything we set our minds to, if we push ourselves outside of our comfort zone. Today, I tell younger women not to let their views of their own limitations stop them from trying something new and challenging.

Whatever the changes in the environment, whatever country you find yourself in, your future is for you to create. For Sidney and me, America was a huge theater of operations. As long as we worked hard we would never go hungry. The Chinese saying is *shi zai ren wei*—"It's people who have the power to make things happen."

But the precondition is that you must always be open to new experiences. As long as you have breath, you have to keep learning. The environment won't adapt to you, you have to adapt to it. *Huo dao lao, xue dao lao*—"study and learn, as long as you live."

We arrived in this huge country empty-handed, obviously at a disadvantage compared to most young Americans. I had to figure out how to make use of the things that I could do best, in order to provide value and to make my contribution.

The key is to keep going, to keep trying, to keep pushing forward, and to look inside yourself for strength and courage. As we said to each other repeatedly in those days, "Whatever happens, never give up!" We never begged, we never borrowed, we never cheated—and we never went hungry or cold. In fact, we thrived in our new American life.

As another Chinese saying goes, *ku jin gan lai*—"After the bitter comes the sweet."

Chapter Fifty

Becoming American

I STILL HAD A lot to learn about the United States, especially life in a big city. One day I walked into a French bakery and stood in line to buy bread. This was one type of foreign food I had come to love. Sidney was browsing at the other end of the shop.

Suddenly I felt a tug. A tall, black man had his hand in my purse, which I had carelessly left unzipped. I grabbed his wrist.

"What are you doing?" I demanded. "Give it back!"

The man was shocked, as were all the Americans standing near me. He started to pull away, but I wouldn't release him. Sidney ran over to where I was standing, and said, in a low voice, "It's okay. Just let him go!" The French proprietor, white as a sheet, was standing behind the counter,

My wallet was still in my purse, so I let the man go. Then I thought of something else in my purse that might be missing. I said, "Wait a minute," and grabbed his arm again. At this point, his buddy, a tall man like him, came up and stood behind me. After checking my purse again, I finally let go.

The would-be thief and his buddy slunk out the door, muttering something about "racism." No one stopped them. No one called the police. The other customers just stared at me as if I had arrived from another planet.

"Is this your wife?" said the shop owner. "Please ask her not to come in here again. Those two come in about once a month, mug my customers, and then leave. I don't want any trouble!" As if I had been the cause of his trouble!

This confounded me. In China, if someone tried to steal money, those nearby would intervene. Someone would call the police, who would come quickly, blow their whistles and chase after the thief. In New York, everyone seemed afraid of the criminals. No one dared report them.

"Don't do that again," Sidney told me on the way home. "This society is different from China. He might have had a gun or a knife. New Yorkers know. If this happens, you don't argue. You just let him take the money."

I shook my head in disbelief. Americans loved to talk about freedom, but in some ways Chinese people had more freedom than they did.

Another time, Sidney was driving us into the city, through the Bronx. The streets were filthy, with empty boxes and bottles on the sidewalks. The driver in front of us opened his window and tossed a beer bottle onto the sidewalk, where it shattered. The people living on the streets seemed lost and abandoned, and the driver scorned them as drunks and thieves. When I was growing up, we were poor, but we worked hard and never stole or drank. Didn't the schools educate these people and teach them to be honest? Though China was a much poorer country, there at least, the government tried to care for people who were struggling, like old Auntie.

~

Other aspects of American life troubled us too, particularly the way older people were sometimes treated. We got a glimpse of this when Jenny started working as a night-shift attendant at a nursing home. It gave her a good environment for learning English, plus some spending money.

Typical of thoughtful Jenny, she took her first wages to a store and picked out a pretty dress to buy for me. This is a Chinese tradition: when you first begin to earn money, you buy a gift for your parents to thank them for all they did while raising you.

But the stories Jenny told us about her job made my blood curdle. Some of the elderly patients were not getting enough to eat and begged her for food. She would bring them biscuits from the kitchen cabinet, for which they were very grateful.

But the person in charge scolded Jenny. "Who told you to feed them? Even if they're hungry, you can't feed them. If they eat all that stuff, they're always having to use the bedpan. Are you going to take care of all that?"

Some of the patients were bedridden and obese, so helping them use the bedpan required a good bit of exertion.

"I can't bear to see them lying there hungry," Jenny told us. "And I can't stand the way some of the people in charge talk to them. How can they be so cruel to those elderly people, who are totally dependent on them?"

Jenny was sleeping poorly and having nightmares. So I told her, "Don't go there any more. You don't have to do that work. We'll manage without it."

Then Shirley's friend Norma Perlman invited Jenny to come stay with her family to work as their helpmate around the house. With this, Jenny struck gold! Norma's husband, Dr. Eli Perlman, was an outstanding Long Island physician, and Norma herself was a highly intelligent, kindhearted social activist. They loved our Jenny, and they announced that they were her godparents. They provided a tremendous amount of support for Jenny as she adjusted to her new country and learned to speak English.

Later, when Sunny arrived in the United States, she worked for that family, briefly, too. She came in 1983, after earning her degree in computer science from Beijing University, the best in China. Toni immigrated in 1982, after earning her medical degree. While we were living in Woodside, Toni studied English but soon found a job in the medical field at Massachusetts General Hospital, doing research on burn recovery. She worked there for four years.

After a year at school in Glen Cove with the Penn family, Sid Junior came back to live with us in Woodside. He entered high school in Long Island City—a school with lots of tough gang activity. I was glad to have him home but worried about him in that school.

He wanted to find a job to help with the family expenses. Shirley's boyfriend, Richie, had an interest in several McDonald's restaurants in Manhattan. Sid wanted to work in the Canal Street location in Chinatown, so Richie referred him to George, the manager there. Sid went for an interview, but several weeks went by and he didn't hear back.

Finally, Richie called George to ask what the problem was. George said, "That Rittenberg kid never showed up."

Richie said, "Check your interview list. His name is Sidney Rittenberg, Junior."

"What!" said George. "That Chinese kid was Sidney Rittenberg, Junior?"

In China, everyone thought our son looked American; in New York, everyone said he looked Chinese.

The next day, Sidney Junior started work on the evening shift at Canal Street. With his first week's pay, he bought me a handsome T-shirt. One Sunday evening, Sidney and I sneaked down to Canal Street to see how he was doing. What we saw shocked us: the other "cooks" were carrying two or three trays of hamburgers, sliding them in and out of the ovens. But our son was lifting more than a dozen trays!

When our son came home that night, Sidney gave him a lecture about not letting the boss exploit him. Why should he accept such a heavy load? As for me, I said, "You're still too young, you're still growing. You shouldn't overexert yourself."

Just like that little boy who had insisted on pushing the wheelbarrow in labor camp, he said, "I need hard work!"

Sid Junior was a sweet-tempered child, not at all combative—but very determined. Back in Beijing, he had begun to train himself in martial arts, learning from a coach at the Chinese Sports Institute.

After coming to America, he trained harder than ever. He studied karate and became so skilled that he was offered a scholarship. But his real love was Chinese martial arts, especially the variety associated with the famous Shaolin Monastery, which he later visited. He trained in many different varieties—including the comical "Drunken Boxer"—and excelled in them all.

In our Woodside flat, we watched him use his bare hand to split a stack of four red bricks in two. Every day, he toughened his fists on bags of green beans, sometimes pounding on them till his hands bled. We saw him train his fingers with sets of steel rings attached to tight springs. At first, he placed the rings around the middle knuckles of his ten fingers, and he could only very slowly close his fist with the rings attached to his fingers. Gradually, he was able to pull the rings together as rapidly as he could move his fingers. Then, he moved the rings to the end knuckles of his ten fingers and began to train all over again, until he could effortlessly pull the rings together.

We both really admired the stubborn determination with which our son was training himself, but we were also curious about his motivation.

"Why are you working so hard to train yourself at martial arts?" I asked him one day.

"I want to be able to take up for people who are being bullied," he said.

Later we found out that this was true. One day, Sid came home over an hour late from school. He wouldn't tell us why, but one of his schoolmates, a Chinese pastor's son, did. At school, there was a gang of Latino kids, some of whom were picking on smaller Chinese kids. Sid Junior warned them repeatedly to lay off, but they paid no attention. Finally, he waited outside for the leader of the Latino gang and gave him a good beating.

He told the defeated gang leader, "I beat you up because you guys pick on the Chinese kids. After this, let's all live in peace. No more fighting, okay?"

After that, there was no more trouble for the Chinese kids.

The other event concerned a big, tough African American kid who was always late to class, and who was a constant threat to the teacher.

One day, the teacher locked the classroom doors, so that this student couldn't come in late. But he came and pounded on the back door, demanding to be let in. Sid Junior was sitting closest to the door, and finally the teacher told him to open it. Sid didn't open it, but pointed through the glass door for him to go around to the front door. When the teacher opened the door, the boy stalked up to Sid and said, "Yo, didn't you hear me knocking?"

"Yes, I heard you," said Sid. "But the teacher didn't want you coming late. It's against the rules."

The big bully glared at Sid for a minute, and then said, "You Chinese?"

"Yes," said Sid. "I'm Chinese."

The big lad broke out in a grin. "Far out!" he said. "Far out!"

The little boy who had been punched in the eye in labor camp and taunted in elementary school had grown up into a young man who could stand up to bullies.

≈

When we first came to the United States, I admitted on my visa application that I had been a member of the Communist Party of China. Because of my honesty at that moment, according to the McCarren Act, I was excluded from ever getting U.S. citizenship or even a green card allowing permanent residence.

But Sidney thought it was important for me to become a U.S. citizen. Although I was proud of my identity as a citizen of China, sometimes it made things hard for me. I never spoke out and criticized Chinese policies, but Sidney sometimes did. Once, when I was in Beijing, some midlevel Chinese bureaucrats refused to let me go back to the United States. Sidney was furious. "Tell them this," he said. "If you're not back here next week, I'll make sure they read their names on the front page of the *New York Times*." Of course, he didn't have that kind of power over reporters, but the Chinese cadres didn't know that. They quickly issued me an exit visa.

Each time I traveled to China, I had to go through Hong Kong. Sometimes, the British authorities there forced me to go through extra questioning. I would often wait for hours in a stuffy, smelly room, crowded with other frustrated Chinese travelers.

Although I didn't like the street crime in America, I did appreciate the freedom. In China in the 1980s, people were increasingly given opportunities to reunite with their families and find better ways to make a living. But they still needed to get permission from the government for almost everything they did. If they were assigned to work in a coal mine, even if it was unrelated to what they had studied, they had to go. If someone overheard them complaining about those in charge, they could get in big trouble. In America, people could say whatever they liked and do whatever they liked, without getting permission every step of the way. After years of oppression, I felt it was my turn. America gave me a chance to make something of my life.

So Sidney took me to meet with a highly regarded immigration lawyer in New York, and he told me there was an exception. I could get a green card on one condition: All I had to do was denounce the Communist Party three times in public places.

But I refused to do that. It's true that I suffered because of bad policies of the Chinese Communist Party. However when I joined the Party and became a youth league member, the situation had been different. In the 1940s and 1950s, the Party had radically improved many lives and their policies had benefited the whole country. For the first time in one hundred years, China became a unified country, with no internal fighting, with a strong central government. The Communist Party treated the urban poor, the peasants, and the workers with dignity and fairness and provided opportunities to go to school and contribute to the country. These are facts. You cannot deny them. In my whole life, I have always abhorred lying. If I lied, I could not live with myself. So I refused to say I opposed the Communist Party of China.

The older I get, the more I understand that if you fall for black-or-white, good-or-bad thinking, you are no better than those people who called me a dog-spy's wife. In the depths of the labor camp, I had learned to think for myself. I had stopped blindly accepting the Party's official judgments. I could see who was acting like a good person and who was not. Now, I could see that some Chinese policies were good and some were bad. Even Chairman Mao, who made some horrible mistakes, also unified and strengthened China. Much as I love America, I can see that not all U.S. policies are good, either. As free citizens, we can use our minds and make judgments for ourselves.

Despite my refusal to denounce the Communist Party, I finally did get U.S. citizenship. One of Sidney's friends knew Patrick Moynihan, then a New York senator, and was a major contributor to his campaign funds. That friend convinced Senator Moynihan to write a letter to the director of the Immigration and Naturalization Service that said, "Yulin Rittenberg is a genuine champion of human freedom."

To get my green card, I had to be fingerprinted by the police. The desk sergeant at the Queens precinct told us that we needed to get a postal money order for twenty-six dollars—no checks or cash accepted, so we went to the post office, got the money order, and then went to the police station.

The desk sergeant was a big Irish cop, who very carefully took me through the process of inking and printing my fingers. As he did, he asked me, "So, what do you think about America, now that you're here?"

"I like lots of things—the convenient shopping, the freeways, the freedom to say what you think," I said. "But there are some things I don't like."

"What don't you like?" he asked.

"Well, there are crooks running around on the streets of New York, mugging old people, committing all sorts of crimes, and yet often nothing happens to them. They're arrested, they go to court, and often they get off with light sentences and go right back to committing crimes. In China, if they're incorrigible, we shoot them!"

The sergeant didn't say anything. But when I finished the fingerprinting, and Sidney handed the money order to the sergeant, he handed it back, and he told Sidney, "Take this nice lady and buy her a good dinner somewhere."

The next week I got my green card.

By then, I had come to love many things about America. Being able to speak my mind was a big one. At first I was careful not to criticize anything about the United States in front of Americans, but by watching Sidney and other American friends, I learned that it was okay to speak out if I disagreed with U.S. government policies. It was even acceptable to criticize President Reagan, and no one would label me a traitor.

Many Americans misunderstood China, but most of the Americans I met were open-minded and willing to listen when I tried to explain.

Most important, the United States is a nation of immigrants and their descendants. So it was possible for me to become a U.S. citizen, loyal to America, and still love my country of origin. No one expected me to stop caring about what happened in my homeland. I could become American without losing my identity as Chinese or turning my back on China.

In some ways, this transition was easier for me, born and raised as Chinese in China, than for my children. In China, they had been called "Americans"—a label often meant as an insult—in the days when they couldn't speak English and had known nothing about the United States. On some level, they had longed to go to America, hoping they would feel at home there. But in America, when they spoke English with a strong accent, they were viewed as outsiders, too. I told them they belonged in both countries, but sometimes they felt at home in neither one.

Meanwhile, Sidney and I worked at Special Tours for Special People till the end of 1982. We resigned in protest when the head man sent out a letter to the Chinese embassy with which we completely disagreed—and he sent it in Sidney's name, without even telling us.

Just at that time, George Vandor, a Hungarian travel agent who had attended some of Sidney's lecture classes, proposed that we set up our own tour service, working with him. George was a perfect gentleman, European in style; he would stay up all night listening to Italian and French soccer games.

The day we set up our own tour company, we became entrepreneurs—the ultimate American dream. Since we had experience leading tours, it didn't seem too risky. We set up our own company, called Pathways to China, and we signed a contract with Inter-Pacific Travel, which managed the tours for us. Over the next six or seven months, we led ten tours to China. The deal was that Inter-Pacific paid us $150 for every tourist that we referred to them, $300 for each member of an organized tour group that we sent them, $450 for each tour member if we personally conducted the tour.

This work provided us a good income—but it was tiring. Working separately, we each led our own tours, lecturing the tourists on China as we went along. But the work required more than just a thorough knowledge of China. We also had to care for the travelers. When the tourists rested, they would come to us with a million questions, so that we got no rest. Finally, Sidney came down with a nasty case of pneumonia in Shanghai and had to be shipped to a Hong Kong hospital because the local antibiotics, in those days, were not working.

As for me, I had a harrowing experience on a tour ship down the Yangtze River. A young American woman who had been studying the Hindu religion in India suddenly came down with a raging fever.

"Yulin! Yulin! Do something!" they cried out.

But what could I do? I could feel from her forehead that she was burning with fever, but on the ship there wasn't even a thermometer, let alone medicine.

I could only do what I had done for my children when they had a fever. "Get me some rubbing alcohol," I said to the captain.

"We don't have any," he answered.

"Well, you must have something," I said. "Don't you have any spirits?"

"We have *baijiu*," he said, a strong, clear liquor, distilled from sorghum or corn.

Using that, I gave her an alcohol rubdown, which broke the fever, but I learned later that she had malaria. Both Sidney and I, worn out after our harrowing experiences, decided to quit the tour business.

Chapter Fifty-One

Computers for China

WE WERE WILLING to do whatever it took to support our family in the United States, as long as it was legal and ethical. But I still resisted Sidney's idea of giving advice to American businesses. I thought, *These big American corporations can hire their own experts on China; what do they need with us? And what do a couple of aging Communists know about business?* Yet corporate executives started to approach us for advice.

Sidney saw this as a great opportunity, and he wanted me to help him. But I wanted to stick to my knitting; at least I knew how to knit and cook and speak Chinese. The business world made no sense to me. From my youth, I had learned that it was populated by greedy landlords and evil capitalists, who were out to cheat workers out of their earnings from honest labor. In America, a man who exploited women willing to pose naked could earn enough to buy his own zoo. I wanted nothing to do with it.

We had a rocky start. An international executive at United Technologies invited Sidney to advise him on their business approach to China. Sidney convinced me to go with him because he pointed out that Americans needed to understand China better. So we went. They were happy to pay for our airfare to their headquarters in Connecticut, but they said nothing about consulting fees. They didn't bring it up, and neither did we.

Sidney's brother-in-law, Art Weinberger, who after a career in the Marine Corps became CFO for Piedmont Shirts, yelled at Sidney. "How can you be so stupid! They'll make hundreds of millions with your help, and you're not getting a penny?"

It's true: we were totally naïve when it came to business. We couldn't get it through our heads that we should demand money for simply giving advice. We didn't have that habit—yet.

In the middle of 1983, just as we were beginning to think we could support ourselves in America, we were invited to ComputerLand to meet with the chair and owner, William H. Millard, who wanted our help to negotiate a deal with a visiting Chinese electronics delegation. This time, I refused to go. What did I know about electronics? But Sidney went, and this trip changed our lives. He returned with a "lifetime contract" as senior consultant to the world's largest retailer of personal computers.

Millard told Sidney he wanted to hire me, too. But I wasn't interested. I had recently accepted an attractive offer for another job in New York, as U.S. general manager of a Hong Kong-Chinese travel company. That was a business I understood. But Sidney insisted I should at least meet Millard, so I agreed to fly to California and accompany him to a dinner at the Millards' luxury mansion in Oakland.

Millard was intense and enthusiastic, an evangelist for personal computers. He had fallen in love with PCs when they were simply hobby kits, in the mid-1970s. ComputerLand was one of the first retailers authorized to sell the early Apple computers and the IBM PCs when they first came out in 1981. By 1982, he had opened hundreds of ComputerLand stores, with sales over $400 million. Later, by 1985, his family-run company would expand to eight hundred locations, including two hundred overseas, with sales close to $2 billion. Prices had come down and technology had advanced so that, for the first time, ordinary Americans could afford to buy computers for their homes. This was a hot new industry.

Over a lavish dinner that night, Millard turned his charm on me. He was passionate about the potential for sales of personal computers in China. He tried to persuade me to join the company, too, with the title of chief corporate representative in China. I smiled and refused, telling him about my other offer. He grew more animated, painting the China market in brilliant colors.

"No, no, no. I can't," I insisted. "I have already promised to take this other job. It's a big job, and I'm very interested in the travel business."

He said he needed my expertise.

I laughed—me, an expert at computers! I refused again, more firmly. Finally, Millard put down his napkin and looked straight at me.

"Yulin! Imagine bringing the power of the personal computer to China. Don't you want to do something that can bring great benefits to the Chinese people?"

According to Sidney, after that I just "melted like an ice cream cone." It was the one argument that touched my heart, so I accepted his offer.

Millard gave us a house in the hills above San Leandro, at very low rent. Our whole family left the cockroaches in New York and moved to California. Jenny and Sunny both began to work at ComputerLand corporate headquarters. Sid Junior eventually entered San Francisco State University. Only Toni did not join us; she found an attractive job, using her medical degree, as a research physician at Massachusetts General Hospital.

The whole family finally settled down and each of us was on our own track. Suddenly, we did not have to worry about where next week's food was coming from. In fact, our financial worries were over from that day onward.

The Millard home in San Leandro was our family's first freestanding house. When we opened the door and walked in, I was stunned by the size of the living room and the roomy interior. The kids raced up and down the stairs, exclaiming over the sauna and the steam bath. They were especially happy that they each had their own room. Sid Junior had a big enough room for his barbells and punching bag.

We had truly arrived in America!

≈

My first duty, after a "China Strategy" conference at corporate headquarters, was to go back to Beijing and open a China office for ComputerLand. There, I found out I had to register with the commercial authorities and get a permit. This normally took years. I checked around and found out that the son of Sidney's old friend General Wang Zhen now handled external relations for the Ministry of Electronics. With his help, I had my permit in a little over a month.

The manager of the Nationalities Hotel offered me a good discount for opening our office there. We signed a one-year renewable lease for enough space for the sales people and for Sidney and myself. In those days, China had no commercial office buildings or apartment complexes available for foreigners, so most foreign business people in Beijing had to live and work in hotel rooms. In today's modern Beijing, that's hard to imagine.

After that, it was an uphill battle. China did not allow foreign companies to open retail stores, and few Chinese people even knew what a personal computer was. I decided that first we needed to hold a "technology exchange fair," at which "foreign experts" from companies could introduce their new systems. So I approached the State Administration of Industry and Commerce officials with my idea. I explained that the exchange fair would be a great way to introduce

state-of-the-art computer technology to China, and that all computers ComputerLand marketed would be supported by service and maintenance centers.
Impressed, they granted approval.

Within a few months, I organized two major computer shows in Beijing. The
main products were personal computers from IBM and Compaq. The stellar attraction was the first Compaq computer: they called it "portable," but actually,
at twenty-eight pounds, it was only "luggable." Still, most people then thought
of computers as huge, room-sized machines with white-coated operators. So a
computer on a desktop was a novel attraction.

Every day of the show, the Compaq technician would raise the hardy computer waist-high and then smash it down on the hard floor. Then he would pick
it up and demonstrate that it still worked perfectly. In fact, one of those much-
dropped computers later became our office computer.

This was China's first large-scale, public introduction to American computer
technology, and the impact was powerful. Mail and phone calls poured in, asking for specifications, prices, and delivery times. Our ComputerLand office got
very busy.

But few Chinese knew how to operate a computer. We needed to figure out a
way to educate people, not just in Beijing but all over China, so I made a proposal
to Millard. I knew that the company had lots of defunct Osborne computers in
its warehouses that could not be sold. I suggested the company donate them to
China and set up computer training schools there. Using financial logic, I explained that ComputerLand would save on warehouse storage costs and also gain
a huge amount of goodwill and positive publicity—far more than if it launched
an expensive advertising campaign.

Millard liked the idea. He shipped more than 360 Osborne computers and
360 printers to China for my ComputerLand training schools. I directed my efforts mainly toward middle and high school students who needed to learn new
technology in order to find good jobs. We set up three computer training schools,
the most successful of which was at the Beijing Ninety-Sixth High School. Millard and the vice-mayor of Beijing cut the ribbon at the opening ceremony.
Drums and cymbals attracted neighbors from all around, the television station
filmed the event, and word of mouth began spreading the news: ComputerLand
was a good company; it donated computers to China.

This school later became the site for China's national student competition
in computer science. The second of the new computer training schools was in

Shanghai, sponsored by the Shanghai Science & Technology Association. The third was sponsored by the China Association for the Handicapped, chaired by Chinese leader Deng Xiaoping's son, Deng Pufang. So China received her first training in personal computers, a gift from William Millard's ComputerLand, and it had a lasting effect.

China was happy to accept free computers. But we still had a big nut to crack: how to get the Chinese to buy computers? In those days, China was a poor country, and the government kept a tight fist on all foreign exchange. At that time, the Ministry of Electronics owned and operated every electronics, computer, and semiconductor plant in China. We decided to ask for the right for ComputerLand to set up "sales and service centers," jointly owned with the electronics ministry. A man in a hurry, William Millard wanted to open these centers all over China.

In the fall of 1983, Millard eagerly made his first trip to Beijing. I managed to get permission for Millard to fly in on his own corporate jet, which was very rare at the time. To do this, I had to go through the Electronics Ministry, the Foreign Ministry, and the general staff of the People's Liberation Army, which controlled China's air space.

Because our chief executive officer had arrived, we were able to set up a meeting with the Minister of Electronics, Jiang Zemin, who later became China's top leader. I arranged for a banquet at the Presidential Dining Room at the State Guest House at Diaoyutai, where China's highest leaders entertained foreign dignitaries. I had learned that Jiang Zemin was fond of bear's paw, so I asked the staff to prepare that delicacy. The little saucers for appetizers at that banquet were antiques from the state collection of imperial tableware, borrowed from the Forbidden City Museum This was a heady experience for someone who grew up hungry. It also gave me direct insight into how China's Communist leaders lived; although the gap in living standards between the leaders and the led was nothing compared to today.

We found Jiang Zemin to be an affable, outgoing man. He was bold enough and spoke good enough English, with a little help from Sidney, to chat cordially with Millard when no other Chinese was present—a violation of China's foreign affairs protocol. There was much joking and laughter in their conversation. But one of his aides, who had become a friend of Sidney's, cautioned us that Jiang was more of a talker than a doer and that we should not take everything he said too seriously.

After three days of negotiations, we signed a contract implementing the letter of intent that Sidney had helped negotiate earlier in San Francisco. Computer-Land and the ministry's computer service company agreed to set up centers all over China, starting in Beijing. Although China called them "sales and service centers," we envisioned them as morphing into retail stores, not unlike the hundreds of stores across America.

We held a final great banquet to celebrate this giant step forward for China's computer technology. U.S. Ambassador Arthur Hummel, Jr. attended and spoke, welcoming this pioneering joint venture between the two countries. Over bear's paw on that Saturday evening, the future looked very bright for ComputerLand China. With one billion people, the China market was ours. Sidney and I toasted each other.

But the contract fell apart. During the negotiations, the president of the ministry's computer company, Mr. Ouyang Zhineng, repeatedly tried to raise various points of objection to the terms, but his minister repeatedly silenced or overruled him. Mr. Ouyang was a manager four levels below the minister in rank, so I figured he would get with the program and follow orders. The ministry signed the contract despite his objections, and he attended the banquet with a stony stare.

Bright and early on Monday morning, Mr. Ouyang appeared in our hotel room doorway. "It's all very well for those great people to sign these fine agreements," he said, "but I'm the one who has to carry them out, and I am telling you that it will never happen."

And it didn't. This was a great lesson for us, new to the business world as we were: China was a country that suffered from both too little and too much freedom. If Mr. Ouyang had been a GE or IBM manager and had defied the decision of his CEO, he would have been looking for a new job immediately. But this was China, and—in those days—it was very difficult to fire an ordinary laborer who was not doing his job, let alone a company president. We realized that Mr. Ouyang's voice should have been heeded during the negotiations. At the time, we thought it was good that he wasn't listened too, but it turned out to be disastrous.

The result was that only one "sales and service center" was actually set up, and that was under the Municipal Commerce Bureau in Guangzhou. Glad to open at least one location, I went to inspect the new store. We provided them with a complete computer service tool kit, with ComputerLand uniforms, and with the specifications for a modern computer retail store. We brought in engineers to train their personnel. When their center conformed to ComputerLand standards, I approved of their putting up our signboard. We were up and running in China!

Surely Mr. Ouyang would see this success and relent.

As a way of thanking them, I proposed that Millard invite representatives from the Electronics Ministry, the Ministry of Commerce, and the Guangzhou Commerce Bureau to go to the United States for "familiarization and training." Chinese officials jumped at the opportunity to travel abroad for free. Mr. Ouyang did not go.

≈

Just a few years after leaving China, I had completed the transition: I was now an American businesswoman. As chief corporate representative for this big American company, I was in charge of ComputerLand China. That meant managing people.

At our office in Beijing, I hired a number of Chinese staff through the government hiring agency. Some of them believed in what they were doing and worked really hard. But others brought old habits with them: they read the paper, sipped tea, chatted and gossiped—and they were entitled to the same pay whether they worked hard or not. I was beginning to understand the shortcomings of a centrally planned economy with guaranteed lifetime jobs. Making a living was tougher in America, but we got things done.

In addition, I had to manage a staff of Americans—and many were much better educated and more highly trained than I was, some with extensive experience in business. They included a Santa Rosa college professor and a number of engineers. At first, I felt intimidated. Who was I, Wang Yulin, to be managing these people? But I gave myself a good talking-to and laid down some rules for myself. First, I would respect all my colleagues, Chinese and American. Second, I would talk things over with them and draw them actively into the work. Finally, I needed to make full use of my advantages: knowledge of China, experience in personnel work, and familiarity with the channels of access to different Chinese departments. I reminded myself that I knew how to talk to prospective Chinese buyers better than my American colleagues did. I had to learn on my feet how to run a business, how to deal with instructions from headquarters, and how to approach all sorts of Chinese bureaucrats and technicians.

With IBM getting nowhere in China, and with us being unable to set up retail stores, I realized we needed to blaze a new trail for computer marketing in this country. The answer seemed obvious: we needed to go out and contact potential users directly and carefully demonstrate why they needed computers and how they could service them. But how to do this? It was a conundrum, and it kept me awake at night.

In December 1983, Sidney flew back to our California home. My plan was to follow him in a week, to enjoy the two-week Christmas break with our son, who was in college. In recent months, we had both been too busy to spend time with him. But, on a sudden impulse, I called Sidney in San Leandro, and said, "China needs PCs, and yet we aren't making any sales. I'm sick and tired of it. Suppose, instead of coming home, I used these two weeks to travel around and see whether I can sell some computers? Would you agree to that?"

What could he say? Of course he agreed. It meant that he and Sid Junior had to spend Christmas vacation alone, but that turned out to be a good thing. Our son had no early memories of his father, and they needed time alone to establish a good relationship. So I took a cold, unheated train to Chengdu, capital of Sichuan Province—thousands of miles from Beijing.

A few months earlier, I had visited Chengdu without making a single sale. At the city electronics bureau, I had demonstrated the new Compaq "luggable," and I had held a marketing show. Everyone I talked with had been interested, but when it came to actually placing orders, the conversation had died down. Buying PCs required foreign currency, which had to be approved by the central government. What's more, they typically had no budget for such purchases.

This time in Chengdu, I didn't have the assistance of the young Chinese American manager who went with me the first time. I had to lug the twenty-eight-pound Compaq and my own baggage everywhere I went. In Chengdu, I asked the electronics people to put me in touch with the local office of the People's Liberation Army, China's military. I knew that the rugged features of the Compaq would interest them. I did my "throw the computer on the floor" demonstration, which impressed them very much, as I had expected. They proposed setting up a joint venture factory with Compaq, but I advised them to first use the machines and see how they met their needs. They ordered a number of Compaq computers, on the spot.

Delighted, I returned to Beijing and set out for Guangzhou. Friends in the Ministry of Commerce had referred me to the Guangzhou City Commerce Bureau, which was interested in getting into the PC business. The director there, Mr. Nie, was eager to buy PCs but hard-bitten: he was addicted to driving very hard bargains. Besides, he couldn't make direct purchases of imported goods; he had to go through the China Foreign Trade Company, which was a trading window in New York for the Commerce Ministry.

We had to fly to New York to negotiate the sale. So early in 1984, Sidney and I met there with a commerce ministry delegation for negotiations on purchasing computers, including several thousand IBMs for Guangzhou. Several high-ranking Chinese trade officials, including the commercial counselor from the Chinese embassy in Washington, arrived for the talks. These big shots bulked out the Chinese team to more than ten people.

On our side of the table, it was just Sidney and myself.

At first, my doubts and fears bubbled up again. Here I was, just a few years out of China, with a newly minted U.S. passport, sitting opposite these "important personages" from China. I was an American citizen, and I represented an American company, but they expected me to take the Chinese side in the talks, implying that otherwise I would be a sellout. Nobody said so, but to me it was very clear.

I was determined not to let my company get the short end of the bargain. So I had to hold the line firmly, and at the same time be careful not to let them walk away so that we lost this huge order. Sidney was no help at all. Although he was terrific at making connections and nurturing relationships, he was hopeless at hard bargaining. During the talks, he barely spoke. Finally, after the second day, Sidney said, "Look, sweetie. They're using me as a soft spot in our team, trying to use me to weaken your position. I'm going to play sick and stay out of the talks, okay? You'll do better by yourself."

I agreed, although I was now just one person against the whole Chinese team. Fortunately, one of the Chinese negotiators was a very down-to-earth man who realized how important this large-lot purchase of computers would be for China. He could see that our prices were reasonable and also that there were definite advantages in dealing with people who understood China. He supported me in persuading the others.

Finally, after a week of tough negotiations, day and night, we signed the largest PC export contract in American history, up to that point. ComputerLand issued me a special memorial plaque to that effect, which is still on display in our home. *Forbes Magazine* wrote up our achievement in selling computers to China, but the reporter attributed our success to Sidney. As if it were beyond the powers of a Chinese woman! Sidney was especially incensed, because he had made it very clear to the reporter that I had done all the work.

I shook my head. For all the talk about feminism in America, it was clear that the business community looked down on women. China, which even then had many women engineers, seemed ahead of the United States in this. I remembered Chairman Mao's phrase I had learned as a schoolgirl: "Women hold up half the sky."

Maybe more than half. In every country, I believe, women have much harder lives than men. In addition to their work, most women take on the responsibility for the family and the home. Most men can forget about their personal lives and focus entirely on their work; they come home and want to have dinner and relax. But women who work can never stop thinking about their husband and children. If their kids are sick or in danger, mothers will give their life to protect them. That's natural. Perhaps this is because during the nine months of pregnancy, the child grows in the mother's body. Whenever something happens to her kids—even after they are grown—the mother worries. Sometimes, her mind overflows with troubling questions, and the burden feels too heavy to carry. I know this feeling. Although my body was traveling around China, my heart was in America, worrying about my four children and their futures.

~

Happy about the sale, Millard embarked on another trip to China to see more of the country and to learn more about the culture. As a CEO, he wanted to take his own corporate jet from Beijing to Shanghai. In those days, it was hard enough getting permission to land a private jet in Beijing, but it was impossible for it to fly from one Chinese airport to another.

I tried to negotiate with the Chinese government, but all I could get was a suggestion that we might—just might—get permission to take Mao Zedong's old special train out of mothballs and lease it for Millard's journey.

This news surprised me. I had heard of this amazing train, specially outfitted with a glass bubble dome in back that allowed him unobstructed views of the passing scenery. Of course, Chairman Mao would never take a public train. Since his death, no one had used it and certainly not a foreign capitalist! If Millard could travel in it, it would be a first.

Others warned me that it would not be easy. I would have to get permission from three different bureaucracies—the Foreign Ministry, the Railroad Ministry, and the general staff of the Chinese armed forces. ComputerLand would have to pay $10,000—plus the cost of having the train cleaned up and redecorated, including new carpeting and curtains. But the minute I mentioned it, Millard urged me to make it happen. He loved the idea of traveling around China in Mao's old train.

So I went all out and tried. In America, if you have money, you can do anything, but in China, you have to get layer after layer of permission. It took more than a month, a lot of persuasion, a lot of contacts. But, with the help of friends, I finally did it!

Sidney joined me and Millard, as we set out from Beijing in the old train with a magnificent glass bubble, easy chairs, full-sized beds, and a private bath, with a tub. There were also elegant compartments for us, for ComputerLand's senior vice president, and for Millard's secretary and security guard—as if that were necessary in China! We even had a private chef to cook for us. Millard had Sidney give a series of lectures all along the way, with me chiming in. We outlined China's history, politics, and culture, as well as issues concerning China's modernization and way of doing business. It felt otherworldly!

Within a year, I had made the transition, from sweater knitter to hard-bargaining businesswoman. Sidney kept reminding me that I had once been a little girl picking up coal embers from the railroad tracks. I surprised myself, some days. What did a Communist cadre, used to pushing papers in an office in Beijing, know about doing big deals? Yet in the 1980s, even experienced negotiators in America didn't know how to do business with China, and China's rules were changing frequently, in unexpected ways. We were all beginners. If you were daring enough to push yourself, it was a time of great opportunity.

Sometimes I think that the suffering in my life made me more adaptable. When I began to sell computers, I recalled my early love of technology. Maybe this work fulfilled my dream of becoming an engineer. Certainly I had never imagined a career in sales! But it helped that I had developed the habits of being persistent and determined, refusing to take no for an answer, and being resourceful about finding other ways when the first way didn't work. Also, for sales, you need to have a thick skin. During the Cultural Revolution, I had learned not to care what other people said about me; I knew who I was and what I stood for.

From my life experience, I learned that you can deal with anything life throws at you. If someone like me can make it through, anyone can. It takes courage. If there are difficulties that seem impossible, ask for help. Don't blame yourself. Don't think, "I am stupid. I cannot do it." Instead repeat this mantra: "I can do it. I can do it." There will always be naysayers; don't listen to them. Friends can help by listening, but nobody can do it for you. Trust yourself. Never give up.

The main reason I achieved some success in business was that I had learned, over the years, to overcome fear. When Sidney was thrown into prison and the children and I were confined to one room, I feared for our future—no one knew when we might get out. After weeping by the window in frustration, I decided to take control of what I could, their education. When forced to carry heavy loads and faced with unfair attacks by my colleagues, I had learned to harden myself. I decided that fear doesn't help solve any problems; it makes things worse. Yes, they beat me and overworked me and harassed me at labor camp. But, in the end, what was the worst they could do? Kill me, that's all. By the time my troubles ended, I was not afraid of anything—except spiders!

Chapter Fifty-Two

_____

Consulting

IN 1985, OUR friends both in the United States and in China urged us to set up our own consulting service, not limited to computers. China was rapidly changing its laws, encouraging foreign trade and allowing more foreign investment. Many U.S. companies viewed China as the last great untapped market, yet they had no idea how to deal with the Chinese cadres who made purchasing decisions. Our friends predicted that Sidney and I would be able to bridge the formidable cultural gaps between Chinese and American companies, and that the growing economic ties between the two countries created a great need for this sort of "matchmaking."

But the very idea of going independent intimidated me. After years of uncertainty, Sidney and I finally had a safety net and monthly corporate paychecks. Sidney held the title of corporate vice chairman for China, and I was chief corporate representative in China. Two of our daughters, Jenny and Sunny, were also working for the company. We no longer had to worry about how we would pay for our next meal. We had a "Mama" to depend on. How could we give that up?

In 1985, ComputerLand was going strong, with eight hundred stores and nearly $2 billion in worldwide sales. It was widely admired as the most successful retailer of the hottest new consumer product, the personal computer. But we could see clouds on the horizon, legal squabbles we didn't quite understand. Capitalist corporations, Sidney explained, were not as stable and dependable as our government jobs had been. He argued that it was time to spread the risk.

Could we really make it as independents? We talked it over many times. Ever since we first came to America, Sidney had believed that business leaders sooner or later would beat a path to our door. They needed our contacts and experience. I felt that those Fortune 500 corporations had their own experts, and some of them were already doing business in China. We, on the other hand, had very limited firsthand business experience. Our success in selling computers did not necessarily qualify us for other business. But Sidney argued that many types of companies needed help entering China, and that we could meet that need. Was I willing to try it and see?

I struggled with this decision. Then, one night I sat bolt upright in bed and looked at Sidney, lying next to me. I had made it through ten long years without even knowing if Sidney was alive. Just having him beside me, restored to health and eager to move ahead, gave me strength. So much had gone wrong for Sidney in China; from now on, I needed to do whatever I could to make things go right.

I took Sidney by the hand, and his eyes fluttered open.

"Nothing to worry about," I said. "As long as we stick together, we can make it work. That's it."

First, we notified Millard that we were leaving his employ to set up our own consulting company, but that we hoped to retain ComputerLand as our first client. Millard was upset. He reminded us that he had made an exception for us: we were the only ComputerLand staffers who actually had a written labor contract and a guarantee of lifetime employment. But we explained our reasons. Finally mollified, he signed a consulting agreement with us.

"Jumping into the sea"—that's the way Chinese described the act of leaving a salaried job to set up your own business. As the 1980s went on, more and more Chinese dared to do this. Sidney and I did it by stages, getting our feet wet before wading into deeper water. We gained confidence and digested our experience as we went forward.

Our first step was to set up an independent consulting company in partnership with Ted Tulley, a trusted friend who had worked as ComputerLand's international vice president. After working well together for several months, we realized we didn't have the facilities or the capital to make a go of it. We couldn't stomach the sudden loss of income.

A close friend of ours, Joan Goldsmith, introduced us to her friend's firm, the prestigious Index consulting group in Cambridge, Massachusetts. The CEO of Index, Tom Gerrity, offered to let us create our own China consulting division, under the name of Index China. Tom was the chairman, Sidney was president, and I was vice president, with very good salaries and various perks. Joan became our partner. This required us to move our home from California to Massachusetts.

My first trip to China for our new company was for our first client—ComputerLand. Sidney was supervising our move from San Leandro to Cambridge.

I had just flown back to California from Beijing and had hardly entered the door when I got a call.

Mr. Nie, the hard-bitten client in Guangzhou, was refusing to pay for several thousand IBM PCs that he had purchased. Though they had already been delivered, he said that they had no foreign exchange with which to pay. Actually, Beijing had announced that they had no disposable foreign exchange and were therefore stopping all international payments.

This was a huge crisis for ComputerLand China, with the payment for several thousand personal computers at stake. I had to turn around the next day and fly right back to Beijing to deal with this issue. Meanwhile, Sidney spoke at a Hong Kong seminar on doing business with China. He said he was confident that our client would get paid, but a leading Chinese financial authority told him flatly that it was impossible.

I couldn't find my winter clothes among the packing cases in our old home, so my first stop in Beijing, direct from the plane, was to a store where I could buy a down overcoat with a hood.

In Beijing, I met with our friend, Jiang Xi, who was the executive vice minister of commerce, a man of sterling integrity. I explained to him that ComputerLand's China subsidiary was facing bankruptcy because of the failure to collect for its deliveries. ComputerLand, I explained, was playing a role in bringing state-of-the-art computers to China. We were also creating new computer training programs for China's youth, preparing unskilled, unemployed youth for good jobs in a key area.

Vice Minister Jiang said that he understood my position, and he knew that we had been doing good work. But he didn't have the authority to decide on the payment of foreign exchange. He had to report the problem to the central leadership and see whether they could solve it.

"I'll come back tomorrow," I said. I had learned the American way of efficiency and persistence.

"What? You can come back tomorrow if you like, but you have to give me several days to get an answer."

I came back the next day—and the next. The result was that after several days Vice Minister Jiang got permission for his ministry to supply the money, since Guangzhou couldn't do it. ComputerLand's people were thrilled. That was our first home run for Index China, at a time when getting paid on time was a major problem for American companies in China.

The next question for Sidney and me was this: Could we expand our business and attract new clients? Our first target was Polaroid, a company well-known and admired in China. When Western tourists first came to China in the 1970s and early 1980s, Polaroid pictures were a big hit with the Chinese people they met, because the photos printed out on the spot. For many Chinese, this was the first photo they ever saw of themselves.

But Polaroid had eluded signing on with any consultants. Executives in our head office bet against our ability to sign them up. Our friend Joan Goldsmith took up our cause, and I learned a lot from watching her super sales techniques in action. She convinced the client that Sidney and I were the answer to their prayers, former insiders who could cut through the red tape and get things done in China. That did it. We signed them up. Still, I could see that solving Polaroid's problems in China wouldn't be easy, and I wasn't sure we could really do what we had promised.

Polaroid already had a joint venture in Shanghai, making circuit boards, which was profitable, but Polaroid was not benefiting. Regulations at the time required all Chinese companies, including joint ventures, to hand over their foreign exchange earnings to the central government, in return for Chinese currency. Our first assignment was to help Polaroid gain access to their earnings in the form of U.S. dollars.

Sidney used his connections to meet with Shanghai's distinguished mayor, Wang Daohan, an old revolutionary with a democratic style of work. Mayor Wang introduced Sidney and me to one of his vice mayors, Liu Zhenyuan. I soon made friends with Liu's wife, Fei Ling, a foreign trade company executive.

I admired Fei Ling; she was the kind of open-minded person China needed to help bring in modern technology. In the world of business, dominated by men, Fei Ling showed me how Chinese women, too, could get things done. I used my powers of persuasion to explain to her that Polaroid was an excellent American company that could transfer important film and camera technology to China, if we could make the right kind of deal.

At dinner with Vice Mayor Liu and his wife, I explained that, if the joint venture could accumulate enough money in U.S. dollars, Polaroid would be willing to open a new manufacturing plant in Shanghai, making their unique film.

With this opportunity at hand, Vice Mayor Liu persuaded the head of the powerful State Economic Commission to approve, as a special case, Polaroid's retention of its foreign exchange earnings, and with that we leaped a major hurdle. What we were able to do for Polaroid in Shanghai taught me that even strict regulations in China didn't have to kill a deal—if you could reach the right people and make a persuasive argument that it was truly good for China.

～

Carefully cultivated relationships don't always solve problems, but sometimes they do make the difference between success and failure. We hoped they would help us in early 1987, when we were representing AIG, the worldwide insurance giant. By then we had joined forces with Ginny Kamsky's China consulting firm, as Kamsky & Rittenberg. Through her we met Maurice "Hank" Greenberg, the well-known CEO of AIG, and soon we were called in to help with a rescue operation on AIG's biggest investment in China.

AIG had invested tens of millions in the building of a huge $175 million dollar hotel and apartment complex designed by Atlanta developer John Portman. Called the Portman Shanghai Center, it boasted a luxury hotel, luxury apartments, offices, shops, restaurants, and a conference facility on Nanjing Road in the heart of Shanghai. The investment was in partnership with the city government's Shanghai Exposition Company.

The problem was that the American partners had accepted lease terms that were much too short. There was no hope of recovering their investment in that period. Yet the Chinese government, from bottom to top, was refusing to lengthen the lease.

In 1987 the newspapers announced that Shanghai would soon have a new mayor: Zhu Rongji. He had been working in Beijing as a vice minister of the State Economic Council, which oversaw all of China's economic development. The day before Zhu Rongji left Beijing to become mayor of Shanghai, I invited him to have dinner with Sidney and me at the Windows on the World restaurant in Beijing's tallest building and explained the investors' plight.

"Foreign investors need to have a return on their investment," I explained. "If the investors lose everything because of bureaucratic treatment, who's going to invest in Shanghai again?"

Zhu Rongji assured us that he would take care of this problem as soon as he got to Shanghai—and he was as good as his word. He granted them a long extension on their lease.

Sidney mentioned that he thought Shanghai was building too many five-star tourist hotels, but Zhu Rongji retorted, "You give me the hotels, and I'll guarantee to fill them!" On this point, too, he was as good as his word.

It was also at this dinner that we suggested Zhu Rongji set up an advisory council of foreign business people, from whom he could draw suggestions and to whom he could explain and consult on investment and trade policies. Before long, Shanghai did set up such a council, with Greenberg as its first chairman, and later other Chinese cities emulated this model.

~

Another big corporate client, Intel, wanted to invest $12 million to set up a software company in Shanghai. At that time, the city of Shanghai required six different levels of approvals. You could not apply for the next level until the previous one was approved. Nobody could predict how many years it would take, but it seemed endless. Intel had already been waiting six months for the second of six approvals.

We invited Chen Zhili, who was Shanghai's deputy Party secretary for high tech, to dinner. I told her, "Look, Intel is prepared to hire a lot of engineers and pay a lot of taxes, and they're being held up." So she called over a young secretary, and said, "Go to the phone and call so-and-so, and tell them I want the certification on my desk by eight tomorrow morning." So finally the deal got the go-ahead, and Intel opened its first software company in China.

We acquired Intel as a client in the same manner that we got all of our clients—through friends and former clients. We never had a website or a brochure, and never made a cold call.

Our first meeting with Intel was in Hong Kong. We flew out to meet with a powerful team of Intel executives, who told us right off that Intel's genius CEO Andy Grove (a Jewish refugee from Hungary) made it a rule never to share technology with "any Communist country."

Sidney and I explained in detail that China was not "any Communist country"—China was China, and the name of the game was to exchange market share for technology. If they simply treated China as a marketplace and refused to share technology, their China business would be limited and short-lived. The whole trick was to build the American corporation into the process of China's modernization, as other great companies like Hewlett-Packard were doing.

"Big Dave" Shrigley, in charge of the China project for Intel International, accepted our argument, and the discussion turned to how to make the most effective entry. Taking part in the discussion was P.Y. Lai, the very talented head of Intel Malaysia, who ran the best Intel chip fabrication plant in the world. P.Y. Lai was placed in charge of Intel China—as its chair.

This was a man who combined a keen sense of the market with a fantastic ability to make friends everywhere. He also understood that any company that is to be a lasting success must pay attention to the welfare and good spirits of its workers.

P.Y. was not even close to being a Communist sympathizer, but he was an ardent Chinese patriot. In accepting his new post as chair of Intel China, he said, "This corporation has always been very good to me, over the more than twenty years that I have worked for Intel. But I want everyone to know—if I am to work in China, I will protect the interests of my company, but I will also do everything I possibly can to help the Chinese people."

P.Y. was as good as his word. In China, he established good relations with schools and other institutions, and did a great deal to help his fellow Chinese. Instead of being split in his loyalties, he found a way to unite his loyalties. I found that inspiring.

In our experience, many, if not most, of the U.S.-China deals that could have succeeded but didn't failed simply because of a failure to communicate. Confused by the marked cultural differences, the two sides couldn't understand each other. This went beyond the translation of words. It was the ability to break the barrier and find out underneath what's really bothering the people on the opposite side of the table.

A clear example was a Chicago company named UCC, which manufactured conveyer belt systems to remove ash from the big boilers that energize power plants. Before we talked with them, we had no knowledge of the fact that coal-fired power plants cannot operate without adequate ash handling.

The busy port city of Ningbo, south of Shanghai, was building a huge power plant, and UCC was bidding to install their ash-handling system. Sidney and I flew to Shanghai to assist the Chicago company in negotiations with the Chinese buyers and their engineers.

When the talks began, each side spoke without really saying anything. The Chinese described their project, Ningbo's Beilungang Power Plant, without revealing exactly what equipment they were interested in. Moreover, they emphasized that they needed to see detailed data on UCC's equipment before they could commit.

UCC read a list of the equipment they could supply, with no details, and gave the price range for their products. But the Chinese continued to demand detailed data, and UCC continued to ask for the detailed specifications of the Ningbo boilers. The whole morning was, as the Chinese say, like "scratching an itching foot through your boot."

Finally, one day before lunch, Sidney and I put our heads together and decided that I would eat with the Chinese while Sidney ate with the Americans, and we would try to find out why they were talking past each other.

What we found out during that short lunch hour amazed us: The UCC people revealed that they were refusing to give the Chinese data on their equipment because they suspected that their hosts' real intention was to get enough details to make the equipment themselves, not to purchase it. As for the Chinese, they told me that they felt UCC's price quotes were suspiciously low, and they were certain that if they signed agreements to purchase it, the equipment would turn out to be inferior and incomplete; also, there would be many hidden costs that would cause losses for the buyers. Sidney and I exchanged notes after the lunch, and then we went back to work.

I explained to the Chinese side that the low prices were owing to the new favorable exchange rate between the Chinese yuan and U.S. dollar. Sidney told the UCC people that the equipment couldn't possibly be manufactured in Shanghai at that time, and that buying ash-handling equipment from abroad was an absolute necessity for the Chinese. If UCC didn't make the sale, a competitor would.

Both sides had new mindsets when they returned to the table that afternoon. First, the leader of the Chinese delegation apologized for stalling, and he presented a full list of the items they needed to purchase. Then UCC gave them all the data they needed on the equipment they were offering. The next day, a purchase-and-sale contract was signed, and the deal was done.

≈

In the 1990s, we formed a consulting relationship and a warm friendship with Craig McCaw, father of cellular phone service in America. We learned a great deal working from this gentle, self-made billionaire, who believes in showing respect for everyone he deals with, and in making broadband service available for the peace and progress of people all over the world. Working with his team of professionals, we were able to negotiate the first digital cell phone network in Shanghai. Later, we represented him in negotiating a uniquely favorable settlement when the Chinese government, to strengthen their bargaining position in the World Trade Organization entry negotiations, shut down China's forty-two foreign joint ventures in cell phone services.

≈

As it turned out, Sidney and I made a good consulting team. Sidney was skilled at attracting and guiding our American clients; I was like a fish in water when we went back to China. I could gain the trust of our Chinese customers and partners because I understood their psyche—the value they put on price, reliability, national identity, and the possibility of an all-expenses-paid business trip to America. They recognized me as an honest, hardworking "Chinese American cousin" who could drive a hard bargain in the interests of my clients, but at the same time was sincerely devoted to helping the modernization of my native China.

I was an American, representing an American company, but, like P.Y. Lai, I would never do anything to betray my motherland. As an American citizen born and raised in China, I was loyal to both my native country and my adopted country. When you marry a foreigner, you have to drop that "win/lose" mentality. As long as the two nations are not at war, I don't have to choose "either/or." I can choose "both/and."

≈

By 1988, Sidney and I had enough clients that we could go completely independent. We set up shop as Rittenberg Associates Inc. and continued to work as consultants, with a substantial income that led to financial independence. Some of our old friends laughed when they saw how Sidney and I enjoyed doing business consulting. On the surface, it seemed like two Communists had turned capitalist.

But we didn't see it that way. Going into business for ourselves did not seem to me like an abandonment of our original Communist values. Running a consulting company did not make us capitalists, since we did not own factories or live off the labor of others. Still, it's true that we were helping others to do business, wheeling and dealing. Once I began selling computers to Chinese customers, I learned to see past my own preconceived notions and realize that doing business did not make me a bad person. In fact, I was helping China by speeding up its move into the modern age.

Even before going into business, Sidney and I had made some decisions. We would not be a part of fraud or deceit on either side. We decided we would never do anything against the law. That meant we never allowed our clients to accept Chinese bribes or kickbacks.

To avoid conflicts of interest, if we were asked to help a Chinese government body or company, we invariably did it pro bono, accepting no reward (except for goodwill). We did things openly, not in secret. We told the Chinese the same things we told our American clients.

Also, we never worked on commission or shared revenues. We aimed for "win/win" agreements, working on straight consulting fees with no commission and no success fees. This meant that if we found that a deal wasn't what we thought it would be, we had no temptation to push it forward anyway. Win, lose, or draw—our income was the same. We stuck to our principles, even if it meant we had to part ways with some clients.

"Win/win" was a concept that worked for me outside of business, too. I did not have to choose either a Chinese identity or an American one. I could be both. I could ensure that my American clients succeeded in China, but also that China benefited from modern technology. I didn't want to see either side lose.

This was alien to the way I had grown up, believing that one political party was evil and the other good, that capitalists became rich only if workers suffered. Wartime analogies of winners and losers didn't bring good outcomes. Revolutionary ideas about class enemies did not make things better. It was liberating for me to realize that I could find—even create—ways that ensured everybody won.

Mostly, Sidney and I just worked hard—really hard. We did anything that was needed for our client's success, even if it meant long hours of typing, copying, and telephoning. That's the advice I always give young people: if you want to be independent, you have to be prepared to work all hours of the day and night. If you need to do something and you don't know how, just ask questions and figure it out. That's how we learned consulting, step-by-step. One big lesson was the importance of not just thinking of our own interests but trying to get inside the minds of our clients and recognize what they needed.

Every time a project succeeded, Sidney and I would go wild. It was the greatest feeling. It's important to take at least a few minutes for self-appreciation, to pat each other on the back for a job well done.

We also gained some great friends, kept long after the client projects were completed or they had retired. Among them were some consulting clients who were not in business— Christian evangelist Billy Graham, Mike Wallace, and CBS reporter Dan Rather.

Sidney and I both loved consulting. We found it meaningful because we thought we were helping not only American companies but also our Chinese partners. During the 1980s and 1990s, China's economy began growing like crazy, and many Chinese people finally had the opportunity to make better lives for themselves. Communist China was learning how to benefit from capitalist business at the same time that Sidney and I were.

And we were successful beyond our imagination. We earned enough not just to support ourselves but to buy our own house, in Woodinville, Washington, surrounded by tall fir trees. We moved to the Seattle area in 1989 because Jenny lived there, and she wanted the whole family to settle in one place. Sunny moved there, too, and Sid Junior, for a time.

At last, I truly had my own kitchen.

Chapter Fifty-Three

Reflections

IN 2013, AT age eighty, I live with Sidney on Fox Island, near Gig Harbor, Washington. From our large picture windows overlooking the Puget Sound, we watch the ever-changing weather in the clouds and the rippling surface of the sea.

In 1997, we bought this house on Fox Island, in part because Sidney grew up in a house overlooking the water. For both of us, it's a dream house. Sidney has his own office, with floor-to-ceiling bookshelves, and I have a good-sized kitchen, where I love making pork dumplings with visitors. An amaryllis plant blooms bright red in the living room. We have three acres of land with almost sixty fruit trees, including apple, plum, pear, peach, persimmon, and a Chinese fruit called *haitang*, similar to crabapple. We also have a grape arbor and plenty of blueberries, blackberries, and huckleberries. We keep our local post office and bank branch supplied with fresh flowers and fruits. Every winter we spend a few months in Arizona. Mama and Papa would be astounded.

Sidney, at 92, refuses to say we have retired. We still do some consulting work, and he does teaching, lecturing, and writing.

Our children have scattered but remain in close touch. Jenny does consulting for Americans in China. Toni and her husband operate a comprehensive pain clinic and three urgent care clinics in North Carolina, where she also practices acupuncture and Chinese Traditional Medicine. Sunny works as a director of administration and information technology for a global builder of power plants. Sid Junior enjoys living in Beijing, where he is vice president and general manager of Greater China operations for a very successful American tech company. All four speak fluent Chinese, and, like me, they are equally comfortable in China and America. We have four healthy, happy grandchildren.

Today, as I sit on my deck, sipping oolong tea and tasting a juicy plum freshly harvested from my own orchard, I stare at the distant shore and think: What have

I learned from all these life experiences? The poverty of my childhood, the joy of Liberation, the humiliation and suffering while Sidney was in prison, the shock of moving to a foreign country at age forty-seven, my startling makeover into a successful business consultant?

My life is unlike any other, but I think others face the same kinds of challenges, in different forms. Life is full of contradictions, twists and turns you cannot anticipate. At times, our difficulties seem insurmountable—and they can be. We all get angry, discouraged, dejected. It's common to feel isolated, despised, alone. I certainly did.

When trouble overtakes you, what do you do? The answers are never easy. People will tell you "don't give up," but sometimes it seems there are no options, no way out.

During the Cultural Revolution, in the camps, I spent years doing backbreaking labor and was cursed and spat upon. My very personhood was denied and I had no rights whatsoever. But that was only one side of what was going on. That was their attempt to break me. But there was another side—my response. I insisted on the truth, on my innocence, at every opportunity, and vowed to perform well at every task I was given, so as to deprive them of excuses for further harassment. I managed to earn secret respect among many of them and to buy time till things changed. If I had only seen the first side—the problem—and not the other side—my path toward a solution—I would not have survived. I had to learn to analyze, to see the many sides in any situation, and to use my head and my will to overcome.

I'm not especially strong. There were times when I considered "taking the short way out"—suicide. But how could I abandon my four children? I knew of many people who gave in or went mad. But the ones who survived made up their mind to power through their troubles. Each time I figured out how to meet a new challenge, I felt myself growing stronger and more capable. By the time Sidney was released, I was ready to wrestle the most powerful authorities in the land to get a full vindication.

Then when I came to America, I was knocked off my feet again. Arriving in a strange country at midlife, I found that everything, even the language, confounded me. I knew some English, but it was hard to keep up with a rapid-fire conversation. I had no clue how to survive in a capitalist economy. What was I to do? Give up and accept an existence on the periphery? No one was shouting insults at me, and I knew I wouldn't starve or freeze, but I also knew that I had to find a way to live in the United States as a free, empowered individual. I could not keep relying on the kindness of others. In order to stand up with dignity, I had to figure out how to make a living, adjust to a totally different system, and learn what it meant to do business. Sidney and I made the transition without abandoning our core values: We never begged, borrowed, cheated, or stole. It helped enormously that we had each other. We stood together, helping each other, loving each other, and learning together how to survive in a strange new world. Now in our elder years, we can sit back and enjoy life, with a sense of accomplishment.

Life is about struggle. You must learn how to struggle. Don't try to run away. There are always issues arising in your life, work, and family. How do you deal with them? Misunderstandings can be cleared up. Difficulties can be overcome. Happiness comes from the struggle with unhappiness.

≈

What if I had chosen a different path once we got to the United States, continuing to design sweaters or running a travel agency? Sidney might have gone into business consulting anyway, perhaps with some success. But he did not have my hard-bargaining skills or my deep understanding of the Chinese psyche. Both of us believe the consulting work succeeded because of our teamwork. And because of our ability to find the good in people, to take pleasure in whatever we did, and to make friends everywhere.

Ultimately, my life would not have been as meaningful if I hadn't done business consulting. It has been lovely to achieve my dream of a comfortable retirement, free of financial worries—an important accomplishment for anyone, but especially for me because I grew up in poverty. But to me, what matters more is the satisfaction of knowing I took risks and acted boldly to bring together the two countries whose separation had caused so much misery in my life and Sidney's.

This is my contribution to humanity: to help bring these two countries closer. For me, that is no abstraction. The continuation of good U.S.-China relations is vital, for the sake of my children and grandchildren. Like our marriage, like me, they are both Chinese and American.